LONDON RECORD SOCIETY
PUBLICATIONS

VOLUME X
FOR THE YEAR 1974

LONDON ASSIZE OF NUISANCE
1301–1431

A CALENDAR

EDITED BY
HELENA M. CHEW
AND
WILLIAM KELLAWAY

LONDON RECORD SOCIETY
1973

© *London Record Society, 1973*
SBN 9009 5207 5

THE SOCIETY IS INDEBTED TO THE CORPORATION
OF LONDON FOR A GENEROUS GRANT TOWARDS THE
COST OF PRINTING THIS VOLUME

Printed in Great Britain by
W & J MACKAY LIMITED, CHATHAM, KENT

CONTENTS

ABBREVIATIONS	vii
INTRODUCTION	
The Assize of Buildings	ix
The Assize of Nuisance: procedure	xii
Nuisances	xx
Public nuisances and the commonalty	xxvi
General observations	xxx
The Rolls and the Calendar	xxxiii
ASSIZE OF NUISANCE	
Misc. Roll DD (1–480)	1
Misc. Roll FF (481–619)	116
Misc. Roll II (620–61)	163
INDEX	184
LONDON RECORD SOCIETY	221

ABBREVIATIONS

Borough customs	*Borough customs*, ed. Mary Bateson (Selden Soc., xviii, 1904; xxi, 1906). 2 vols.
C.E.M.C.R.	*Calendar of Early Mayor's Court Rolls 1298–1307*, ed. A. H. Thomas (1924)
C.I.P.M.	*Calendar of Inquisitions Post Mortem*
C. Letter-Book (A–L)	*Calendar of Letter-Books . . . A–L*, ed. R. R. Sharpe (1899–1912). 11 vols.
C.P.M.R.	*Calendar of Plea and Memoranda Rolls preserved at Guildhall, 1323–1437*, ed. A. H. Thomas; *1437–82*, ed. P. E. Jones (1926–61). 6 vols.
C.P.R.	*Calendar of Patent Rolls*
Cal. Wills	*Calendar of Wills proved and enrolled in the Husting*, ed. R. R. Sharpe (1889–90). 2 vols.
Chronicles of London	*Chronicles of the mayors and sheriffs of London*, transl. H. T. Riley (1863)
H.C.P.R.	Husting of Common Pleas Rolls
H.P.L.R.	Husting of Pleas of Land Rolls
H.R.	Husting Rolls (of wills and deeds)
Lib. Alb. } *Lib. Cust.*	*Munimenta Gildhallae Londoniensis*, ed. H. T. Riley (1859–62). 3 vols. in 4
London Eyre of 1244	*The London Eyre of 1244*, ed. H. M. Chew and M. Weinbaum (London Rec. Soc., vi, 1970)
London possessory assizes	*London possessory assizes*, ed. H. M. Chew (London Rec. Soc., i, 1965)
Memorials	*Memorials of London and London life*, ed. H. T. Riley (1868)
Novae narrationes	*Novae narrationes*, ed. Elsie Shanks and S. F. C. Milsom (Selden Soc., lxxx, 1963)
Ricart's Kalendar	*The maire of Bristowe is Kalendar*, by Robert Ricart, ed. L. Toulmin Smith (Camden Soc., new series, v, 1872)

All records cited are in the Corporation of London Records Office unless otherwise stated.

The following abbreviations are used in the calendar:
def.	defendant
pl.	plaintiff
par.	parish
within 40 days etc.	For explanation see p. xviii and **35**.

INTRODUCTION

The Assize of Buildings

London was much afflicted by fire in the eleventh and twelfth century. In a period of less than one hundred and fifty years there were, perhaps, as many as five major conflagrations.[1] According to City tradition, in 1189 during the mayoralty of Henry fitz Ailwin (probably from 1192 *or* 3 to 1212), some regulations were provided for settling disputes between neighbours concerning boundaries and other matters, and for encouraging the use of stone in building.

A number of questions concerning the antiquity of these regulations, apart from the obvious discrepancy in dates, are posed by the surviving texts. Well known to students of London history, the Assisa de Edificiis (hereafter referred to simply as the *Assize*) has often been printed, both in its original latin and in translation.[2] It was also frequently copied by compilers of the City custumals: in Liber de Antiquis Legibus, ff. 45–8; Letter-Book C, ff. 13v–15; Liber Horn, ff. 227–229v, 231; Liber Custumarum, ff. 208–210v; and Liber Albus, ff. 210v–212v as well as in Liber Dunthorn, the Elizabethan Liber Albus, and in Ricart's Kalendar (a particularly corrupt and unsatisfactory version). Apart from the text in Liber de Antiquis Legibus there are only minor variations between the other texts which clearly derive from one another or from a common exemplar. Letter-Book C contains the cleanest text with the smallest number of corrections, and probably dates from the beginning of the fourteenth century. Liber Horn was not earlier than 1311, the year in which Andrew Horn caused the book to be made, and its text of the *Assize*, which has many insertions, was corrected from the text in Letter-Book C. Liber Custumarum is at least two decades later in date and contains a number of obvious slips and copying errors. Liber Albus, is, of course, early fifteenth century and the other texts, which are later still, need not

---

1. The chronology of these fires presents difficulties, see William Page, *London* (1923), 42, 74–6, 78. Even the fire said to have been in the first year of Stephen's reign was probably in 1133 (*Chronicle of John of Worcester, 1118–40*, ed. J. R. H. Weaver (Oxford, 1908), 36–7). *Cartulary of Holy Trinity Aldgate*, ed. G. A. J. Hodgett (London Rec. Soc., vii, 1971), no. 31 (app.) describes two 12th-century fires, one in the time of Prior Norman, 1108–47, and another in the time of Prior Ralph, 1147–67. John Stow assumed that the second of these referred to the fire of 1135 or 1136 (*Survey*, ed. C. L. Kingsford, i (1908), 22, 139, 224). We are indebted to Professor C. N. L. Brooke for advice on this topic.
2. *De Antiquis Legibus Liber*, ed. T. Stapleton (Camden Soc., xxxiv, 1846), 206–11; T. H. Turner, *Some account of domestic architecture in England*, 2nd edn., i (1877), 275–81; *Chronicles of the mayors and sheriffs of London*, transl. H. T. Riley (1863), 179–87, which like Turner, was from Liber de Antiquis Legibus. The printed text to which reference is made throughout this volume is *Liber Albus*, ed. H. T. Riley (*Munimenta Gildhallae Londoniensis*, i, 1859), i, 319–32. Riley also published a translation, *Liber Albus* (1861), 276–87.

Introduction

concern us. The earliest text of the *Assize* is contained in Liber de Antiquis Legibus which may have been so called for that reason. The volume also contains a chronicle (ff. 63v–144v) part of which is clearly in the same hand as the *Assize* and which, according to Riley, was written before or in 1274.[1] This version of the *Assize* contains everything which was in the later texts with the exception of one paragraph[2] and the word 'aldermanni' after 'xii viri' in the description of how the assize was to be constituted. One paragraph was added in a margin[3] and two at the foot of ff. 45v and 46[4] but all in the same hand as the rest. Only the last paragraph of the text is in a later hand.[5] After mentioning the fire in Stephen's reign this text adds: 'ut in cronicis in hoc libro prescriptis notatur' (f. 47v), a reference to a short chronicle of Stephen's reign on f. 35.

The regulations contained in the *Assize* are remarkably elaborate; they set out not only the rules concerning walls, gutters, privies, windows, and pavements but also the procedure to be followed in assizes. On the other hand their arrangement is far from systematic and suggests compilation from more than one source. There are two widely separated passages touching upon the origin of the *Assize* (*Lib. Alb.*, i, 319, 328–9), some of the regulations being summarised in the second of these (*ibid.*, 329). The regulations concerning both walls and gutters are also separated and somewhat repetitious (*ibid.*, 321–3; 329–30; 331–2). It is unfortunately not possible, with one notable exception, to establish which parts of the *Assize* belong incontestably to a period earlier than the twelve-seventies. The exception concerns the regulations relating to stone walls (*ibid.*, 321–2). The London custumal of John's reign, under the heading, Lex de Assisa, laid down in words very similar to those used in the *Assize*[6] that neighbours wishing to build a party-wall should each give $1\frac{1}{2}$ ft. of land and share the cost of building a stone wall 3 ft. wide and 16 ft. high, and also share the cost of a gutter; that arches should be only 1 ft. deep so that 1 ft. of wall would remain between them; that if one party did not wish to, or could not afford to, build a wall, that party should provide the land and the other party should build upon it; and that he who gave the land should have half the wall and the right to build upon it. The Lex de Assisa is preceded by a list headed 'Nomina iuratorum ad assisam muri lapidei' consisting of the mayor (unnamed) and ten men, some of whom may be identified as aldermen;[7] they were performing the work allotted by the *Assize* to twelve alder-

---

1. *Chronicles of London*, p. v.
2. Si vero domus . . . mancipentur (*Lib. Alb.*, i, 320).
3. Eodem modo . . . recipientibus (f. 46) (*Lib. Alb.*, i, 324).
4. Et licet . . . vacuam (f. 45v) and Et si . . . conducta (f. 46) (*Lib. Alb.*, i, 331–2). Riley in *Lib. Alb.* thought that these paragraphs and the one mentioned in n. 2 above did not appear in Liber de Antiquis Legibus; in *Chronicles of London*, 179 he noted correctly that only the paragraph mentioned in n. 2 above was lacking.
5. Et sciendum quod . . . unum diem (f. 48).
6. M. Weinbaum, *London unter Eduard I. und II.*, ii (Stuttgart, 1933), 46–8 prints the Lex de Assisa in parallel columns with the *Assize* (from Liber de Antiquis Legibus); M. Bateson, 'A London municipal collection of the reign of John', *English Hist. Rev.*, xvii (1902), 506–7.
7. We are indebted to Mrs. Gillian Keir and Miss Susan Reynolds for allowing us to consult their index of Londoners before 1215. See also, Reynolds, 'The rulers of London in the 12th century', *History*, vol. 57 (Oct. 1972), 335–7.

Introduction

men chosen in full Husting. In 1244 aldermen are found serving as jurors in a plea of intrusion[1] and aldermen were certainly serving on assizes in 1301, when our rolls begin. In the provision concerning privies, we find that the period of limitation, the first year of Richard I, coincides with the year in which the *Assize* was said to have been drawn up.[2] The only other clause in the *Assize* which contains any apparent indication of date concerns pavements (*Lib. Alb.*, i, 331); as the term 'ballivos civitatis' is used rather than 'vicecomites' it is possible that the passage belongs to a period during which the City was in the king's hand (i.e. possibly in 1239 or more likely 1265–70).

The *Assize* made no mention of the great fire in John's reign, but equally a series of regulations drawn up under Henry fitz Ailwin, immediately after the fire in July 1212, made no reference to the *Assize*.[3] They were directly concerned with fire-prevention and rebuilding after the fire and were apparently all framed at one time. It is here, and not in the *Assize*, that we find provisions concerning roofing and roofing materials; no building should be covered with reeds, rushes, straw or stubble but only with tiles, shingles or boards and buildings roofed with reeds or rushes should be plastered over within eight days. It was also ordered that all the wooden houses in Cheap which endangered the stone houses there should be removed, by view of the mayor, sheriffs and discreet men of the City. The regulations concerning roofing were later incorporated in the articles of wardmote;[4] evidence of presentments under this article survive for 1377 and 1422[5] and in an interesting instrument of 1302 a citizen indemnified the City against the peril of fire arising from his houses roofed with straw and undertook to correct the matter within a period amounting to five months.[6] On the other hand, pleas concerned with thatched roofs were never dealt with in our records.[7]

The Lex de Assisa may have originated in the twelfth century and anyway cannot be later than 1216; the *Assize* in the form we know it is almost certainly of a later date. The mention of 1189 as the period of limitation for privies, a familiarity with the regulations of 1212 which were undeniably promulgated by Henry fitz Ailwin and a liking for any story which lent antiquity to City custom,[8] may well have stimulated the *Assize*'s compiler to explain its origins as he did. In any case, it was this compilation which provided the basic rules of procedure for assizes of nuisance in London.

1. *London Eyre of 1244*, no. 240.
2. In 1275, the first year of Richard I was fixed as the extent of legal memory for writs of right, Statute of Westminster I, c. 39 (*Statutes of the Realm*, i (1810), 36).
3. *Lib. Cust.*, i, 86–8.
4. *Lib. Alb.*, i, 334, specified lead, tiles or stone; *Ricart's Kalendar*, 113, prohibited shingles.
5. *C.P.M.R. 1364–81*, 237; *1413–37*, 125.
6. *C. Letter-Book C*, 105.
7. Straw roofs may have been outside the scope of the assize of nuisance because, however great the potential danger of fire, they could not be shown to be to a neighbour's damage until after the event. The number of pleas in which the danger of fire was mentioned is remarkably small but see **77** and **141**.
8. Cf. the tradition that the City had developed a possessory procedure of its own which was already fully developed by the reign of Henry II (*Lib. Alb.*, i, 114).

Introduction

The Assize of Nuisance: procedure

The assize of nuisance[1] according to Glanvill had its origins in a variant writ of novel disseisin.[2] A freeholder might be disseised of some part of his tenement and the injury was said to be 'ad nocumentum liberi tenementi'. Bracton wrote at length on the subject and mentioned the assize of nuisance by name for the first time. He explained that no one might complain of nuisances unless he was a freeholder, so that the assize was denied to any who held only for a term of years. Further, the nuisance must both have caused damage and be of a kind condemned by the law. He also emphasised that the tenement in question must be viewed.[3]

In the thirteenth century assize of nuisance proper, which concerned the making or removal of ditches, pools, hedges, the diversion of watercourses and the obstruction of ways, were heard by the justices of assize. Viscontiel writs of nuisance, described as 'de parvo nocumento', concerning houses, mills, weirs, privies and other matters (perhaps including doors and windows), were used in county courts.[4] Little is known of the process in boroughs but it is clear that custom concerning nuisances had developed in several places before 1300. The earliest record of such custom dates from the late twelfth century and relates to Northampton: in disputes between neighbours concerning a wall, building, or gutter, the bailiffs and good men of the pleas ought to view the tenement by men of the neighbourhood and their finding should stand without essoin and delay.[5] London custom preserved in Lex de Assisa, although dating from the early thirteenth century, may well have been as old or older than Northampton's. However, an assize concerning a party-wall, gutters and pipes of 1290-1 vouched to warranty in a later plea (**283**) appears to be the earliest reference to an assize of nuisance in London.[6] Only from 1301 when the rolls here calendared begin is there ample evidence, both direct and indirect, of how the assize of nuisance functioned in London and how the *Assize* was applied in practice.

---

1. On the history of the assize of nuisance, see S. F. C. Milsom's introduction to *Novae narrationes*, pp. xcvi-civ; C. H. S. Fifoot, *History and sources of the common law* (1949), ch. i, and C. T. Flower, *Introduction to the Curia Regis Rolls* (Selden Soc., lxii, 1944), pt. 2, ch. xviii. The origins of the assize have been studied by Dr. Janet S. Loengard, 'Free tenements and bad neighbours: the assizes of novel disseisin and nuisance in the king's court before the Statute of Merton (1236)' (Unpublished doctoral dissertation, Columbia Univ., 1970).
2. Glanvill, *Tractatus de legibus*, ed. G. D. G. Hall (1965), 34–6.
3. Bracton, *De legibus et consuetudinibus Angliae*, ed. G. E. Woodbine, iii (1940), 189-99. Cf. *Fleta*, iii (Selden Soc., lxxxix, 1972), 110-18.
4. *Novae narrationes*, pp. xcvii-xcviii. For examples of a variety of writs, see *Early Registers of Writs*, ed. E. de Haas and G. D. G. Hall (Selden Soc., lxxxvii, 1970), especially Hib. 7, CA55, and R 468, R 658-9.
5. *Borough customs*, i, 245. Bateson also found customs of later date for Ipswich, 1291; Waterford, *c.* 1300; Bury, 1327; Fordwich, 15th century. Custom in Ludlow concerning windows appears to have been not unlike London's (*Novae narrationes*, p. cii, B149). Although Canterbury does not appear to have had an assize of building, it is significant that strict provision was made (perhaps as early as 1177-9) that material used for the repair of shops should be non-inflammable (W. Urry, *Canterbury under the Angevin kings* (1967), 206–7, 207 n. 8).
6. A dispute of 1276-7 concerning adjoining tenements was settled by the mayor and good men summoned for the purpose (**318**) but it is not said to have been an assize.

Introduction

The *Assize* (*Lib. Alb.*, i, 321–1) laid down that the action should be initiated in full Husting, or, if the Husting was not sitting, at a congregation of the mayor and aldermen. Bills of complaint, which were written in French (**574, 591**), were rarely entered upon the rolls but it is sometimes stated that the assize was sought in the Husting (**460–1, 593, 661**) or at a congregation (**287, 658–60**). A random search of the rolls of Husting of Common Pleas and Pleas of Land[1] shows that assizes of nuisance were noted upon both, from time to time, but usually in small numbers; and from 1448, in the earliest Husting Book only very occasionally. Such records of congregations as exist for the fourteenth and early fifteenth century are to be found in the Plea and Memoranda Rolls[2] and these contain scattered plaints of nuisance. It is likely, however, that the greatest number of pleas originated at congregations, especially as the Husting was held only on Mondays. According to the *Assize* (*Lib. Alb.*, i, 320) the defendant could be prohibited from further building operations during the time of petition (in tempore petitionis) and workmen or owners continuing to build after such prohibition would be sent to prison. No example of this regulation appears on our rolls.

The *Assize* (*Lib. Alb.*, i, 320) provided for the election of twelve aldermen in full Husting; the greater part of those so elected was to be present with the mayor in holding assizes. The mayor nearly always presided; his inability to attend, for a variety of reasons, was a frequent cause of adjournment (**314, 323, 373, 629**). The appearance of Hamo de Chigwell in August 1327 as *locum tenens* (**286–7**) was exceptional. The mayor, Richard de Betoyne, had gone to Nottingham in an attempt to persuade the king not to remove the exchequer from London to York and Hamo, who had been deposed only nine months earlier, took the opportunity of reasserting himself.[3] In practice, the mayor and six aldermen[4] apparently constituted a quorum and an insufficiency of aldermen was a frequent cause of adjournment or respite (**37, 146, 151, 192, 407–8, 506**). On the other hand, unless we assume clerical negligence, there were assizes at which fewer than six aldermen were present (e.g. 16 Feb. 1358, **492**; 7 Nov. 1365, **524**); on 22 May 1360 a defendant objected that there were fewer than six aldermen present but he was ordered to make another answer (**510**). Even at the end of our period the mayor and sheriffs, taking with them six aldermen, go to the site (**645**). It is clear that the duty of serving on the assize was by no means evenly shared amongst the aldermen: most of them appeared at some time but it was left to a minority to perform what must have been a time-consuming duty. On one occasion an assize was adjourned because certain well-informed aldermen were absent (**54**). The alderman who served most regularly was the recorder; he is not mentioned by office until 1328 (**272**) and not frequently until after 1369. As an alderman he was normally entered in the headings of the record either after the mayor or after the mayor and past-mayors and before the other aldermen (an order preserved

---

1. e.g. H.P.L.R. 50, m. 7 and 61, m. 10; H.C.P.R. 62, m. 3; H.C.P.R. 64, mm. 2, 6, 9, 17, 20, 24d. would appear to be exceptional in containing a dozen or more.
2. e.g. *C.P.M.R. 1323–64*, 141–2, 209, 216, etc., and subsequent vols.
3. *C. Letter-Book E*, 222–3; *C.P.M.R. 1323–64*, 25–30.
4. In 1302 it was ordained that six aldermen should be present in the court of Husting when judgments were given (*C. Letter-Book C*, 14; Liber Horn, f. 270).

Introduction

in modern ceremonial practice).¹ The aldermen were often joined on the assize by the sheriffs. From time to time the assize is described as consisting of the mayor, the aldermen, sheriffs, 'and others', 'and all the others belonging to the assize', 'and others sworn to keep the assize', or 'etc.' (**67, 87, 154–5, 181, 277, 310**) which may have referred to the carpenters and masons sworn to the assize (**430**) or even to the commonalty (**85**). In 1309 a defendant declared that an assize ought to be held by the mayor and aldermen and 'other good men of the City elected and sworn for the purpose'; 'the mayor and good men' were later said to have been insufficiently advised and the assize was accordingly adjourned (**146**).

The plaint having been made, the mayor was to assign a day within the following week, which in practice was always a Friday. A bill embodying the plaint was prepared by the common clerk and forwarded to the sheriffs. On the Wednesday following the day on which the plaint was made, the sheriff or his serjeant summoned, by view of two neighbours, the defendants named in the bill to appear *super terram* on the following Friday.² Should the defendant default, it had to be testified that he had been summoned (*Lib. Alb.*, i, 327). This was normally done by the sheriff (**10, 50, 57, 62, 132**) but sometimes by his clerk (**494**). A similar procedure obtained for persons pleaded in aid by defendants (**219**). Should the defendant be out of the City at the time of the summons, a contingency provided for in the *Assize* (*Lib. Alb.*, i, 328), the sheriff was to order those living in the tenement in question to warn the defendant to appear in a fortnight. The sheriff or his clerk often testified that the defendant was out of town when he was summoned (**51, 170, 299**) but sometimes it was the tenants or neighbours who testified to his absence (**273–4, 294, 306**). Increasingly, in the later pleas, the names of two summoners were given (**266, 292–3, 305**) and sheriffs frequently testified elsewhere, perhaps in the Husting, that defendants had been summoned (**528, 605–6, 608, 611**).

On the appointed day the mayor and aldermen came to the site and the plaintiff explained his case. The defendant frequently made default, or if he came, said nothing to delay the verdict of the assize (**50, 60, 84, 110, 126**). Alternatively, there were a variety of arguments he might put forward aimed either at excluding the plaintiff from the assize or simply to delay judgment. The defendant frequently pleaded that the freehold was not his and that his interest was only for life or for a term of years (**6, 87, 104, 219, 258, 608**) or that he held by courtesy of England (**14**). Similarly he might plead that the joint-feoffee was not mentioned in the plaint (**54, 76, 449**). In such cases the assize was normally adjourned so that the freeholder might appear, either freely (**6**) or after being summoned (**219**).³ Conversely the defendant might argue that the plaint was defective because a tenant for life had not been named (**102**) or for some other reason (**109**).

The *Assize* specified the period of limitation in the case of privies as the

---

1. For a list of the recorders appearing in the rolls, see index under 'Recorder'.
2. *Ricart's Kalendar*, 96; *Lib. Alb.*, i, 48. The process was very similar to the one adopted for pleas of intrusion (*London possessory assizes*, pp. xvii–xviii).
3. According to the Statute of Westminster II, c. 24 (*Statutes of the Realm*, i, 83), a grantor who had created a nuisance might be sued with the grantee in cases concerning houses and walls.

Introduction

first year of Richard I. It had also been laid down that the plaint must be raised within a year and a day (*Lib. Alb.*, i, 324, 331). But according to a regulation[1] in Liber de Antiquis Legibus not included in the *Assize*, a man might make his plaint long after his wall had been encroached upon provided he did so as soon as the encroachment had been noticed. It was sometimes asserted that a plaintiff was not entitled to an assize because the plaint had not been raised within a year and a day (**61, 232, 261, 313**). One plaintiff in reply to the charge that the period of limitation had been disregarded claimed that it applied only to 'stone walls and the like' (**261**) but on at least one occasion the plaintiff was advised to seek another remedy (**61**). A defendant who cited the appropriate provision of the *Assize* did so to no avail (**313**). Long seisin was often pleaded by defendants (**2, 69, 96, 243**) but in an assize of 1306 it was expressly stated that long seisin could not prejudice the plaintiff's case or give the possessor the right and fee (**105**).

A defendant might plead that a nuisance was not apparent to the view of the assize (**20, 111**). Alternatively, he might plead that the assize had no cognisance of the matter in question (**52**) because it was a case of trespass (**55**) or intrusion (**510**) and not of nuisance. If there had been a previous assize he might assert that the plaintiff should not be allowed another (**528**). The *Assize* (*Lib. Alb.*, i, 330) stipulated that a defendant who claimed to have a deed from the plaintiff, or from an ancestor of the plaintiff, should be allowed to produce it. This could be used simply as a means of delaying proceedings (**37–8, 282, 313, 376, 389, 399**) but documents were often actually produced both by defendants (**85, 255, 261, 305, 574, 619**) and by plaintiffs to support their case (**146, 219, 272**). Both plaintiffs and defendants also vouched to warranty proceedings in previous assizes (**371, 476, 528, 631**) or wills proved in the Husting (**233**). The defendant might make complaint concerning the plaintiff's tenement (**11, 31**) and this was commonly the practice when the plaintiff's building operations had been prohibited (**13, 35, 204, 236**), a process dealt with below. The *Assize* was occasionally cited by the litigants, the surveyors or the court (**230, 235, 313, 323**).

Attorneys were employed much less often than in assizes of fresh force.[2] Attorneys for defendants occur from time to time (**34, 70, 102, 125, 488**) and at least once a defendant was given permission to appear by attorney on account of illness (**233**).[3] Plaintiffs also appeared by attorney but infrequently until the late fourteenth century: an Italian plaintiff was allowed an attorney, possibly because he was an alien (**12**); the mayor was petitioned to send two aldermen to receive the attorney of the abbess of the Minoresses (the plaintiff), because she was enclosed (**80**); one party appearing as both plaintiff and defendant was also allowed an attorney (**27**). The *Assize* (*Lib. Alb.*, i, 330) made special provision for minors to appear by their guardians (**312, 493**).

Both parties were allowed one essoin (*Lib. Alb.*, i, 326). But for every essoin by a plaintiff (e.g. **6–8**) there were dozens by defendants (e.g. **21–3**,

---

1. Dated 1292 by M. Bateson (*Borough customs*, i, 247–8).
2. *London possessory assizes*, pp. xix–xx, xx n. 1.
3. According to the *London Eyre of 1244*, nos. 234, 238, all tenants impleaded in City courts were free to appoint an attorney but plaintiffs were specifically denied the privilege.

Introduction

58–9, 531–3). In the early fourteenth century there is some evidence of restraint in allowing essoins: a defendant was refused an essoin because he had already had one (**37**), the essoin of a wife was quashed because her husband had been essoined in the same plea at the previous court (**26**), while the essoin of another defendant was held not to lie because he was seen in court (**71**). In the same period there appear to have been professional essoiners, William de Brainford and William de Reyle being those most frequently employed. At an assize in 1311 (**169**) the latter offered to essoin the defendants but afterwards denied having done so on the ground that he had not been asked. In the second half of the fourteenth century some essoiners' names suggest that the office may have become fictitious, for example, John, Robert, Thomas and William (atte) Rose or Russe (**443, 466→539**); William (atte) Grosse (**467–8**); James and William (atte)Posse or Pusse (**465→542, 549**); most appropriately for a building assize, Adam, Alan, Thomas and William Post (**573, 575, 578, 580**); and perhaps Adam Potelle (**579**) and Richard Postek (**564–5**). On the other hand, even in the later period, it is possible to identify some essoiners, for example, Ralph Coo and Gilbert Meldebourne who were attorneys and William Sewale who was afterwards serjeant of the Chamber. Essoiners might be asked to produce their warrant at the quindene (**488, 510, 525, 604**) and after 1357 this became common form. One essoin was allowed not only to each of the parties or their attorneys (**488**) but also to defendants not named in the bill (**76**). After an adjournment to produce his muniments, a defendant was allowed one essoin (**510, 566**) in accordance with the *Assize* (*Lib. Alb.*, i, 330). Our calendar omits very many essoins[1] in the interests of economy.

Essoins were not the only cause of delay in the settlement of disputes. Adjournments on various pretexts were very frequent. The *Assize* (*Lib. Alb.*, i, 328) stipulated that if the mayor and aldermen did not come upon the land, the plaintiff must demand another assize in the Husting or at a congregation and occasionally resummons was necessary (**37, 53**), in one instance because of the proximity of Easter[2] (**149**). But resummons could be, and usually was avoided. According to the *Assize* it was necessary for some of the aldermen to view the land in the presence of the parties, but in practice two aldermen (**312–14, 319, 328**), an alderman and the mayor's serjeant (**151**) or an alderman and the common clerk, Hugh de Waltham (**329**), might go to the site and adjourn proceedings, a procedure which provoked a scandalised marginal comment from a student of the rolls (**312**). As we have seen, adjournments for lack of aldermen were numerous (**146, 192, 407–8, 416, 502, 506**). A variety of reasons was given for the absence of the mayor and aldermen: because the mayor was occupied with the collection of money for the king's gift[3] (**314**), or was delivering Newgate gaol (**313, 323**), or because he and the aldermen had been summoned to the king at Westminster (**373, 629**), or were engaged upon his business (**313, 328, 331**), or had to appear before the treasurer and council (**174**), or because they were occu-

---

1. For the principles upon which they have been omitted, see below p. xxxiv.
2. The feasts of Christmas, the Nativity of St. John the Baptist, Whitsun and All Hallows also gave grounds for adjournment (**313, 321, 507, 614**).
3. The adjournment was in Sep. 1333; in the following year the City granted the king 1,200 marks for raising troops (*Memorials*, 187–90).

Introduction

pied with important City business (**389, 441, 593, 614**). The *Assize* (*Lib. Alb.*, i, 330) provided for adjournment in the event of the defendant claiming that he had muniments bearing upon the case and this rule was much used both for its proper purpose and as a means of delaying judgment. The plaintiff too was allowed respite to produce documents (**38, 313, 631**). Adjournments or respites were also given at the request of (**430**) or with the consent of parties (**389, 479, 510**). Occasionally a special reason for an adjournment on behalf of a defendant was given: to produce a husband (**51**), to consult (**44**) or because the defendant's counsel had left when noon struck before the assize had come (**104**). Perhaps the most frequent cause of adjournment was that the mayor and aldermen wished to be more fully advised (**37, 146–7, 346, 400, 483**); in due course this became common form for adjournments. No doubt there were occasions when the assize genuinely sought further information, for example when an adjournment was made so that the mayor and aldermen might consult the sworn masons and carpenters (**522**) or because there was some important business touching the plea (**618**). Finally there were adjournments to hear judgment, which in the later fourteenth and fifteenth century, became the normal practice. The proceedings were adjourned to Guildhall, before the mayor and aldermen, often in Husting, where the record and process were recited (**426, 431, 436, 500–2**) and judgment given; but sometimes the mayor and aldermen found it necessary to return *super terram* before giving judgment (**430, 631, 635**).

From time to time certain questions were referred to juries which were summoned either by the sheriff (**43**) or by the serjeant of the Chamber (**608, 614, 618**), frequently at the request of the the parties (**375, 381, 387, 396, 510**). There were normally twelve jurors (**109, 375, 381, 396, 483**); exceptionally eighteen or twenty-four were summoned (**234, 401, 511**), but only twelve came. Only once are the jurors said to have made default (**510**). They were described variously as being of the venue or neighbourhood (**387**), of a lane or street (**511, 483**), of a parish (**488**) or of a ward or wards (**261**). Such questions were asked of them as, whether or not a defendant had stopped up a gutter or ditch (**258, 375, 614**), to which party an easement belonged (**317, 381, 488, 510, 660**), or whether a lane was common to both parties (**396**). In one assize where a plaintiff pleaded a deed, without apparently producing it, a jury was summoned to test the truth of his allegation (**511**) and in another a jury found that a plaintiff had given a wrong measurement (**309**). An assessment of a plaintiff's damages (**660**) was exceptional.[1] Juries were summoned for four pleas in which the commonalty were plaintiffs (**375, 387, 396, 483**) but in one of these the jurors were asked about only one of the charges (**387**). In one of the most interesting pleas in which jurors feature, a jury was summoned because the interests of the City were involved and the parties were suspected of fraud and trickery (**618**). In 1347 an assize ruled that the custom of the City did not allow the reference to a jury of the point at issue (**399**) which turned upon the ownership of a lane. Returns by juries in favour of both plaintiffs (**261, 309, 375, 381, 483**) and defendants (**109, 396**) feature upon the rolls. In an unusual plea (**145**) an inquest consisting of six men of the neighbourhood

1. Plaintiffs sometimes pleaded damages (**313, 613, 617, 632**) but they were rarely assessed (**71**).

Introduction

was elected and sworn by consent of the parties to certify the mayor and aldermen concerning certain doubtful points in an assize which they could not determine by view. Arbitrators were not often appointed (**61, 534, 632**), presumably because arbitration was the normal task of the mayor and aldermen and the masons and carpenters sworn to the assize.

According to the *Assize* (*Lib. Alb.*, i, 325) a neighbour's building operations might be impeded provided a pledge to prosecute was given to the sheriff; thereupon building was to cease until the assize had considered whether such building was unjust. The rolls abound in pleas of this kind (**11, 13, 35, 92, 212, 282–3, 305, 381**) in some of which the sheriff's serjeant rather than the sheriff prohibited the building work (**253, 269, 317, 346, 348**). The defendant usually brought a counter charge attempting to justify the prohibition in which he might succeed (**13, 35**) but was much more likely to fail and be amerced for unjustly impeding the plaintiff's building work (**308, 313, 333, 348, 405**).

Amercement of one or other party was by no means the inevitable outcome in pleas of nuisance. Apart from amercement of a defendant for unjustly impeding building to which we have just referred, a plaintiff (**13, 290, 358, 371, 392**) or a defendant (**11, 169, 282**) was liable to amercement for making a false plaint or defence. To demolish part of a wall held in common without the consent of the parceners (**272**); to neglect or refuse to repair such a wall (**18, 256, 482**); or to allow it to be damaged by a cesspit (**19**) might, but generally did not, result in amercement.

The *Assize* (*Lib. Alb.*, i, 326) ordained that if the plaintiff should default, he and his pledges were to be amerced by the sheriffs. Suits of this kind, where the plaintiff was adjudged *non prosecutus*, appear on our rolls, often before the parties had been heard (**46, 342, 374, 425, 596**) but occasionally after lengthy proceedings (**488**). On the other hand, licence to agree (**24, 31, 184, 193, 391**) and agreement between parties (**337, 531, 588, 623**) were not uncommon. If the defendant should default, the *Assize* continued, the mayor and aldermen were to proceed to give judgment and the sheriffs were to warn him so that the judgment should be carried out within forty days (**117, 119, 525, 537, 566, 609**). Only rarely do we find a longer period allowed; in one plea the period appears to have been six months; a wall was declared by the sworn carpenter and mason to be ruinous but not to need repair before the summer (**53**); in another, the repair was to be carried out when the weather was suitable (**281**). It was equally rare for less than forty days to be allowed but one defendant was ordered to repair a gutter 'without delay' and remove his corbels from his neighbour's walls within eight days (**184**). Occasionally the task of warning the defendant was entrusted to the serjeant of the Chamber (**483**).

In the earliest pleas the period of forty days was not always specified in the judgment but by about 1320 its omission was exceptional. Likewise, the penal clauses to the effect that the sheriffs would act at the expense of the defaulting party and fine him 40s. were not always fully entered in the record. In the event of judgment remaining unexecuted after forty days, the *Assize* (*Lib. Alb.*, i, 326) laid down that complaint might be made to the mayor, whereupon, by his precept, two or three aldermen were to proceed to the site; if they saw that judgment had not been executed, the defendant

Introduction

was to be amerced by the sheriff who was to put it into effect at the defendant's expense. Complaint that the judgment had not been executed was apparently made either in the Husting (**272, 292**) or, perhaps, at a congregation of the mayor and aldermen (**291**). Of the consequent visit to the site by two or three aldermen prescribed by the *Assize* there is but one example (**284**). The sheriffs might be ordered to summon the defendant before the mayor and aldermen to show cause why judgment should not be put into execution (**442**) but normally the sheriff was simply ordered to put the judgment into effect at the defendant's expense and to fine him 40s. for contempt (**353–4, 367–8, 370**), a fine which he levied to his own use (**284, 347**). How successful the penal clauses were in assuring that judgments were executed is difficult to ascertain. While threatened action by the sheriff may have spurred some defendants to the correction of nuisances, enforcement cannot have been easy. Plaintiffs normally waited from three to nine months before complaining that judgment had not been executed (**174, 279, 292, 367, 390, 439**). Occasionally they were less patient and we find complaints made seventy-six and fifty-four days after judgment (**353, 291**) and once within six days of the statutory period of forty days, that is, forty-six days after judgment (**429**). When the commonalty were plaintiffs (or an interested party) the sheriff was ordered to report upon the action he had taken (**292**) and the correction of a nuisance might be entered on the roll (**536–7**). On the other hand, sheriffs encountered difficulties in enforcing judgments or were dilatory in doing so (**390, 398**). In one plea, the plaintiffs did not complain of non-execution until five years after judgment (**272**). Early in the fourteenth century plaintiffs were sometimes advised to seek a remedy by another process (**20, 36, 52, 55, 61, 287**) which suggests that the scope of the action was less clearly defined than it became later in the century when such advice was given less frequently (**386, 400, 492**).

When a nuisance could quite literally not be seen by the assize the plaintiff's case was likely to fail (**11, 20, 111**). Perhaps for this reason, increasing use was made of professional viewers during the fourteenth and fifteenth century. Four such viewers, two master carpenters and two master masons, were sworn to consider matters concerning buildings. On a Monday in 1301 (presumably in the Husting) a mason was sworn to give due consideration to stone walls between neighbours, party-walls and others in bad repair as often as he was required to do so and two carpenters took a similar oath concerning boundary-walls and gutters.[1] Twelve years later masons and carpenters sworn to make and supervise assizes and partitions of tenements are found making partition of a debtor's tenements with the City chamberlain.[2] Later appointments of sworn masons and carpenters appear in the Letter-Books.[3] Our record first mentions these officials in 1303 (**53**) in a dispute concerning a ruinous wall. The regulations in the *Assize* relating to party-walls and gutters were often difficult to apply and in such cases, the expertise of the masons and carpenters was valuable. They were increasingly relied upon by the mayor and aldermen to give

1. *Lib. Cust.*, i, 100; *C. Letter-Book C*, 86.
2. *C. Letter-Book B*, 15.
3. In the 16th century the appointments were entered in the Repertories, e.g. 2, ff. 58v, 172; 7, f. 46v, and at least once in the Journals 5, ff. 217, 220.

Introduction

advice (**310, 501, 522**) as well as, at the request of the parties, to settle disputes that depended upon view (**518**). Measurements made by the masons and carpenters were accepted and were sometimes given to within a quarter of an inch (**527**) or even represented diagrammatically on the roll (**304**). Once the carpenters were ordered to correct a nuisance with the plaintiff's carpenters (**271**). In 1384 the mayor and aldermen initiated what must be one of the earliest archaeological excavations in London by ordering the masons and carpenters to uncover foundations in order to discover how wide a path had been (**631**). After 1366, with increasing frequency, their reports were made in the form of a bill or certificate addressed to the mayor and aldermen in French (**526–7, 566**), a language used until at least 1428,[1] but in English some twelve years later.[2] The certificates were filed (**604, 645**)[3] and sometimes enrolled at the request of the parties (**526–7**). There is little evidence that the advice or findings of the masons and carpenters was ever over-ridden. But in a plea of 1373 (**591**) the defendants denied that a wall was partible, although at their request, a certificate to that effect had been enrolled about seven years earlier (**526**). An indenture of 1406 concerning the apportionment of rent in accordance with the testament of Thomas Noket, late citizen and draper, was presumably only entered (**647**) because the masons and carpenters were among the parties to it. A similar reason may explain the enrolment of a view concerning fixtures (**583**), which appears at the foot of a membrane containing two other certificates. The plea to which it relates was enrolled on the Plea and Memoranda Rolls[4] and concerned damage done to the fixtures of a house by a tenant. The task of partitioning tenements fell, as we have seen, to the masons and carpenters from an early date. A partition arising out of a plea of dower was cited by a defendant (**160**) and in a plea between co-heirs (**233**) a mason and carpenter were sworn to make partition and report in full Husting.[5] Once more, the presence of such pleas in our record can be explained most readily by the rôle of the masons and carpenters in the proceedings.

Nuisances

The *Assize* laid down elaborate regulations for the settlement of disputes between neighbours, concerning walls, gutters, windows, privies and paving.[6] Some of those concerning walls (*Lib. Alb.*, i, 321–3) were, as we have seen, modelled upon the Lex de Assisa: stone walls between neighbours were to be 3 ft. thick and 16 ft. high; each party was to give 1½ ft. of his land and the cost of building was to be shared between them; or, if one party could not

---

1. *C.P.M.R. 1413–37*, 218–19.
2. *C.P.M.R. 1437–57*, 23.
3. Viewers' certificates of the 16th and 17th centuries are preserved in the Corporation Records Office: 1509–46 (general file); *c.* 1508, and *c.* 1547–57 (1 box) Misc. Mss. Box 91; a roll, 1623–36. After about 1547 until 1557 a master tiler made view with masons and carpenters.
4. *C.P.M.R. 1364–81*, 150.
5. **234** concerns the same partition. **233–4** occupy two sides of one membrane (DD, m. 29).
6. For medieval building in general, see L. F. Salzman, *Building in England down to 1540* (1952); Margaret Wood, *English mediaeval house* (1965).

Introduction

or would not build jointly with the other, he was to give 3 ft. of his land and the other was to build at his own expense and the wall so built was to be shared equally between them. Judgments based upon these regulations usually offered the parties the choice implied by the rules (**32, 34, 278, 288, 590**); if a defendant pleaded poverty (**279**) no alternative was offered. According to the *Assize* (*Lib. Alb.*, i, 329–30), a party wishing to build the whole of a wall upon his own land who had an assize brought against him, might either join with his neighbour in building a wall in common or continue building his own wall; the neighbour might then build a similar wall for himself. Once again we find the parties are offered a choice (**93, 165**).

Party-walls were often the subject of litigation. Owners of stone walls held in common were forbidden by the *Assize* (*Lib. Alb.*, i, 323) to pull down or alter any part of the wall without the consent of the other party (**74, 272**). Disputes frequently arose when one or other party was rebuilding or repairing his tenement. Complaints were usually made because one party had placed his timber upon the wall (**92, 146, 156, 211, 282–3**), because the wall had been pierced and beams or corbels placed in it (**37, 506**) or, less usually, because one party had deforced and overthrown the building work of the other alleging that the wall was his (**38**). Such disputes were normally settled by view, in accordance with various regulations laid down in the *Assize* (*Lib. Alb.*, i, 325–7). If a person owned a wall covered at the top with his own roofing or timber, his neighbour, even though he had corbels and joists in the wall, could not claim more than he already had possession of, without the consent of the wall's owner; if a person owned two parts of a wall and his neighbour owned the third part, his neighbour could use his part freely (but presumably only by consent). When the nuisance was viewed, the mayor and aldermen and later the masons and carpenters sworn to the assize noted the position of the old timber or corbels in deciding how much of the wall belonged to each party (**90, 92, 146, 211, 253**). The part shared might be very unequal: for example, the assize found that a plaintiff was formerly seised of a wall to a depth of 6 inches and it was adjudged that he might place his posts and timber upon the wall only to that depth (**269**). The *Assize* (*Lib. Alb.*, i, 322) contained a regulation, also in the Lex de Assisa, concerning the building of arches and cupboards in party-walls. Although the building of arches was never a matter of dispute on our rolls, interesting use was made of the regulation: the mayor and aldermen found after diligent scrutiny that, when a certain wall was first built, it had had arches 1 ft. deep on both sides, with 1 ft. of wall in the middle, thus establishing that it was divisible between the parties (**308**). Arches were used as evidence of ownership on other occasions but without the same clear implication of age (**526, 591, 597**).

Walls or houses overhanging a neighbour's land, which prevented him from building, frequently gave rise to litigation (**118, 149, 265, 301, 304, 377–9**). Such disputes were often settled with the aid of a plumb-line (**76, 271, 295, 388**). Walls leaned by as much as 2 ft. but one two-storeyed solar overhung a churchyard by as much as 6 ft. (**502**) while one over a street projected 10 ft. (**536**). Ruinous walls were another source of trouble. One party might refuse to repair his part of a wall (**256**). Plaintiffs alleged that ruinous walls were a danger to inhabitants and passers-by (**50, 53, 131, 264**)

Introduction

and that they themselves suffered damage thereby: their gardens are said to have been trampled down, their fruit taken and their private business watched (**34, 446, 496**); dogs, pigs, cocks, hens and children came too, over the ruinous walls (**66, 293, 595**). Such walls were described as *clausture*, a term usually rendered as 'fences'[1] in our calendar, but it is clear that *murus* was often used to describe a boundary wall of the same kind.

The record does not always specify the material of which walls were made. Stone was, of course, a common material and, as we have seen, one of the purposes of the *Assize* was to encourage its use. But many walls were made of earth (**25, 165, 218, 281, 293**). These appear to have been thicker than stone walls, measuring as much as $4\frac{1}{2}$ ft. (**307**) and were generally fences. Plastered walls (**164, 505, 521, 595, 607**), wooden walls (**501**) with stone foundations (**149**) or palings of wattle and daub (**278–9**) are occasionally mentioned. The *Assize* laid down that walls of stone were to be 16 ft. high, presumably high enough to accommodate a two-storeyed house, and this height was generally given in judgments. One plaintiff, contrary to the *Assize*, undertook to provide a wall 10 ft. high on a defendant's land (**180**). Sometimes it was adjudged that fences should be rebuilt in stone according to the *Assize* (**93, 217, 278**) but, more often, that the wall, even though earthen, should be repaired or rebuilt in that material (**218, 307, 380, 418, 496**).

The *Assize* made no mention of chimneys, a fact which might argue for its antiquity.[2] When chimneys were complained of, it was rarely on account of the risk of fire (**77, 658**), unless by implication in the case of a forge (**617**), but rather because they overhung a neighbour's property (**265, 447, 527**); such were a chimney built upon a corbel (**629**) and a double chimney (**655**). The only other chimneys mentioned were in an indenture (**205**) and by a plaintiff who was hindered from repairing one (**331**).

Other causes were given for the ruin of walls: the building of a turret (**31**), the stacking of firewood (**55, 60, 183,** cf. **524**), and the building of pigsties (**263, 332**) against them, or, in the case of a wattle and daub paling, the piling of earth against it (**278**). Seeping sewage from cess-pits was, as we shall see, a further cause of ruinous walls and rotting timbers but so too was water. It is not surprising then, that gutters feature prominently in the *Assize* and upon the rolls.

The subject is difficult because the terms used for gutter are confusing; indeed, it is often impossible to visualise the form of gutter to which the record refers. The most generally used word was *guttera* (gotterum, gutera, etc.) which might be made of lead[3] (**283, 336, 370**), attached to a wall (**184, 236, 331**) or in, or under, the ground (**11, 20, 111, 618**). *Stillicidium* was the term used by the *Assize* and was also commonly used on our rolls (**71, 163, 183, 222, 230, 344**) to describe a gutter above ground level, often under the eaves. Frequently it is used interchangeably with *guttera*. Exceptionally, however, *stillicidium* is used to designate a spout of the kind still seen pro-

---

1. An enclosure or barrier (e.g. a hedge, wall, railing, etc.) along the boundary of any place which it is desired to defend from intruders (*O.E.D.*, sb. 5).
2. *Lib. Alb.*, i, p. xxxiii.
3. The soldering of a gutter and the candles used for the purpose are itemised in an account of 1359 (*Memorials*, 305).

Introduction

truding from the mouths of gargoyles (**521**). A pipe from the middle of a gutter (**486**) and two other pipes jutting out from a house (**424**) may have served the same purpose. *Filettum*, which we have translated as fillet-gutter, was used with more discrimination. Once we hear of a 'filettum plumbeum ad modum guttere' (**267**) and these gutters were often made of lead (**222, 267**). It seems likely that they were long strips of lead bent so as to form a gutter. In one plea (**616**) a concave leaden gutter (filacium plumbeum concavatum) upon the eaves of a house received the water from the house and conveyed it into a leaden underground channel (fistula). In another (**222**) all three words occur: *stillicidium* is used to describe a rain-gutter; *gutterum* seems to describe a gutter on the ground while a leaden *filettum* carries the water from the *stillicidium* into a sink. Gutters (guttere) might be as much as $1\frac{1}{2}$ or 3 ft. wide (**222, 501**). 'Down pipes' of a kind familiar to the reader are seldom, if ever, mentioned; a possible exception may be four leaden pipes draining from the roof of a house into a leaden gutter (**283**). Gutters spilled on to waste ground or into cess-pits or into the street but sometimes their contents were received by sinks or soakaways (**222, 277, 572, 584**). From the streets the water might be carried away in street gutters or kennels (**140, 358, 577**). These in turn might feed the *rivolus* leading to the Moor (**266, 292, 375**), the Fleet, the Walbrook or the Thames itself. A kennel near Houndsditch was allegedly liable to overflow so that the children of the inhabitants were often drowned (**618**).

The provisions of the *Assize* about gutters were no less elaborate than those concerning walls and far more confusing. When a wall was held in common by neighbours (*Lib. Alb.*, i, 321, 322), whether in equal or unequal shares (*ibid.*, 327), the parties were either to combine to provide a rain-gutter to carry off the water from their houses, or each was to provide his own gutter to convey the water from his own house on to his own land or into the street (*ibid.*, 321). If one of the parties heightened his portion of the wall he was to make a rain-gutter for it at his own expense (*ibid.*, 321–2). Should one party be unable or unwilling to participate in the building he was to give 3 ft. of his land, and his neighbour was to build thereon a wall of the prescribed height and breadth, half of which was to belong to the donor of the land, and between them they were to provide for drainage (*ibid.*, 322). On the other hand, if an individual built a wall upon his own land at his own expense he was to possess it *libere et digne* (*ibid.*, 329). His neighbour was to have no right in it, but was to provide a rain-gutter under the eaves of the house built upon it and receive the water upon his own land or convey it into the street (*ibid.*, 323).[1] If in such a case the neighbour brought an assize against the builder, the latter was free to choose whether to join him in building a wall in common, or to adhere to his original plan; but he could not prevent the plaintiff from building a wall of the same height next his, and they would then have to provide for the

---

1. *Lib. Alb.*, i, 326 recognises that certain individuals have acquired a prescriptive right to have corbels and beams and even arches and cupboards in walls which are 'private' property, and lays down that in future no such claims must be recognised without the express consent of the owner of the wall and insists that all claiming such rights must receive the water draining from the house built on the wall, through a gutter beneath the eaves.

Introduction

drainage either jointly or severally (*ibid.*, 329–30). If it happened that water had been allowed to drain for a long time from a house not walled in stone on to a neighbouring vacant plot of land, the owner of the plot might nevertheless build upon it at will, removing the overhanging eaves of the adjoining house; but thereafter he would be responsible for carrying off the water from it. The same rule was to apply to gutters discharging on to vacant land. When a gutter discharged into that of a neighbour or ran through the midst of his tenement the neighbour might not obstruct it, and even if he demolished his house with the intention of rebuilding it, he must continue to receive the water and convey it away, as had been customary; but the assize should be notified of what had been done (*ibid.*, 331–2).

In most of the pleas concerning gutters, the plaintiff complains that the water from the defendant's roof falls upon his land, flooding it, rotting his timber, etc.,[1] either because the defendant had no gutter or because his gutter was defective in some way (**77, 132, 163, 336, 343–4, 349–50**). Gutters held in common were the cause of litigation when one party refused to share the cost of repair (**183**) even if there was a written agreement (**71, 476**). The obligation to receive and carry off the water from a neighbour's roof (**54, 61, 95, 252**) must always have been likely to cause disputes. For example, a plaintiff complained that the defendants had built a gutter to carry off the water from their own house, whereas they ought to have received the water from his house, as he had provided the stone wall enclosing their land; but it was found that part of the wall was held in common and therefore adjudged that the defendant should provide the gutter where the wall was owned solely by the plaintiff but that it should be provided jointly or separately where the wall was held in common (**94**). The tearing down of a neighbour's gutter might result in a plea of trespass in the mayor's court,[2] or in an assize of nuisance (**184, 236,** cf. **589**). Sewage thrown into gutters was another ground of complaint (**370**). Gutters which passed through a neighbour's tenement and were blocked (**70, 258, 438, 607**) may have been below ground (**11, 20, 111**). Elsewhere on the rolls gutters running under houses are specifically mentioned (**214, 614, 616, 654**).

Intense and drastic rebuilding at various times since the middle ages has left little of medieval London either above or below the ground. Archaeologists find medieval pits, cess-pits, rubbish-pits and wells, and these are, perhaps, the only physical remains of the nuisances with which we are concerned. The ground of the medieval city was honeycombed with pits,[3] often of considerable size, measuring as much as 12 ft. across and 12 ft. deep (**485**).[4] Into them went much of London's sewage and rubbish;[5] and they gave rise to many disputes between neighbours.

The provision in the *Assize* (*Lib. Alb.*, i, 323–4) for these disputes did not

---

1. Cf. *Novae narrationes*, C108.
2. *C.E.M.C.R.*, 104.
3. W. F. Grimes, *Excavation of Roman and mediaeval London* (1968), 151–2; a lined square pit is illustrated on plate 74. For an illustration of a lined round pit, see 'Archaeological finds in the City of London', London & Middx. Archaeol. Soc. Trans., xxii, pt. 1 (1968), plate 4.
4. Cf. Grimes, 160.
5. E. L. Sabine, 'Latrines and cesspools of mediaeval London', *Speculum*, ix (1934), 303–21; and 'City cleaning in mediaeval London', *Speculum*, xii (1937), 19–43.

Introduction

feature in the Lex de Assisa but may well have been as old. The assize might be demanded for any pit, except those made before the first year of Richard I, i.e. theoretically, the year in which the assize was enacted. If the cess-pit of a privy was lined with stone its mouth should be $2\frac{1}{2}$ ft. from a neighbour's land even though there were a stone wall between them; if not so lined it should be $3\frac{1}{2}$ ft. from a neighbour's land. Pits of all kinds, for receiving clean or foul water, were to be subject to this rule.

The complaint most frequently made was that the cess-pit of a privy was too close to a party-wall and that the sewage from it was penetrating the wall, ruining it, rotting the timber or running into a neighbour's cellar.[1] Judgments strictly in accordance with the *Assize* were common (**2, 44, 60, 69, 96, 98**) and when it was simply a matter of a pit's distance from a wall, little room was left for elaborate pleading, which perhaps explains the small number of incomplete pleas of this kind. A pit might be found to be far enough away (**26**); or when a stone wall was alleged to have been ruined, the defendant might be ordered to repair the wall (**19**). But on one occasion when a plaintiff said that his earthen wall had been rotted and his house inundated with sewage, the defendant successfully claimed that the pit in question was held in common; and it was adjudged that the parties clean it and rebuild the wall in stone at their common charge (**165**). Occasionally the distance from the plaintiff's wall specified in judgments varied, e.g. $1\frac{1}{2}$ ft. (**3**) or 3 ft. (**191**).

A few details concerning sanitary arrangements are noteworthy. A privy might be enclosed by party walls and provided with seats but have a cess-pit shared with neighbours (**325**). A public convenience in Queenhithe was cleansed by the flow of water collected in a gutter for that purpose; the flow was obstructed by sewage from a wooden pipe connected to the seat of a householder's privy (**214**). The stench from such places was not greatly complained of (**364, 585, 644**).[2]

Apart from walls, gutters, privies and pavements[3] the only other category of nuisance for which the *Assize* provided, was windows (*Lib. Alb.*, i, 324). It ordained that a view from a window, despite long possession, could be fully obstructed by a neighbour who built opposite it on his land, unless it were protected by a deed. But the plaint most frequently found was made by plaintiffs whose neighbours had windows or other apertures, or even doors, overlooking their land (**14, 129, 163, 167, 216, 231–2**). Complaint of evils arising from such windows was commonly made: that the private business of the plaintiff, his household and servants could be seen by the defendant, his tenants and servants (**407, 419–23**); that filth and rubbish were thrown out on to the plaintiff's land (**81, 407, 426, 445, 514, 525**); that the stench of a defendant's privy came through apertures in his wall (**364**).[4] The height at which windows overlooking a neighbour's land were tolerable appears to have been settled in 1316. In a plea of that year it was adjudged that a defendant should have no window at a height of less than 16 ft. facing the plaintiff's land (**230**). This judgment seems to have been duly noted in later

1. Cf. *Novae narrationes*, C107.
2. Cf. *ibid.*
3. For pavements, see p. xxx below.
4. Cf. *Novae narrationes*, B149.

Introduction

plaints which gave the height of windows as 13, 7 or 4½ ft. from the ground **(261, 340–1)**[1] but by 1339 it was common form to complain that they were less than 16 ft. from the ground **(349–50, 359, 363, 371–2)**.[2] In such cases it was normally adjudged that the defendant should block the windows or apertures in question. In one plea of this kind, the parson of St. Stephen Walbrook who had made a great aperture in the stone wall on the south side of his church was obliged to repair it **(174)**; in another, doors and apertures opening on to an alley adjoining the defendant's house and leading to the plaintiff's garden were to be blocked up **(464)**.

A view from a window less than 16 ft. from the ground cannot have been easy to retain. An unexceptionable grant of view and light from a house was almost a prerequisite. A plaintiff, whose view had been blocked by a stack of firewood, successfully supported her suit with a deed granting her 'visum, aperturam, lumen, aerem et claritatem' of a window in the gable of her house, 2½ ells, 1 inch above the ground and barred with wood or iron **(312)**; another produced a deed guaranteeing him the light into and out of (cum libero introitu et exitu luminis) his windows and upheld his plaint against a neighbour who had begun to build a house opposite **(430)**; yet another, whose apertures lighting his kitchen had been blocked, had them reopened because he was able to produce a deed granting the light to his predecessor **(203)**.[3] Sometimes, if a view were obscured by a new building, the building was prohibited but when complaint was made concerning the prohibition, defendants seldom had success in protecting their view **(255, 305, 317, 381, 417)**. But jetties or pentices which obscured a view **(77)** or blocked the light into a workshop **(548)** were treated as nuisances.

Many of these windows were presumably unglazed. The earliest glazed window to which reference is made occurs in a deed of 1263–4 **(255)**; other examples are not numerous **(81**, cf. **648)**; once we hear of windows with broken glass through which a neighbour's affairs can be seen **(362)** suggesting that the glass itself was translucent rather then transparent. Unglazed windows were sometimes barred with wood or iron **(312, 370)** or shuttered **(206)**. A defendant in 1427 hopefully alleged that according to the custom of the City, it had always been permissible for windows to overlook a neighbouring tenement provided they were 8 ft. from the ground and glazed with thick glass or barred with iron (cum vitro spisso vel fermentis ferreis includere) but in accordance with the custom of the City she was ordered to block her windows **(652)**.

Public nuisances and the commonalty

Apart from the disputes between neighbours with which our record is primarily concerned, the Nuisance Rolls also contain a number of pleas which sought to correct public nuisances. But the assize of nuisance was never used extensively for this purpose.

The vast majority of public nuisances were dealt with by wardmotes. A

1. Cf. **268** in which windows or apertures less than 9 ft. from the ground or the storey to which they belong, are alleged to be contrary to custom.
2. A complaint concerning windows 16 ft. from the ground **(243)** may have been a clerical error.
3. See also **351, 370**.

Introduction

few presentments have been preserved, notably those for 1422 and 1423 enrolled upon the Plea and Memoranda Rolls, but fragments of earlier presentments and the evidence provided by the custumals show that the procedure dated from a much earlier period.[1] The range and variety of matters dealt with was considerable and many of the presentments were not unlike the nuisances appearing on our rolls. Apart from purprestures, the wardmotes dealt with ruinous houses or walls which endangered passers-by, defective paving, ruinous chimneys, low pentices, obstructions of paths or lanes, blocking of ditches, noisome privies, the tipping of ordure or rubbish into the streets or watercourses and many other matters that need not here concern us. Our rolls contain not only several pleas initiated by presentment (**449–50**) at wardmote, but also one membrane (DD, m. 68) consisting of seven presentments made at three different wardmotes (**453–9**), which may have been especially copied for the use of the assize.[2]

In 1309 two entries occur (**140–1**) which probably arose from wardmote presentments; judgment was given because the nuisances had been found by the testimony of the neighbours and were apparent to the men of the assize. These nuisances may well have been dealt with in this way in order to impress the dean and canons and the master of the bakehouse of St. Paul's who had perpetrated them.

Purprestures, or encroachments upon the king's highway, were commonly enquired into, during the thirteenth and early fourteenth century, by the justices itinerant in their sessions of crown pleas at the Tower; in 1246 a special session was held there and many purprestures were rented from the king while the remainder were ordered to be amended.[3] The normal procedure at such sessions,[4] according to a note in Liber Custumarum,[5] was to amerce anyone who made a purpresture but to allow him or his heirs or assigns to rent it from the king for a fixed annual rent provided the dozens (duodene) of the ward should agree that it was not a nuisance to the neighbours but if it was not so agreed, the sheriffs were to throw it down. A further proviso allowed the tenant of such a purpresture to place himself upon the verdict of the mayor, aldermen and commonalty as to whether his purpresture was to the nuisance of the neighbours.

The purprestures dealt with by the justices itinerant were basically concerned with free passage along the king's highway, streets, lanes, paths or waterways. They were normally presented at wardmotes, but in the fourteenth century they were also sometimes inquired into by the assize of nuisance. Even before the Eyre of 1321 the mayor and aldermen were using the process to settle what might well have been treated as purprestures by the justices (**15, 97, 188**). During the Eyre itself no assizes were held (**254**)

1. *C.P.M.R. 1413–37*, pp. xxiv–xxx, 115–41, 150–9.
2. The medieval numeration of the membrane and the position of the holes at its head show that it anciently formed part of the roll. Although two of the presentments (**455, 457**) relate to pleas (**449–50**) another (**453**) is twelve years earlier than the rest and the matters presented are various.
3. *London Eyre of 1244*, nos. 349–486.
4. For purprestures at the Eyres of 1276 and 1321, see B. M. Add. Ch. 5153, m. 16d; and P.R.O. J1/547A.
5. *Lib. Cust.*, i, 366; *Eyre of London, 1321*, ed. H. M. Cam (Selden Soc., lxxxv, 1968), i, 65.

Introduction

but thereafter the commonalty had frequent recourse to the assize for this and other purposes (**260, 292, 334, 390, 487**). The most common ground for complaint by the commonalty was ruinous stone walls (**299, 302–3, 361, 390**), sometimes described as being in danger of collapsing to the peril of neighbours and passers-by (**264, 334**). After judgment had been given in one such plea, the defendant's wife, who was present in court, warned her husband to repair the wall lest evil befall someone (**28**). The mayor had warned the owner of a wall near the entrance of Guildhall to repair it but when he failed to do so, the commonalty brought an assize against him (**213**). Ruinous houses[1] also gave offence: one was said to be so ruinous that great and small, horsemen and pedestrians feared to pass by, while its lack of a roof and rotten timbers were the scandal and disgrace of the City (**300**). Walls or houses, ruinous or otherwise, which overhung a road, street, or lane and other things, including pentices, which obstructed the free passage of pedestrians, horsemen or horses and carts were among the nuisances which the commonalty sought to correct by the assize (**97, 396, 408, 536, 547**). Pentices, jetties and solars which overhung the street were a perennial problem to the City authorities. Regulations controlling them are numerous: they were to be high enough for a man on a great horse to pass beneath,[2] and later, more precisely, they were to be 9 ft. from the ground; otherwise they were to be corrected within forty days under penalty of 40 shillings.[3] When it was adjudged that a solar of this kind should be removed 'iuxta formam statuti editi de edificiis' (**536**) this regulation, although never part of the *Assize*, may have been intended. Other pleas concerned forges (**483, 547**), the fencing of a vacant plot in the parish of St. Bartholomew by the Exchange because robbers lurked there at night and attacked passers-by[4] (**394**); the blocking of ditches (**292, 375**); and pigsties built over, and other encroachments upon, the Walbrook (**15–16, 188, 382–3**).

The City officials presumably found the assize useful when the wardmote process had failed, when religious houses or difficult or powerful men were perpetrating nuisances or where there was some call for urgency in the correction of a nuisance. Nearly every plaint by the commonalty resulted in judgment for the plaintiffs: only once did a defendant win his case (**396**) and very few of these pleas were incomplete (e.g. **97, 299, 387**). No doubt the mayor and aldermen seldom bothered their heads with theoretical matters but one development of the fourteenth century may possibly have coloured their views and this concerned the common soil or *solum communitatis*.[5] The arrentation of purprestures was probably never very profitable to the crown[6] and in any case, after 1341 there were no further

---

1. For a regulation on this subject, see *Ricart's Kalendar*, 106.
2. *Memorials*, 35.
3. *Lib. Alb.*, i, 271. For the most detailed regulations see *Ricart's Kalendar*, 107; but see also *Lib Alb.*, i, 336, 432; *C. Letter-Book A*, 217. In 1381 a grant of an hautpas between tenements on either side of a street stipulated that it should be 14 ft. from the ground (*Memorials*, 452–3).
4. For an unsuccessful defence on the same grounds, cf. **260**.
5. For a history of common soil, see P. E. Jones's introduction to *C.P.M.R. 1437–57*, pp. ix-xxii.
6. *London Eyre of 1244*, pp. xvi–xix, xxvii–xxxii.

Introduction

London sessions of crown pleas at the Tower. There was then nothing to inhibit the idea that the commonalty owned the streets and lanes. Thus, it is striking that the phrase *solum communitatis* first appears on our rolls in 1344 (**387**) when a defendant is charged with having built upon the commonalty's soil next the City Wall[1] within Newgate;[2] further pleas (**450, 487, 493–4**) and two ward presentments (**453, 455**) are also concerned with nuisances upon the common soil. No mention of the common soil was made in 1305 when an assize (**85**) found that the Black Friars had built too close to the City wall and forbade them thenceforth to build within 16 ft. of it.

The commonalty were normally represented as plaintiffs by the common serjeant,[3] the City's professional pleader (**260, 334, 483**) although he was sometimes simply described as attorney (**292, 299, 302, 449–50**). Ralph Pecok, the first attorney to appear for the commonalty (**15**) was common serjeant in all but name.[4] Reginald Wolleward[5] who pleaded for the commonalty from June to August 1328 may have been another holder of the office but Adam de Acres, who is only described as attorney, is known to have been the common serjeant from other sources.[6] No holder of the office is known between Ralph Pecok in 1301 and Gregory de Norton in 1319, during which period the commonalty were represented by the City chamberlain (**167, 188, 213–14**) and, quite exceptionally, by an alderman, John de Gisors, prosecuting a suit on his own as well as on the commonalty's behalf (**179**). In pleas concerning Bridge House property the commonalty were represented by the wardens of the bridge (**51–2, 416**).

The commonalty never had an assize brought against them although one complaint is entered upon the rolls (**544**). The parson of St. Clement Eastcheap and his parishioners complained of a tenement bequeathed to the mayor and commonalty with two jetties one above the other between the church and the churchyard. After view, the complainants released and quitclaimed all plaints and demands concerning the tenement and in return the mayor and aldermen undertook to provide wax torches on the vigil of the Assumption, at the elevation of the Body of Christ and on appropriate occasions when the Lord's Body was carried through the parish.

One other form of entry on the rolls deserves comment although there are only four examples of it. The perambulation of the mayor and aldermen is twice described as being at the instance of a complainant (**64, 250**); and on the other two occasions it is likely that it was made because the mayor and aldermen happened to be in the parish for holding an assize (**114, 119**). They do not conform to the *Assize*'s rules of procedure; there appears to have been no summons, and no essoins or adjournments, but

1. At a perambulation in 1352 the mayor and aldermen viewed and evalued purprestures upon *solum communitatis* within and without Ludgate (*Lib. Cust.*, ii, 454–5).
2. In 1435, the common soil of the City was said to extend 16 ft. from the Walls or Gates, according to the laws and customs of the City (*C. Letter-Book K*, 188).
3. For a discussion of this office and a list of those who held it, see B. R. Masters, 'The Common Serjeant', *Guildhall Miscellany*, ii, no. 9 (1967), 379–89.
4. He is found pleading on the City's behalf between 1293 and 1301 (*Lib. Cust.*, i, 116; *C. Letter-Book C*, 13–14, 107; *C.E.M.C.R.*, 80).
5. He is also described as attorney at the Guildhall in 1309 (*C. Letter-Book C*, 165).
6. Masters, 'Common Serjeant', 383.

Introduction

the judgments follow the same pattern as those used in the assize. In other cases not described as perambulations, the assize apparently took action without the usual preliminaries: peremptory orders were given to remove obstructions from the course of the Walbrook (**198–200**)[1] and the owners of a ruinous wall spontaneously agreed to repair it (**201**).[2]

Another matter sometimes dealt with peremptorily by the mayor and aldermen was paving. The *Assize* (*Lib. Alb.*, i, 331), contained a regulation whereby anyone unjustly making a pavement in the king's highway to the nuisance of the commonalty or a neighbour could be prohibited from doing so by the City's bailiffs[3] and that the matter could then be discussed by the men of the assize.[4] In one instance the course of a stream (probably a kennel) had been changed by raising the level of the pavement (**140**); in another the level of the pavement was to be lowered because it endangered private persons and strangers walking or riding there (**142**); and in another it was alleged that for lack of paving great damage was daily incurred by the citizens and, it was curiously added, could arise in case of fire (**141**). Each was to pave in front of his own tenement (**141–2, 186, 369**). Only once do we find a party impleaded by his neighbour concerning the repair of paving (**249**). It was normally a matter dealt with by the commonalty.[5]

General observations

Two-thirds of the pleas on the rolls were heard in the first half of the fourteenth century. Although only one plea was entered in 1349, the number of pleas in the few years immediately after that date differed little from those before it, thus serving to confirm the impression given by the possessory assizes[6] that the Black Death had little effect upon the level of business in City courts.[7] Between 1379 and 1431 when the rolls end, only forty pleas were enrolled. Complaint was made of nuisances in most City parishes. They were most numerous in the parishes surrounding Guildhall (especially in St. Lawrence Jewry); along the Thames (especially in St. Michael Queenhithe and St. Dunstan in the East) and also along the course of the Walbrook (especially in St. John, St. Martin Vintry and St. Stephen). Indeed, to keep the Walbrook flowing without obstruction or excessive filth, was a task which greatly exercised the City authorities:[8] Londoners stacked their firewood above it (**16, 199**), built pig-sties and privies over it (**200, 382–3**) and otherwise encroached upon its course (**15, 55**).

During the first few decades of the fourteenth century aldermen or

---

1. Cf. **16, 85**.
2. Cf. **209**.
3. For possible implications of the term 'bailiff', see p. xi above.
4. In 1372 it was ordered that no one might raise his pavement higher than his neighbour's without the consent of the mayor and aldermen (*C. Letter-Book G*, 301).
5. In the mayoralty of Gregory de Rokeslee (1274–81) an ordinance was made whereby each wardmote was to elect four men 'a garder les pavimens e les desturbances' (*C. Letter-Book A*, 183; cf. *Lib. Cust.*, i, 100). In 1302 four paviors were sworn for the whole City according to the ordinance (*C. Letter-Book C*, 115). In 1311 four persons were appointed to survey the pavements in Langbourn ward (*C. Letter-Book D*, 312).
6. See *London possessory assizes*, p. xxxi (chronological list).
7. Cf. Sabine, 'Latrines', *Speculum*, ix, 320.
8. e.g. *Memorials*, 23, 379, 478.

Introduction

members of aldermanic families were the predominant class among the parties to the assize. No doubt their great wealth goes far to explain their taste for litigation but the possibility that they could indulge this taste without payment of fees cannot be overlooked. Certainly, at a later date, when a fee of six pence payable to the common clerk was fixed for each bill of assize of nuisance or intrusion, aldermen were specifically exempted from it.[1] The rule that no one can be at the same time a party and a judge[2] was not observed by the aldermen who held the assizes in the early fourteenth century. Frequently aldermen are found on the assizes in which they were plaintiffs (**29–30, 44, 50, 66, 96**). Nor were sheriffs and mayors blameless in this respect (**9, 53**).

The City clergy with their parishioners or churchwardens often made use of the assize to rectify nuisances around their churches and churchyards (**63, 81, 308, 546, 574, 623, 659**) and conversely, were frequently impleaded (**50, 125, 259, 298, 487, 631**). Apart from many pleas which concern churchyards, particular mention should be made of several entries touching upon parochial processions (**43, 544, 639**), chantries (**385, 498, 647**) and a small window in a party-wall of St. Leonard Eastcheap through which the owner of an adjoining house could watch the celebration of Mass (**574**). Religious houses both within the City and outside were also parties to assizes, particularly in the second half of the fourteenth century and the fifteenth century (**386, 399, 570, 613, 642, 656**), and were frequently represented by their heads in person, even the abbot of St. Albans appearing upon the site of the nuisance himself. Apart from the heads of religious houses outside the City a number of other parties, who were not Londoners, are noteworthy: several members of the nobility (the earls of Gloucester and Suffolk, the countess of Hereford and Aymer de Valence) as well as a number of knights who were 'foreigners'.

The number of pleas which arose through the practice of a craft is strikingly small. Most nuisances of this kind were probably corrected by the wardmote, but a handful resulted in assizes: a chalk-pit for tanning hides (**251**); dyers' workmen who carried their dripping wet cloths up and down steps allegedly belonging to a neighbour (**488**); a tenter-yard (**589**); tenting-frames which damaged a wall (**643**); the work-shop of Queen Philippa's tailor (**417**); a scalding-house in St. Nicholas Shambles in which pigs and other animals were slaughtered (**569**);[3] forges built in the public highway (**483, 547–8**) and most intriguing of all, the forge of an armourer (**617**) whose sledgehammers shook the neighbours' walls, disturbed their rest and spoiled their wine and ale, while the stench and smoke from the sea-coal used in his forge penetrated their hall and chambers. The picture of the social life of fourteenth and fifteenth century London which the rolls present is in sombre colours and no doubt distorted, but the fact remains that many of the parties to assizes were from the more well-to-do sections of society and nuisances and squalor would hardly have been confined to their tenements.

1. *Lib. Alb.*, i, 48.
2. *London Eyre of 1244*, no. 236.
3. For a study of nuisances associated with this trade, see E. L. Sabine, 'Butchering in mediaeval London', *Speculum*, viii (1933), 335–53.

Introduction

Malice, although difficult to detect with certainty, may well have been the root cause of some pleas. It was only once alleged by a party to an assize (**591**) but clearly little love was lost between the neighbours Joan de Armenters and William de Thorneye on the one hand and Andrew Aubrey and his wife on the other. The trouble apparently started when Joan hired masons to build a door in her cellar and Andrew prohibited it (**323**) and at the same time prohibited William from building a privy (**324**). Six weeks later Andrew complained that Joan and William had removed the fence and roof from their privy (**325**) and that they had made a hole in their room over William's cellar through which his private business could be seen by those in the room above (**326**). Matters seem only to have been resolved by the death of Joan (**316**).

Outside London the assize of nuisance was available for actions concerning rights of way from an early date.[1] The *Assize*[2] made no mention of rights of way but the process was used both by individuals (**125, 399–400, 511, 606, 631**) and by the commonalty (**64, 259, 449**) to correct nuisances concerning them. Access to the private quays (**392, 453, 637**) and wharves along the Thames was a likely cause of such disputes (**327, 396, 459**).

Although even in the early fourteenth century plaintiffs sometimes complained of several apparently separate nuisances at one time, this practice became common after about 1341 (**370** *et seq.*). There was, in such pleas, a distinct air of trying to tidy up everything in a neighbouring tenement about which complaint could possibly be made. For the plaintiff such a course was obviously economical both of money and time while the risk of overloading his bill does not appear to have been great. If he sometimes over-reached himself he might still succeed on most counts and face amercement only on one (**371**).

'Nocumenta vero infinita sunt' wrote Bracton; although not infinite, the nuisances on our rolls are undoubtedly varied. The *Assize* may originally have clearly marked the scope of the action, but a high proportion of the entries fall wholly or partly outside that scope. Pleas concerning chimneys, leaning walls, windows overlooking a neighbour's land, and rights of way, as well as most of the actions in which the commonalty were plaintiffs, provide striking examples. During the century and a quarter covered by our records changes in procedure can also be seen. Even in the early fourteenth century essoins and adjournments sometimes delayed the process unduly but by the end of our period its summary character had almost disappeared. There can be little doubt, however, that the assize of nuisance provided the freeholder in London with a convenient means of solving some of the problems of urban life.

---

1. See p. xii above; cf. *Novae narrationes*, C112.
2. One somewhat obscure clause in the *Assize* may be dealt with here. The Lex de Assisa contained the sentence: 'Debet autem fieri et teneri ubi usseriam vel introitum aut exitum vel s[h]opam non auferat'. M. Bateson suggested that this referred to the twelve jurors who met on the spot (*Borough customs*, i, 247). The following clause in the *Assize* presumably derived from it: 'Hec autem assisa non conceditur alicui per quod husseria, introitus vel exitus vel schopa ad nocumentum vicini sui extricetur vel arctetur'. No plea on our rolls appears to be based upon this rule.

Introduction

The Rolls and the Calendar

The records of the assize of nuisance are preserved in the Corporation of London Records Office in three rolls, known as Miscellaneous Rolls DD, FF, and II. Misc. Roll DD (**1–480**), covering the years 1301–56, consists of 73 membranes (most of which are roughly $8\frac{1}{2} \times 28$ inches), filed together at the head. The membranes have been numbered in pencil mm. 1–17, 17a, 18–72 and these are the numbers given in the calendar. They were also numbered in a late fourteenth-century or early fifteenth-century hand 1–44 (= mm. 1–17, 18–44) and 45–71 (= mm. 46–72); mm. 17a and 45 were not numbered, probably being overlooked because they are short. A note at the head of m. 38 explains that mm. 38–9 were found among the memoranda of John de Burton, clerk of the Chamber, after his death,[1] which perhaps accounts for the duplication of entries on mm. 39 and 40. The roll has been repaired in recent years but there is no reason to suppose that mm. 17a and 45 are modern additions. The piece of parchment sewn to the foot of m. 12 (as a roll cover) and the endorsement upon it shows that mm. 1–12 at one time formed a separate roll and endorsements[2] on mm. 13–15, 17, 18, 20–2, 27, 32 and 35 suggest that these membranes may once have been filed separately as rotulets. Misc. Roll FF (**481–619**) covering the years 1356–78 consists of 40 membranes measuring from $10\frac{1}{2}$ to $11\frac{1}{4}$ inches in width and from 18 to 30 inches in length. A few membranes are damaged, rubbed or faded and several have been repaired. The stitching at the head of the roll and the numbering of the membranes is modern but there appears to be no reason to doubt that the roll was anciently made up in this way. Misc. Roll II (**620–61**) consists of 17 membranes measuring $9\frac{1}{2}$ to $10\frac{1}{2}$ inches in width and 15 to 29 inches in length. It contains the record of assizes and certain other matters between 1378 and 1431. Some membranes are much damaged and have been extensively repaired and there is considerable chronological disorder in the arrangement. But the numbering of the membranes shows that this disorder was not of recent making. The roll differs from DD and FF in failing to give an impression of the process's continuity; matters such as essoins and respites are not separately entered upon it.

The rolls tell little of how they were kept, but it is clear that they must generally have been written up after the assize had been held. It is unusual to find proceedings for one assize entered in more than one place on the rolls even though judgment was sometimes greatly delayed. Essoins and respites that were separately entered frequently appeared also in the record of the proceedings. The rolls appear to have been well kept; incomplete entries are not uncommon but cannot be attributed to clerical negligence. Apart from contemporary *notae* indicating essoins, respites, judgments or amercements at least two students (probably of the late fourteenth or early fifteenth century)[3] have made comments in the margins of DD and FF. Such comments are seldom more than a brief summary of some point in the record and have not been calendared here, except in a few instances

---

1. ? before 1332 (he was assessed in the lay subsidy of 1319 but not in that of 1332).
2. These have not been calendared in order to save space; they merely note the regnal years of the pleas on the membranes concerned.
3. One noted that St. Werbourge was the ancient name of the parish (**81**).

Introduction

where the commentator was clearly surprised or scandalised at his findings.

The compression of records occupying 130 membranes into the present calendar has imposed a difficult task upon the editors. Our aim has been to eliminate 'common form' as far as possible while retaining significant details of fact and procedure. The normal form 'B summonitus fuit ad respondendum A de placito assise nocumenti. Et unde A queritur quod . . .' has been calendared 'A complains that B', while the more unusual form 'A optulit se versus B' has been rendered 'A appears against B' (e.g. **10–12, 24, 28**).[1] Dates have been rendered in days, months and years, the latter reckoned to begin on 1 January. Where a word or phrase seemed obscure or of particular significance it has been enclosed in round brackets after the suggested translation. Illegible words or phrases have been indicated thus: (—). Latin forenames have normally been translated; the original spelling of surnames and places has been retained but Latin place-names have been translated. Suspension marks at the end of names have generally been ignored. Separately entered essoins and respites have been calendared only when they are the sole evidence that a plaint had been raised; where proceedings of the assize appear elsewhere on the roll essoins and respites have been omitted.

The Index contains entries for persons, places and subjects. H. A. Harben, *Dictionary of London* (1918), E. Ekwall, *Street-names of the City of London* (1954) and the appropriate volumes of the English Place-Name Society have generally been used to establish the modern forms of place, street and parish names. Certain subjects occur too frequently in the text to make indexing profitable; these are dealt with in the Introduction, and the Index makes reference to the discussion of them there. Subjects of legal interest have not been entered separately in the Index but have been brought together under the heading 'Legal matters'. For subjects grouped under the headings, 'Buildings & parts thereof' and 'Trades & occupations', cross-references have been provided. References in Roman numerals are to the pages of the Introduction; Arabic numerals denote entries in the calendar (and not pages) unless printed in italics when they refer to the heading of an entry in the calendar. In indexing headings only the first and last appearance of mayors, aldermen and sheriffs have been given.

1. In one plea **(230)** the normal form was deleted and the second form substituted. For an inconclusive discussion of the significance of these forms, see *Cal. Exchequer of the Jews*, iii. *1275–7*, ed. H. Jenkinson (Jewish Hist. Soc., 1929), pp. xxxiii–xxxiv.

ASSIZE OF NUISANCE
MISC. ROLL DD

[m. 1] *Fri. 10 Feb. 1301. Elias Russel, mayor, Geoffrey de Nortone, Walter de Finchingfeld, William le Marezerer, Thomas Romeyn, John de Dunstaple, Solomon le Coteler, John de Canterbury (Cantuaria), Simon de Paris, Hugh Pourte, Nicholas Pycot, aldermen.*

1. William de Stertford essoins himself against William de Gartone by Stephen de Wetheresfeld.

2. William de Béthune (Betonia) complains that the cess-pit of the privy (puteum cloace) of William de Gartone adjoins so closely his stone wall that the sewage penetrates his cellar (celarium). The def. says that he and his ancestors have been seised of the privy in question time out of mind, and prays that the assize do nothing in prejudice of his free tenement. The pl. says that long seisin contrary to the statute ought not to prejudice his case. After adjournment the assize comes upon the land on Fri. 3 Mar. 1301, and it is adjudged that within 40 days the def. remove his cess-pit 2½ ft. of masonry (de petra) from the pl.'s wall.

3. The same William makes a like complaint concerning the cess-pit of the privy of William de Sterteford. The sheriff testifies that the def. was summoned but he makes default. The assize comes [as in **2**], and since it is found that the def. owns a moiety of the stone wall in question it is adjudged that within 40 days he remove his cess-pit 1½ ft. of stone (de opere petre) from the same.

Fri. 17 Feb. 1301. Elias Russel, mayor, Geoffrey de Nortone, William de Leyre, Thomas Romeyn, John de Canterbury, Martin Box, Solomon le Coteler, Simon de Paris and Luke de Haveryng, sheriff.

4. Richard Tayllehaste essoins himself against Thomas de Bannebury and Joan his wife by Thomas de Tatesfeld.

Fri. 3 Mar. 1301. Elias Russel, mayor, Geoffrey de Nortone, William de Leyre, Thomas Romeyn, John de Canterbury, Solomon le Coteler, Simon de Paris, Nicholas Pycot.

5. Hugh le Blund, kt., complains that Walter de Wanlok. [Entry incomplete.]

Fri. 14 July 1301. Lord (per dominum) Elias Russel, mayor, Geoffrey de Nortone, William de Béthune (Betonia), Thomas Romeyn, Walter de

Assize of Nuisance

Finchingfeld, John de Vintry (Vinetria), Adam de Fulham, Hugh Pourte and Nicholas Pycot.

6. Henry le Galeys complains that Gerard Dorgoyl has ruined his stone wall and disturbed him in the easement of his privy in the par. of St. Martin in the Vintry. The def. says that he has only a 16 year interest in the tenement in question and that it is the free tenement and fee of Arnold Barage and Christine his wife without whom he cannot answer. Arnold and Christine come freely and the parties are given a day at the quindene. Afterwards, on Fri. 1 Sep. 1301, the assize comes by Elias Russel, mayor, John le Blund, William de Leyre, Thomas Romeyn, John de Canterbury, John de Dunstaple, Simon de Paris, aldermen. The pl. essoins himself by William de Braynford.

7. The same Henry, pl., essoins himself against Ralph Hardel, def., by William de Braynford.

8. The same Henry, pl., essoins himself against Arnold Barage and Christine his wife, defs., by the same.

9. Elias Russel complains that the house of Amice Horn in the par. of St. Michael Candelwykstrete is ruinous and the water falls from it upon his land and that she has a view into his tenement. The def. says she has no counsel (non habet consilium). The parties are given a day at the quindene. [m. 1d. Blank.]

[m. 2] *Fri. 1 Dec. 1301. John le Blund, mayor, William de Leyre, Walter de Finchingfeld, Nicholas de Farndon, Simon de Paris, John de Dunstaple, Solomon le Coteler, Henry de Gloucestre, Geoffrey de Nortone, Hugh Pourte, Nicholas Pycot, William de Betoyne, Adam de Fulham.*

10. Henry Poteman and Denise his wife, pls., appear against (optulerunt se versus) John Pykeman, rector of the church of Wykham, and Thomas his brother, defs. Thomas comes but John does not, and because his is the fee the sheriff is ordered to summon him for the quindene.

11. Sabine relict of Philip le Tayllour by John son of the said Philip, her attorney, and the same John, pls., appear against Richard de Chigewelle, def. They complain of the unjust prohibition by the sheriff at the instance of the def. of their rebuilding of a party wall (parietis). The def. counters by charging them with the obstruction of a gutter (goterum) conveying the water from both their tenements through the midst of his house into Westchep; but because the gutter is not apparent to the view of the assize (non constat aspectui assise de gotero predicto) it is adjudged that the pls. complete their building operations. Def. in mercy for a false plaint.

12. Orlandino de Podeo and Thomas son of Guydicio (Guydicionis), merchants of the society of the Ricardi of Lucca, pls., appear against Robert de Multone, tailor, and Agnes his wife and Walter de Northwyc and Cecily his wife. The pls. complain that the defs. have built a new house obstructing their view contrary to the terms of their feoffment. After adjournment, Robert and Agnes essoin themselves by Stephen de Wetheresfeld, and Walter and Cecily by Robert de Leycestre; Orlandino appoints Laude Ruffini his attorney. They are given a day on Fri. 9 Feb. 1302. [Judgment was then respited and on Fri. 23 Feb. 1302 it was referred to the Husting of Common Pleas.][1]

Fri. 8 Dec. 1301. [No entry.]

Fri. 15 Dec. 1301. John le Blund, mayor, Geoffrey de Nortone, Walter de Finchingfeld, Thomas Romeyn, Solomon le Coteler, John de Dunstaple, Nicholas Pycot, William de Leyre.

13. Peter le Ireys, [tailor], complains that William de Leyre has unjustly prohibited him from building upon his moiety of the party-wall between their tenements in the par. of St. Lawrence Jewry. The def. justifies his action on the ground that the pl.'s workmen demolished his part of the wall without his consent. After sundry adjournments the parties appear on Fri. 8 Feb. 1302 and judgment is given that the pl. rebuild within 40 days the wall which he has demolished and be in mercy for a false plaint. Def. *sine die.*

14. Richard de Chigewelle complains that the water draining from the houses of Geoffrey de Conduit and Imanya de Brauncastre in the pars. of St. Peter de Wodestrete and St. Matthew de Fridaystrete falls upon his land; and that they have windows (fenestras) and other apertures (foramina) overlooking his land. Adjourned until Fri. 19 Jan. 1302 because the defs. claim to hold by the courtesy of England (per legem Anglie) and say that they cannot answer without Philip son of John le Bailiff to whom the fee and right belong.

15. The commonalty complain by Ralph Pecok, their attorney, that Anketin de Gisors has newly constructed a building (edificium) above the common course of the Walebroke in the par. of St. Martin in the Vintry. The def. pleads that he has no interest in the tenement in question, which is held by Thomas le Noreys for life; but it is adjudged that the building be taken into the hand of the City.

16. It is found by the assize that John de Talworthe stacks his firewood above the course of the Walbroke in the same par. He is ordered not to remove it until he has given satisfaction to the City. On Fri. 15 Nov. 1303 the assize comes and finds 575 faggots stacked above the common course of the Walbroke.

[m. 2d.] *Fri. 9 Feb. 1302. John le Blund, mayor, Elias Russel, Geoffrey de Nortone, Thomas Romeyn, William de Leyre, Adam de Fulham, Richard de Gloucestre, John de Dunstaple, Solomon le Coteler, Nicholas Pycot.*

1. H.C.P.R. 27, mm. 8, 12d, 15.

Assize of Nuisance

17. Avice relict of Thomas Kary, def., v. Robert de Molton and Agnes his wife, pls., are given a day at the quindene.

18. John de Vintry, clerk, complains that Henry le Galeys has a ruinous stone wall which is to the damage of his tenement in the par. of St. Martin in the Vintry. The def. does not deny the charge and it is adjudged that he rebuild the wall within 40 days and be in mercy.

Fri. 23 Feb. 1302. John le Blund, mayor, Elias Russel, Geoffrey de Nortone, Thomas Romeyn, William de Leyre, Walter de Finchingfeld, John de Armenters, John de Dunstaple, Solomon le Coteler, Nicholas Pycot, Richer de Refham.

19. John Duly, kt., pl., appears against John le Riche and Rose his wife, defs., complaining that the stone wall which he holds in common with them in the par. of St. Nicholas Shambles is ruinous because the cess-pit of their privy adjoins it too closely. The sheriff testifies that the defs. were summoned but they make default. It is adjudged that they rebuild the wall within 40 days etc. and be in mercy.

20. Adam Molgas, tailor, complains that Lawrence de Totenham has obstructed a gutter (goterum) running through the midst of his tenement, which from time out of mind has conveyed the water from his premises into the street, in consideration of a yearly quit-rent of 1d. The def. pleads that the assize has no cognisance in the matter since the nuisance is not apparent to its view (non constat eius aspectui etc.), nor does the pl. produce any deed to show that his tenement is bound to render the service alleged. He denies that he has ever been seised of the rent in question and utterly repudiates all claim to it for himself and his successors. It is therefore adjudged that the pl. be quit in perpetuity of the payment aforesaid and have his recovery by another process of law. Def. *sine die*. [*Margin*: Nota de stillicidio per medium tenementi alterius.]

Fri. 16 Mar. 1302. Lords (per dominos)[1] John le Blund, mayor, Elias Russel, Geoffrey de Nortone, William de Leyre, Thomas Romeyn, Walter de Finchingfeld, Richard de Gloucestre, John de Dunstaple, Simon de Paris.

21. Adam de Hallingbury, def., essoins himself against John Somery and Margery his wife, pls., by William de Derteford.

22. John son of Lawrence Duket, def., essoins himself against John de Salisbury (de Sar'), 'barber', and Margery his wife and Christine Duket daughter of Margery, pls., by William de Braynford; and Sibyl relict of the said Lawrence and Roger atte Harpe appear.

23. Gilbert Pynnote, def., essoins himself against Isabel de Estre, pl., by Robert de Leycestre.

---

1. This phrase which occurs intermittently until 1309 is not calendared hereafter.

Assize of Nuisance

24. Master Philip Walrand, pl., appears against Thomas and Richard de Meldeburne, defs., concerning the building of a fence (claustura) between them in the par. of St. Olave de Silvirstrete. The parties are to appear at the quindene unless they can reach an agreement in the meantime.

Fri. 6 Apr. 1302. John le Blund, mayor, Elias Russel, Geoffrey de Nortone, William de Leyre, John de Vintry, John de Dunstaple, Henry de Gloucestre.

25. John le Leuter complains that whereas Simon de Paris guardian of John son of Walter le Blund, a minor, is bound to repair an earthen wall (murum de terra) between their tenements in the pars. of St. Stephen Walebroke and St. Antonin, he refuses to do so. The def. denies the obligation on the ground that the wall stands wholly upon the pl.'s land. Since neither party can produce a deed or other evidence of ownership, it is adjudged that they rebuild the wall on its present site at their common charge.

Fri. 13 July 1302. [Essoin only.]

[m. 3] *Fri. 27 July 1302. John le Blunt, mayor, Geoffrey de Nortone, William de Béthune, Thomas Romeyn, Solomon le Coteler, Nicholas Pycot, Simon de Paris, William de Leyre.*

26. The essoin of Agnes wife of Simon son of (fiz) Robert le Pesshoner, pl., by Robert de Leycestre, is quashed because Simon was essoined at the last court. The same Simon and Agnes complain that John le Bonde and Joan his wife have built the stone cess-pit of a privy too close to their tenement. The def. denies the charge and a day is given to the parties to hear judgment at Guildhall on Tues. 31 July. Afterwards, on Fri. 3 Aug. 1302, the assize comes upon the land by John le Blunt, mayor, William de Béthune, Walter de Finchingfeld, Geoffrey de Nortone, Richard de Gloucestre, Solomon le Coteler, Simon de Paris and Nicholas Pycot, etc.; and because it is found that the cess-pit is at a sufficient distance from the pls.' tenement it is adjudged that the defs. complete their building operations. Pls. in mercy for a false plaint.

27. William de Mabely and Alice his wife, pls., in a plea of assize of nuisance, are given a day at the quindene to meet the objection of the def., Lucy relict of Thomas de Leukenore, that they have no fee or free tenement in the tenement in respect of which the nuisance is alleged; and to make good their claim that the def.'s tenement should receive the water falling from their houses. Lucy as both pl. and def. (tam querens quam defendens) appoints Reginald Wolleword her attorney.

Fri. 7 Sep. 1302. John le Blunt, mayor, Elias Russel, Geoffrey de Nortone, William de Leyre, Thomas Romeyn, John de Canterbury, John Darmenters, John de Dunstaple, Solomon le Coteler, and Nicholas Pycot.

28. The commonalty, pls., appear against Adam Rose, 'potter', def., concerning a stone wall in the par. of All Hallows Bredstrate which is alleged

Assize of Nuisance

to be ruinous. The sheriff testifies that the def. was summoned but he makes default and the assize proceeds in his absence. Judgment that he rebuild the wall within 40 days. He is warned by his wife to obey lest evil befall someone. (Et preceptum est predicto Ade per uxorem suam quod reficiat dictum murum infra xl dies ne malum alicuius inde adveniat.)

29. Solomon le Coteler, pl., appears against William le Servat, def., concerning an alleged nuisance in the def.'s tenement in the par. of St. Mildred;[1] but it is testified that the def. has no free tenement or fee there and he is accordingly *sine die*.

30. Solomon le Coteler complains that Michael de Tullesan has broken down the fence (claustura) of his house in the same par., so that his tenants have a view into his courtyard (respectum habere possint infra curiam suam) and can see his private business; and that the water from the def.'s house floods the courtyard and submerges his trees and plants (herbas). The def. comes and agrees to do all that he ought to do. He is given a day at the quindene but afterwards the parties agree out of court.

31. Amice Horn complains that the house of William de Stertford is ruinous and overhangs her land in the par. of St. Michael de Candewyk-strete by more than $1\frac{1}{2}$ ft., so that she is unable to build thereon. The def. claims that a turret (turellus) built upon the pl.'s tenement is the cause of ruin of his house. They are given a day at the quindene unless they agree together in the meantime. On Fri. 21 Sep. the assize comes, as appears below, but the def. makes default. Judgment that he evacuate the pl.'s land within 40 days.

Fri. 21 Sep. 1302. John le Blunt, mayor, William de Béthune, Walter de Finchingfeld, Thomas Romeyn, Solomon le Coteler, Nicholas Pycot, Geoffrey de Nortone, William de Leyre, Richer de Refham.

32. Gilbert le Mareschal complains that Gilbert de Colcestre refuses to rebuild his part of a common fence (clausture) between their tenements in the par. of St. Edmund the King. The def. says that he is ready to do all that he ought to do and the pl. likewise. It is adjudged that the parties build between their tenements upon land held in common a stone wall 3 ft. wide and 16 ft. high and that the same remain to them in common in perpetuity.

33. John son of Roger le Lunge complains that Richard le Sowyer and Richard Golde. [Entry incomplete.]

[m. 3d.] *Fri. 5 Oct. 1302. John le Blunt, mayor, Geoffrey de Nortone, William de Béthune, Walter de Finchingfeld, Thomas Romeyn, John de Canterbury, Nicholas de Farndon, Richard de Gloucestre, Henry de Gloucestre, William de Leyre, and Simon de Paris, sheriff.*

1. St. Mildred Poultry, cf. **66**.

Assize of Nuisance

34. Brother Henry de Suttone, guardian of the Friars Minor, and his brethren complain of the dean and chapter of St. Martin le Grand, Master Robert de Staundone, clerk, and William de Hottokeshathere that their fence (clausturam) adjoining the pls.' garden is ruinous and broken down so that the fruit and plants (herbe) are carried off and trampled down and other evils and enormities are inflicted upon them and that the defs. utterly refuse to repair the fence in whole or in part. The dean comes by Charleto de Sayssello, his attorney, and the chapter by John de Witham and Giles of the Wardrobe, canons, and other vicars [choral]. They say that the land concerning which the friars make complaint was given them in pure and perpetual alms by the progenitors of the present king without whom they cannot answer; and they pray that the assize give no judgment in prejudice of their free tenement. Robert de Staundon comes and says that William de Hottokeshathere is dead, and proffers a charter showing that the free tenement, fee and right in the tenement in question are his alone. The pls. say that they do not challenge the right of the defs. but pray that the assize compel them to rebuild their fence according to the law and custom of the City. Since, however, neither party produces any deed to prove the obligation of the other to repair the fence, it is adjudged that within 40 days they may either build a stone wall upon land held in common at their common charges, or one or other of the parties find the land and the other build the wall. If either party fails to carry out his part of the bargain, the sheriff is to carry out the work on behalf of the defaulter and in addition to fine him 40s. Saving to either party an action of title as of right belongs to him (Salva utrique parti accione de terra sua adquirenda que de iure ei competi etc.).

35. Simon son of Robert and Agnes his wife complain that at the instance of John le Bonde and Joan his wife the sheriff has prohibited them from building a house upon their land. The defs. say that they found the pls. demolishing their part of a stone wall common to both parties. The assize finds that the pls. had no right to demolish the wall since they can produce no evidence of ownership. It is therefore adjudged that they repair it at their own charges within 40 days otherwise the sheriff is to have the work carried out at their expense and fine them 40s. in addition for contempt.[1]

[m. 4] *Fri. 23 Nov. 1302. [Essoins only.]*

Fri. 7 Dec. 1302. John le Blund, mayor, Simon de Paris and Hugh Pourte, sheriffs, William de Béthune, William de Leyre, Walter de Finchingfeld, John de Dunstaple, Nicholas de Farndon, Elias Russel, Richer de Refham, Ralph de Honilane.

36. Henry le Moyne complains that Gregory le Botoner has constructed a gate (portam) in the tenement he holds of him in the par. of St. Alban in Wodestrete, too narrow and low, contrary to the terms of his feoffment.

---

1. Hereafter this formula has been calendared simply as *within 40 days etc.* See above p. xviii.

Assize of Nuisance

The def. pleads that the assize has no cognisance in the matter, since the work is already complete. Judgment that the pl. take nothing for his plaint, but have his recovery by another process of law. Def. *sine die*.

37. Anketin de Gisors complains that the prior of the hospital of St. Mary without Bisshopesgate (called elsewhere the new hospital) pierced and broke his stone wall in the par. of All Hallows at Hay, inserting his beams (trabes) and corbels (corbellos) therein. The def. claims the wall as his own, and offers to produce documents in proof of his claim. Both parties are thereupon given a day at the quindene to produce all the evidence necessary for the information of the assize. On Fri. 8 Feb. 1303 the assize comes, but the def. essoins himself by William de Reyle. On Fri. 8 Mar. he seeks a further essoin, but it is held not to lie. On Fri. 3 May he fails to appear, and it is decided to continue in his absence. On Fri. 17 May the assize comes, but further adjournments follow because it is not yet fully advised, until Fri. 20 Sep. when the def. once more makes default,[1] and the proceedings are adjourned because there are insufficient aldermen present (non habentur de aldermannis ad plenum).[2] Finally, on Fri. 15 Nov. the assize, resummoned, comes by John le Blound, mayor, John de Burreford, sheriff, William de Leyre, William de Béthune, Walter de Finchingfeld, Adam de Fulham, Nicholas de Farndon, Richer de Reffham, Hugh Pourte, Solomon le Coteller, John de Dunstaple, Simon de Paris, Nicholas Picot, Richard de Gloucestre, Henry de Gloucestre, and Thomas Sely, but because it is found that the resummons had not been considered either in the Husting during term, or by the mayor and aldermen out of term, it is adjudged to be null, and the pl. is recommended to seek a further resummons at the next Husting.

38. Rose daughter of Clarekin Fylin complains that when she wished to build upon the stone wall belonging to her tenement in the par. of St. Michael de Candelwykstrete William le Bole deforced her and overthrew her work. The def. says that the wall is his; and since both parties claim ownership, they are given a day to produce their muniments and other evidences and to hear judgment.

Fri. 8 Feb. 1303. John le Blunt, mayor, William de Leyre, William de Béthune, Thomas Romeyn, Walter de Finchingfeld, and Simon de Paris, sheriff.

39. John de Gildeford, def., essoins himself against Thomas Romeyn, pl., by William de Reyle.

40. Thomas Basset and Isabel his wife, defs., essoin themselves against Richard de Wyrhale and Juliana his wife by William de Braynford.

41. Thomas de Leukenore, Henry de Gildeford and John Cleymunt,

---

1. Document continued on a strip of parchment (of which the dorse is blank) sewn across the membrane.
2. But according to the entry under that date there were eleven in addition to the mayor.

executors of the will of Alice de Bavente, essoin themselves against Alan de Dalstone, 'potter', by William de Reyle.

42. John de Ovesseye, def., essoins himself against Henry Hauteyn, pl., by William de Braynford.

Fri. 8 Mar. 1303. John le Blunt, mayor, William de Leyre, William de Béthune, Walter de Finchingfeld, Nicholas de Farndon, John Darmenters, Solomon le Cotiller, John de Dunstaple and Simon de Paris then sheriff.

43. Roger Hosebonde and Maud his wife and Thomas de Brauncestre complain that William de Caustone and Denise his wife have built their cistern (cisternam) on the common plot (placia) belonging to the pls. in the par. of St. Matthew de Fridaystrete. The defs. say that they and their predecessors have had a cistern there time out of mind, and that the place where the cistern stands and the whole path (via) there belong entirely to their tenement, except that the pls. have the right of entry and exit thereby, and the rector and parishioners of St. Matthew's have the right of way for their procession four times a year. The pls. say that the place in question is common to others as well as to themselves, and that the cistern built there is to the damage of their free tenement. They ask that enquiry be made at the next Husting, and the defs. likewise. The sheriff is ordered to summon a jury (bonam patriam).

[m. 4d.] *Fri. 3 May 1303. John le Blunt, mayor, Elias Russel, William de Leyre, John le Coroner, Richer de Refham, John de Dunstaple, Hugh Pourte, Simon de Paris, sheriff, Solomon le Cotiller.*

44. Elias Russel complains that the cess-pit of the privy of Adam de Coumbe and Alice his wife adjoins too closely his land in the par. of St. Martin Orgar in Candilwickestrete. The defs. ask a day to consult and it is granted by consent of the pl. After adjournment the assize comes on the land on Fri. 24 May 1303, and it is adjudged that *within 40 days etc.* the defs. remove the cess-pit from the pl.'s land a distance of $2\frac{1}{2}$ ft. of masonry or $3\frac{1}{2}$ ft. of earth.

Fri. 17 May 1303. John le Blunt, mayor, Simon de Paris, sheriff, Elias Russel, William de Béthune, Walter de Finchingfeld, Adam de Fulham, Nicholas de Farndon, Richer de Refham, Nicholas Pycot.

45. The abbess of Our Lady of the New Place without Alegate[1] appoints Peter de Shordich her attorney against Peter Berneval and Maud his wife.

46. Walter de Wanlok, def., v. Hugh le Blunt, pl., by William de Reyle. Pl. in mercy for not prosecuting his plaint. Def. *sine die.*

Fri. 24 May 1303. John le Blunt, mayor, Elias Russel, William de Leyre, Walter de Finchingfeld, John de Armenters, John de Dunstaple, Adam de

1. i.e. St. Clare without Aldgate (Minoresses).

Assize of Nuisance

Fulham, Nicholas Pycot and Simon de Paris, sheriff, Thomas Romeyn, William de Béthune.

47. Gilbert de Asshendone, def., essoins himself against John Lorence, pl., by William de Braynford.

48. William de Hanningtone, def. [Entry incomplete.]

Fri. 2 Aug. 1303. John le Blund, mayor, William de Leyre, Walter de Finchingfeld, William de Béthune, Solomon le Cotiller, John de Dunstaple, Adam de Foleham, Nicholas Pycot, and Hugh Pourte sheriff, and Simon de Paris, sheriff, John de Armenters.

49. Robert de Multone and Agnes his wife essoin themselves against William Servat by William de Braynford.

50. William de Leyre complains that Master John de Egemere, rector of All Hallows the Less upon the Cellar, and his parishioners have a stone wall at the west end of the church on the verge of ruin, to the great peril of the pl. and other inhabitants and passers-by. The sheriff testifies that the rector was summoned but he makes default; the parishioners come but show no reason why the verdict of the assize should be delayed. Judgment that the defs. rebuild the wall *within 40 days etc.*

Fri. 16 Aug. 1303. [No entry.]

[m. 5] *Fri. 6 Sep. 1303. John le Blund, mayor, Simon de Paris and Hugh Pourte, sheriffs, William de Béthune, William de Leyre, Thomas Romeyn, Richard de Gloucestre, John de Dunstaple, John de Canterbury, Henry de Gloucestre, Ralph de Honilane, Adam de Foleham.*

51. Robert the Chaplain and John le Benere, wardens of London Bridge, prayed an assize (petierunt assisam de nocumento) in the name of the commonalty against Henry Poteman and Denise his wife concerning a free tenement of the Bridge in the par. of St. Magnus the Martyr. The sheriff testifies that the def. was not in town when the precept was delivered. Denise appears and is given a day to produce her husband, ready to receive and do what the assize shall direct. On Fri. 18 Oct. 1303 the assize comes but the def. essoins himself by William de Reyle. He is given a day at the quindene, but since on that day the assize does not come he is *sine die*.

52. The same wardens of London Bridge complain that Adam de Foleham, alderman, has built his house upon land belonging to the Bridge in the same par., obscuring the view from the windows of the houses of the Bridge and impeding the course of the Thames. The def. says that the assize has no cognisance in such matters and that he is not bound to answer to the plaint. He asks for a precise judgment (iudicium precise), and the pls. likewise. It is adjudged that the pls. take nothing for their plaint, but have their recovery by another process of law. Def. *sine die*.

Assize of Nuisance

53. Hugh Pourte and Margaret his wife complain that the stone wall of the house of Robert de Foleham and Albreda his wife next their entrance in the same par. is ruinous, to the danger of the lives of the pls. and of all those passing by. The defs. deny that the wall is ruinous, and say that it stands as it has for the past hundred years. The matter is referred to the masons and carpenters sworn to the assize. On Fri. 18 Oct. 1303 the assize comes, but the masons do not appear. On Fri. 13 Dec. 1303 the assize comes by resummons, but the defs. make default. Richard de Wytham, mason, and Robert Osekin, carpenter, appear and declare upon oath that the wall threatens ruin, but that there is no danger before the summer. Judgment that the defs. rebuild the wall about the feast of the nativity of St. John the Baptist [24 June]. If they should fail to do so, the sheriff is to act, and in addition is to fine them 40s.

Fri. 20 Sep. 1303. John le Blund, mayor, William de Leyre, Walter de Finchingfeld, Thomas Romeyn, Richard de Gloucestre, Nicholas de Farndone, Henry de Gloucestre, Richer de Refham, John Darmenters, Solomon le Cotiller, Nicholas Pycot, Simon de Paris, sheriff.

54. Osbert de Braye and Isabel his wife complain that whereas they have a stone wall 16 ft. high in the par. of St. Michael in Wodestrete, which acts as an enclosure (claustura) to Adam de Hallingbury, who is bound to receive beneath their eaves (severunda) the water falling from the same wall and the house built thereon, and convey it at his own charges to the street, he is now making a gutter (goterum), and nailing (clavis firmare) it to his timber (meremium). Adam prays judgment concerning the plaint, because his son Bartholomew, who is enfeoffed jointly with him, is not named therein; and he asks a day to produce documents to show that the gutter ought to be made in the form in which it has been begun. Afterwards the assize comes on Fri. 18 Oct. 1303, but because certain aldermen who are well informed on the matter (et quia quidam aldermanni qui de assisa predicta certiorati sunt) are absent, the case is adjourned to the octave. [Cf. **61**.]

55. The prior of the hospital of St. Mary without Bisshopesgate complains that Margery relict of John de Gysorzs and John and Anketin her sons and their tenants encroach upon the course of the Walebroke, which is common to the City and stack their firewood too near the pl.'s party-wall (parieti), in the par. of St. Martin in the Vintry, which is thereby broken and his house damaged. The defs. say that the case is one of trespass, and is not within the cognisance of the assize. Judgment that the pl. have his recovery by another process of law.

[m. 5d.] *Fri. 18 Oct. 1303. John le Blund, mayor, William de Leyre, John de Wangrave, Thomas Romeyn, Solomon le Cotiller, Adam de Foleham, Hugh Pourte, John de Canterbury, Simon de Paris, John de Dunstaple, Nicholas Pycot, and William de Combemartyn, sheriff.*

56. Walter de Wenlok essoins himself against Roger Sthorn by William de Reyle.

57. The prior of Holy Trinity complains that the house of Richard de Routon in the par. of St. Mary atte Nax threatens ruin, to the damage of his free tenement and the manifest peril of those dwelling therein. The sheriff testifies that the def. has been summoned to appear upon the land. Judgment, in his default, that he rebuild the house within 40 days so that the prior and the common people suffer no damage or peril.

[m. 6] *Fri. 13 Dec. 1303. John le Blund, mayor, John de Wangrave, William de Béthune, William de Leyre, Thomas Romeyn, Adam de Foleham, Hugh Pourte, Richard de Gloucestre, John de Canterbury, John de Dunstaple, Henry de Gloucestre, Nicholas Pycot, aldermen.*

58. Richard de Bedeforth, def., essoins himself against John de Laufare, 'cordwaner', pl., by William de Reyle. Isabel wife of Richard appears.

59. Henry Poteman and Denise his wife, defs., essoin themselves against Robert the Chaplain and John le Benere, wardens of London Bridge, by William de Reyle.

Fri. 31 Jan. 1304. [*Essoins only.*]

Fri. 14 Feb. 1304. John le Blund, mayor, John de Wangrave, William de Béthune, Walter de Finchingfeld, Thomas Romeyn, Richer de Reffham, Ralph de Honilane, aldermen.

60. Alice atte Stakes complains that the cess-pit of the privy of Adam de Lindesseye and Christine his wife adjoins too closely her land in the par. of St. Mary Wollenoth, and that the defs. stack their firewood against her wall, which is thereby broken and damaged. The defs. say nothing to delay the verdict of the assize. Judgment that *within 40 days etc.* they rebuild the cess-pit at a distance of $2\frac{1}{2}$ ft. of stone wall or $3\frac{1}{2}$ ft. of earthen wall from the pl.'s land, and remove the firewood.

Fri. 21 Feb. 1304. [*Essoin only.*]

Fri. 29 May 1304. [*Essoin only.*]

Fri. 29 May 1304.[1] *John le Blond, mayor, William de Combematin, sheriff, John de Wangrave, William de Béthune, Walter de Finchingfeld, Richer de Refham, Richard de Gloucestre, John de Dunstaple, Nicholas de Farndone, Thomas Romeyn, Ralph de Honilane, Nicholas Pycot.*

61. Osbert de Braye and Isabel his wife complain that the water draining from the house of Adam de Hallingbury through his gutter (gotera) falls upon the tiles (tegulos) of the side (costera) of their house in the par. of St. Michael de Wodestrete and that whereas they own the stone wall 16 ft. high, for which reason he ought to convey away the water falling from their house under their eaves, he has constructed a gutter and nailed it to the

1. Same date as previous assize; one is presumably an error.

beams (tingnos) above their wall aforesaid. The def. says that the pls. are not entitled to an assize, because he and his predecessors have been seised of the gutter and fall of water (aquecasu) for many years, and the plaint ought to have been raised within a year and a day. Afterwards the parties agree to the arbitration of four aldermen, the pls. choosing John de Wangrave and William de Leyre, and the def. Walter de Finchingfeld and Richer de Refham. On Fri. 26 June 1304 the parties come, but the arbitrators say that they have not yet met. The assize is further adjourned until Fri. 10 July, when the pls., because they cannot deny that the def. has been seised for many years of the gutter and fall of water, are advised to seek a remedy on that count by another process of law. Since, however, the stone wall 16 ft. high belonging wholly to the pls. is opposite the def.'s kitchen where the gutter is to be newly built it is adjudged that *within 40 days etc.* the def. make it so as to receive the water from the pls.' house and convey it into his own, beneath the pls.' eaves and so onto his own land. [Cf. **54**.]

[m. 6d.] *Fri. 19 June 1304. John le Blound, mayor, John de Burreforth, sheriff, John de Wangrave, William de Leyre, William de Béthune, Walter de Finchingfeld, Thomas Romeyn, Richer de Refham, Simon de Paris, Solomon le Cotiller.*

62. Adam de Horsham complains that Martin Shenche has caused John de Burreforth, sheriff, to prohibit his new building work in the par. of St. Lawrence Jewry. The sheriff testifies that the def. has been summoned, but he makes default. It is therefore adjudged that the pl. continue with his building.

63. Luke, parson of St. Benet Fink, and his parishioners complain that Roger de Euere has overthrown the fence (clausturam) of the churchyard, so that pigs and other animals and even men enter it by night and day, and carry off the plants growing there (crescentia), and commit other enormities in contempt of God and to the great damage of the church. The def. admits his obligation to rebuild the fence, and asks to be given until Michaelmas to do it. The pls. agree, on the understanding that, in the event of his failure, they are to be given 3 ft. of his land on which to erect a wall. To this he freely consents.

64. On the same day the mayor and aldermen made a perambulation to the churchyard of St. Mary de Wollecherchehawe, because the bailiffs of the earl of Gloucester complained that the paling (palicium) erected by the rector and parishioners around the churchyard had greatly narrowed the path (via) at the entrance to the earl's house. It is found that the path has been recently narrowed to the damage of the earl and of the citizens carrying on business there, and the rector and parishioners are therefore ordered to remove the paling as far as the elms growing nearby. The neighbours and those dwelling round about complain that the earl's bailiffs have enclosed with an earthen wall a lane (venellam) on the south side of the churchyard. They are ordered to reopen it as it used to be *within 40 days etc.*

Assize of Nuisance

Fri. 26 June 1304. John le Blund, mayor, John de Burreforth, sheriff, John de Wangrave, William de Leyre, Walter de Finchingfeld, Adam de Foleham, Richer de Refham, John de Dunstaple, Solomon le Cotiller, Nicholas Pycot, Thomas Sely, William de Béthune.

65. Henry le Keu, 'peintour', def., essoins himself against William atte Delle, pl., by William de Brainforth.

66. Solomon le Cotiller complains that the party-wall (paries) of the house of Michael de Tholosan in the par. of St. Mildred in the Poultry is broken down and overhangs his land, so that dogs and other animals enter his herb-garden (herbarium) and trample down and tread underfoot the plants growing there, and do much other damage. This is so manifest that the def. cannot deny it. Asked by the assize whether he is willing to enclose with stone he refuses to do so, either individually or in common. The pl. says that he is prepared to build. It is therefore adjudged that the def. give 3 ft. of land on which the pl. is to build a stone wall 16 ft. high and 3 ft. thick, the same to remain to him and his heirs to build upon.

Fri. 10 July 1304. John le Blound, mayor, John de Burreforth, sheriff, William de Leyre, Walter de Finchingfeld, Nicholas de Farndon, Nicholas Pycot, Thomas Sely, etc.

67. James de Moun, def., essoins himself against Walter de Finchingfeld, pl., by Thomas Golde. Walter appears.

68. Henry le Keu, 'peintour'. [Entry incomplete. Cf. **65, 71.**]

Fri. 7 Aug. 1304. [Essoin only.]

[m. 7] *Fri. 28 Aug. 1304. [Essoins only.]*

Fri. 11 Sep. 1304. John le Blound, mayor, William de Combemartin, sheriff and alderman, John de Wangrave, Walter de Finchingfeld, Nicholas de Farndon, Nicholas Pycot, Solomon le Cotiller, Thomas Sely.

69. Hugh de Oxford (Oxonia), Maud his wife, and Lucy and Katherine their daughters, complain that the dean and chapter of St. Paul's, Thomas de Aveynes, Isolde his wife and Lucy their daughter have built the cess-pit of their privy too close to their stone wall and their land in the par. of St. Michael le Querne (ad bladum). The dean and chapter make default. The other defs. come and say that they did not build the cess-pit, which was made long before they were born (antequam ipsi in rerum natura existerant). It is nonetheless adjudged that *within 40 days etc.* they remove the pit $2\frac{1}{2}$ ft. of stone-work or $3\frac{1}{2}$ ft. of earth from the pls.' land.

Fri. 30 Oct. 1304. [Essoin only.]

Fri. 13 Nov. 1304. John le Blound, mayor, John de Wangrave, William de

Leyre, Walter de Finchingfeld, Nicholas de Farndon, Nicholas Pycot, John de Vintry, Ralph de Honilane, Adam de Rokesle, Solomon le Cotiller and John de Lincoln and Roger de Paris, sheriffs.

70. Ymayne de Brauncestre complains that whereas Peter de Bristoll, goldsmith, in a deed which she produces, undertook to convey away in perpetuity through a gutter (goteram) in the midst of his shop in the Goldsmithery in the par. of St. Peter de Wodestrete the water draining from the herb-garden (herbarium) of the shop sometime belonging to David de Enefeld, goldsmith, and now in her possession, Sabine relict of Philip le Tayllour has obstructed the said gutter to the damage of her free tenement. The def. appears by attorney and says that she has only a life interest in the shop in question, of which the right and fee belong to Henry son of Philip le Tayllour without whom she cannot answer. She asks for his aid, which is granted. She is given a day at the quindene.

71. Hawyse de Rothyng complains that whereas Henry le Ku, 'peintour', was previously ordered by the assize to provide for the carrying off of the water (aque conductu) from his house and that of the pl., according to the terms of an indenture dated 21 Sep. 1301, whereby they agreed to combine to make a gutter (stillicidium) running above the kitchen and stable of the pl., and along the stone wall between their houses to Wodestrete, and to share the cost of upkeep, he refuses to fulfil his part of the agreement in defiance of the former verdict of the assize and to her damage 20s. The def. essoins himself by John de Brackelee, but because he is seen in court the essoin is held not to lie. Judgment that he pay the pl. the damages assessed by the court and be in the sheriff's mercy, and that *within 40 days etc.* he make the gutter (goterum) in accordance with the terms of the deed.

[m. 7d.] *Fri. 20 Nov. 1304. John le Blound, mayor, John de Wangrave, William de Béthune, Walter de Finchingfeld, Thomas Romeyn, Simon de Paris, Nicholas Pycot, William de Combemartin, Thomas Sely, aldermen, and John de Lincoln, sheriff.*

72. William le Mareschal. [Entry incomplete.]

[m. 8] *Fri. 27 Nov. 1304. [Essoins only.]*

Fri. 11 Dec. 1304. [Essoin only.]

Fri. 22 Jan. 1305. John le Blound, mayor, William de Leyre, Walter de Finchingfeld, John de Dunstaple, Simon de Paris, Ralph de Honilane, John de Vintry and John de Lincoln, sheriff.

73. Joan wife of William de Hedersete appoints the same William her attorney.

74. William de Hedersete and Joan his wife complain that John Amizs has

broken down the stone wall common to them in the par. of St. Michael de Paternostrestrete. The def. says that he broke down only the part of the wall belonging to him; but because the custom of the City does not permit anyone, even though having a share in a stone wall, to demolish his part of it without the consent of his coparcener, it is adjudged that *within 40 days etc.* the def. rebuild the wall as it was before.

Fri. 19 Feb. 1305. [Essoins only.]

Fri. 5 Mar. 1305. John le Blound, mayor, John de Wangrave, Thomas Romeyn, William de Leyre, Richer de Refham, Adam de Rokesle, Simon de Paris, Thomas Sely, Richard de Gloucestre, John de Dunstaple, John de Lincoln and Roger de Paris, sheriffs.

75. Fulk de St. Edmunds appoints James his son, his attorney.

76. William de Caxtone and Maud his wife complain that Fulk de St. Edmunds and Agnes his wife have prohibited their new building operations, and that part of their houses overhang their land in the par. of St. Swythun in Candelwykstrete. The defs. come and Fulk says that he has no interest in the tenements in question save in right of his wife Agnes; she says that she holds for life by bequest of Peter de Brauhingg, her late husband, and cannot answer without John, Peter's son, to whom the right and fee belong. The assize comes on Fri. 12 Mar., and Fulk and Agnes appear, but John essoins himself by Bartholomew de Brauhing. On Fri. 26 Mar. the assize again comes, and having heard the allegations of both parties and seen the nuisances concerning which the dispute arose, adjudges that the pls. set up the posts (postes) of the house they are building adjoining and in alignment with (directe) those of the defs., and that *within 40 days etc.* the defs. rebuild by plumb-line (per plumbum) those parts of their houses which overhang the land of the pls.

Fri. 12 Mar. 1305. John le Blound, mayor, John de Wangrave, William de Leyre, John de Dunstaple, Richer de Refham, Hugh Pourte, Thomas Romeyn, Solomon le Cotiller, John de Lincoln and Roger de Paris, sheriffs, William de Combemartin, Adam de Rokesle.

77. Robert le Barber complains that William le Mareschal has constructed a gutter (goterum) from which the water falls at his door (hostio), and has built a jetty (jacticium) above (ultra) his beams (trabes) opposite his door and windows (fenestrarum) which obstructs his view, and that his chimney (caminum) is too near the pl.'s party-wall (parieti), causing danger of fire to his house in the par. of All Hallows de Grascherch. The def. comes but says nothing to delay the verdict of the assize. Judgment that *within 40 days etc.* he remake the gutter in dispute so that the water falls within his own tenement; that he remove all that part of the jetty which obscures the pl.'s view; and that he rebuild his chimney so that neither the pl. nor any other neighbours are in danger from fire.

Assize of Nuisance

78. [Inverted at the foot of the m. appears the following list of names in two columns] Peter de Edelmetone, John Fairhead, Walter de Hakeneye, Thomas de Hales, Thomas le Blound, Geoffrey de Hales, Geoffrey le Barbour, Robert de Kent, John Sewale, fishmonger, Walter de Colecestre, Henry de Somersete, Richard le Cordwaner.

[m. 8d.] *Fri. 26 Mar. 1305. John le Blound, mayor, John de Wangrave, William de Leyre, Walter de Finchingfeld, Thomas Romeyn, Richer de Refham, Nicholas de Farndon, John de Dunstaple, Solomon le Cotiller, Thomas Sely, aldermen, and John de Lincoln and Roger de Paris, sheriffs.*

79. Ralph Godchep and Margery his wife essoin themselves against William de Arondel by William de Braynford. William [de Arondel] appears.

Fri. 7 May 1305. John le Blound, mayor, John de Wangrave, Walter de Finchingfeld, Thomas Romeyn, Richer de Refham, Nicholas de Farndon, Henry de Gloucestre, William de Leyre, William de Combemartin, aldermen, and Roger de Paris, sheriff.

80. The abbess of St. Clare brings an assize against Gilbert de Asshendone. Richer de Refham petitions the mayor to send two aldermen to her to receive her attorney, since she is enclosed. The def. is given a day at the octave.

Fri. 14 May 1305. [Essoin only.]

Fri. 21 May 1305. John le Blound, mayor, John de Wangrave, Richer de Refham, John de Dunstaple, Simon de Paris, Ralph de Honilane and Solomon le Cotiller, and John de Lincoln, sheriff.

81. William, parson of St. Werbourge in Fridaystrete, complains that Adam atte Rose, potter, has built his windows opening upon the land of his church, and his tenants throw filth and refuse through them on to the land consecrated to God, and the water from Adam's house floods it. Judgment that *within 40 days etc.* the def., who says nothing to delay the verdict of the assize, block up or glaze (vitro claudere) the windows, and convey away the water from his house on to his own land or into the street.

Fri. 28 May 1305. [Respite only.]

Fri. 4 June 1305. John le Blond, mayor, Walter de Finchingfeld, John de Wengrave, Richer de Refham, Solomon le Cotiller, Simon de Paris and John de Lincoln, sheriff.

82. Adam de Horsham, pl., appears by Reginald Wolleward, his attorney, against Martin Shenche, def., who prohibited his building-work. The def., given a day to appear by William de Reyle, his essoin, makes default. Judgment that the pl. be *sine die* and the def. in mercy.

Assize of Nuisance

Fri. 30 July 1305. John le Blond, mayor, John de Wengrave, Walter de Finchingfeld, John de Dunstaple, Richer de Refham, Simon de Paris, Nicholas de Farndon, Nicholas Pycot, Thomas Sely, aldermen, and John de Lincoln and Roger de Paris, sheriffs.

83. William de Wynton' complains that Adam de Horsham has overthrown his stone wall in the par. of St. Lawrence Jewry and built a new house on the site. The def. claims that the wall is his and says that he built on his own land. Since, however, neither party was seised of the wall of old (quai murus predictus a neutra parte seysitus est ex antiquo) they are given a day upon the land at the octave, without essoin, to hear judgment and produce any muniments that may be of profit to them (utraque pars habeat tunc ibi munimenta sua que in premissis sibi viderit proficere).

Fri. 10 Sep. 1305. [Essoins only.]

[m. 9] *Fri. 24 Sep. 1305. John le Blund, mayor, John de Wengrave, William de Leyre, Walter de Finchingfeld, John de Dunstaple, Richer de Refham, Solomon le Cotiller, Adam de Fulham, Simon de Paris, and Roger de Paris, sheriff.*

84. Fulk de St. Edmunds complains that William de Caxtone and Maud his wife have prohibited his building operations at the north end of their house in the par. of St. Swythun in Candelwikstrete. The defs., asked if they can show any cause why the pl. should not build his house adjoining theirs, say nothing to delay the assize. It is therefore adjudged that the pl. build his house adjoining theirs, straight by plumb-line (directe per plumbum), and of any height he chooses.

85. The assize comes on Fri. 1 Oct. 1305 by John le Blound, mayor, John de Wengrave, William de Leyre, Walter de Finchingfeld, Richer de Refham, Nicholas de Farndon, Simon de Paris, John de Dunstaple and Henry de Gloucestre, aldermen, and Reginald de Thunderlee, sheriff; and because it is found that the prior and brethren of the Order of Preachers have built their house opposite the church of St. Martin within Ludgate too close to the City Wall, they are forbidden to build henceforth within 16 ft. of the wall until etc. Afterwards the assize comes on Fri. 8 Oct. by John le Blound, mayor, John de Wengrave, William de Leyre, Walter de Finchingfeld, Nicholas de Farndone, William de Combemartin, aldermen, and William Cosin, sheriff, and William de Helvetone, John de Burreforth, William de Bydik, Simon Gut, Robert de Uptone, Robert de Pipehirst, Roger de Lintone, Roger Hosebonde, Stephen de Pancrich, Robert le Convers, goldsmith, Thomas de Farndon, Nicholas le Brun, Henry de Kele, Elias de Suffolk, Robert de Worstede, Roger le Viroler, John le Botoner, Richard de Caumpes, John Dode, Walter de Bardeneye, Walter Grapefige, Peter de Sparham, Ranulph Balle, John de Wyndesore, William Bernard, Adam Absolon, Andrew de Staunforth, Alexander le Coffrer, Daniel de Ciltre, William Poyntel, Alexander Pung, William de Hundesdich, and others of the commonalty, summoned for the purpose. The prior and brethren

Assize of Nuisance

come and show letters patent of Edward I,[1] dated 10 June 1276, confirming a grant by Gregory de Rokesle, mayor, and the barons of the City to Archbishop Robert [Kilwardby] and his assigns, for the enlargement of his place at Baynards Castle and the Tower of Munfichet, of two adjoining lanes, on condition that he substitutes for them a better road, more convenient for the citizens. The prior and brethren say that the archbishop made a convenient road leading to the Thames, at Baynard Castle, and adjoining their stone wall, and that they are therefore entitled to block up the lane aforesaid.

[m. 9d.] *Fri. 17 Dec. 1305. John le Blund, mayor, John de Wengrave, Richer de Refham, Simon de Paris, Nicholas Pycot, Richard de Gloucestre.*

86. Walter de Harewe, Hugh de Oxford, tailor, and Maud his wife essoin themselves against the prior of the hospital of St. Mary without Bishopesgate by Roger son of Thomas.

Fri. 28 Jan. 1306. John le Blound, mayor, William de Leyre, Walter de Finchingfeld, William de Coumbemartin, Richard de Gloucestre, Henry de Gloucestre, John de Dunstaple, Adam de Fulham, aldermen, and Reginald de Thunderle, sheriff, etc.

87. The wardens of London Bridge complain that the water from the house of William le Mitere in the par. of St. Mary atte Hulle floods the area of the Bridge so that they can have no profit from it, but suffer deterioration and damage. The def. says he has only a life interest in the tenement in question.

Fri. 11 Feb. 1306. [No entry.]

Fri. 4 Mar. 1306. John le Blound, mayor, John de Wengrave, William de Leyre, Walter de Finchingfeld, Richer de Refham, Nicholas de Farndon, Richard de Gloucestre, Simon de Paris, aldermen, and Reginald de Thunderle, sheriff.

88. John le Mareschal of Walebrok, def., essoins himself against Simon de Broutone, pl., by William Brainford.

Fri. 18 Mar. 1306. John le Blound, mayor, John de Wengrave, William de Leyre, Walter de Finchingfeld, Thomas Romeyn, Richer de Refham, Nicholas de Farndon, John de Dunstaple, Richard de Gloucestre, Simon de Paris, Solomon le Cotiller, Thomas Sely, Richard de Chigewelle, Richard de Wylehale, Nicholas Pycot.

89. John Trentemars and Gilbert de Lesnes complain that Robert de Uptone and Margery his wife have broken down the stone wall common to the parties in the par. of St. Mary le Bow (de Arcubus). The defs. say that the pls.. have no share in the wall; but because it is clearly apparent to

---

1. Cf. *C.P.R. 1272–81*, 147–8, and for the background of the case W. A. Hinnebusch, *Early English Friars Preachers* (Rome, 1951), 22, 35–55.

the view of the assize (quia evidenter aspectui assise apparet) that for a long time past the pls. have been seised with their timber (maeremio) of the greater part of the wall, it is adjudged that they have for their share as far as their timber extends, measuring straight by plumb-line, and that *within 40 days etc.*, the defs. rebuild the wall as it was before.

90. Elias le Chaucer complains that Robert de Uptone and Margery his wife have inserted their corbels (corbellos) in his stone wall in the same par. and have taken possession of it with their timber (maeremio). The defs. say the wall is theirs; but since it is found by view of the assize that they have no share in it, it is adjudged that they remove their timber *within 40 days etc.*

91. Simon Turgis, pl., v. Cecily atte More and John Starre and Mary his wife, defs., are given a day at the quindene to agree (concordandi).

[m. 10] *Fri. 22 July 1306. John le Blound, mayor, John de Wengrave, William de Leyre, Walter de Finchingfeld, Nicholas de Farndone, John de Dunstaple, Richer de Refham, John de Vintry, Ralph de Honilane.*

92. Ralph le Coupere and Celestria his wife complain that the prioress of Haliwelle has caused the sheriff to prohibit their building operations in the par. of St. Mary Wolnoth. The prioress comes and says that she caused the work to be prohibited because the pls. took possession with their timber (meremium) of the whole stone wall, which is common to them; but it is found that she has no right therein save for her corbels (corbellos) and summer (someria), and it is therefore adjudged that the pls. complete their building operations, taking possession of the wall at will.

93. Rose de Coventre complains that the land of John, prior of St. Bartholomew de Smethefeld, adjoining hers in the par. of St. James de Garlekhethe is not enclosed, so that she suffers deterioration and damage. The sheriff testifies that the def. was summoned but he makes default. The pl., asked whether she is willing to build a fence (clausturam), agrees. It is therefore adjudged that either each party provides $1\frac{1}{2}$ ft. of land, and together they build a stone wall 3 ft. thick thereon; or that one party provides 3 ft. of land and the other builds the wall at his own cost; or that one party builds the wall upon his own land at his own charges and it remains to him in perpetuity.

Fri. 5 Aug. 1306. John le Blound, mayor, John de Wengrave, William de Leyre, Walter de Finchingfeld, John de Dunstaple, Richer de Refham, Solomon le Cotiller, Hugh Pourte.

94. William le Spicer, 'peleter', complains that Nicholas Pycot and Alice his wife have built the gutter (goteram) receiving and carrying off the water from their house in the par. of St. Michael upon Cornhulle upon his land, which it floods, whereas they ought to receive and carry off the water from his house since he provides the stone wall enclosing their land. The defs.

after essoin make default. It is found by the assize that in some places the pl. is sole owner of the wall, but in others it is common to the parties. Judgment that *within 40 days etc.* the defs. receive the water from the pl.'s house in their own gutter and convey it on to their land wherever the stone wall of the pl. extends, but where the wall is common they are either to act jointly, or each separately is to convey away his own water.

95. John de Langeleye complains that whereas Richer de Refham used to receive and convey away the water falling from his house in the par. of St. Michael de Paternostrecherche in his own gutter (goteram) beneath the stone alure (aluram) of his wall[1] he has now pierced the alure and inserted a new gutter through the aperture, and diverted (evertit) his other gutters, so that the roof (coopertura) of the pl.'s house is damaged and his place (placea) flooded. The def. says that he provides the stone wall which encloses the land of the pl. who ought therefore to receive the water draining from his house upon his own land. The pl. admits that he ought to receive the water falling from the def.'s eaves (severunda), but says that he is not bound to receive that falling from the newly constructed gutters. After adjournment because the def. essoins himself by Robert de Heresseye the assize comes on Fri. 2 Sep. 1306, and since it is found that the def. provides the stone wall and no other water falls upon the pl.'s land save from that part of the roof (summitatis) of his house which extends towards it (ulla alia aqua cadit super terram predicti Johannis preterquam de parte sumitatis domus se extendente versus terram eiusdem Johannis) it is adjudged that the pl. receive the said water and convey it wherever he wishes.

96. Richer de Refham complains that the cess-pit of John de Langeley's privy adjoins his stone wall in the same par. The def. pleads that the pit was built more than forty years earlier and before the building of the wall, but the pl. says that the assize has cognisance of all cases of privies and suchlike pits and gutters, even where seisin is of long duration. Judgment that *within 40 days etc.* the def. remove the cess-pit 2½ ft. of stone from the pl.'s wall.

97. [m. 10d.] The commonalty complain that the prior of St. Bartholomew has narrowed Medelane, which is common to the citizens by 1½ ft. in some places and in others by less, whereas the lane ought to measure in width 1½ ells 1 inch between the corner of the stone house formerly belonging to John de Stratford and Belisant his wife and the Thames, as appears in an indenture between Adam son of Peter son of Nevelon (Neuelonis) and John and Belisant which is in the possession of Henry de Montquoy, the present tenant of the tenement of John and Belisant. Further the prior has removed the wharf (pontem) extending into the Thames.

Fri. 19 Aug. 1306. John le Blound, mayor, John de Wengrave, William de Leyre, Walter de Finchingfeld, Thomas Romeyn, Richard de Gloucestre, Nicholas Pycot, John de Dunstaple, Thomas Sely, aldermen, and William Cosyn, sheriff.

1. The wall may possibly have been crenellated (**158** n.).

Assize of Nuisance

98. Ralph le Cuver and Celestria his wife complain that the cess-pit of the privy of the prioress of Haliwelle adjoins their stone wall in the par. of St. Mary Wulnoth. The prioress after essoin makes default. Judgment that *within 40 days etc.* she remove the cess-pit from the pls.' wall a distance of 2½ ft. of stone or 3½ ft. of earth.

99. Thomas de Kent, tailor, and Juliana his wife complain that Hugh de Derby, rector of St. Leonard de Eschep, Richard Sharp, Boydin atte Grene, William Molling, John Sharp, William de Craye, Roger de Wautham and other parishioners have dug a ditch (foveam) on their land, by reason of which their house in the par. of St. Leonard is ruined, and they produce a deed, enrolled in the Husting,[1] reciting the gift to them by the executors of Adam de Blakeneye of a tenement extending from the king's highway on the west to the wall of the church on the east. The defs. say that the land between the pls.' house and the church has been in their possession time out of mind; but it is found as well by the above-mentioned deed as by view of the assize that the land in question belongs to the pls. and the church has no right in it. Judgment that *within 40 days etc.* the defs. restore the ditch to its former condition.

Fri. 2 Sep. 1306. John le Blound, mayor, John de Wengrave, William de Leyre, Thomas Romeyn, Richer de Refham, Richard de Gloucestre, Simon de Paris, Solomon le Cotiller, Thomas Sely, Nicholas Pycot, aldermen, and Reginald de Thunderle, sheriff.

100. Nicholas Pycot and Alice his wife complain that John de Cotes, Robert de Farweberwe, Walter de Bardeneye and Agatha relict of Walter de Reyle have diverted (everterunt) the gutters receiving their water and that from Richer de Refham's house into their gutter, so that their house in the par. of St. Mary de Colchirche is flooded and damaged. John de Cotes makes default. Walter de Bardeneye says that he has no interest in the tenement in question save at the will of Agatha. Agatha and Robert come but show no cause save length of seisin why the water from their gutter should be diverted into that of the pls. Judgment that *within 40 days etc.* John, Robert and Agatha receive and convey on to their own land or into the street, at their own expense, the water from their own houses and from that of Richer de Refham, who provides the stone wall enclosing their land.

Fri. 9 Sep. 1306. John le Blound, mayor, John de Wengrave, William de Leyre, Walter de Finchingfeld, John de Dunstaple, Simon de Paris, Nicholas Pycot, Richard de Wylehale, aldermen, and William Cosyn, sheriff.

101. Geoffrey de Brokhampton complains that Andrew de Staunford has cut off (cidit) his timber (maheremium), so that his beams (tingna) are in danger of ruin, and occupies and takes possession of his land in the par. of St. John de Walebrok with his timber. The def. makes default. Judgment that he restore the timber he has cut to the same state as before, and that the parties, both of whom have a share in the stone wall, combine to make

1. On Mon. 23 Jan. 1296 (H.R. 25(8)).

a gutter to convey their water into the street, or elsewhere as they think best.

[m. 11] *Fri. 16 Sep. 1306. John le Blound, mayor, John de Wengrave, William de Leyre, Walter de Finchingfeld, Richer de Refham, Nicholas de Farndon, Nicholas Pycot, Simon de Paris, Solomon le Cotiller, aldermen, and Reginald de Thunderle, sheriff.*

A day is given to the parties in a plea [109] concerning the obstruction of the Walebroke and the sheriff is ordered to summon all who have lands abutting on the Walebrok.

102. Gilbert de Asshendon complains that the privy of the abbess and sisters of St. Clare without Alegate adjoins his stone wall. The defs. appear by John de Colecestre, their attorney, and say that Henry de Stokes holds for life the tenement about which the dispute has arisen and is not mentioned in the plaint. This the pl. cannot deny. Judgment that he take nothing for his plaint. Defs. *sine die.*

Fri. 23 Sep. 1306. John le Blound, mayor, John de Wengrave, Walter de Finchingfeld, Nicholas de Farndon, John de Dunstaple, Solomon le Cotiller, Henry de Gloucestre, Hugh Pourte, aldermen.

103. John de Bauquelle and Cecily his wife essoin themselves against Gilbert de Asshendone, pl., by William de Graftone and the same Gilbert by William Slomo.

Fri. 21 Oct. 1306. [Essoins only.]

Fri. 4 Nov. 1306. John le Blund, mayor, John de Wengrave, William de Coumbemartin, Hugh Pourte, Adam de Rokesle, John de Dunstaple, Solomon le Cotiller, Richard de Gloucestre, Richer de Refham.

104. Richer de Refham, mercer, complains that Ranulph Balle and Isabel his wife have constructed the gutter carrying off the water from their houses so that it runs through the midst of his house in the par. of St. Mary Colcherche. The defs. say that Isabel has only a life interest in the tenement in question, which she holds by bequest of her late husband, Adam de St. Albans, and that the fee and right belong to Richard, Adam's son. Adjourned that she may have him in court. On Fri. 18 Nov. the assize comes, but Richard makes default. The defs. say that they are without legal advice, since their counsel left them because noon struck before the assize came (consilium suum ab eis recesisse eo quod nona pulsabatur ante adventum assise). After further adjournments the assize comes on Fri. 16 Dec., and the parties, with their consent, are given a day to hear judgment on Fri. 20 Jan. 1307.

105. Isabel relict of Estmar de Wynton' complains that Peter de Hatfeld and Juliana his wife have built the gutter (goterum) carrying off the water from their houses in the par. of St. Lawrence de Candelwykstrete leading into hers, which is unable to contain or convey away so great a quantity of water, so that it rots her timber (meremium) and floods her house. Peter after essoin makes default. Juliana comes and says that her father, Fulk de St. Edmunds, gave her the tenement, built as at present, and that she and her father before her were seised of the said fall of water (de predicto aqueductu); but because long seisin cannot prejudice the pl.'s case or give to the possessor the right and fee (quia diutina seysina huiusmodi aqueductus parti querenti non preiudicat neque parti illum possidenti ius nec feodum adquirit), it is adjudged that *within 40 days etc.* the defs. receive the water from their houses and convey it on to their own land without damage to the pl. and her free tenement.

106. [m. 11d.] The same Isabel makes a like complaint in respect of John atte Gate and Avice his wife. The defs. make default. Judgment [as in **105**].

Fri. 18 Nov. 1306. [No entry.]

Fri. 2 Dec. 1306. John le Blund, mayor, John de Wengrave, William de Leyre, Walter de Finchingfeld, Nicholas de Farndone, Richard de Gloucestre, John de Dunstaple, Simon de Paris, John de Gysors, aldermen.

107. Robert son of Walter essoins himself against John le Chaundeler of Colemanstrete by Thomas de Kent.

108. William Pykeman essoins himself against Robert son of Robert le Treyhere by Gilbert Russel.

Fri. 16 Dec. 1306. John le Blund, mayor, John de Wengrave, Thomas Romeyn, Walter de Finchingfeld, Richard de Gloucestre, Nicholas de Farndone, Simon de Paris, John de Dunstaple, Richer de Refham, Solomon le Cotiller.

109. Daniel de Ciltre complains that John de Laufare, 'cotiller', has obstructed the course of the Walebrok by filling it with earth, to the nuisance of his free tenement in the par. of [St. Mildred] de Bradestrete. The def. says it is not the Walebrok that is concerned, but a ditch (fovea) dug with the consent of his neighbours. He asks that enquiry be made by a jury, and the pl. likewise. The jury comes by William atte More, Richard de Hundeslowe, Peter le Batour, Richard le Megucer, John le Megucer, William le Kyng, Walter Grapefige, Hugh le Kissere, Richard le Maunchier, Robert de Braye, William atte Peu and Adam Painter (Pictorem), who confirm upon oath the def.'s statement. Judgment that the pl. take nothing for his plaint. Def. *sine die*. [For an adjournment see above under 16 Sep.]

[m. 12] *Fri. 3 Mar. 1307. John le Blund, mayor, John de Wengrave, William de Leyre, Walter de Finchingfeld, Nicholas de Farndone, Richard de Gloucestre, Thomas Sely, Richer de Refham, aldermen.*

Assize of Nuisance

110. John Heyron complains that John de Paris, saddler, and Alice his wife, John le Lung and Agnes his wife and Guillotin le Sautreour have built the cess-pit of their privy adjoining his stone wall, so that his house in the par. of St. Alphege beside Crepelgate is flooded by the sewage. Guillotin makes default. The other defs. come but say nothing to delay the verdict of the assize. Judgment after view that *within 40 days etc.* they remove the cess-pit by 2½ ft. of stone wall or 3½ ft. of earthen wall from the pl.'s land.

Fri. 17 Mar. 1307. John le Blund, mayor, Walter de Finchingfeld, Adam de Rokesle, John de Dunstaple, Richard de Gloucestre, John de Gysorz, Richard de Wylehale, Thomas Sely, aldermen.

111. William Bernard, William de Bykele, Richard Jordan, Richard le Barber of Bredstrete, and John le Mazerer, goldsmith, complain that Roger de Frowyk and the prior of Crutched Friars have stopped up (obturarunt) a gutter (goteram) through which their water used to run into the street, so that the houses of the pls. in the par. of St. Olave by the Tower are flooded. The defs. say that the assize does not lie, and ask judgment whether, since the nuisance concerning which the dispute has arisen is not apparent to the view of the assize (non apparet aspectui assise), they ought to have cognisance of it. It is adjudged that the pls. take nothing for their plaint. Defs. *sine die.*

Fri. 2 June 1307. John le Blund, mayor, John de Wengrave, Walter de Leyre, Nicholas de Farndone, Richard de Gloucestre, Walter de Finchingfeld, Henry de Gloucestre, Richer de Refham.

112. The dean and chapter of St. Martin le Grand essoin themselves against the prior of Holy Trinity by Robert de Leycestre.

113. Elias, prior of Austin Friars, essoins himself against John de Sodingtone by Thomas Fykeys.

114. In the perambulation made that day it was found that the stone wall of Thomas Dew on the east side of Brackelelane is ruinous. He is ordered to repair it within 40 days.

Fri. 16 June 1307. John le Blund, mayor, John de Wengrave, Walter de Finchingfeld, Richer de Refham, Nicholas de Farndon, Richard de Gloucestre, John de Gysors, Solomon le Cotiller, aldermen.

115. Roger de Ely and Margery his wife, Robert son of Thomas Sely and Joan his wife, Henry de Thele and Maud his wife, Roger de Balesham and Isabel his wife, Gilbert the Surgeon and Felicia his wife, William de Hedersete and Joan his wife essoin themselves against John Leutour by Henry de Excestre. John appears.

116. Robert son of Thomas Sely and Joan his wife essoin themselves against William Trente by Henry de Excestre. William appears.

117. [m. 12d.] Gilbert de Tondeby, pl., appears against Gregory son of Robert de Rokesle, Walter Morice and Sarah his wife concerning the defs.' fence (claustura), which is broken down, to the nuisance of the pl.'s free tenement in the par. of St. Brigid in the suburb of London. The defs. make default. Judgment, by view of the assize that the sheriffs warn them to repair the wall *within 40 days etc.*

118. Thomas Dieu complains that the stone wall which he and Fremond de Houthtone and Margery his wife have in common in the par. of All Hallows atte Heywharf is ruinous and overhangs his land by almost 1 ft. so that he cannot raise (levare) the timber for the building of his new house. He asks that the defs. be compelled by judgment of the assize to repair their part of the wall.

119. In the perambulation made that day it was found that a stone gable (gabulam) of the house of Stephen de Abyndone in the Ropery (corderia) in the same par. is ruinous, to the danger of the neighbours and passers-by. The sheriff is ordered to warn him to repair the wall *within 40 days etc.*

Fri. 21 July 1307. John le Blound, John de Wengrave, William de Leyre, Walter de Finchingfeld, Richer de Refham, Richard de Wylehale, Henry de Gloucestre, Thomas Sely, Simon Bolet.

120. William de Leyre and Idonea his wife essoin themselves against Gilbert le Mareschal and Amice his wife by Richard Scot.

121. Master Gilbert the Surgeon and. [Entry incomplete.]

122. Roger de Balesham and. [Entry incomplete.]

123. William de Hedersete and. [Entry incomplete.]

[On a piece of parchment sewn to the foot of the m.]: 'Originales rotuli'. 'Communitas'. This roll contains pleas of assizes of nuisance for 29–35 Edward.

[m. 13] *Fri. 17 Nov. 1307. John le Blound, mayor, John de Wengrave, Nicholas de Farndone, William de Combemartin, Adam de Rokesle, Richard de Gloucestre, Solomon le Coteler, Simon de Paris, John de Wyndessore, Nicholas Pycot and Nigel Drury.*

124. John de Wynton', 'barber', def., essoins himself against Paul le Potter, pl., by Robert de Leicestre. Paul appears against Solomon de Basing who does not come.

Fri. 22 Dec. 1307. John le Blound, mayor, John de Wengrave, William de Leyre, Henry de Durham (Dunolm'), Nicholas de Farndon, John de Gysorz, Geoffrey de Conduit, Thomas Romeyn, William de Coumbemartin, Nicholas Pycot, sheriff, Simon de Paris, Solomon le Cotiller, aldermen.

125. Denise relict of John Bacheler complains that William de Gatewyk, rector of All Hallows de Berkingecherche, John de Stratford, Peter de Blakeneye, Robert le Maderman and William de Finchingfeld have enclosed with gates (per clausturam portarum) the path (viam) giving access to her free tenement in the par. aforesaid. William de Gatewyk says that the path is a dedicated place and free alms of his church. The other defs. say nothing to delay the verdict of the assize. They are given a day on the morrow at Guildhall to hear judgment. William de Gatewyk appoints William le Clerk his attorney. On Sat. 23 Dec. the parties come and the defs. are ordered to remove the nuisance by the next day, and restore the path to the condition in which it was when the sheriff forbade the erection of the gates (clausturam nocumenti). Both parties are given a day to hear judgment at Guildhall on Mon. 8 Jan. 1308; but the mayor and aldermen being then unable to attend there is a further adjournment to Fri. 12 Jan., on which day Denise appears but the defs. make default. The sheriff is ordered to distrain them to remove the gates (clausturam nocumenti) complained of, and to cause them to appear on Mon. 15 Jan. to make fine for their trespass. At the court held on that day, the pl. again appears, but the defs. do not come. Judgment, by view of the assize, that within 40 days they remove the nuisance, so that the path remains common, as it used to be; and that the sheriffs have their bodies before the mayor and aldermen on Fri. 19 Jan. to make fine for the trespass, of which they have been found guilty by inquest, of erecting the gates aforesaid in defiance of the sheriffs' prohibition.

Fri. 26 Jan. 1308. [Essoins only.]

[m. 13d.] *Fri. 9 Feb. 1308. John le Blound, mayor, John de Wengrave, William de Leyre, Henry de Durham, Thomas Romeyn, Nicholas Pycot, John de Wyndesore, William Cosyn, John de Gysorz, William de Combemartyn, aldermen.*

126. The abbot of Stratford complains that the water draining from the houses of Ralph le Coupere and Celestria his wife rots his timber and the stone wall which they have in common in the par. of St. Mary Wolnoth. The defs. say nothing to delay the verdict of the assize. Judgment, after inspection by the assize that within 40 days the defs. receive their water and convey it on to their own land or into the street, unless the parties can agree together to carry off their water at their common charges in a single gutter.

[m. 14] *Fri. 12 July 1308. John le Blound, mayor, John de Wengrave, William de Leyre, John de Wyndesore, Richard de Gloucestre, Richard de Wylehale and Nicholas Pycot, sheriff, aldermen.*

127. Ralph le Balauncer, Adam Bray and Tiffany his wife essoin themselves against Robert de Keleseye, pl., by William de Brainford.

128. The prioress of Haliwelle and Henry de Shorne, defs., essoin themselves against Richard de Littleton, clerk, pl., by William de Braynford.

Assize of Nuisance

Fri. 19 July 1308. [Essoins only.]

Fri. 2 Aug. 1308. John le Blound, mayor, John de Wengrave, William de Leyre, John de Wyndesore, Nicholas de Farndon, Nigel Drury, sheriff.

129. Cecily relict of John de Bauquelle complains that the apertures (aperturas) in the house of Avice la Sackere overlook her land in the par. of Holy Trinity the Less. The def. after essoin makes default. Judgment, by view of the assize, that *within 40 days etc.* she block up the aperture.

Fri. 20 Sep. 1308. John le Blound, mayor, John de Wengrave, William de Leyre, Thomas Romeyn, Nicholas de Farndon, John de Wyndesore, Simon de Paris, Nicholas Pycot.

130. The prior of St. Bartholomew de Smethefeld complains that Adam Wade. [Entry incomplete.]

Fri. 27 Sep. 1308. John le Blound, mayor, William de Leyre, John de Wyndesore, Thomas Romeyn, Nicholas de Farndon, Simon de Paris, Thomas Sely, Henry de Gloucestre, aldermen.

131. Idonea de Cambridge (Cantebrigia) complains that the stone wall of Richard de Mompesson (Monte Pessulano) and Raymond de la Brouwe is ruinous, to the danger of the lives of her tenants and others dwelling there (conversancium), and to the nuisance of her free tenement in the par. of St. Mary Magdalen de Melkstrete. [*Margin:* dies oct'.]

[m. 14d.] *Fri. 15 Nov. 1308. Nicholas de Farndon, mayor, John de Wengrave, William de Leyre, Thomas Romeyn, John de Wyndesore, John de Gysorz, Henry de Durham, Simon Bolet, aldermen.*

132. Thomas Broun complains that the water falling from the houses of Stephen de Uptone and Sybil his wife rots the timber of his house in the par. of St. Sepulchre without Newgate. The sheriff testifies that the defs. have been summoned, but they do not come. Judgment, after inspection by the assize, that *within 40 days etc.* they make a gutter (goteram) to convey their water on to their own land or into the street.

Fri. 7 Mar. 1309. Nicholas de Farndon, mayor, John de Wengrave, John de Wyndesore, Henry de Durham, William de Leyre, Nicholas Pycot, Simon de Paris, Geoffrey de Conduit, William de Coumbemartin, aldermen.

133. Master John de Sodingtone essoins himself against the prior of the Austin Friars by Robert de Leycestre.

134. Roger Chauntecler essoins himself against Amice relict of Walter de Flete by William de Brainford.

Fri. 14 Mar. 1309. Nicholas de Farndon, mayor, John de Wengrave, Thomas

Assize of Nuisance

Romeyn, William de Leyre, John de Wyndesore, Henry de Durham, Richard de Gloucestre, Geoffrey de Conduit, Simon Bolet, Simon de Paris, William Servat, Richard de Wilehale, and Henry de Gloucestre, William Cosyn, Thomas Sely and Nicholas Pycot, aldermen.

135. Hugh le Blound, kt., and Henry Lisson essoin themselves against Robert son of Walter, pl., by Robert de Leycestre; Hugh brother of the aforesaid Henry essoins himself against the same Robert by William de Braineford.

136. Henry de Bluntesdon and William Trente, defs., essoin themselves against John Heyroun, pl., by William de Reyleye.

Fri. 18 Apr. 1309. Nicholas de Farndon, mayor, John de Wengrave, William de Leyre, John de Wyndesore, Nicholas Pycot, Henry de Durham, Henry de Gloucestre, William Trente, aldermen.

137. Sabine relict of Philip le Taillour essoins herself against Henry de Durham, pl., by J. de Brackele.

Fri. 25 Apr. 1309. Nicholas de Farndon, mayor, John de Wengrave, William de Leyre, John de Wyndesore, Henry de Durham, Richard de Gloucestre, Nicholas Pycot, Simon de Paris, William Cosyn, William de Coumbemartin.

138. Adam de Cobham and Agnes his wife, defs., essoin themselves against Alice relict of Richard de Chingeford, pl., by Robert de Leycestre.

139. A day is given to Ralph de Billingesgate, taverner, pl., and Adam Ludekyn, def., at the prayer of the parties.

140. Because it is found by testimony of the neighbours and is apparent to the men sworn to the assize that the master of the bakehouse of St. Paul's and Master John de Silverstone changed the course of the stream (cursum aque) formerly running through the street leading to St. Paul's Wharf by raising the level of their pavement (pavimentum), it is adjudged that the master of the bakehouse and the tenants of the tenement formerly belonging to the said Master John, be warned that *within 40 days etc.* they lower (ad deprimendum) the pavement so that the water can follow its former course.

141. Because it is found by presentment of the neighbours and is apparent to the mayor and the men sworn to the assize that for lack of a pavement in the road by (sub) the close of St. Paul's great damage is daily incurred by the citizens and could arise in case of fire, it is adjudged that the sheriff warn the dean and canons living near the bakehouse, the master of the same, the abbot of Peterborough and others living there (ceterosque vivos) that *within 40 days etc.* each make a pavement outside his tenement.

142. The mayor and the men sworn to the assize order that *within 40 days etc.* John de Waledene lower the pavement which he has built too high

Assize of Nuisance

opposite his house, to the nuisance of private persons and strangers walking and riding there.

143. Because Roger de Rokesle, William Cros. [Entry incomplete.]

144. Peter le Ireys, tailor, complains that Roger le Mineter. [Entry incomplete.]

[m. 15] *Fri. 22 Aug. 1309. [Essoins only.]*

Fri. 5 Sep. 1309. Nicholas de Farendon, mayor, John de Wenegrave, John de Wyndesore, Richard de Gloucestre, William Trente, Henry de Gloucestre, William de Leyre, aldermen.

145. The assize of William de Toppesfeld [and Joan his wife, v. Giles son of Nicholas Broun and Richard le Broun his guardian (custos)] on the Fri. following because it could not be terminated by view of the mayor and aldermen. It is adjudged that an inquest be held concerning certain doubtful points. The parties and the jury duly appear and are given a day at the octave. On Fri. 19 Sep. the assize comes upon the land by Nicholas de Farndon, mayor, John de Wenegrave, John de Wyndesore, Nigel Druri, Simon de Parys, Henry de Gloucestre, Thomas Sely, aldermen, and six men of the neighbourhood, viz. Thomas le Paumer, Henry de Amoundesham, Walter le Chaundeler, Richard Levesone, Robert de Weleford and Adam le Forbour, elected and sworn by consent of the parties to certify the mayor and aldermen concerning those matters which they could not determine by view. The mayor and aldermen having been duly certified the parties were given a day at the quindene to hear judgment.

Fri. 14 Nov. 1309. [Essoins only.]

Fri. 28 Nov. 1309. Thomas Romeyn, mayor, Nicholas de Farndon, John de Wengrave, William de Leyre, Nicholas Picot, Nigel Drury, William Servad, Henry de Gloucestre, Henry de Durham.

146. Christine de Compton complains that when she wished to repair the stone wall of her tenement next the land of John de Rameseye in the par. of All Hallows de Berkyngchurch and sought to place her timber upon it and her carpenters began to build, the def. prohibited the work. John says that a moiety of the wall is his. The pl. says that he cannot claim anything in it, because the tenement of which it is part belonged formerly to Avice daughter of Richard and Thomas her brother who gave it to Robert de Cokfeld, kt., whose heir she is; and it lies between the tenement of William Clerk on the east and that of Master Arnold de Tulio, which belonged to Elias le Mariner on the west, and contains in breadth on the side where the wall is, 10 ells. She produces as evidence the deed of gift of Avice and Thomas to Robert, and says that Robert and all subsequent tenants have been seised of the wall in its entirety. She asks that the plot of land opposite the wall from the tenement of William Clerk be measured, and says that she will not consent to put herself upon any assize outside the bounds contained in her charter (petit quod dicta placea exopposito dicti muri a tenemento dicti Willelmi Clerici mensuretur, quia extra bundas in carta sua contentas super aliquam assisam ad ponendum se non vult consentere). The def. says that this is an assize, and ought to be held upon the land and determined by view of the mayor and aldermen and other good men of the City elected and sworn for the purpose, and that he can produce various evidences and arguments in support of his claim to own half of the wall. The mayor and good men being insufficiently advised as to whether the land should be measured for the bounds contained in the pl.'s charter, or whether the assize should proceed notwithstanding the production of her title-deed, give the parties a day at Guildhall [on Fri. 5 Dec.]. Further adjournment follows, until the next Tues. [9 Dec.] for lack of aldermen, and again until Fri. 12 Dec. because the mayor and aldermen are still insufficiently advised as to the judgment to be given. On that day the assize comes and the parties likewise, and because it appears to the view of the assize that a plate (plata) of old timber belonging to the pl.'s house lies upon half the wall in dispute, it is adjudged that the measurement for which she asked shall not be proceeded with, but that she retain the moiety of the wall upon which her old timber rests, and *within 40 days etc.* remove the timber newly placed upon the moiety not so built upon (hospitata).

[m. 15d.] *Fri. 12 Dec. 1309. [Heading cancelled: no entry.]*

Fri. 27 Feb. 1310. Thomas Romain, mayor, Nicholas de Farndon, John de Wengrave, William de Leire, Simon de Paris, Henry de Durham, John de Wyndesore, Thomas Sely, William Coumbemartyn, William Servat, John de Lincoln, aldermen.

147. William de Hanyton, skinner, pl., appears against John, rector of St. John upon Walebrok, Robert Persone, John le Marchal, Robert de Dodeford, Andrew de Stamford, Hugh de Wircestre, Henry le Forbour, Robert Liger, Adam de Burton, Robert le Purtreor and John de Eynesham, parishioners, defs. The rector comes and the sheriff testifies that the parishioners have been summoned, but they make default. The assize is accordingly adjourned to the quindene. On that day the parties come but two more adjournments follow because the mayor and aldermen are insufficiently advised as to the judgment to be rendered.

148. Walter Cross, pl., appears against Reginald Deumars and Isabel his wife, defs. The sheriff testifies that the defs. have been summoned but they do not come, and the assize is accordingly adjourned to the quindene.

Fri. 10 Apr. 1310.

149. The prior of Merton, def., essoins himself against William Amys by William de Realle. At the quindene [24 Apr.] the sheriff is ordered to cause the assize to be resummoned for Fri. 1 May because of the proximity of Easter. On that day the parties come, but for lack of aldermen the assize is

Assize of Nuisance

adjourned until Fri. 8 May, when the parties come in the presence of Thomas Romayn, mayor, J. de Wengrave, W. de Leire, H. de Durham, William Servat, J. de Wyndesore, and Nicholas Picot and James de St. Edmunds, sheriff. Judgment, after view by the assize, that the party-wall (paries) of the prior's house be demolished, because it does not stand straight (lineatura, *rectius* lineatur) but leans towards the pl.'s land, and that the pl., at his own charges, lay the foundation (fundamentum) in stone of a new wall, the def. finding the timber to complete it. The pl. to meet the entire cost of building and the wall to remain to the def.

[m. 16] *Fri. 15 May 1310. T. Romayn, mayor, J. de Wengrave, William de Leire, William Servat, H. de Durham, J. de Windesore, and Nicholas Picot, aldermen, and James de St. Edmunds, sheriff.*

150. William de Hakford, Avice his wife and Walter their son, defs., essoin themselves against Alan le Cordwaner and Joan his wife by W. de Reile.

Fri. 22 May 1310.

151. Pleas of assize between Ralph de la Penne, pl., and Peter de Wymbourne, clerk, living at Smethefeld; Robert de Gloucestre, goldsmith, pl., and William atte Wolde and Isabel his wife; Alice relict of Gerard de Brye, pl., and Robert son of Robert le Treier respited by Henry de Durham, alderman, and Thomas de Kent (Kancia), serjeant, for lack of aldermen.

Fri. 19 June 1310. [Essoins only.]

Fri. 26 June 1310.

152. The bishop of Hereford essoins himself against Geoffrey Scot, junior, by Adam Pye.

[m. 16d.] *Fri. 7 Aug. 1310. [Essoins only.]*

Fri. 14 Aug. 1310. [Essoins only.]

[m. 17] *Fri. 10 July 1310.*

153. William de Hackeford essoins himself against Alan le Cordewaner and Joan his wife by W. de Reyle. Avice wife of William appears. [Cf. **150.**]

Fri. 17 July 1310.

154. On that day Simon Corp, pl., and Peter Adrien, def., appear before Thomas Romain, mayor, John de Wengrave, John de Lincoln, Simon de Paris, William de Combemartyn, Nicholas Pikot, Simon Bolet, Richard de Wyrhale, William Servat, Richard de Gloucestre, Thomas Seely and William Trente, aldermen. The pl. complains that when he sought to repair his house, the def. prohibited him from placing his timber upon his part of the wall between their tenements. Judgment, after inspection by the mayor and aldermen and all the others belonging to the assize, that the pl. have 1½ ft. of the wall for its entire length, viz. 21 ells 1½ ft. from the tenement of Henry de Bouden on the east to Soperelane on the west, and that the space left between the parties for a gutter be common to them and repaired at their joint expense.

Fri. 7 Aug. and Fri. 14 Aug. 1310. [Entries as on m. 16d.]

Fri. 21 Aug. 1310.

155. On that day the mayor and aldermen come and Gilbert de Taunton likewise. J. de Pelham, by his attorney, complains that the def. in building upon his land, placed his timber too close to his house. The def. puts himself upon the view of the mayor, aldermen, sheriff and others of the assize, who give judgment in his favour.

Fri. 28 Aug. 1310. Thomas Romayn, mayor, Nicholas de Farndon, John de Wengrave, William de Leire, William Trente, John de Lincoln and William Servat, aldermen, and James de St. Edmunds, sheriff.

156. On that day Roger le Palmere, pl., and Thomas Gisorz, def., appear before the mayor and aldermen, and Roger complains that, when building his house in the par. of St. Mildred in Bredestrete he sought to place his timber upon the wall between his land and that of the def., the latter prohibited the work and overthrew the timber. Thomas claims that the wall is his. He puts himself upon the view of the assize and the pl. likewise. A day is given to the parties on Mon. 31 Aug. and further adjournment follows until Fri. 4 Sep. for lack of aldermen. Finally the parties come on Wed. 16 Sep. at Guildhall and because it appears to the mayor and aldermen that the south part of the wall, next to the wall of the church of St. Mildred, stands upon the land of the pl. and the rest upon that of the def., who has an old post above in his kitchen adjoining the wall about which the dispute has arisen, it is adjudged that the pl. have the wall, measuring by scantling (per scantilonem) from the outside of the said post to the corner of the church, and the def. from inside the post.

[m. 17d.] *Fri. 23 Oct. 1310.*

157. Nicholas de Westmulne and Margaret his wife, defs., essoin themselves against Francis de Kaleys by P. le Keu.

158. Gilbert de Taunton, pl., appears against John de Pelham, def., concerning a nuisance to his free tenement in the par. of St. Olave in S[ilver]-strete. Henry de Passenham produces royal letters of protection[1] on behalf of the def., and asks that the protection be allowed. The pl. produces royal

1. *C.P.R. 1307–13*, 16. For a licence to crenellate granted to John de Pelham, 2 Nov. 1311, see *ibid.*, 398. Cf. grant to William Servat, *C.P.R. 1301–7*, 379. For the only possible reference to a crenellated building in the rolls, see **95**.

Assize of Nuisance

letters promising him maintenance and protection in his affairs, and likewise asks that they be allowed. And because the mayor and aldermen are insufficiently advised concerning the premises a day is given to the parties.

Fri. 6 Nov. 1310.

159. Alice de Molers essoins herself against William Trent by H. de Exeter (Exon').

160. William Busshe complains that Maud relict of John le Heaumer, William de Basing and Richolda his wife have broken down the party-walls (parietes) of the privy in a room in the par. of St. Dunstan by the Tower of which he has been seised for ten years and more, declaring that it belongs to them, and that he receives upon his land the rainwater from the defs.' house, whereas they ought to do so. The defs. come and Maud, as tenant of the tenement in question, says that she lately brought a writ of dower against the pl. in the Husting, and the privy was included in the third part assigned to her by the carpenters and masons (homines carpentarios et lapicidas) sworn to make such partitions. The pl. says that the partition was made three years ago, and the privy was not included in Maud's share, but remained in his possession until within the last month she laid claim to it. Because it appears to the mayor and aldermen, on Maud's own showing, that the pl. retained the privy from the time of the partition until the present, and it seems to them that he could not have done so had it been included in her third part, they give judgment that within 40 days she rebuild the party-walls as they were before under a penalty of 40s. As to the reception of the water, it is adjudged that, since no plaint has yet been raised, nothing be done at present.

[m. 17a][1] *Fri. 9 May 1309. Nicholas de Farndon, mayor, John de Wengrave, John de Wyndesore, Thomas Romeyn, Richard de Gloucestre, Geoffrey de Conduit, aldermen.*

161. Roger le Mineter and Gregory de Basingg, defs., essoin themselves against Peter le Hirreys, tailor, pl., by John de Brackele.

[m. 18] *Fri. 20 Nov. 1310.*

162. Robert [de Chiggewelle] essoins himself against Roger de Frowik by W. de Reyle.

Fri. 27 Nov. 1310. Richer de Refham, [mayor], Nicholas de Farndon, John de Wengrave, Henry de Durham, William Trente, Thomas Seely, Nicholas Picot.

163. William Busshe complains that the water draining from the house of William de Basyng and Richolda his wife and Maud relict of John le Heaumere in the par. of St. Dunstan by the Tower, falls upon his land,

1. A narrow strip of parchment the dorse of which is blank.

and that the defs. have a door and a window opening upon it. The defs. though summoned make default. Judgment after view that they make a gutter (stillicidium) to receive and carry off their rainwater, and block up the apertures complained of *within 40 days etc.*

164. William de Leire complains that Simon de Abyndon has recently made an aperture in the plaster (luteo) wall of his house in the par. of All Hallows the Less, opposite the pl.'s hall. The def. comes and submits to the judgment of the assize. After view, the mayor and aldermen adjudge that he block up the aperture *within 40 days etc.*

Fri. 4 Dec. 1310.

165. John le Luter complains that the cess-pit of Robert de Chiggewelle's privy adjoins too closely his earthen wall in the par. of St. John Zachary, so that his house is inundated and his wall rotted by the sewage. The def. says that the cess-pit is common to both parties, since their respective tenements were formerly a single whole; and the wall simply marks the boundary between their pourparties. Judgment after view that they clean the cess-pit at their common charges; and, at their discretion, either combine to build a stone wall in place of the earthen one, or each build a stone wall on his own pourparty. The cleansing of the cess-pit to be carried out within 40 days. Otherwise the sheriff is to act at the expense of the defaulting party. [Entry deleted. *Margin:* vacat hic quia intratur inferius.]

[m. 18d.] *Fri. 7 May 1311.*

166. Isabel relict of Roger de Higham essoins herself against Luke de Havering, chamberlain of London, on behalf of the commonalty by William de Reille.

167. The commonalty, by Luke de Haveryng, chamberlain, appear against Thomas de Campes, John Dode, John de Dallyng, Robert de Fulsham and Master Peter le Cirugien. Master Peter makes default. The sheriff is ordered to warn him to be prepared within 40 days to combine with the commonalty to build a wall between them, in accordance with the *Assize*. Thomas de Campes, John Dode and Ralph de Fulsham come and agree to build their respective portions. John de Dallyng is ordered to block up his apertures overlooking the land of the commonalty, and to make a fillet-gutter (filettum) to receive his rainwater.

Fri. 14 May 1311. R. de Refham, mayor, S. de Corp, sheriff, J. de Wengrave, N. de Farndon, Thomas Romayn, H. de Gloucestre, N. Pikot, S. de Paris, H. [sic] de Gloucestre.

168. John de la Barnette, minor, essoins himself against John le Botoner by William de Braynford.

169. John de Triple, pl., appears against Peter le Blund, parson of St.

Assize of Nuisance

Stephen Walebroke, and William de Hanyton, John Cotun, John de Cornwall (Cornubia), Gilbert atte Herst, Roger de Ely, fishmonger, Elias de Thorp, Geoffrey de Shropshire (Salop), Adam de Harewebrewe, Peter de Newcastle (Novo Castro), Roger de Netlestede, Robert de la Marche, tailor, and Andrew Brunne, parishioners. William de Reylle comes and offers to essoin the defs. but afterwards he denies doing so on the ground that he had not been asked. Peter appears in person. John de Triple complains that the part of his stone wall between his tenement and the church, with the house built thereupon, was ruinous and dangerous, and he began to demolish it with a view to its repair, whereupon the defs. caused the sheriff to prohibit the work. It is found by view of the mayor and aldermen and the others sworn to the assize that the part of the wall in question viz. that situated on the south side of the church, between the altar of the Blessed Virgin on the east and the corner where John Adrien, late citizen, is said to be buried on the west, stands wholly on the pl.'s land, and the gutter (stillicidium) thereon belongs solely to him, whereas the church has its own gutter (stillicidium) to receive its own water, situated upon its own land. It is therefore adjudged that the pl. continue his building operations. Peter and his parishioners in mercy for a false plaint. [Cf. **174**.]

Fri. 11 June 1311. R. de Refham, mayor, Nicholas de Farndon, John de Wengrave, Henry de Durham, William Servat, Richard de Gloucestre, Nicholas Pikot, John Lincoln, Thomas Sely, aldermen.

170. The mayor and commonalty appear against Thomas Perceval, and the sheriff attests, by Richard de Crofton, clerk, that he was not in the City at the time of the summons. The sheriff is instructed to order those living in the tenement concerning which the assize is sought, to warn him to be upon the land at the quindene; and the same day is given to the mayor and commonalty.

171. Mayor and commonalty, pls., v. Isabel relict of Stephen Asshwy, def., are given a day at the quindene.

[m. 19] *Fri. 18 June 1311. R. de Refham, mayor, J. de Wengrave, William de Leire, Henry de Durham, Simon de Paris, Nicholas Picot, William Servat and Thomas Sely, aldermen.*

172. Hugh Picard and Sabine his wife, defs., essoin themselves against Geoffrey de Bordeslee and Albreda his wife by H. de Passenham.

173. Robert Person, 'peleter', def., essoins himself against William de Bristoll and Denise his wife by William de Reyle.

174. John Triple, pl., appears against Peter le Blund, parson of St. Stephen Walebrok, William de Hanyngton, John Coton, Roger de Nettlestede, John de Cornewaille, Geoffrey de Shropshire, and Gilbert atte Hierst, parishioners, defs., who first essoin themselves and then make default. The pl., by Henry de Passenham, his attorney, complains that the defs.

acting on their own authority, have made a great aperture in the stone wall on the south side of the church, overlooking his tenement. The mayor and aldermen, after viewing the premises, give the parties a day at the octave [25 June] at Guildhall to hear judgment; but on that day they had to appear before the treasurer and council, and the assize was therefore adjourned until Wed. [? 14 July 1311]. On the following Fri. the parties come, and judgment is given that since the wall in question forms the fence between the parties, and for the past thirty years and more there has been no aperture in it, the defs. must block up *within 40 days etc.* the aperture they have made.

Afterwards, on Sat. 11 Mar. 1312, the pl. comes and complains that judgment has not been executed. The sheriffs, Richard de Welleford and Simon de Corp are ordered to put it into execution in accordance with the custom of the City. [Cf. **169**. m. 19d. Blank.]

[m. 20] *Fri. 18 July 1311. Richer de Refham, mayor, Nicholas de Farndon, John de Wengrave, William de Leyre, Nicholas Pikot, Thomas Sely, Simon Bolet, aldermen, Simon de Corp, sheriff and others sworn to the assize.*

175. On that day it was adjudged by the mayor and aldermen that *within 40 days etc.* William de Hackeford and Avice his wife should pave the outside of their tenement in the par. of St. Stephen de Colemanstrete from their gate (porta) along the earthen wall in the lane leading to the church of St. Margaret de Lotheberi.

176. The widow of Geoffrey de Vescy was likewise ordered to pave outside her tenement within the same period and subject to a like penalty.

Fri. 30 July 1311. Richer de Refham, mayor, Nicholas de Farndon, John de Wengrave, William de Leire, Nicholas Picot, Thomas Sely, Simon de Paris, Simon Bolet, aldermen, and Simon Corp, sheriff.

177. John de la Barnet, def., essoins himself against John le Botoner by W. de B[raynford].

178. William de Coumbemartyn and Margery his wife, defs., essoin themselves against Adam Hunteman by the same.

179. William Trente essoins himself against John de Gisors (Gysorcio) prosecuting for himself and the commonalty by Adam Prat.

180. On that day Roger Poyntel, pl., and Ellen de Clouton came, and Roger undertook to build a stone wall 10 ft. high between them extending from Ellen's land on the west to his own on the east.

181. On the same day the parishioners of St. Mary Aldermanbury appeared against the same Ellen de Clouton concerning her wall next the churchyard of that church. Judgment by the mayor, aldermen, sheriffs and others sworn to keep the assize that *within 40 days etc.* the parishioners demolish the wall in question and rebuild it at their own cost upon land provided by Ellen to a width of 3 ft. and a height of 16 ft. according to the *Assize* of the City.

Fri. 10 Mar. 1312. John de Gisors (Gisorcio), mayor, Nicholas de Farendon, Henry de Durham, William Trente, William Servat, Nicholas Picot, Anketin de Gisorz, aldermen, and Richard de Welleford, sheriff.

182. Simon de Mereworth, def., essoins himself against John son of Roger de Essex by W. de Reile.

183. Francis de Vilers, kt., complains that by default of Henry le Brewere the gutter (stillicidium) between their tenements in the par. of St. Dunstan Fletestrete, which ought to be repaired at their common charges, is so broken that the timber of his house is rotted and the party-wall is ruinous, and that the cess-pit of the def.'s privy adjoins the earthen wall of his hall too closely; and further that he stacks his firewood in his garden too near the pl.'s stable wall so that it is broken and damaged. Judgment that since all the nuisances complained of are manifest, the parties repair the gutter *within 40 days etc.* at their common charges, and that within the same period the def. remove his cess-pit $3\frac{1}{2}$ ft. from the pl.'s wall, and remove his firewood from his stable wall and repair the damage caused to it under a penalty of 40s. etc. [m. 20d. Blank.]

[m. 21] *Fri. 13 Oct. 1312. John de Gysors, mayor, John de Wengrave, Nicholas de Farndon, Richard de Gloucestre, Nigel Druri, Anketin de Gisors and Simon Bolet, aldermen, and Richard de Welleford, sheriff.*

184. Isabel relict of Richard de Horemade complains that Master John Wylemyn, in rebuilding his house in the par. of All Hallows de Grascherche upon the site adjoining the pl.'s tenement, placed his timbers upon the stone wall which belongs wholly to her house, tearing down (eradicavit) the gutter (guteram) on the same wall which received and carried off her rainwater into the street, and breaking and cutting through (abscisit) the tiles and timber. The def. comes and asks for licence to agree. He undertakes to repair and replace the gutter in its former position; and the pl. agrees to remit to him all the trespass and damage done to her. The def. is ordered to repair the gutter without delay and to remove his corbels from the pl.'s wall within eight days.

Fri. 22 Dec. 1312. J. de Gisors, mayor, N. de Farndon, John de Wengrave, William de Coumbemartyn, William de Leire, William Servat, Henry de Gloucestre, Simon Bolet, Henry de Durem, John de Wyndesore, Nigel Druri, Roger de Paris, Richard de Wyrhale, John Lambyn, alderman and sheriff, Richard de Willehale [sic], Anketin de Gysorz and Stephen de Abyndon, aldermen.

185. Master William de Meleford, archdeacon of Colchester, pl., appears against Ralph son of William Mabely, surgeon, John de Laufare and

Edward de Macchyng, defs., complaining that they have apertures in the earthen walls of their houses in the par. of St. Benet Fink overlooking his garden. The sheriff testifies that the defs. were summoned, but they make default. Judgment, after inspection of the premises that *within 40 days etc.* the defs. block up the apertures complained of.

186. On Fri. 2 Mar. 1313 it was adjudged by J. de Gisors, mayor, and the aldermen that John de Watford and John Knyght, tailor, should *within 40 days etc.* remake the pavement outside their tenements in the par. of St. Sepulchre in the suburb of London, which in its present state is to the damage of John de Chibenherst and the other neighbours.

Fri. 27 Apr. 1313. J. de Gysors, mayor, Nicholas de Farndon, John de Wengrave, William de Leire, Roger de Frowik, John de Lincoln, Anketin de Gysors, aldermen, and Adam Ludekyn, sheriff.

187. Richard Ussher, Geoffrey de Chelchehethe, Gervase de Houndesdiche, Philip de Houndesdiche, Geoffrey Drie, Simon atte Smalebregge, Lawrence de Hadham, Walter de Hadham, Walter de Shenefeld, Roger de Chipstede, Roger de Edelmeton, John Swift, Walter de Chipstede, William de Hakeneye, William le Meleward, Richard Beryng, William de Mymmes and Stephen de Hadham, tanners, pls., appear against Philip fitz Herves', William de Forsham, Thomas de Luda, John le Botoner and Henry le Callere and other tanners, defs., concerning their free tenement in the par. of St. Mary le Bow (de Arcubus). Philip fitz Herves' and Thomas de Luda do not come, because they were not in the City at the time of the summons. The sheriff is ordered to summon them for the quindene, and meanwhile the assize proceeds. The pls. complain that they have a common seld in the par. which is in disrepair, but they cannot repair it because the defs.' wall which adjoins their tenement is ruinous and must first be demolished and rebuilt. William de Forsham comes and says that he has no interest in the wall in question except by demise of Philip fitz Herves'. John le Botoner and Henry le Callere come.

Fri. 1 June 1313.

188. John le Mazeliner, chamberlain, appears on behalf of the commonalty, pls., against the prior and brethren of the Austin Friars, defs., complaining that whereas, time out of mind, there was a ditch (fovea) outside the old hedge (sepe) enclosing their garden in the par. of All Hallows London Wall which served to receive and carry off the water of the Walebrok, the defs. have stopped up the ditch and built an earthen wall around their garden on the other side of it, thus narrowing the king's highway to the damage of the whole City, and obstructing the course of the Walebrok. The defs. come and are given a day.

Fri. 6 July 1313. Mayor, the aldermen and sheriff.

189. William de Meltone, dean of St. Martin le Grand, the chapter of the

Assize of Nuisance

same and William de Beverle, chaplain, essoin themselves against the mayor and citizens prosecuting for themselves and for the guardian of the Friars Minor by W. de. Westwode.

190. Robert de la March, tailor, essoins himself against John le Luter and Isabel his wife by J. de Westwode.

[m. 21d.] *Fri. 8 June 1313.*

191. John de Preston, 'zeinturer', pl., appears against William Spot and Muriel his wife and Margery la Fundour, defs., complaining that the cess-pit of the privy they have made in their house in the par. of St. Lawrence Jewry adjoins too closely the pl.'s tenement and so undermines it that his house and timbers are ruined. The defs. do not come. Judgment after view that *within 40 days etc.* the cess-pit complained of be well and firmly blocked up and another made 3 ft. from the pl.'s land.

192. The assize between William Trente, pl., and Alice la Molere respited for lack of aldermen.

Fri. 15 Mar. 1314. Nicholas de Farndon, mayor, sheriffs and the aldermen.

193. On that day Hugh de Waltham, pl., and Richard Dask, def., agreed by licence of Nicholas de Farndon, mayor, the sheriffs and aldermen. The tenor of the agreement [French] follows. [*Margin:* Scriptum irrotulatum.] Richard acknowledges that he is bound to maintain in repair a gutter (gotere) between his house and Hugh's in the par. of St. James Garlekhethe, and to receive upon his land the water draining from Hugh's house; the pl. granting him in return the right to affix his transoms (traverseyns) to his timber (meryn), and to convey the water from his house through his tenement. The def. further undertakes that whenever the pl. wishes to repair his house he may remove the said transoms and gutter (gotere), and divert or stop up the water flowing through his tenement, and promises to claim no right in the pl.'s wall or timber. Penalty for breach of the agreement £20 payable to the pl., his heirs or assigns. Dated 13 Oct. 1312. Witnesses: John de Birdene, Peres Maupyn, John de Taleworth, William le Bret and others. The def. comes and acknowledges the above deed as his, and grants for himself, his heirs and assigns that if at any future time it is contravened, the £20 shall be levied by the City officers to the use of Hugh, his heirs or assigns or to whomsoever the tenement in question shall come; and he puts himself in mercy [*sic*].

[m. 22] *Fri. 5 Oct. 1313.*

194. Roger Sauvage, kt., and John de Chesthonte essoin themselves against Robert de Hagham and Idonia la Blunde his wife by William de Reile.

Fri. 19 Oct. 1313.

Assize of Nuisance

195. The prioress of Halywelle and Robert de la Marche, tailor, defs., essoin themselves against John le Luter and Isabel his wife by John Scot.

196. John de Coton essoins himself against Margery de Basyng and Reginald de Basyng her son by John Devineys.

197. Alice de Lincoln complains that Idonea daughter of William de Leire. [Entry incomplete, but see **205**.]

Fri. 4 Jan. 1314. Perambulation by Nicholas de Farndon, mayor, and the aldermen to inspect the course of the Walebrok.

198. Roger de Eure and Ranulph, rector of St. Margaret Lotheberi, were ordered to remove within 40 days all the obstructions they have placed in the course of the Walebrok and to enlarge the watercourse beside their tenements where they have narrowed it.

199. Robert de Asshe, 'cordewaner', is ordered to remove his firewood from the course of the Walebrok.

200. Likewise John de Paris, 'seler', is ordered to remove certain beams (trabes) and timber lying across the Walebrok next his house; and William de Fourneis to remove a privy built above it within 15 days. Otherwise the sheriff is to act.

Fri. 1 Feb. 1314. [Essoins only.]

[m. 22d.] *Fri. 1 Mar. 1314. Nicholas de Farndone, mayor, John de Wengrave, Henry de Durham, John de Lincoln, Henry de Gloucestre, Roger de Frouwyk, Roger de Paris, aldermen, and Robert Burdeyn, sheriff.*

201. It is adjudged by the assize that the stone wall common to the tenements of Robert de Keleseye and Katherine relict of William de Staunford in the par. of St. Mary de Colchurch in Cheap, which is ruinous, be repaired within 40 days at their common charges. Both agree spontaneously to do the work. If they fail the sheriff is to act at the expense of the defaulter.

Fri. 15 Mar. 1314. Nicholas de Farndon, mayor, and the other aldermen, etc.

202. Richer de Refham complains that John le Botoner. ['Vacated because elsewhere'. See **206**.]

203. Hugh de Waltham, clerk, complains that John le Tailleur of Grascherch has caused his masons to cut through the foundations of the stone wall between the tenement formerly belonging to Ralph le Blund, goldsmith, in the par. of St. Benet Garscherche, now held by Peter de Herlyng, called le Taverner, and the pl.'s own tenement, beneath his joists (gistis) and planks (planchetis) and under the entrance to his house, and has blocked up the apertures in his party-wall which formerly gave light to his kitchen, and which John de Beverley, tailor, the def.'s father, granted to Edmund Horn, predecessor of the pl. After inspection by the mayor, sheriffs, aldermen and others sworn to the assize, it is adjudged that *within 40 days etc.* the def. repair the wall in question, and reopen the apertures in accordance with his father's deed.

Fri. 29 Mar. 1314. Nicholas de Farendon, mayor, John de Gisors, John de Wengrave, Richard de Gloucestre, John de Lincoln, William Servat, Henry de Durham, Roger de Paris and Simon de Paris, aldermen, and Robert Burdeyn, sheriff.

204. William de Cornehulle, parson of St. Mary Aldermanberi, complains that William de Salesbury, clerk, has caused the rebuilding of his house, which adjoins that of the def., to be prohibited. The def. says that the pl. sought to attach his timbers and a brace (bracea) to a post in his house, in which he has no right. The assize finds that as alleged by him the brace of the pl.'s old house was affixed to the post in question and that his wall-plate (pannam) rested upon it. It is therefore adjudged that he affix his new brace and timber in like manner, provided it be not to the detriment of the def.'s tenement.

[m. 23] *Fri. 26 Oct. 1313.*

205. Alice de Lincoln complains that Idonea daughter of William de Leire, citizen, in repairing her house in the par. of Holy Trinity the Less, placed her timber upon the stone wall between their tenements, half of which belongs to the pl., who thereupon prohibited the work. Idonea says that the assize has no jurisdiction in the matter, because the tenement now held by the pl. was formerly in the possession of John de Halghford, citizen, between whom and the def. a dispute arose concerning the wall in question, and she produces the indenture made between them on Thurs. 19 Oct. 1301, and witnessed by Elias Russel, then mayor, Robert le Callere and Peter Bosenham, sheriffs, Ralph de Honylane, alderman of the ward [of Bread Street], Walter de Fynchyngfeld, junior, John le Blund, N. de Farndone, R. de Gloucestre, H. de Gloucestre, aldermen, John de Lincoln, Roger le Palmere, Simon le Blund, baker, and others, according to which the parties agreed that the wall, extending from the tenement of John de Gisors on the east to the royal highway on the south, and measuring 30 ells, not counting the odd inches, should be common between them in perpetuity, and maintained in repair at their common charges, half remaining to John and his heirs and assigns, and half to the def., with the right to build thereon; saving to John his chimney on the said wall. Idonea says that she claims nothing more than is allowed by the indenture, but asks that the masons and carpenters appointed for the purpose come and measure the wall in length, breadth and depth to determine the extent of her share. Master Simon de Pabenham [?Pakenham] and Michael de Canterbury, masons, and Master Robert Norhampton and Simon de Canterbury, carpenters, come on the following Mon. [29 Oct.] and report their findings at Guildhall.

Judgment that the wall, throughout its length, is common to the parties, and that Alice may build upon her half without obstruction from Idonea.

Fri. 29 Mar. 1314. Enrolled on the rolls of pleas of assize of nuisance in the Chamber of Guildhall.

206. John le Botonner is summoned to answer Richer de Refham in a plea of assize of nuisance. Richer says that buildings in the City one, two or three storeys high have come into the possession of divers persons, two or three living in them according to the number of cellars and storeys, having acquired their right by inheritance, purchase or bequest; and that such persons ought, according to the custom of the City, to maintain their portions in repair and rebuild them if destroyed by fire or other cause. He complains that whereas he lately bought a shop on the corner of Soperislane next Cheap (forum), the def. has a very small shop in the corner of the same, under the first storey, which threatens ruin to the danger of passers-by and the scandal of the City; and he has refused for three years and more to repair it. The def. appears and says that his shop is in sufficiently good condition and does not need repair: but the mayor and aldermen find that it is ruinous and dangerous, and must be demolished and rebuilt. Since, however, the shop will remain for the greater part to Richer, it is adjudged that if possible within 40 days he provide subject to the prescribed penalty, a new post at the corner next Cheap and Soperislane of the same thickness as the previous one, together with the joists (gistas), plates (platas) and planks (planchea) and everything else necessary, excepting only the wall (claustura) between the def.'s premises and those of the pl., the cost of which they are to share equally. Further, the def. is to be allowed to affix the iron hooks (uncos) for hanging his shutters (fenestras) to the timber of the pl.'s shop, and is to be allotted the same space as he formerly enjoyed, according to measurements taken in the presence of Nicholas de Farndone, mayor, Hugh de Gartone and Robert Burdeyn, sheriffs, John de Gysors, John de Wengrave, William de Leyre, Henry de Durham, John de Lincoln, Simon Corp, Roger de Paris, and other aldermen and citizens and of the parties, viz: from the corner of the shop next Cheap to the pl.'s land on the south $1\frac{1}{2}$ ells 3 ins.; from the same corner to the pl.'s land on the east $1\frac{1}{2}$ ells less 2 ins.; in breadth on the east side $1\frac{1}{2}$ ells 3 ins.; on the south side $1\frac{1}{4}$ ells 2 ins.; in height from the pavement on the west side next Soperislane 2 ells 6 ins.; and from the pavement next Cheap beneath the pl.'s solar $2\frac{1}{2}$ ells 3 ins.; thickness of the post 12 ins.[1]

207. [m. 23d.] Royal writ[2] to the mayor and aldermen, dated 4 May 1314, to enforce the repair of tenements parts of which are occupied by different tenants.

208. Richard and Walter Crepyn, pls., appear against John, parson of St. Dunstan, def., complaining that the fences (clausture *sic*) between their

1. Assize transcribed in Liber Horn, ff. 259–260v.
2. This writ, upholding Richer's plea (**206**), was much copied: Liber Horn, f. 260v; *Lib. Alb.*, i, 469–70; Liber Dunthorn, ff. 30v, 31v; Letter Book E, f. 17.

Assize of Nuisance

tenement and that of the def. are broken down. The def. makes default. Judgment that the fence [*sic*] be repaired at the common charges of the parties within 40 days.

209. It is likewise adjudged that within 40 days an earthen wall $3\frac{1}{2}$ ft. thick be built at their common charges between the land of the same Richard and Walter and that of Thomas de Spain (Ispania) and Christine relict of Alan de Neuberi in the par. of St. Dunstan by the Tower, and between their land and that of John son of Lawrence Albyn. Otherwise the sheriff is to act at the expense of the defaulting party, and fine him 40s.

Fri. 15 Mar. 1314. [No entries but see above on m. 22d.]

[m. 24] *Fri. 26 July 1314. Nicholas de Farendone, mayor, John de Wengrave, William de Leire, Richard de Gloucestre, Anketyn de Gisors.*

210. John Tedmar essoins himself against Richard de Gloucestre, by Richard Bird.

211. Roger de Hortone, attorney of the abbess of St. Clare, pl., appears against John Hardel, def., complaining that he caused the repair of her house in the par. of St. Martin Vintry, to be prohibited. The def. comes and says that his house adjoins that of the pl. and that when she began to build she placed her timber on his land and affixed it to his wall. The mayor and aldermen find, after viewing the premises, that her old timber lay upon part of the wall in question, of which she is therefore seised, and that her posts and timber used in her new building do not encroach on the pl.'s land. She is therefore told that she may proceed with the work, and the pl. is forbidden to put any further obstacle in her way. Further, he is told that if he wishes at any time to demolish the wall, he may do so only as far as the pl.'s timber extends, and without threatening ruin to her house.

212. Cambin son of Fulbert (Fulberti) complains that whereas the solar above the entrance to his house is built upon the posts and timber of the party-wall between his tenement and that of Geoffrey de Blith and Cecily his wife in the par. of All Hallows de Grascherche, they caused the sheriff to prohibit the work when he sought to repair it. After viewing the premises the mayor and aldermen adjudge that the wall, posts and timber are common to the parties, and the pl. is to have half upon which to build his solar at will.

Fri. 9 Aug. 1314. Nicholas de Farndon, mayor, John de Gisors, John de Wengrave, William de Leire, Richard de Gloucestre, Roger de Paris and John de Lincoln, aldermen and Robert Burdeyn and Hugh de Garton, sheriffs.

213. The mayor and commonalty, by John Dode, chamberlain, complain that Walter le Benere has a house in the par. of St. Lawrence Jewry of which the stone wall extends from the outer gate (forinceca porta) of the Guildhall to the middle gate of the entrance (mediam portam introitus) of

which part is ruinous, to the great danger of the passers-by, and although warned by the mayor he has not troubled to repair it. Judgment that he repair it *within 40 days etc.*

214. The mayor and commonalty, by John Dode, chamberlain, complain that whereas of old in the par. of St. Michael Queenhithe, a gutter (gutera) running under certain of the houses was provided to receive the rainwater and other water draining from the houses, gutters and street, so that the flow might cleanse the privy (camera privata) on the Hithe, Alice Wade has made a wooden pipe (pipam ligneam) connecting the seat (sedile) of the privy in her solar with the gutter, which is frequently stopped up by the filth therefrom, and the neighbours under whose houses the gutter runs are greatly inconvenienced by the stench. Judgment that she remove the pipe *within 40 days etc.*

[m. 24d.] *Fri. 16 Aug. 1314. Nicholas de Farndon, mayor, John de Gisors, John de Wengrave, William de Leire, Simon de Paris, Simon Corp, Anketyn de Gisors, aldermen, and Robert Burdeyn and Hugh Garton, sheriffs.*

215. William de Hakford and Avice his wife, pls., appear against John de Sabrichesworth, junior, def., complaining that the earthen wall between the garden of the pls. and the land of the def., extending from the corner of their kitchen on the north to the corner of the def.'s house on the south in the par. of St. Stephen de Colmanstrete is ruinous, and the def. refuses to share in the cost of repairing it. The def. comes and says that he is prepared to repair the wall in accordance with the judgment of the assize, and the pl. says likewise. It is adjudged that it be rebuilt at their common charges to a width of 3 ft. The pls. further complain that the rainwater from the west side of the def.'s house falls upon their land. Judgment that the def. convey it into the street or on to his own land. Further, the pls. say that the def. has apertures in his party-wall overlooking their premises. Judgment that he block them up *within 40 days etc.*

216. Reginald de Walsyngham and Mary his wife complain that William de Hedersete and Joan his wife prohibit them from repairing their house in the par. of St. Thomas the Apostle; and that the water from the def.'s house falls upon their land and floods it and their house; and that they have a window overlooking their premises. Judgment that the pls. rebuild the walls of their house as they were formerly, and have possession of as much of the wall between the houses of the parties on the north side as was occupied by their old timber. The defs. are ordered to convey the water from their house on to their own land and to block up the aperture complained of *within 40 days etc.*

217. Walter Crepyn complains of John Aubyn that the fence (claustura) between his plot of land and the def.'s tenement in the par. of St. Dunstan by the Tower is completely pulled down (disrupta) and demolished (prostrata) and the def. refuses to rebuild it. Judgment that each of the parties contribute half the land and build a stone wall between them at their

Assize of Nuisance

common charges of the height and thickness required by the *Assize*. Otherwise the sheriff is to act at the expense of the defaulter.

218. The prior of Holy Trinity complains of William Wastel that the earthen wall built of old between the land and garden of the prior in the par. of St. Botolph without Alegate in the suburb of London on the north side, and the lands and tenements of the same William, Adam de Bocton and Peter de Grascherche on the south side is for the greater part pulled down and demolished, so that men and animals enter the pl.'s garden and carry off the fruits and tread down the grass (herbagium). Judgment that within 40 days the parties combine to repair the wall. Otherwise the sheriff is to act at the expense of the defaulter, and fine him in addition 40s.

[m. 25] *Fri. [? 6 Sep.; the vigil of the nativity of the B.V.M.] 1314. [Essoins only.]*

Fri. 20 Sep. 1314.

219. Margery de Somery complains that she has a tenement in the par. of St. Michael de Wodestrete, with right of free entry and exit as well by night as by day through a great entrance (introitus) adjoining the tenement of William le Chaundeler and Christine his wife; but they have so filled it with stalls (truncis),[1] timber and other impedimenta that she cannot go freely in and out to transact her business; and that she and the defs. had a well (fontem) in the entrance, common to both their tenements, from which to draw water, but the defs. have obstructed it; and, further, that the rain-water from their house falls upon her land and floods it. The defs. come and say that they hold their tenement for life only, and that the reversion belongs to Robert Burdeyn, goldsmith, without whom they cannot answer. The sheriff is ordered to summon him for the quindene [4 Oct.]. On that day the pl. appears but the sheriff testifies that Robert has not yet been summoned. He is ordered to summon him for the octave [11 Oct.] when the mayor and aldermen and the parties duly come. The pl. proffers a deed in which Philip the Palmer of Wodestrete granted to Maud de Bentele, his sister, and to all Christians acquiring it by inheritance, gift, sale or bequest, the great hall with its appurtenances which she now holds, with free entry and exit through the gate (portam) with horses and other beasts of burden (averiis) and carts, by day and by night, and with the right to draw water from the well (puteo) by the hall door (hostium). Robert can say nothing in rebuttal of her claim and it is therefore adjudged that *within 40 days etc.* the well be repaired at the common charges of Robert and the pl., and that he allow her free entry and exit by the gate and entrance aforesaid and further, since the cess-pit of the defs. adjoins too closely the pl.'s wall, Robert is ordered to remove it to a distance of $2\frac{1}{2}$ ft. if it is walled in stone or $3\frac{1}{2}$ ft. if in earth.

Fri. 4 Oct. 1314.

1. Probably boxes or stands placed in the street for the sale of wares (*Memorials*, 20n, 34n).

Assize of Nuisance

220. Walter atte Lee, clerk, essoins himself against Robert le Kallere by J. Pride, and Sabine wife of Walter appears.

Fri. 11 Oct. 1314. [Essoins only.]

(m. 25d.) *Fri. 10 Jan. 1315. John de Gisors, mayor, Stephen de Abyndon and Hamo de Chiggewelle, sheriffs, John de Wengrave, William de Leire, William Servat, Anketin de Gisors, Roger de Frowik, Simon Corp, aldermen.*

221. Oliver Brounyng, pl., appears against John de Bolyngton and Isabel his wife, defs., complaining that when he sought to repair his house in the par. of St. Nicholas de Coldabbeye, adjoining that of the defs., and to rest his timber upon half the post common to their tenements, the defs. caused the work to be prohibited. The defs. say that the post belongs wholly to them. After the premises have been viewed by the mayor, aldermen and sheriffs, the parties are told to come to an agreement, if possible, within the next eight days. Otherwise the pl. may lawfully (licencialiter) build there, on condition that he set up the post before and behind, having half the ground throughout his shop, as the half of the post in the front part between the tenements of the parties requires (predictus Olyverus postem predictum ex proprio custu levare fac' ante et retro, habendo medietatem fundi terre per totam shopam suam, prout medietas postis predicte que est in anteriori parte inter dicta tenementa sua expostulat). He is to do nothing to the detriment of the defs., who are forbidden to impede his work under a penalty of 40s.

[m. 26] *Fri. 13 June 1315. John de Gisors, mayor and other aldermen and sheriffs.*

222. William de Tanrigge complains that Master Thomas Gernoun refuses to convey the rainwater from his gutter (stillicidium) and house in the par. of St. Alphege Creplegate on to his own land, so that the pl.'s tenement is often flooded; and further that the cess-pit of his privy adjoins too closely the pl.'s land. The def. denies that he is obliged to receive his rainwater on his own land, because the tenements of both parties formerly belonged to Reginald de Meldebourne and Gunnilda his wife, and in their deed enfeoffing him, which he proffers, they granted him 1½ ft. of their own land to make a gutter (guteram) running the length of the pl.'s tenement to convey the water into his garden. The pl. says that he is not thereby bound to receive the water draining from the def.'s gutter (stillicidio) and roof (summitate domus), since nothing is said to that effect in the deed; but the def. ought to receive the pl.'s water in a sink (puteo) in his garden in return for the easement he enjoys in having his gutter (gutera) on the pl.'s land. This the def. concedes. As far as the cess-pit is concerned, he says that it is surrounded by a stone wall, but he does not know how thick it is. Judgment that *within 40 days etc.* the def. make a leaden fillet-gutter (filettum) running from his gutter (stillicidio) along his house, to convey his water into the sink in his garden; and that he make his cess-pit 2½ ft. from the pl.'s land if walled in stone, and 3½ ft. if in earth. [m. 26d. Blank.]

Assize of Nuisance

[m. 27] *Fri. 19 Dec. 1315. Stephen de Abyndon, mayor, Nicholas de Farendon, John de Gisors, John de Wengrave, William de Leire, Simon Corp, Roger de Paris, John de Camera and Hamo de Chiggewelle.*

223. Richard le Cordewaner, def., v. Robert de Torkeseye, 'barbier'. [Entry incomplete.]

Fri. 20 Feb. 1316.

224. Peter de Grascherche, def., essoins himself against Juliana Romeyn by J. Baroun.

Fri. 19 Mar. 1316. Stephen de Abyndon, mayor, John de Gisors, Nicholas de Farendone, William de Leire, Elias de Suffolk.

225. Thomas Brangweyn, def., essoins himself against William Mabely by Adam Pre.

226. Francis de Luco, John de Luco his brother and John son of the same John, defs., essoin themselves against William de Cornehill, parson of St. Mary de Aldermanberi, by William de Mounby.

227. Cecily de Bauquelle, def., essoins herself against John Wilemyn by William Robert. John Wylemyn, def., [*sic*] appears by Roger de Broune, attorney.

Fri. 2 Apr. 1316. Stephen de Abyndone, mayor, John de Gisors, John de Wengrave, William de Leire, Robert de Keleseye, Elias de Suffolk, Henry de Gloucestre, John de Lincoln, aldermen.

228. John de Kressyngham, 'ioignour', pl., appears against the dean and chapter of St. Paul's, and Master Walter de Thorp, canon, defs. The defs. make default. The pl. complains that when he began to erect his timber for building his house on his own land, adjoining that of the defs., they caused the work to be prohibited. The mayor and aldermen, being unprepared to give judgment immediately by reason of certain difficulties (causas difficultatis), give him a day at Guildhall on the following Wed. [7 Apr.]. On that day, Master Walter de Thorp appears and says that he is the sole tenant of the land on which the pl. proposes to build, as he is prepared to prove; and he prays that judgment be not given against him. A further adjournment follows, by consent of the parties, until [Mon.] 19 Apr.

Fri. 18 June 1316. [*Essoins only.*]

Fri. 2 July 1316.

229. Reginald de Conduit brings an assize against Simon de Hakeneye concerning a tenement in the par. of St. Mary de Fancherche. [m. 27d. Blank.]

Assize of Nuisance

[m. 28] *Fri. 19 Nov. 1316. John de Wengrave, mayor, Nicholas de Farendon, John de Gisors, Robert de Keleseye, John de la Chaumbre, Roger de Paris, Simon de Abyndon and Richard de Willehale, aldermen, and Ralph le Balauncer, sheriff.*

230. Master John de Sodyngton, pl., appears against (obtulit se versus)[1] Hugh Garton, def., who makes default. The pl. says that he has a tenement adjoining the newly-built houses of the def. in the par. of St. Peter the Less in Bradestrete; and that the def. ought to convey the rainwater from them on to his land or into the street in accordance with the statute of assizes of the City;[2] but that, although frequently prohibited by the mayor at the instance of the pl., he has built his eaves (severundas) overhanging his land, so that it is flooded; and that he has made many windows and other apertures in his party-wall overlooking the pl.'s land. Judgment that, since the nuisance is manifest to the view of the mayor and aldermen, and it appears from the records that the pl. sought an assize while the def. was building, the def. have no apertures facing the pl.'s land except at a height of 16 ft.; and that *within 40 days etc.* he make a gutter (stillicidium) on his house to convey his rainwater on to his own land or into the street.
Afterwards the pl. came and complained that the def. had not attempted to execute the judgment, and William de Causton, sheriff, was ordered to put it into execution.

231. The same Master John, pl., appears against William Syward and Juliana de Brounford, defs., who make default. The pl. complains that the rainwater from the tenement and houses of the defs. in the same par. falls upon his adjoining land, which is thereby flooded; and, further that they have windows and other apertures overlooking his land.

Fri. 4 Feb. 1317. [*Essoins only.*]

[m. 28d.] [*1317.*] *John de Wengrave, mayor, Nicholas de Farendon, John de Gisors, William de Leire, Richard de Gloucestre, Simon de Paris, Hamo Godchep, Elias de Suffolk, John de Lincoln, Henry de Gloucestre and Roger de Paris, aldermen.*

232. Hugh de Garton complains that the rainwater from John de Sudington's tenement in the par. of St. Peter the Less in Bradestrete falls upon his land and floods it, and that he has windows and other apertures in his party-walls overlooking his tenement. The def. comes and says that he and all the tenants of the tenement in question have been seised of the easement of the fall of rainwater (de distillatione aque pluvialis) and the apertures from time out of mind, and that he understands that the assize has no cognisance in such matters after a year and more. He asks judgment, and the pl. likewise.

---

1. Two lines above the entry concerning the parties in this plea and using the form 'summonitus fuit ad respondendum' have been erased.
2. *Lib. Alb.*, i, 331–2.

Assize of Nuisance

[m. 29] *Mon. 17 July 1318.*[1]

233. Osbert de Bray and Isabel his wife complain that whereas a cellar with solars and shops above in Bredstrete, formerly held by William de Paris, draper, and Maud his wife, Isabel's sister, by inheritance of the same Maud, passed on her death to Isabel and William le Neve, son of Avice, sister of Isabel and Maud, as co-heirs, William refuses to agree to a partition of the premises in accordance with the custom of the City, and withholds the rent due to the pls. Osbert and Isabel produce a royal writ [**239**] in their favour addressed to the mayor, and dated 15 June 1318. The def. is given permission, on account of illness, to appear by his attorney, John de Waltham, who says that Isabel has no claim to a share in the premises, because Anastasia Buntyngs, mother of Isabel, Maud and Avice, granted them in fee tail to Maud, with reversion to Avice, whose son the pl. is; but when asked to produce the deed he says he has not got it to hand. The pls. say that, in any case, the deed cannot affect their claim, because, in her will proved and enrolled in the Husting[2] on Mon. 2 May 1300, Anastasia devised the premises to William de Paris and Maud his wife, her daughter, and Maud's heirs, and they vouch the roll to warranty. It is adjudged that the premises be duly partitioned between the co-heirs, and Master Simon de Pakenham [*sic*], mason, and Master Adam de Rothyng, carpenter, searw in the presence of J. de Wengrave, mayor, Nicholas de Farndon, John de Gisors, Robert de Kelseie, William de Leire, Hamo de Chiggewelle, John Lambyn, Elias de Suffolk and Anketin de Gisors, aldermen, and John Priour, sheriff, to make the partition with the help of those appointed and sworn to assist them, and to report the result in full Husting on the following Mon. [17 July]. The measurements having been made on Sat. 15 July, half the cellar, measuring from the stone wall of the master and brethren of the hospital of St. James on the south northwards, viz. $5\frac{1}{2}$ ells 3 ins. along Bredestrete on the west, and $4\frac{3}{4}$ ells 7 ins. on the east; and, above, in the shops and solars, measuring from the tenement of the hospital of St. James on the south northwards, $7\frac{1}{4}$ ells $3\frac{1}{2}$ ins. along Bredstrete on the west, and $7\frac{3}{4}$ ells $3\frac{1}{2}$ ins. on the east, were assigned by lot to Isabel and Osbert, and the remaining equivalent portion to William le Neve. The value of teh portion assigned to the pls. is estimated at £6.9.4., and that assigned to the def. at £6.12.0., not including two shops paying an annual rent of 36s. to the prioress of St. Helen's. Judgment that Isabel and William have the portion assigned to them, with all the easements pertaining thereto. William in mercy for an unjust impediment.

[m. 29d.] *Fri. 20 Oct. 1318. John de Wengrave, mayor, John de Dallyng, sheriff, and the aldermen.*

234. Judgment between Hugh de Waltham, clerk, and Juliana his wife, pls., and William le Neve, 'furbour', respited until Fri. 3 Nov.; on which day the pls. appeared against the def., complaining that, whereas they hold a cellar with a shop above, in Bredestrate, purchased of Osbert de Bray and Isabel

---
1. The date of the Husting at which judgment was given.
2. *Cal. Wills*, i, 145.

Assize of Nuisance

his wife, the def., who holds a solar above the same, on Thurs. 12 Oct., cut down, demolished and carried away without warning, a pentice (appenticium) affixed to the solar above the doors of the cellar and shop of the pls. The def. makes default; and it is ordered that he be attached to appear at the octave [? 10 Nov.], together with a jury of eighteen [sic] of the venue of Bredestrate. After adjournment until the following Mon. [? 13 Nov.] the jury come in full Husting by William de Speresholte, John atte Crouche, John de Codestone, Thomas de Wygth, 'taverner', William le Cergere of Bredstrate, William atte Roche, Peter le Barbier, Adam le Sackere, Hugh de Depeden', Walter de Barkeworthe, Richard de Berdefeld and Henry le Mareschal, and say upon oath that at the time of the partition between the def. and Osbert and Isabel, the pentice served to protect from rainwater the windows and steps of the tenement, and was ordered to remain for the benefit of both parties; and that when Hugh and Isabel enfeoffed the pls. with their portion the pentice was entire, but that the def. cut down, demolished and carried away without warning the part above the cellar and shop belonging to the pls. The parties are given a day to hear judgment on Wed. next following [? 15 Nov.] before the mayor and aldermen in the Chamber, but, after further adjournment, the jury, on Mon. [? 20 Nov.] in full Husting, find for the pls. Judgment that within 40 days the def. restore the pentice at his own cost, and by view of the carpenters sworn to the assize, to the condition it was in when he demolished it under a penalty of 40s. payable to the sheriff.

[m. 30] *Fri. 21 Oct. 1317. John de Wengrave, mayor, John de Gisors, Nicholas de Farendon, William de Leyre, Robert de Kelesey, Richard de Gloucestre, Simon de Paris, Anketyn de Gisors and Roger de Paris, aldermen, John Priour, sheriff.*

235. The prior of the hospital of St. Mary without Bisshopesgate and Cecily de Bauquelle complain that, when in the course of repairing their houses and buildings (domos et edificia), they affixed their new corbels to the stone wall between their tenement and that of Richard Godchep and Margery his wife, defs., in the par. of St. Mary le Bow, which adjoins it on the west side, the defs. on Wed. last [19 Oct.], on their own authority, overthrew them by night, and caused the work to be prohibited. The defs. say that the pls. have no right in the wall in question, but the pls. argue that the contrary is evident from the position of their old corbels. Judgment, after consultation of the ordinance of the *Assize*,[1] that the pls. may lawfully affix to the wall as many corbels as they previously had, provided that they are not thicker than the old ones. Defs. in mercy for an unjust impediment.

Fri. 23 Dec. 1317. John de Wengrave, mayor, John de Gisors, Nicholas de Farendon, William de Leire, Robert de Keleseye, Richard de Gloucestre, Simon de Paris, John de Lincoln, John de la Chambre, Anketyn de Gisors, William Servat, Hamo Godchep.

236. Simon Corp complains that when, by reason of the age of the timbers

1. *Lib. Alb.*, i, 325. De corbellis.

and the ruinous state of the stone wall, 11 ells long and 3 ft. wide, extending from his house in the par. of St. Pancras, bought of Alice de Arraz and Henry de Boudene, on the north, to another of his tenements on the south, and situated between his tenement and those of Roger de Paris, mercer, def., which his wall overhangs, he sought to effect repairs, the def. caused the work to be prohibited. The def. claims that the wall is common to the parties, and strong enough to support his house, and that the pl. infringed the assize by undermining and weakening (suffodere et attenuere) it, and tearing down and carrying off a leaden gutter (guteram) affixed to part of another wall running from Simon's place on the south to the street on the north and conveying away the def.'s rainwater. The mayor and aldermen, wishing to be more fully advised concerning the view made of the wall in question, give the parties a day on Fri. 20 Jan. 1318. After a further adjournment until Fri. 27 Jan. the assize comes by John de Wengrave, mayor, Nicholas de Farndon, John de Gisors, William de Leyre, Robert de Celeseye, Richard de Glowcestre, Simon de Paris, John Lambyn, Elias de Suffolk, Anketin de Gisors and John de Lincoln, aldermen, and John Priour, sheriff, and the parties likewise. Judgment that the part of the wall in length and breadth upon which is affixed the def.'s wall-plate (platam) upon which his house rests, is his, and that it is sufficiently strong and does not need repair; but that the pl. may repair and strengthen and heighten his part as seems good to him, without damage to the def.; and *within* the next *40 days etc.* he must restore to its former state the gutter removed by him.

[m. 30d.] *Fri. 3 Mar. 1318. John de Wengrave, mayor, John Priour and William de Fourneys, sheriffs.*

237. Jordan de Langgele and William le Mareschal, defs., essoin themselves against William de Leire by R. de Rothyng.

238. John de Pikenham, def., essoins himself against William le Chaundler by the same.

239. Royal writ to the mayor and sheriffs (fieri faciatis), dated 15 June 1318, on behalf of Osbert de Bray and Isabel his wife. [See **233**.]

240. Plea of intrusion (querele intrusionis) before John de Wengrave, mayor, John Priour and William de Fourneys and before the aldermen on Wed. [? 5 July 1318 (before the feast of the translation of St. Benedict, 11 Ed. II)]. John son of John le Riche complains of intrusion, v. Philip son of Philip de Beauveys concerning his free tenement in the pars. of St. Mary de Aldermarecherche and St. Mildred de Bredstret.

Fri. 23 June 1318. [*Essoins only.*]

Fri. 30 June 1318. [*No entry.*]

Fri. 7 July 1318. Mayor and the aldermen.

Assize of Nuisance

241. John de Pikenham, def., essoins himself against William le Chaundler by William Reyle. Emma wife of John appears.

Fri. 21 July 1318. [Essoins only.]

Fri. 4 Aug. 1318.

242. Juliana wife of William Rabot, def., essoins herself against William de Hockele by Thomas Orpedeman.

[m. 31] *Fri. 8 Dec. 1318. John de Wengrave, mayor, John de Dallyng, sheriff.*

243. Assize of nuisance brought at the instance of Henry le Palmere, who complains that William de Hallyngburi has made a gutter (guteram) upon a stone wall on his land in the par. of St. Michael de Paternostercherch into which he and his household throw water and all kinds of refuse, which flows out on to the pl.'s land, so that his timber and all his other property (necessaria) are rotted; and that by reason of the same gutter he cannot build on his land adjoining the same wall; and that the def. has made windows therein 16 ft. from the ground [*sic*]. The def. says that the gutter has been *in situ* for sixty years, and was not therefore made by him, and he puts himself upon the view of the mayor and aldermen.

[m. 31d.] *Fri. 8 Feb. 1320. Hamo de Chigwell, mayor, Simon de Abyndon and John de Prestone, sheriffs.*

244. Assize of nuisance brought at the instance of Thomas de Cobham, woodmonger (buscarius), who complains that when he wished to build a house upon his half of the stone wall between his tenement and that of Thomas de Brakkele in the par. of All Hallows at Hay, as upon his perpetual fief (feodum suum perpetuum), the def. prohibited the work.

[m. 32] *Fri. 6 Oct. 1318. John de Wenegrave, mayor, John de Dallyng, sheriff and the aldermen.*

245. Richer de Refham, kt., pl., appears against the prior of Blakemore, def., who does not come, because he was not in the City at the time of the summons. His tenants are ordered to warn him to appear at the quindene.

Fri. 20 Oct. 1318. John de Wengrave, mayor, John de Dallyng, sheriff and the aldermen.

245 cont. Pl. essoins himself by Gregory de Norton, who appears for him, but the def. does not come and is not represented. A day is given to the pl. to hear judgment on Mon. 23 Oct. in the Husting of Common Pleas.[1]

246. Ralph le Gildere, def., essoins himself against John Michel, 'lorymer',

1. Cf. H.C.P.R. 43, m. 5d.

Assize of Nuisance

by Thomas Orpedeman. Amice wife of Ralph is summoned (exigatur) and comes.

247. [This entry is identical with **234**, except for slight verbal differences, and the omission of the date of the alleged nuisance.]

[m. 32d.] *Fri. 17 Nov. 1318. [Essoins only.]*

Fri. 24 Nov. 1318. [Essoin only.]

Fri. 1 Dec. 1318. John de Wengrave, mayor, sheriffs and the aldermen.

248. Aymer de Valence, pl., appears against Simon de Abyndon, def., concerning a tenement in the par. of St. Mary atte Hull. Simon comes in person and the parties are given a day on Sat. 2 Dec. to hear judgment before the mayor in the Chamber of Guildhall.

249. The same Aymer, pl., appears against Richard de Hakeneye, Richard le Miter and Thomas Prentiz, defs., in an assize concerning his free tenement in the same par., asking that each repair the pavement outside his property on the west side. The defs. come in person and are given instructions to carry out the repairs by the view and labour of paviors chosen and sworn by Aymer's serjeant (serviente).

250. Perambulation by the mayor, sheriffs and aldermen of the land of the dean and chapter of St. Paul's in the par. of St. Dunstan [? in the East], on complaint of Thomas de Neusom, clerk of sir Ralph de Monthermer, that because the tenement of the dean and chapter adjoining that of Ralph is not built up along the street, vagabonds crossing the tenement by night break down Ralph's party-walls and enter and do damage there. The dean and chapter do not come and are not represented. Judgment that they be compelled to build a wall on their property, along the street, to a height of 16 ft.

251. Margery relict of William de Coumbemartyn complains that Adam Hunteman has made a chalk-pit for tanning hides on his land in the par. of St. Mary de Berkyngechapel, adjoining too closely her party-wall, so that the water therefrom penetrates it. Judgment that the def. who can say nothing in his defence remove the pit further from the pl.'s wall; and that within 40 days he build a stone wall $2\frac{1}{2}$ ft. thick between the pit and the wall under a penalty of 40s.

[m. 33] *Fri. 16 Nov. 1319.*

252. William de Spersholte, pl., appears against William de Canefelde, def., complaining that, whereas he has a stone wall 16 ft. high joining his tenement in the par. of St. Michael Queenhithe to that of the def., who ought therefore to receive the water draining from his house, the def. fails to do so for lack of a leaden gutter (guttere plumbei) 14 ft. and more in length, which he ought to provide. The def., summoned by Robert le Hetherent

Assize of Nuisance

[*sic*] and Henry atte Swan, makes default. Judgment that he make the gutter in question *within 40 days etc.*

253. Thomas de Cobham complains that, whereas he has a stone wall 50 ft. long and 3 ft. wide between his tenement and that of Thomas de Brakkele in the par. of All Hallows at Hay in Douegate ward, and wished to demolish and build upon it, the def., by William Pykeman, serjeant of John de Dallyng, sheriff, on Wed. 26 Sept. 1319, caused the work to be prohibited. The def. claims that half the wall is his. The pl. says that his beams (trabes) extend into the midst of the wall, so that they can be clearly seen from the pl.'s land, and his wall-plate (plata) lies upon it, and his supporting timber occupies the whole breadth. Judgment after view that he have the whole wall. Def. in mercy.

254. Memorandum quod anno xiiii° nulle assise de nocumenta presente fuerunt, quia illo anno sedebant justiciarii itinerantes apud Turrim London' ad placita corone.

Mon. [? 17 Aug.] (Mon. after the feast of St. Lawrence) 1321. Hamo de Chiggewell, mayor, and the aldermen, William Prodhomme and Reginald de Conduit, sheriffs.

255. Thomas de Berkyngge, goldsmith, complains that when he began to build a house, ready for roofing (ad cooperiendum paratam) on the east side of the house of Henry atte More, goldsmith, the latter caused William Prodhomme, sheriff, to prohibit the work. The def. says that the prohibition was justified, because his tenement was formerly held by Ralph de la More, who enfeoffed his daughter Beatrice with the portion now held by the pl., on condition that neither she nor her heirs should at any time obscure the light from two glazed windows on the west side of his house by building within 10 ft. of it. In support of his claim he produces a deed of Ralph de la More, granting to John de Pontefract, goldsmith, and Maud atte More, daughter of the grantor, a portion of his land in Wodestrete in the par. of St. Michael, situated between the messuage he gave to his daughter Beatrice on the north and the house (managium) of John le Blount, goldsmith, on the south, and between the street on the west, and the land of Peter de Haverhull, clerk, on the east, on the conditions quoted above. Witnesses: Thomas fitz Thomas, mayor, Thomas de la Forde and Gregory de Rokeslee, sheriffs, Stephen Bucr', alderman of the ward,[1] John de la Blakethorn, Henry de Frowyk, Ralph le Blount and others [1263–4]. The pl. says that his case cannot be prejudiced unless the def. produces the deed enfeoffing Beatrice; to which the def. replies that Beatrice was enfeoffed on the same conditions as John and Maud, and that the pl. holds her portion. The parties are given a day on the following Wed. to hear judgment. After further adjournments the assize comes on Fri. [? 4 Sep.] and the parties likewise; and it is adjudged that the pl. continue his building operations, notwithstanding Henry's defence, and that the def. be in mercy.

1. ? Cripplegate.

Assize of Nuisance

Fri. 4 Sep. 1321. [Essoin only.]

[Day and feast omitted, 1321–2.] Hamo de Chigewelle, mayor, and the aldermen. [Essoin only.]

[The same heading repeated.]

256. John de Acre, pl., appears against Nicholas son of Alan de Suttone called Ballard, def., by William de Reile his attorney, and complains that the def. refuses to repair the stone wall dividing their tenements, to the nuisance of the pl. and his household. The def., after essoining himself, makes default. Judgment that *within 40 days etc.* he remove the nuisance and be in mercy.

[m. 33d.] *Fri. 4 Sep. [1321].*

257. John de Kyngeston and Sabine his wife complain that the cess-pit of the privy of John Mounde, baker, and Avice his wife, adjoins too closely their party-wall and rots it; and that the defs. allow the eaves of their house to remain unroofed (discoopertas), so that the water therefrom falls upon the wall. Judgment after view that *within 40 days etc.* the cess-pit be removed to a proper distance from the pls.' wall, and that the defs.' eaves be repaired and roofed, and that they receive their water upon their own land.

258. Richard Andreu complains that John de Thunderle has stopped up (obturavit)[1] a gutter (gotteram) passing through his tenement, which used to convey the water from the pl.'s house into the street, in accordance with a grant made to him by Adam de Thunderle, which he produces. The def. says that he has only a life interest in the tenement in question, of which the reversion belongs to Adam, without whom he cannot answer. Given a day at the quindene, the parties come, and John and Adam unite in declaring that the gutter was already stopped up when the pl. was enfeoffed, and has always been so. A jury, summoned for the following Fri. [? 11 Sep.], comes by Stephen de Preston and others on the panel, and finds that the gutter was stopped up by the def. Judgment that *within 40 days etc.* he remove the obstruction.

Fri. 19 Mar. 1322. Hamo de Chigewelle, mayor, and Robert de Swalclyve, Simon de Abyndon, John de Prestone, Henry de Secheford, Robert Sely and Edmund Lambyn, aldermen.

259. The commonalty complain of the obstruction by Walter, parson of All Hallows de Berkynggecherche, John Priour and Walter le Milward, parishioners, of the free passage by the gate (portam) near the tenement of Denise relict of John le Bacheler. The parson and Walter make default, but John Priour comes and says that the place is dedicated, and he does not think that it should come within the purview of the assize; but it is adjudged that the defs., *within 40 days etc.*, remove the obstruction, so that the path (via) remain common as it used to be.

1. Corrected from 'opstupavit'.

Assize of Nuisance

260. The commonalty complain that Roger, parson of All Hallows de Garscherche, Arnold le Chaundeler, Robert le Barber, Richard le Cordewaner, Robert de Stratford, Cambin Fulberd, Peter de Herlyng, taverner, and John Scot have obstructed with a stone wall and a gate a path (via) near the churchyard of All Hallows, turning south towards the royal highway. The defs. say that the place is dedicated, and belongs to the church of All Hallows; but Gregory de Norton, common serjeant, prosecuting for the commonalty, says that there has always been a common way there for both horsemen and pedestrians, as far as the turning to the north. The defs., asked if they have anything to add to defer judgment, say that they blocked up the path because evil-doers used to lurk there by night to waylay passers-by. Judgment that *within 40 days etc.* they remove the nuisance.

[*No heading.*]

261. On Fri. 22 July 1323, William de Dalby complained that the house of Alan de Asshendon and Margery his wife overhangs his land by 5 ft. and more so that he cannot build; and that the defs. have two windows only 13 ft. from the ground and unglazed; and that the water from their eaves, 9 ells long, and from two gutters (gutteris), falls upon his land. The def. says his wife has no interest in the tenement in question, and that, as far as the overhang (superpendenciam) and the windows and eaves are concerned, the assize has no competence, because according to the custom of the City, complaint must be made within a year and a day of the nuisance arising. As to the gutters, he doubts whether an assize lies, because the pl. holds the tenement formerly belonging to Robert de Paris, mercer, and he himself that held by Adam de Beverly, 'peleter'; and he produces a deed which purports to show that Adam covenanted with Robert to make two gutters, one $11\frac{1}{4}$ ells in length between their respective kitchens, and another, 3 ells long between Adam's house and Robert's new chamber, Robert undertaking to receive the water from both and convey it away towards the west. The pl. argues that the limitation of a year and a day applies only to stone walls and the like; and, as regards the gutters, he says that Adam de Beverly never had any interest in the tenement he now holds; and that the gutters mentioned in the def.'s deed are not those of which he complains. The case is referred to a jury of the wards of Bassieschaw and Colmanstrete, who find for the pl. Judgment that each of the parties receive and convey away his own water, and that the def. build a gutter upon his eaves. The pl. is to be free to build if he so desires, the def.'s eaves having been removed.

[m. 34. *No heading.*]

262. On Fri. 3 Sep. 1322 John Pycot, son of Nicholas Pycot, pl., appears against Ralph son of John de Boctone, def., complaining that the def. has a wall dividing his tenement in the pars. of St. Bartholomew the Less and St. Michael upon Cornhulle from the pl.'s house, and has allowed the gutter (guttera) thereon to be broken, and the wall is so damaged (prostratus) by the water that it no longer forms a fence (claustura) between the adjoining houses. The def. makes default. Judgment that *within 40 days etc.* he rebuild the wall and gutter as they used to be.

263. Joce de Spaldinge and Joan his wife complain that Rose relict of Walter le Hert has built her pig-sty (porcariam) so close to their wall that it is overborne by the weight. The def. says that it is not the pig-sty that has caused the collapse of the wall, which was already falling into decay. Judgment after view that the pls. repair the wall, and that *within 40 days etc.* the def. remove the pig-sty $3\frac{1}{2}$ ft. from it, if it is of earth, and $2\frac{1}{2}$ ft. if it is of stone.

264. Gregory de Norton, common serjeant, on behalf of the commonalty, pls., appears against Thomas Frembaud and Joan his wife, defs., complaining that the stone wall in front of their house towards the east in the par. of St. Matthew de Frydaystrate is ruinous, and in danger of collapsing, to the peril of all living there or passing by. The defs. make default. Judgment that *within 40 days etc.* they demolish the wall.

Fri. 1 Oct. 1322. Mayor, and the aldermen.

265. John Preston, corder, pl., appears against Robert de Hereford, def., complaining that he cannot build upon his plot of land adjoining the def.'s house in the par. of All Hallows at Hay, because the def.'s chimney (chimineus) overhangs it by 8 ins. for a distance of 48 ins. The def. makes default. Judgment after view that *within 40 days etc.* he remove the nuisance so that the pl. can build.

Fri. 5 Nov. 1322.

266. Christine Tylly and Henry de Denecombe, pls., appear against Nicholas de Perndon, def., complaining that whereas an open drain (rivolus) used to carry off to la More the water from their adjoining houses and those of other neighbours, the def. has so obstructed it that when it rains the pls.' garden and the plants growing therein are flooded to a depth of $1\frac{1}{2}$ ft. The def., summoned by Robert de Dunmowe and Roger de Wyndesore, makes default, and no one appears for him. Judgment after view that *within 40 days etc.* he remove the obstruction so that the water can be carried off to la More as formerly.

[m. 34d.] *Fri. 3 Sep. 1323. Pleas of assize held before N. de Farndone, mayor, the aldermen and others sworn to the assize, on the scene of the nuisance in the par. of Hoggenlane in Crepelgate Ward.*

267. John Hauteyn, pl., appears against Matthew de Essex, def., who essoins himself and then makes default. The pl. complains that the water draining from the def.'s house falls upon his land for a depth of 22 ft. Judgment after view that *within 40 days etc.* the def. make a leaden fillet in the form of a gutter (filettum plumbeum ad modum guttere) along the whole length of his house to receive his water and convey it on to his land or into the street.

268. The same John, pl., appears against Bartholomew de Hallyngebery, def., who makes default. The pl. complains that he has infringed the custom of the City, whereby no windows or other apertures facing a neighbouring house may be less than 9 ft. [*sic*] from the ground or the storey to which they belong (*a terra sive a stagio*). Judgment after view that *within 40 days etc.* the def. block up the windows and apertures complained of.

Fri. 25 May 1324. Hamo de Chigewell, mayor, and the aldermen.

269. Thomas Doget complains that when he demolished part of the wall between his tenement and that of Henry Prodhomme in the par. of St. Leonard Estchep in order to repair it, placing his new timber where the old had been, the def. caused the work to be prohibited by Ralph Borgard, serjeant. Henry says that the assize does not lie, because Thomas was formerly seised of the tenement which he (Henry) now holds, and Maud daughter of Christine Sperelyng and Felicia her sister brought an action *de rectis serviciis* against him in the Husting, in 19 Edward I [1290–1], claiming the tenement as *gavelet*, and because he made default, it was awarded them as *forshard*;[1] and he says that the wall upon which the pl. claims to build belongs to the said tenement. The pl. says that Edward son of Martin Sperling gave the messuage in Estchep which he now holds, lying between the church on the north and the land of Ralph [? Sperling] on the south, and measuring in front along the street towards the west $15\frac{1}{2}$ ells, and on the side next the church $15\frac{3}{4}$ ells, and in width in the middle $16\frac{1}{2}$ ells 1 in., on the south $17\frac{3}{4}$ ells and on the east $16\frac{1}{2}$ ells, to Stephen (—), a minor and Richard Russel. Afterwards Stephen quitclaimed his rights in the messuage to Richard, who enfeoffed therewith the prioress of Wyntoneye, who, with the consent of her chapter, enfeoffed John Doget, the pl.'s father, who, throughout his time, enjoyed the right to affix to the wall in question the posts upholding his house. The mayor and aldermen, having viewed the premises, find that the pl. was formerly seised of the wall to a depth of 6 ins. Judgment that he may place upon it his new posts and timber up to that width, removing anything that exceeds it. Def. in mercy.

[m. 35. *No heading*.]

270. Margaret relict of John Vivien complains that Stephen atte Holte has prohibited, through the sheriff, the building of her house in the par. of St. Michael upon Cornhulle. The def. says that he purchased a portion of land for building from Peter de Waltham, including half an old post, with the right to place his timber thereon, and the pl. now seeks to appropriate parts of it, measuring in length from the post of the house of Nicholas le Chaundeler and Alice his wife on the north to a post of his own house on the south $3\frac{7}{8}$ ells, 1 in., and in width $\frac{1}{2}$ ft. and more. The pl. says that the

1. Variant form of 'shortford' (*O.E.D.*) or 'shartford' (*Lib. Alb.*, i, 63, 468–9, where the procedure is described).

land in question belongs by right to her, because the old house which she demolished was built upon it, as can be seen from an old post still standing there. The mayor and aldermen, having viewed the premises, find that her claim is correct. Judgment that she have and hold the portion of land in question and build upon it at will. Def. in mercy for an unjust impediment.

271. The same Margaret complains that Nicholas le Chaundeler and Alice his wife have a post of their house in the same par. standing partly upon her land, so that she cannot build. The defs. say that the land where their house is situated and where the post stands formerly belonged to Peter de Waltham, who sold it to Stephen atte Holte, who sold it to John de Bekles, from whom they bought it, and they claim no more than is due to them according to the metes and bounds in the deed of feoffment. The mayor and aldermen and others, having viewed the premises, find that the post in question is too near the pl.'s land and is not straight, but leans over somewhat at the top. It is therefore adjudged that the carpenters sworn to the assize, together with those of the pl. measure the post by plumb-line to see how far it is out of alignment (et in summitate eiusdem postis lineam cum plumbe protendant deorsum), and, according to their findings, cut it back below or above so that the pl. can build, and the defs. retain what is theirs.

Fri. 22 July 1323. [Essoins only.]

Fri. 5 Aug. 1323.

272. The abbot and convent of Waldene complain that Thomas de Brackele and Alice his wife have demolished half the stone wall, about 40 ft. long, which is common to their tenements. The defs. claim that they were entitled to do so, because their half of the wall was not built upon, or occupied by the pls.' timber. The pls. argue that their action is contrary to the custom of the City, since it was taken without their consent, and add that about 92 years before, Andrew Bokerel being then mayor [1231–7], a covenant was made between the abbot and convent for the time being and John de Coudres, then tenant of the def.'s tenement, in which he quitclaimed to them the corbels which he had upon the rabbet (rebattum) of the stone wall between their tenements in the par. of St. Botolph without Aldresgate and all his rights in the same wall, saving only the rabbet aforesaid; and they proffer the relevant indenture. Judgment after view that, since the defs. have manifestly infringed the custom of the City by demolishing part of a wall held in common without the consent of their parceners, they rebuild it *within 40 days etc.*

Afterwards, at the Husting of Common Pleas held on Mon. 6 June 1328, the pls. come by Henry Wrenge, their attorney, and complain that judgment has not been executed. After inspection of the rolls of assize for 1323–4 it is agreed by the mayor and aldermen that the parties be warned to appear on the following Fri. [10 June] at the place where judgment was given. On that day Hamo de Chigwell, mayor, Gregory de Norton, recorder, Anketin de Gisors, Reginald de Conduit, John [de Preston] and Henry de Combemartyn, Henry de Seccheford, John de Causton and

John de Pulteneye, aldermen, come, and the sheriffs testify that the defs. have been summoned by Geoffrey de Heston and Richard in the Lane, but they make default. Judgment that without delay the sheriffs cause the wall to be rebuilt at the expense of the defs., who are in mercy. [m. 35d. Blank.]

[m. 36] *Fri. 24 May 1325. Hamo de Chigewell, mayor, John de Caustone and Benedict de Fulsham, sheriffs, and the aldermen.*

273. Hugh de Waltham and Juliana his wife, pls., appear against Robert Mustrel of Tonebregge, def.; but it is said that the def. was not in town at the time of the summons or later. His tenants are ordered to warn him to appear at the quindene.

274. The same Hugh appears also against Adam de Rothyng, carpenter; but his tenants and neighbours testify likewise that he was not in the City at the time of the summons or later. They are ordered to warn him to appear at the quindene.

275. A day at the quindene is given to the same Hugh, pl., and Thomas de la Marche, and to John de Wymondham and Joan his wife and Adam de Rothyng concerning the reception of water and the view from the defs.' houses upon the pl.'s land.

276. John de Gisors complains that the earthen wall between his land and that of the prior of Holy Trinity in the par. of St. Mary atte Naxe is so decayed and broken that it no longer serves as a fence between them; and the def.'s tenants and others enter his garden and do much damage there. He asks that the wall, which stands wholly upon his land, be removed and rebuilt in accordance with the assize. The def., by Reginald Woleward his attorney, says that the wall is common to the parties and ought to be repaired at their common charges. After careful inspection of the site at both ends and in the middle, and of the metes and bounds of the tenements next the street of St. Mary atte Naxe, together with the paling (palicio) of the def. which adjoins the western end of the wall, it is adjudged that *within 40 days etc.* the wall be removed and rebuilt, the parties either each contributing 2 ft. of land and sharing the cost of building, or one of them providing 4 ft. of land and the other bearing the entire expense. The same arrangement to hold if, instead of an earthen wall, they prefer a paling or some similar form of enclosure. Otherwise the sheriffs are to act at the expense of the defaulting party, and fine him 40s.

Fri. 14 June 1325. Hamo de Chigewell, mayor, John de Causton and Benedict de Fulsham, sheriffs, Nicholas de Farndon, John Prior, Richard de Hakeneye, Anketin de Gisors, John Cotun, John Poyntel, Hamo Godchep, Richard Costantyn and Henry de Sescheford, aldermen, and others.

277. Hugh de Waltham and Juliana his wife, pls., appear against Robert Mustrel of Tonebregg, def., who makes default. They complain that the cess-pit of his privy and a pit called 'swelugh' receiving the water from his cistern and from a well not walled in stone adjoin their land too closely. On viewing the premises the mayor and aldermen find that the cess-pit and the 'swelugh' receiving the water from the well and from a great vessel called a 'Thityngtunne', are not walled in stone, and are too near the pls.' foundations. Judgment that *within 40 days etc.* the defs. remove them to a distance of 2½ ft. at least or 3½ ft. if they are not walled in stone. [Cf. 273.]

278. [m. 36d.] The same Hugh complains that his paling of wattle and daub (palicium de ligno et daubicio) is on the verge of ruin, and broken down in divers places because of the earth thrown up against it by Thomas de la Marche, whose land it adjoins; and he asks that it be replaced by a suitable fence (claustura) in accordance with the custom of the City. The def. agrees to abide by the judgment of the mayor and aldermen and others sworn to the assize, who, after viewing the premises, adjudge that within 40 days either both parties provide 1½ ft. of land and share the cost of building thereon a stone wall, or the one provide 3 ft. of land and the other bear the whole cost of building: under a penalty of 40s. to be levied from the land and chattels of the defaulter by the sheriffs, who, in addition, are to cause the work to be done at his expense. [Cf. 275.]

Fri. 19 July 1325. Mayor, sheriffs, and the aldermen.

279. The same Hugh complains that Katherine relict of Adam de Rothyng has likewise piled earth up against the wattle and daub paling (palicium de ligne et daubicio), 40 ft. long between their tenements so that it is on the verge of ruin, and it is further broken down in many places by the water falling from a worthless tree (arbore nugario) belonging to her. He declares his readiness to build a new wall of stone, earth or wattle and daub, in accordance with the assize. The def. says she holds her tenement jointly with Joan, daughter of Clement le Settere, without whom she cannot answer. Joan comes, and together they affirm that they cannot afford to build a wall. Asked whether they can show any cause why they should not be compelled to do so, they say no. Judgment that, in accordance with the custom of the City, they provide *within 40 days etc.* 3 ft. of land upon which the pl. can build.
Mandate of the mayor and aldermen to the sheriffs ordering them to inspect the tenor of the above judgment, and cause it to be put in execution without delay, 18 Apr. 1326.

[m. 37] *Fri. 6 Dec. 1325. Hamo de Chigewell, mayor, John Cotun and Gilbert de Mordon, sheriffs, Robert de Swaleclive, John Hauteyn, Roger le Palmere and others, aldermen.*

280. William de Stanford essoins himself against John de Hemenhale by Richard Scot.

281. John de Hemenhale complains that the earthen wall between his land and that of John de Havering in the par. of St. Ethelburga within Bisshopesgate, which stands wholly on his land, is ruinous and broken down, so that

Assize of Nuisance

men and dogs, pigs and other animals can come in and out freely; and he asks that the wall be rebuilt in accordance with the assize. The def. comes and the parties agree together, the pl. undertaking to build the wall at his own expense, and the def. to provide the land. The work is to be done within 40 days when the weather is suitable. At present it cannot be done because of wintry conditions. [m. 37d. Blank.]

[m. 38] Note that the two following membranes were found among the memoranda of John de Burton, clerk of the Chamber, after his death, and record the proceedings between William de Burgh, pl., and John de Refham, def., [283] in an assize of nuisance; and between the same William and Richer de Refham [282] in a like plea.

[m. 38d.] *Mon. 5 May 1326. Husting of Pleas of Land, the following pleas of assize of nuisance were sought:*

282. William de Burgh v. Richer de Refham concerning a tenement in the par. of St. Mary de Colchurche. Parties summoned for the following Fri. [Continued below.]

283. The same v. John son of Richer concerning a tenement in the same par. Parties summoned for the same day. [Continued below.]

William de Burgh appoints John de Staynton his attorney in both pleas.

Fri. 9 May 1326. [Essoins and adjournment only.]

Fri. 23 May 1326. Mayor, and the aldermen.

282 cont. William de Burgh, clerk, complains that Richer de Refham unjustly claims half his stone wall, which is wholly occupied and covered by his timber. The def. says he has a deed proving his right and asks for time to produce it. A day is given to the parties at the quindene. [Continued below.]

Fri. 6 and 27 June 1326. Mayor, and the aldermen. [No entry.]

[m. 39. *No heading.*]

283 cont. William de Burgo complains that whereas he is the sole possessor of a stone wall in the par. of St. Mary de Colechirche in Chepe, adjoining the tenement of John de Refham on the west side, and extending from the street in front to the tenement of John de Preston at the back, and carrying the potts (postes) and puncheons (punchones) supporting the wall-plate (pannam), joists (gistas) and timber of his house, the def. has of a sudden inserted his posts, puncheons, joists and summers (someria) into the same wall, and attached them to the pl.'s posts and puncheons; and has placed a summer 2 ft. long and 8 ins. wide in front of his house, next the street, on the east side of the pl.'s tenement under the lower storey of his

solars, to carry his party-walls (parietes), gable (gabulam) and joists; and when, because of the ruin caused thereby to his house the pl. sought to rebuild it, the def. had the work prohibited by Gilbert de Mordon, sheriff. Further, the def. has four leaden pipes draining from the roof (de summitate) of his house into the pl.'s leaden gutter (gutteram plumbeam), which is frequently flooded by his rainwater. The def. comes in person and says that the assize does not lie, because the pl.'s tenement was formerly held by Isabel de St. Albans between whom and his feoffor, Richer de Refham, an assize of nuisance was held in 1290–1 before Henry le Galeys, mayor; when it was adjudged by the assize and agreed by the parties that Richer and all his successors in the tenement should hold it exactly as it is now as regards the wall and timber of the pl. and the pipes and gutters, and he vouches the record to warranty. A day is given to the parties in the Husting on the following Mon. but the def. makes default. After viewing the premises the mayor and aldermen find that the pl.'s allegations are correct. Judgment that all the nuisances complained of be removed within 40 days etc. so that the pl. be no longer impeded in his building. [See also **284**, **286–7**.]

282 cont. William de Burgo complains that whereas he has a house in the same par. adjoining that of Richer de Refham, kt., on the west side, and built upon his stone wall carrying his wall-plate (pannam), joists (gistas) and timber, and measuring in length from the street on the south to the tenement of Katherine de Staunford on the north 78 ft., and in width 4 ft., and was compelled to rebuild it, because the roof of his house was ruinous and was adjudged by the mayor and aldermen to be a danger to passers-by and residents, the def. caused the work to be prohibited by Gilbert de Mordon, sheriff. Richer comes in person and says that the wall claimed by the pl. as his is common to the parties, as is expressly contained in his charter of feoffment, which he undertakes to produce. A day is given to the parties at the quindene, and the proceedings are afterwards adjourned until Fri. 28 June. The pl. comes, and the def. appears by his attorney, Reginald Wolleward, who produces no deed or other evidence in support of Richer's claim; and because it is manifest to the mayor and aldermen that the wall in question is wholly occupied by the pl.'s timber, it is adjudged that he have and hold the same as his free tenement and build upon it at his pleasure. Def. in mercy for a false defence. [See also **285**.]

[m. 39d. Entries under 5 and 9 May 1326 as on m. 38d.; m. 40 Entries as on m. 39d. and under 23 May 1326 as on m. 39 and under 10 June 1328 as on m. 39.]

284. Mandate to the sheriffs on behalf of the king by the mayor and aldermen, after reciting the findings in the plea of assize of nuisance between William de Burgo and John de Refham [**283**] and the judgment pronounced [m. 40d.]; and the report of Reginald de Conduit and Hugh de Garton, aldermen, who had been present at the view, that no action had been taken in pursuance, to go in person to the tenement and without delay cause the nuisance complained of to be removed at the expense of the def., and to levy from his goods and chattels, lands and tenements to their own use the accustomed amercement.

285. The like in the case of William de Burgo v. Richer de Refham [282].

286. Afterwards, on Tues. 11 Aug. 1327, John de Refham appeared before Richard de Beton, mayor, and the aldermen, complaining that William had made a purpresture on his tenement after the judgment given in the recent assize [283]. The sheriffs were accordingly ordered to prohibit William from further action, and to summon him to appear on the site on the following Fri. [14 Aug.]. The proceedings were adjourned until the following Mon. [17 Aug.] because of the absence of the mayor. The assize then came by Hamo de Chigwell, locum-tenens of the mayor, John Poyntel, John de Grantham, Reginald de Conduit, Hamo Godchep, Anketin de Gisors, Richard de Hakeneye, John de Preston, John de Causton, John de Oxford and Henry de Sescheford, aldermen, and Richard de Rothing, sheriff, and the record and process of the assize were read before them and confirmed by them; but because John declared that William had since taken possession of a strip of land $2\frac{1}{2}$ ft. wide which had belonged to his father and feoffor, Richer, and to his feoffor before him for many years past, it was adjudged that this remain as his defence, and that William seek an assize if he so desire.

287. Afterwards, in a congregation of the mayor and aldermen at Guildhall on Mon. 17 Aug. 1327, William de Burgh seeks an assize against John son of Richer de Refham concerning his tenement in the par. of St. Mary de Colcherch. Thomas de Morle, clerk of Richard de Rothing, sheriff, returns that the def. has been summoned by John de Redign [sic] and John Bray for the following Fri. [21 Aug.]. On that day the assize comes by Hamo, locum-tenens of the mayor, Reginald de Conduit, Anketin de Gisors, Richard de Hakeneye, Richard Costentyn, John de Oxford, John Poyntel, Hamo Godchep and Hugh de Garton, aldermen, and William complains that, in spite of the previous judgment in his favour, the def. has again prohibited him from building. The def. says that his action is justified, because the pl. has, since the previous assize, made a purpresture of $2\frac{1}{2}$ ft. on his land, cutting down and carrying away part of a shop which has stood there for 22 years and more, and of which the def. and his father have been continuously seised. The locum-tenens of the mayor and the aldermen, having viewed the site of the alleged purpresture, find that while William has built foundations and a wall there, there is no building of the def. now standing on which they can base a judgment. It is therefore adjudged that the def., if he so desire, seek a remedy by another process of law, and that the pl. be not hindered from completing his building operations.

[m. 41] *Fri. 3 June (tercio die Junii) 1328.* Hamo de Chigwelle, mayor, Henry Darci, sheriff, Nicholas de Farndon, Anketin Gisors, Reginald de Conduit, Gregory de Norton, John de Grantham, Richard Costantyn, John Poyntel, Richard de Hakeneye and others.

Assize of Nuisance

288. Hamo de Chigwell complains that the fence (claustura) between his plot of land in the par. of St. Peter the Less by St. Paul's Wharf in Castle Baynard ward, and that of Joce de Spaldyng and Joan his wife and Benedict Reyner and [blank] his wife which adjoins it in length between his house on the north and the Thames on the south, is ruinous and in great part broken down, to his damage and that of his tenants. Judgment that if the parties agree to rebuild in stone, either each shall provide 1½ ft. of his land and pay half the cost of building, or one shall provide 3 ft. of his land and the other meet the entire charges; the wall in either case to be partible between them.

Fri. 10 June 1328. H. de Chigwell, mayor, Henry Darci, sheriff, Gregory de Norton, Anketin Gisors, Reginald de Conduit, John de Preston, Henry Combemartyn, Henry de Seccheford, John de Causton and John de Pulteneye, aldermen.

289. Benedict Shorn is summoned to answer Robert le Treyere in a plea of nuisance. The pl. appears and says that William de Canefeld came before the chamberlain of Guildhall on Thurs. 18 July 1325 and acknowledged himself bound to him in 20 marks, payable at a fixed term, but failed to pay at the appointed time. An extent of his land and rents having been made by the chamberlain, it was found that he held a quit-rent of 40s. payable from a shop in les Stokkes in the par. of St. Mary de Wolcherchehawe, and half of this was delivered to Robert to hold as his free tenement in settlement of the debt; but the def. has stopped up the entrance of the shop so that the pl. cannot enter to distrain for the rent. The def. comes and acknowledges his offence. Judgment that he open the entrance under the penalty etc. Otherwise etc.

290. William Noyl complains that Geoffrey le Boteler, draper, has built a stone wall 4½ ells long and ½ ft. wide upon his land in the par. of St. Mary de Bothawe. The def. claims that the wall stands on his own land, and not on that of the pl., and puts himself upon the assize. The mayor and aldermen, after viewing the premises, find that his claim is correct. Judgment that the pl. take nothing for his plaint, but be in mercy. Def. *sine die*. He is to be free to continue building, any impediment being removed.

291. The same Geoffrey complains that the water from the same William's gutter (gutteram) in the same par. falls upon his land. The mayor and aldermen find by view that this is so and the def. does not deny it. Judgment that *within 40 days etc.* he receive the water upon his own land.
Mandate of the mayor to the sheriffs, dated in the Chamber of Guildhall, 3 Aug. 1328, reciting the above judgment and the failure of the def. to act upon it, and ordering them to put it into execution at the def.'s charges.

Fri. 17 June 1328. Hamo de Chigwell, mayor, Henry Darcy, sheriff, Nicholas de Farndon, Gregory de Norton, Anketin de Gisors, Reginald de Conduit, John de Preston, Henry de Combemartyn, John de Causton and John Poyntel, aldermen.

Assize of Nuisance

292. The commonalty complain by Reginald Wolleward, their attorney, that whereas the rainwater descending from the fields behind the hospital of St. Mary without Bisshopesgate on the east side used to flow through a ditch (*fossatum*) in the midst of the royal highway outside Bisshopesgate in the par. of St. Botolph to the tenement of Thomas de Blakeneye, draper, called 'le Breggehous', and thence along his wall at the north and beneath the tenement of the New Hospital to la Moore, whence it was carried by the Walbroke into the Thames, the said Thomas has obstructed the flow to the prejudice of the citizens. The sheriff, by John de Hardyngham, his clerk, testifies that the def. was summoned by Simon le Barbier and John le Peyntour, but he makes default. Judgment after view that he remove the obstruction *within 40 days etc.* and do not again impede the flow of water. Mandate of the mayor to the sheriffs in the Husting of Common Pleas, Mon. 24 Oct. 1328, reciting the above judgment, and the failure of the def. to execute it; and ordering them, on behalf of the king, to put it into effect without delay, reporting on the action taken and returning the present bill in full Husting on Mon. 7 Nov.

[m. 41d.] *Fri. 1 July 1328. Mayor, Richard de Betoyn, Benedict de Fulsham, Gregory de Norton, Thomas de Leyre, John de Causton and John de Coton.*

293. The prior of Austin Friars complains that the earthen wall of the garden (*ortum*) of William le Mareschal and Margaret his wife, belonging to certain sheds (*domunculas*) of theirs in the par. of All Hallows bi the Walle, and extending in width from their house on the north to the prior's garden (*gardinum*) on the south for 6 ells, and in length from the tenement of [blank] on the east to the south end of the priory garden on the west for $14\frac{1}{4}$ ells, is so ruinous and broken down in divers places that dogs, pigs, cocks and hens as well as men, women and children are able to enter the prior's garden and do damage there. John le Ry, sheriff's serjeant, reports that the defs. have been summoned by William Vauntage, 'gerdeler', and Warin de Hodesdon, but they make default. The mayor and aldermen find, on viewing the premises, that the allegations of the pl. are correct; and since decorum particularly requires that the enclosure between religious and others should be strong and well founded, it is adjudged that the parties combine to build a stone wall, either each contributing $1\frac{1}{2}$ ft. of land and sharing the cost of building, or one providing 3 ft. of land and the other building the wall at his own charges. The same to be done within 40 days; otherwise the sheriffs are to act at the expense of the defaulter and fine him 40s.

Fri. 15 July 1328. Mayor, John Hauteyn, sheriff, Nicholas de Farndon, Reginald de Conduit, John de Grantham, John Poyntel, John de Preston, Thomas de Leyre, Benedict de Fulsham, John Priour and Gregory de Norton, recorder, aldermen.

294. Richard de Rothyng and Joan his wife, pls., appear by William de Grenstede, their attorney, against John de Cherleton, kt., def., concerning a tenement in the par. of St. Sepulchre without Neugate, but the def.'s tenants and neighbours come and say that he was not in town at the time of the summons. They are ordered to warn him to appear at the quindene, and the same day is given to the pl.

295. Reginald de Thorp complains that when he sought to repair and heighten his house next that of John le Bokbyndere in the par. of St. Brigid beyond Flete Bridge, John had the work prohibited. The def. comes and says that the pl., in building, occupied a strip of his land, $5\frac{1}{3}$ ells long and $\frac{1}{2}$ ft. wide, and removed his posts and puncheons (punchones). The mayor and aldermen, on viewing the premises, find that the wall and foundation belong for the greater part to the pl., and it is adjudged that he have and hold as much as is his, as indicated by the old post on the north side of his house, and his joists above, so that his house may be raised and propped up (suppodatur) and stand straight by plumb-line (per lineam et plumbum); and that the def. have what is indicated by his old timber. Another wall, common to the parties, is ruinous and overhangs the pl.'s land. Judgment that it be repaired at their common charges, since its condition does not appear to be the fault of the def.

Fri. 22 July 1328. Mayor, Henry Darci, sheriff, Nicholas de Farndon, Gregory de Norton, Thomas de Leyre, Anketin de Gisors, John Hauteyn, John de Causton, John Poyntel.

296. The abbess of St. Clare without Alegate essoins herself against James Beauflour by Nicholas de Cranle.

297. William Sprot complains that the cess-pit of Adam and William, sons of Geoffrey Merre is too near his tenement, and is so full of sewage that it overflows and penetrates his stone wall, and enters his house and collects there, causing a great stench. The defs. make default. The mayor and aldermen and other members of the assize find that the pl.'s allegations are correct. Judgment that *within 40 days etc.* the defs. wall the cess-pit with stone and remove it $2\frac{1}{2}$ ft. from the pl.'s wall.

[m. 42] *Fri. 5 Aug. 1328. Hamo de Chiggewell, mayor, Gregory de Norton, John de Preston, Nicholas de Farndon, John de Grantham, Henry de Secheford, Richard Costantyn and John Poyntel, aldermen and Henry Darcy, sheriff.*

298. Roger de Depham and Margaret his wife complain that, whereas they hold a plot of land in the par. of St. Michael de Crokedelane called 'le Tythyngwowes'[1] as Margaret's dower, received from her late husband, James Folk, and it was enclosed, at his own expense, by Fulk de St. Edmunds, James's father, with a stone wall measuring, between the land formerly belonging to Robert le Lung and afterwards to John de Harewe on the south and the churchyard of St. Michael's on the north, 128 ft. in length and 2 ft. in thickness, and in height beneath the ridge-tile (?)

---

1. i.e. tighting or tenter walls (OE verb 'tyhtan', 'to draw, pull, stretch'; OE sb. 'wāg', 'a wall'). We owe this etymology to Mr. J. McN. Dodgson.

(cresta) on the east side next 'Tyghtyngwowes' 6 ft., and on the west side next the churchyard 8 ft., the rector and parishioners for the time being providing the land so that the wall is common to the parties, and neither can lawfully make any alteration to it without the consent of the other: Ralph, parson of St. Michael's, Walter de Moredon, John Lovekyn, Robert de Braye, William atte Lanende, Richard Gubbe, John Gubbe, Peter de Ware and Henry de Braughyng, parishioners, eight days since demolished 78 ft. of it and began to demolish the rest to the damage of the pls. and of John son of Fulk to whom the reversion belongs. The parson and John Lovekyn, Robert de Bray, Peter de Ware and many other parishioners come and say that the assize does not lie, because the wall was built by the rector and parishioners for the time being, and is wholly theirs; but asked whether they can produce any evidence in support of their claim they say no, and put themselves upon the view of the assize. The mayor and aldermen find that the wall stands wholly upon the land of the churchyard, and was built by Fulk, predecessor of the above-named John, and is thus common to the parties. Judgment that *within 40 days etc.* the defs. restore it to the condition in which it was before they demolished it.

Fri. 19 Aug. 1328. The aforesaid mayor, Henry Darcy, sheriff, Nicholas de Farndon, Richard de Betoin, Anketin de Gisors, John de Preston, John de Causton, Gregory de Norton, Richard Costentyn and John Poyntel, aldermen.

299. The commonalty, pls., by Reginald Woleward, their attorney, appear against Nicholas de Clare, kt., def., concerning the ruin of a stone wall on the royal highway in the par. of St. Mary de Wolcherchehawe. The sheriff testifies that the def. was not in town when he issued his precept. He and the def.'s neighbours are ordered to warn him to appear at the quindene.

300. The commonalty, pls., by the same Reginald, appear against Walter le Bret and Juliana his wife, defs., complaining that their house in the same par., which abuts upon the royal highway, is so ruinous that great and small, horsemen and pedestrians, fear to pass by; and that the house is roofless and its timber rotten, to the scandal and disgrace of the City. The sheriff testifies that the defs. were summoned by Geoffrey de Shrovesbery and Robert de Bregges, but they make default. Judgment that *within 40 days etc.* the house be demolished and removed.

301. John de Grantham complains that $13\frac{1}{4}$ ells of the stone wall common to him and Alice relict of William de Speresholte in the par. of St. Michael ate Quenehethe overhang his land by 1 ft. and more so that he cannot build his house straight by plumb-line (per lineam et plumbum). Afterwards the pl. (dictus Johannes) rebuilt the wall and repaired it where it was defective, and raised it (exaltavit) for the convenience of both parties.

[m. 42d.] *Fri. 2 Sep. 1328. The aforesaid mayor, Henry Darcy, sheriff, Gregory de Norton, Anketin Gisors, John de Causton, John de Polteneye, John Poyntel, Richard Costentyn and John Priur, aldermen.*

Assize of Nuisance

302. The commonalty, pls., by Reginald Woleward, their attorney, appear against Thomas de Clare, kt., def., complaining that he has a ruinous stone wall in the par. of St. Mary de Wolcherchehawe, of which the corner is opposite the churchyard; and it extends in width from the same corner to Walebroke lane for 8 ells, and in length towards the east for 22 ells. They ask that for the benefit of the people of the City, and more particularly because of the great danger to men and women passing day by day, the wall be either repaired or demolished. And because it appears on inspection of the rolls[1] that Thomas was summoned to appear on Fri. 19 Aug. but was not then in the City, and although warned by his tenants he now makes default, it is adjudged that the wall be repaired or demolished *within 40 days etc.*

303. A like judgment was given for the commonalty in respect of two ruinous shops belonging to John son of John de la Chambre in the par. of St. Augustine at the east door of St. Paul's.

[m. 43] *Fri. 24 Mar. 1329. [Essoins only.]*

Fri. 7 Apr. 1329. Mayor, Nicholas de Farndon, Gregory de Norton, Reginald de Conduit, Thomas de Leyre, John de Causton, Henry de Seccheford, John Poyntel, Richard de Hakeneye, Anketin Gisors, aldermen, Henry de Combemartyn and Simon Frаunceys, sheriffs.

304. John de Pountoyse and Alice his wife and John de Castelacre and Isabel his wife are summoned to answer Andrew Aubrey in an assize of nuisance. John de Pountoyse and Alice essoin themselves but afterwards make default. John de Castelacre comes in person and Isabel by John de Horewode, her attorney, but they show no cause why the assize should be delayed. The pl. complains that the stone wall of the defs. adjoining his plot of land in the par. of All Hallows de Bredestrete, measuring in length $6\frac{7}{8}$ ells, and in height 12 ft. and more, according to the measurements of Masters Simon de Canterbury and John de Totenham, carpenters, and Master Simon de Pabenham, mason, sworn to the assize, overhangs his land so that he cannot build. The mayor and aldermen, having viewed the premises, and measurements having been taken by the mason and carpenters above-named, it is found that the defs.' wall overhangs the pl.'s land by $5\frac{3}{4}$ ins. at the north end, and 5 ins. at the south end, as represented diagrammatically on the roll. Judgment that the defs. remove the nuisances *within 40 days etc.*

Fri. 9 June 1329. Mayor, Nicholas de Farndon, Gregory de Norton, Reginald de Conduit, Henry de Combemartin, John de Caustone, Henry de Secheford and John de Cotoun, aldermen.

305. The same Andrew complains that the same John and Isabel have caused his building operations against their wall in the same par. to be prohibited. John comes, but Isabel makes default, although the sheriff

1. Respite (on m. 42) because Thomas was not in the City.

testifies that both were summoned by Thomas le Barber and Albert le Keu of Bredstrete. The assize proceeds in her absence. John says that the pl. may not build against his wall because the tenement which he and Isabel hold is of her inheritance, and formerly belonged to William fitz Isabel, who, as appears by an indenture which he produces, granted it, viz. the stone house in Cheap between the land of Richard Travers and the land formerly belonging to Baldewyn Crispin, with a view extending 16 ft. to the rear and 6 ft. on the side facing the house of Richard Travers, to John de Braughyng, Walter Gernoun and Ralph Bataille, who with all the other tenants and the defs. have enjoyed the same without disturbance until the pl.'s building threatened to obscure the entire view. The pl. says that this answer cannot prejudice his case because the defs. cannot claim a greater estate in the tenement they hold than was enjoyed by Deodonatus the goldsmith, Isabel's father, who was granted it by John de Vaux, goldsmith, with free light on the south towards the tenement of Walter de Beverle and on the north towards Westchepe. John says that he has other muniments supporting his claim and asks for time to produce them. Because the mayor and aldermen wish to be more fully advised, the parties are given a day on Fri. 23 June, but the def. proffers no new evidence; and since it appears to the view of the assize that the defs. cannot lawfully proceed against the pl. by an assize of nuisance (edificationem . . . per aliquam assisam de nocumento possunt de iure perturbare), it is adjudged that he complete his building operations against the defs.' wall without further impediment. Defs. in mercy.

[m. 43d.] *Fri. 18 Aug. 1329. Mayor, Nicholas de Farndon, Richard de Betoin, Anketin de Gisors, John de Causton, Henry de Sescheford, Gregory de Norton, John Poyntel and Henry de Coumbemartyn, aldermen, and the same Henry, sheriff.*

306. Henry de Newenton, rector of St. Mary Magdalene in Melkstrete, John de Enefeld, kt., Robert de Kelseye, Adam de Burgoyne and other parishioners, pls., appear against John de Charleton, Adam de Burgoyne [*sic*], John de Assheby, John de Lifton and William de Pontfreit, defs. concerning a free tenement of the church. John de Charleton and Adam come, but John de Assheby, John de Lyfton and William make default. The neighbours testify that they were not in the City when the summons was issued. They are ordered to warn them to appear at the quindene, and the same day is given to the other parties.

Fri. 8 June 1330. Simon de Swanlond, mayor, Nicholas de Farndon, Gregory de Norton, Richard Costantyn, Thomas de Leyre, Robert de Ely and Henry de Seccheford, aldermen, and Richard le Lacer, sheriff.

307. Hugh de Waltham and Juliana his wife complain that Thomas de la Marche has prohibited them from building an earthen wall between his garden and theirs in the par. of St. Andrew de Cornhulle. Both parties agree to abide by the decision of the mayor and aldermen, who adjudge that Thomas provide 4½ ft. of land, and that Hugh and Juliana undertake

Assize of Nuisance

the cost of building. The wall runs from the corner of the pls.' house next a well there, on the south, to the garden of the prioress and convent of St. Helen's on the north and is 31½ ells in length.

Fri. 7 Sep. 1330. Simon de Swanlond, mayor, Nicholas de Farndon, Hamo de Chigwell, John de Grantham, Reginald de Conduit, John de Preston, Henry de Coumbemartyn, Anketin de Gisors, John Priour, Thomas de Leyre, Henry de Seccheford and Richard de Hakeneye, aldermen.

308. William, rector of St. Stephen de Walebroke, Peter de Newcastle (Novo Castro), Adam de Braye, Elias de Thorp, Roger de Ely, and other parishioners complain that when they proposed to rebuild their bell-tower (clocherium), and rested part of it on the church wall at the west end, Isabel relict of John le Leuter had the work prohibited. Isabel comes and says that the wall in question belongs wholly to her and not to the church. It is found by the mayor and aldermen after diligent scrutiny above and below and on both sides of the wall that of old, when it was first built, an arch of free stone 1 ft. deep was built on the side of the church, and another of the same depth on Isabel's side, with a foot of wall between. It is therefore adjudged that the wall is, according to the custom of the City, divisible between the parties. Isabel and pledges to prosecute in mercy for causing the work to be impeded. The rector and parishioners *sine die*, with authority to complete their building.

[m. 44] *Fri. 21 Dec. 1330. John de Pulteneye, mayor, Nicholas de Farndon, John de Grantham, Richard de Betoyne, Gregory de Norton, Reginald de Conduit, Thomas de Leyre, Richard Costantyn and Henry Darcy, aldermen, Robert de Ely and Thomas de Harewold, sheriffs.*

309. John Melf, 'nakerer', and Joan his wife complain that, whereas they possess an easement belonging to their free tenement on the land of William Abel, 'bocher', and Joan his wife in the par. of St. Nicholas Shambles, whereby they have access by an enclosed place 7½ ft. long and 4 ft. wide to a privy (garderoba), with a pipe leading to the defs.' cess-pit, and they have a door (ostium) in their solar opening on to the said place, the defs. have completely removed the privy and pipe and fence (claustura) and replaced them by joists and other constructions. The defs. come in person and say that the pls.' claim is contrary to common right (contra communem ius), unless they can show a special grant. The pls. say that they and all previous tenants of the tenement they now hold have been seised of the easement time out of mind. The case is referred to a jury, which comes by William Pykerel and others on the panel. They say upon oath that the pls. were seised of the easement in question until the last quarter, and that they and their predecessors had been so seised for 50 years and more; but that the width of the enclosed space is only 3½ ft. and not 4 ft. as alleged. Judgment that *within 40 days etc.* the defs. repair the fencing (claustura), with the privy and pipe, and that the pls. continue to enjoy their easement as before but be in mercy for giving the width of the enclosure as 4 ft. instead of

3½ ft. Note that the inquisition was held in the church of St. Nicholas. [m. 44d. Blank.]

[m. 45] *Fri. 8 June 1330. Simon de Swanlond, mayor, and the aldermen and sheriff, etc.*

310. Assize brought at the instance of Richard atte Pole concerning a fence (claustura) formerly existing between the land which he recently bought of the prioress and convent of St. Helen's in the par. of St. Michael de Cornhull and the garden of Roger de Leukenore. The pl. asks permission of the mayor and aldermen to build there the foundation to support his new house. Roger is summoned, but makes default. After viewing the site and taking counsel with the carpenters and masons sworn to the assize the mayor and aldermen tell Richard that he may lay his foundation whenever he pleases, in accordance with the ancient metes and bounds.

311. Afterwards, at another assize held on Fri. 31 Aug. at the tenement of the same Richard, Roger de Leukenore again makes default. It is found by view of the mayor and aldermen and the carpenters and masons sworn to the assize that the stone wall carrying Richard's new house and extending from the churchyard of St. Michael on the north to the corner of his parlour (parlorii) on the south, stands wholly on his land, and belongs to him and no one else, as appears by the former judgment of the mayor and aldermen. The wall adjoins the garden of Roger de Leukenore on the east side, and is 35⅜ ells long including the post at the north end; and Richard and his heirs and assigns are to hold the same, as above said. [m. 45d. Blank.]

[m. 46] *Fri. 12 July 1331. [Essoin only.]*

Fri. 26 July 1331. John de Pulteneye, mayor, Nicholas de Farndon, Gregory de Norton, John de Preston, John Priour, Anketin de Gisors, Henry de Seccheford and Robert le Bret, aldermen.

312. Isabel relict of Hamo Goldchep, pl., appears against Geoffrey son of Geoffrey Beauflur, def., who has a day to appear by essoin, but makes default. The pl. says that on 1 Apr. 1299, Isabel relict of John Brother, senior, late citizen, granted to Richard Wolmar, citizen, whose heir she is, the view, opening, light, air and clarity (visum, aperturam, lumen, aerem et claritatem) of a window in the west gable of her house, adjoining his land in the par. of St. Botolph Billyngesgate; the same to be barred with wood or iron and to be 2½ ells 1 in. above the ground, 1½ ells 6 ins. in length from south to north, and ¾ ell 5 ins. in width, not counting the inches (absque pollicibus mensuratis), as appears by a deed which she produces in court, witnessed by Henry le Waleys, mayor, Thomas Saby [*rectius* Sely] and Richer de Refham, sheriffs, Elias Russel, alderman of [Billingsgate] ward, Stephen Pykeman, Robert le Treyere, Gilbert Cros, William Pykeman, Peter de Combe, Richard Sharp, John de Fulmere, Robert Pikeman,

Assize of Nuisance

John de la Barre, beadle (serviente) of the ward, and others. She complains that John Ruddok, who recently rented the house from Robert de Barsham, guardian of the def., who is a minor, has piled up his firewood against her window so high above the upper stone frame (superiorem superficiem lapidum) that it is completely obscured, and the light, view, air and clarity impeded. The mayor and aldermen agree that John Ruddok be ordered, on behalf of the king, to remove the firewood, before Fri. 2 Aug., from the window, so that it is below the lower stone frame, and then $3\frac{3}{4}$ ells to the west, where he may stack it to a height of $1\frac{1}{4}$ ells and no more; the same to be done so that they may satisfy themselves concerning the light etc. before giving judgment. On the appointed day the assize comes by Nicholas Farndon, mayor, Richard de Beton, Gregory de Norton, Robert de Ely, John de Preston, John Priour, John de Causton and Henry de Seccheford, aldermen, and Thomas Harewold, sheriff, and the pl. appears by Hugh de Waltham, her attorney; but judgment is deferred until 9 Aug. to allow the mayor and aldermen to take further advice. On that day Gregory de Norton and John de Causton come to the site and again adjourn the proceedings until 16 Aug., when they are once more adjourned until 23 Aug. by the same Gregory and Henry de Seccheford. [*Margin* (in a later hand): Nota, quia contra consuetudinem ut michi videtur.] On that day Gregory de Norton and Henry de Seccheford come and see that the firewood has been removed from the window, and on Fri. 30 Aug. they testify to that effect before the mayor and aldermen at Guildhall in the presence of the pl. Judgment that in future nothing be done contrary to the tenor of the deed produced by the pl., under a penalty of 40s. payable to the sheriffs. Gregory in mercy for the impediment caused by his tenant, John Ruddok; but because he is a minor the amercement is pardoned by the mayor. [m. 46d. Blank.]

[m. 47] *Fri. 15 May 1332. John de Pulteney, mayor, John de Mockyng, sheriff, Nicholas de Farndon, Gregory de Norton, Simon de Swanlond, Benedict de Fulsham, John de Causton, Henry de Seccheford and William de Causton, aldermen.*

313. Henry de Cobeham, kt., complains by John de Horewode, his attorney, that whereas he has a plot of land in the par. of St. Dunstan by the Tower, enclosed by stone walls upon which his house is built, and because of the ruinous state of the house he proposed to rebuild it, removing the old timber and replacing it by new, Joan relict of John de Braye and Edmund her son who hold the adjoining tenement, caused the work to be prohibited by John de Mockyng, sheriff, to his damage, 20 marks. The defs. come, and Edmund, who is under age, says that he claims nothing at present in the tenement, which, according to Joan, was devised to her for life by her late husband, with reversion to Edmund, together with the plot of land claimed by the pl. She declares that she has documents proving her right, and asks for time to produce them, in accordance with a certain article of the statutes and ordinances made of old for the holding of assizes of nuisance. The parties are given a day on the following Tues. [19 May] in the Husting of Common Pleas, and an article is inspected of which the tenor is as

Assize of Nuisance

follows: 'Si autem dixerit . . . procedat assisa';[1] but because the mayor and aldermen wish to conclude the assize, according to custom, on the site of the dispute, the parties are given a day there on Fri. 29 May. The def., Joan, essoins herself by John Scullard, and the proceedings are adjourned until the quindene [12 June]; but because the day fell in Whitsun week when no pleas are held, Gregory de Norton and John de Causton, aldermen, went to the site, and in the presence of the attorneys of the parties, adjourned the proceedings until Fri. 19 June. On that day, because the mayor was engaged in business concerning the king, the same Gregory and Benedict de Fulsham, aldermen, again adjourned the assize until 26 June, when the mayor, as one of the justices, was occupied in delivering the Neugate gaol and so could not be present. Finally, on Fri. 3 July the assize came by John de Pulteneye, mayor, John de Mockyng, sheriff, Nicholas de Farndon, John de Grantham, Benedict de Fulsham, Gregory de Norton, Reginald de Conduit, John de Causton, Henry de Seccheford and Henry de Gisors, aldermen, and likewise the parties, and Joan said for herself and her son that the tenement which she now holds formerly came by escheat into the hand of Henry III, who gave it to William le Taillour his serjeant, who gave it to Richard le Tailleur, who gave it to Richard le Taillour and Margery his wife; and that the pl.'s plot of land has been parcel of the tenement ever since Henry III gave it to William le Taillour. The pl. says that the land in question is his by inheritance, and has belonged to him and his predecessors for 60 years and more, and he asks judgment because the def. has not produced the written evidence for which an adjournment was granted. The relevant article is again recited, together with another prohibiting interference with any occupation which has lasted for more than a year and a day (Et sciendum est . . . unum annum et diem).[2] [m. 47d.] Judgment that the prohibition made by the sheriff at the instance of the def. be annulled, and that the pl. continue his building operations on the plot of land in dispute at his good pleasure and without further impediment. The def., and Edmund her son, who is present in court, in mercy.

[m. 48] *Fri. 20 Aug. 1333. John de Preston, mayor, and the aldermen, etc.*

314. Alice wife of John de Brycheford essoins herself against William de Causton and Denise his wife by Robert de Stratford. The parties are adjourned until the quindene. On that day, viz. 3 Sep., they are again adjourned by Henry de Coumbemartyn and John Priour, senior, aldermen, because the mayor and aldermen are occupied at Guildhall with business concerning the collection of the money for the king's gift (exhennio), until the octave [10 Sep.]. [Entry incomplete. Cf. **318**.]

Fri. 27 Aug. 1333. John de Preston, mayor, and Gregory de Norton, Reginald de Conduit, John Hautayn, Anketin de Gisors, Nicholas de Farndon, Henry de Secheford, aldermen.

315. John de Godeston and Lucy his wife essoin themselves against Isabel relict of John Paas by John de Salisbury. Afterwards on Fri. 3 Sep. because

1. *Lib. Alb.*, i, 330.   2. *Lib. Alb.*, i, 331.

Assize of Nuisance

the mayor and aldermen were not free to hold an assize the parties were adjourned until the octave.

316. Since it is testified that Joan relict of John de Armenters, who brought an assize against Andrew Aubrey and Joan his wife, is dead the assize falls to the ground (cadit assisa). [See **328**.]

317. Richard de Keselyngbury complains that on Thurs. 5 Aug. Richard de Bromyerd caused the sheriff's serjeant to prohibit him from repairing his houses in Cordewanerstret in the par. of St. Mary le Bow. The def. says he did so on account of the light pertaining to a shop there which belongs to his wife Cecily, who comes and joins him in declaring that the shop which they have held for many years past, adjoining that of the pl. on the south side, formerly belonged to Robert Broke, citizen and hosier (calligarius), who gave it, with the light pertaining to the east end, to Alexander le Settere, by a deed dated Tues. 30 Nov. 1311. Alexander granted it to Matthew de Essex and Matthew to William de Stanes by deeds which they produce in court. On William's death Richard and Cecily entered in her right and were peacefully seised of the light in question until it was obscured by the pl.'s building operations. The pl. says on the contrary that on 1 Oct. 1304, Thomas Broke granted to William de Upton, draper, a shop and solar in Cordewanerstrete which Henry de Kent used to hold, and which are situated between the tenement formerly belonging to Robert de Kydemenstre on the south and that of Philip Broke on the north. William de Upton died seised of both shop and solar, and was succeeded by his son Matthew, who granted them to the def.; but he denies that any light was reserved when Thomas Broke enfeoffed the above-named William or later, and he asks that the case be referred to a jury. The pl. does likewise. Richard appoints Simon de Kelshull his attorney. The jury comes on Fri. 10 Sep., but because the mayor and aldermen are unable to be present, it is adjourned to the octave. Further adjournments follow on the same pretext until 10 Oct.

Fri. 20 Aug. 1333. Continuation.

318. John de Brycheford and Alice his wife are summoned to answer William de Causton and Denise his wife who complain that, whereas a dispute occurred between Walter le Waleys, citizen, and Thomas de Brauncestre, citizen, in 1276–7, when Gregory de Rokesle was mayor, and Robert de Arraz and Ralph le Feure, sheriffs, concerning their adjoining tenements, and was settled by the mayor and other good men summoned for the purpose, the parties agreeing that Thomas and his heirs and assigns should have and hold in perpetuity a new building (edificamentum), with the use of a courtyard (curie) and well, and with the right of free entry and exit towards Westchepe and the church of St. Matthew de Fridaistrete, as appears in an indenture made between them; and the pls. hold the tenement which then belonged to Walter, and John de Brycheford and Alice his wife that of Thomas, the same John and Alice have obstructed the courtyard by building there and have placed a cistern in an inconvenient position,

Assize of Nuisance

reducing the space available to the pls. The defs. come and say that the courtyard is not common to the parties, because in the time of Henry III the tenement which the defs. now hold belonged to Henry fitz Stephen, with half the adjoining courtyard or plot of land, and he granted the same to Hugh de Rokyngham, goldsmith, who granted it to Thomas de Brauncestre, who, in his will, provided for it to be sold by his executors [names omitted], who sold it to John de Dallyngg, mercer, from whom the defs. bought it. On Fri. 22 Oct. the assize comes by J. de Preston, mayor, Nicholas de Farndon, J. de Granthan, Gregory de Norton, Reginald de Conduit, Benedict de Fulsham, H. de Cumbemartyn, J. de Causton, J. Priour and Henry de Sechford, aldermen, and John Hamond and William Hanisard, sheriffs, and the parties likewise; but because of various difficulties the proceedings were adjourned to the next Husting of Common Pleas to be terminated there. On Mon. 6 June 1334, the parties come and ask for the record and judgment. The customary discussion (colloquium) having been held between the mayor and aldermen the record is read, and the allegations of the parties considered together with the indenture between Walter le Waleys and Thomas de Brauncestre previously produced by the pls., and it appears to the court that the courtyard and well are common to the parties, and that no partition was made at the time of, or subsequent to, the drawing up of the indenture. Afterwards the mayor and aldermen go to the site and find that the defs., as alleged, had moved the cistern from the place where it used to stand and built a fence (claustura) in a new position without the consent of the pls. Judgment by view of the carpenters and masons sworn to the assize, that *within 40 days etc.* they replace the cistern in its former position, and rebuild the fence as it was before.

[m. 48d.] *Fri. 18 Feb. 1334. Mayor, sheriff and the aldermen.*

319. Henry le Cheyner, mercer, pl., appears against William son of William de Leyre, def., concerning a tenement in Mylkstrete in the par. of St. Lawrence Jewry. The sheriff testifies, by the neighbours, that the def. was not in town when the summons was issued. They are ordered to warn him, wherever he may be near the City, to appear at the quindene on the site where the assize was sought. The same day is given to the pl.

Fri. 4 Mar. 1334. Mayor, sheriff and the aldermen.

319 cont. Def. essoins himself by John de Salisbury. And he comes before Gregory de Norton, alderman and recorder, and appoints William de Rasne his attorney.

Fri. 18 Mar. 1334. Mayor, sheriff and the aldermen.

319 cont. The pl. complains that the def. has prohibited him from repairing the wall 60 ft. long and 3 ft. wide, joining their tenements in the same par. William appears by his attorney and says that he has written evidence to support his claim to the wall, and asks for time to produce it. He is given a day on Fri. in Easter week; but because pleas cannot be held at that time,

Assize of Nuisance

the proceedings are adjourned by Gregory de Norton and William de Causton, aldermen, until 14 Apr. [*sic*], when the assize comes by the mayor, Nicholas de Farndone, Gregory de Norton, Reginald de Conduit, John de Causton, Henry de Sechford, William de Causton, Andrew Aubrey, John de Hyngeston, aldermen, and John Hamond, sheriff, and the parties come likewise. The def., asked whether he can show cause why the wall should not be assigned to the pl., says only that the wall-plate (plata) of his house hangs above it (supra pendet), and used to rest upon it and be carried by it until the wall was demolished. It appears to the mayor and aldermen after carefully viewing the site that the def. can claim nothing whatever in the wall. Judgment that the pl. do what he will with it, notwithstanding the previous prohibition. Def. in mercy.

Fri. 3 June 1334. J. de Pulteneye, mayor, and the aldermen.

320. Thomas atte Rededore, 'brewere', essoins himself against William Gylle by John de Rasne.

Fri. 10 June 1334. The aforesaid mayor, and the aldermen.

321. Michael Mynot essoins himself against Hugh de Waltham, clerk, by Robert Prat. Since the quindene fell on the feast of the nativity of St. John the Baptist [24 June], the proceedings were adjourned until the octave [1 July]. Further adjournments followed until 22 July, because of the absence of the mayor.

[m. 49] *Fri. 30 Apr. 1333. John de Preston, mayor, John Husebonde and Nicholas Pyk, sheriffs, Nicholas de Farndon, Richard de Betoyne, John de Grantham, John de Pulteneye, Gregory de Norton, Reginald de Conduit, Richard de Hakeneye, John de Oxford, John de Causton, Henry Darcy and other aldermen.*

322. Joan wife of Andrew Aubrey essoins herself against John de Lyndewode by John Prest. Andrew appears.

323. Joan Darmenters appoints Thomas de Bury or Simon de Kelshull her attorney.

Fri. 14 May 1333. John de Preston, mayor, John de Pulteneye, John de Grantham, Nicholas de Farndon, Richard de Betoyne, Henry Darcy, Gregory de Norton, John Priour, Robert le Bret, Robert de Ely, Benedict de Fulsham, Anketin de Gisors and William de Causton, aldermen.

323 cont. Joan complains that when she hired masons to build a door in the stone wall of the cellar beneath her house in the par. of St. Antonin, Andrew Aubrey and Joan his wife caused the work to be prohibited. The defs. say that the wall is theirs from the foundation upwards, and supports their wall-plate (platam) and roof (cumulum), and that their plates, joists and timber rest upon it as well below in the cellar, as above in their chamber (camera). They argue that it is not permissible for anyone to make a hole in such a wall, or demolish it or diminish it in any way without the consent of the owner, even if they have corbels and beams in it to uphold their solar, or arches or cupboards (almaria); and they refer to an article of the *Assize*.[1] The proceedings are adjourned to the Husting of Common Pleas on Tues. 15 June. Further adjournments follow on such pretexts as the absence of the mayor, his occupation in delivering Newgate gaol, and the absence of certain of the aldermen who had been present at the previous view, until 13 Aug. [See **316**.]

324. William de Thorneye complains that when he hired workmen to build the cess-pit of a privy in his house in the par. of St. Mary de Aldermaricherche, Andrew Aubrey and Joan his wife had the work prohibited. The defs. say that the cess-pit is not built in accordance with the custom of the City, since the fence (claustura) is not 2½ ft. from their wall. After repeated adjournments, the mayor and aldermen come on Fri. 25 June, and having viewed the cess-pit, find that it is not to the nuisance of the pl., but sufficient and tolerable according to the custom of the City. Judgment that the pl. continue his building in stone without further impediment.

Fri. 4 June 1333. [*Essoin only.*]

[m. 49d.] *Fri. 25 June 1333. Mayor, Nicholas de Farndon, John de Grantham, Richard de Betoigne, John de Pulteneye, Gregory de Norton, Benedict de Fulsham, Anketin de Gysors, William de Causton, John de Causton, Henry de Gysors and Robert le Bret, aldermen, John Husebonde and Nicholas Pyk, sheriffs.*

325. Andrew de Aubrey and Joan his wife complain that whereas they possess an easement in the use of a cess-pit common to their tenement and those of Thomas Heyron and Joan relict of John de Armenters, and the same was enclosed by a party-wall (pariete) and roofed with joists and boards (bordis), so that the seats (cedilia) of the privies of the pls. and the others could not be seen, Joan de Armenters and William de Thorneye have removed the party-wall (clausturam) and roof so that the extremities of those sitting upon the seats can be seen, a thing which is abominable and altogether intolerable. Judgment, after the site has been viewed, that the defs. roof and enclose the cess-pit as it was before, under the penalty prescribed by the law and custom of the City in such cases.

326. As regards the aperture which the same Andrew and Joan his wife made in their room over the cellar of John de Armenters, now held by William de Thorneye, through which his private business (secreta) can be seen by those in the room above, and concerning which Joan de Armenters and the above-named William have made complaint, it is adjudged by the mayor and aldermen that it be blocked up.

Mon. [*rectius Fri.*] *25 June 1333. Continuation.*

1. *Lib. Alb.*, i, 326–7. De corbellis et trabibus.

Assize of Nuisance

327. William Rabot complains that Adam Lucas has caused the rebuilding of his house and stone walls in the par. of St. Magnus to be prohibited by the sheriff. Adam comes and says that the pl., in rebuilding his walls has made a purpresture upon the lane (venella) leading from Thamestrete to the river, and serving him and others living there. The pl. says that his tenement adjoining the lane in question, formerly belonged to Henry Sudbery and Alice his wife, relict of Stephen de Oistergate, and by an indenture enrolled in the Husting[1] on Mon. 22 Jan. 1274, they granted it, with free entry and exit by the lane, which measures $1\frac{1}{2}$ ells 2 ins. in width throughout its length, to Adam de Bekenesfeld called de Fulham and Alice his wife, whose estate he, William, now holds. Afterwards, Clarkin de Wolcherchehagh and Agnes his wife, daughter of Henry de Sudbery and Alice de Oystergate, granted to Adam and Alice, his predecessors, by a deed enrolled in the Husting[2] on Mon. 13 Mar. 1290, a quit rent of $\frac{1}{2}$ mark, with the right of free entry and exit by the lane for loading and unloading at their wharf (kayum) on the Thames, and because the wall carrying his house was ruinous he began to demolish and rebuild it, but without narrowing the lane as the def. alleges. The assize comes on Fri. 16 July by John de Preston, mayor, Nicholas de Farndon, John de Grantham, Gregory de Norton, Reginald de Conduit, Richard de Hakeneye, John de Causton, Benedict de Fulsham, aldermen, and the parties likewise appear. After viewing the site, it is adjudged that the pl. rebuild his wall upon the old foundations, and if they cannot be traced, he is to dig a new foundation, taking possession (saisiando) of his own land as far as 'le Campete kaij', as reason and custom require.[3]

Fri. 16 July 1333. John de Preston, mayor, Nicholas de Farndon, John de Grantham, Benedict de Fulsham, Gregory de Norton, Reginald de Conduit, Richard de Hakeneye and John de Causton, aldermen.

328. Joan relict of John de Armenters essoins herself against Andrew Aubrey and Joan his wife by Alan de Hormede. William de Thorneye appears. The parties are adjourned to the quindene. A further adjournment follows and on Fri. 13 Aug. the parties are adjourned by Henry de Sescheford and Robert de Ely, aldermen, because the mayor and aldermen are preoccupied with the king's business. [See **316**.]

Fri 23 July 1333.

329. The prior and convent of Holy Trinity essoin themselves against John de Gysors by Ralph Wayte. After an adjournment by Anketin de Gysors, alderman, and Hugh de Waltham, the pl. comes but the defs. do not come and are called in the presence of Robert de Benstede, William de Wedon and William atte Herst, neighbours.

Fri. 13 Aug. 1333.

1. H.R. 6 (10).
2. H.R. 19 (22).
3. Cf. *Lib. Cust.*, ii, 447–8.

Assize of Nuisance

330. Richard de Bromyerd essoins himself against Richard de Keselyngbury, hosier, by Robert de Pyrynton. [See **317**.]

[m. 50] *Fri. 1 Mar. 1336. Reginald de Conduit, mayor, Gregory atte Shire, John de Causton, John de Oxford, William de Causton, Richard de Berkyng and Walter de Mordon.*

331. Adam de Kyngeston, 'fisshmongere', is summoned to answer John Abel in an assize of nuisance. Walter de Mordon, sheriff, testifies that he was summoned by William Oliver and Thomas atte Wyche, but he makes default. The proceedings are adjourned until the quindene because the mayor and aldermen are engaged in urgent business concerning the king and the City and cannot attend. On Fri. 26 Apr. the pl. appears and Adam also, but he says nothing to delay the assize. The pl. complains that whereas he has a house 28 ft. long in the par. of St. Michael de Crokedelane adjoining that of the def., he receives on his wall the water draining from the latter's house, 14 ft. of which overhang his wall on the east side so that he cannot do the necessary repairs to the chimney (chiminum) standing upon it or to his gutter (guterum) or house. After viewing the premises the mayor and aldermen adjudge that the nuisances complained of be removed *within 40 days etc.*

332. On the same day the above Adam was ordered by the mayor and aldermen to remove a pig-sty adjoining John Abel's wall on the north side.

Fri. 1 Mar. 1336. [Essoin only.]

Fri. 14 June 1336.

333. William de Lyouns, 'heremite', of the Crepulgate hermitage, complains that when he wished to repair the wall of the hermitage Thomas Sporon, 'goldsmyth', whose tenement it adjoins, caused the work to be prohibited. The def. says that he holds the land upon which the pl. proposes to build by the courtesy of England, with reversion to John son of John de Ludgershale, without whom he cannot answer. On Fri. 12 July the assize comes by Reginald de Conduit, mayor, Gregory atte Shire, John de Causton, Richard de Hakeneye, John Hamond, Henry Darcy, Richard Lacer and Ralph de Upton, aldermen. The pl. appears, and likewise Thomas and John, but they show no cause why the assize should be delayed. After the premises have been viewed by the mayor and aldermen, it is adjudged that the pl. repair his wall without further impediment. Def. in mercy.

Fri. 18 Oct. 1336. Reginald de Conduit, mayor, John de Grantham, Gregory de Norton, John Hamond, Andrew Aubre, Richard de Rothyng, Simon Fraunceys and Richard de Hakeneye, aldermen.

334. William de Iford, common serjeant, complains on behalf of the commonalty, that the stone wall on the north side of the house of Henry de Sutton and Isabel his wife, facing the street in the par. of St. Mary de

Assize of Nuisance

Aldermarichirch, is ruinous and on the point of collapsing, to the terror of the neighbours and passers-by. Judgment by the mayor and aldermen that *within 40 days etc.* it be demolished, and, if the defs. so desire, rebuilt.

[m. 50d.] *Fri. 7 Feb. 1337. John de Pulteneye, mayor, Reginald de Conduit, Gregory de Norton, Henry Darcy, John Hamond, Andrew Aubrey, Richard Costantyn, John de Causton, Richard Lacer, Richard de Hakeneye, Simon Fraunceys, John de Oxford, Richard de Rothyng, Henry de Coumbemartyn, Ralph de Upton, Richard de Berkyngg and Nicholas Crane, aldermen.*

335. William de Iford, common serjeant, complains on behalf of the commonalty, that Michael Myngihot has erected a paling (palicium) and three staples (stapulas) in the street opposite his tenement in the par. of St. Mary de Aldermannebury, to the nuisance of citizens and passers-by. The sheriff testifies that the def. has been summoned by William atte Stake and Henry de Gloucestre. He comes in person but says nothing to delay the assize. It is adjudged that *within 40 days etc.* the paling and staples be removed.

Fri. 23 Jan. 1338. Henry Darcy, mayor, Gregory de Norton, John Hamond, Richard Lacer, Richard de Hakeneye and Nicholas Crane, aldermen.

336. John de Horwode and Maud his wife complain that for lack of a leaden gutter (gutere plumbee) 26½ St. Paul's ft. long, which Peter Cosyn, Roger le Cartere and Juliana his wife ought to provide, the water from their tenement in the par. of Holy Trinity the Less falls upon their land and rots their timber. Peter and Juliana make default. John comes but shows no cause why the assize should not proceed. Judgment after view that *within 40 days etc.* the defs. convey away their water as seems best to them without nuisance or impediment to the pls.

Fri. 20 Feb. 1338. Henry Darcy, mayor, Gregory de Norton, John de Causton, Richard de Hakeneye, John Hamond, William de Causton, Richard de Berkyng, aldermen.

337. John de Cologne (Colonia) complains that when he sought to demolish and rebuild an earthen wall in his messuage in the par. of St. Peter upon Cornhull, John de Yakesle, whose tenement adjoins it, caused the work to be prohibited, claiming the wall as his own. The def. comes in person and says that the wall is the boundary between the pl.'s messuage and his, and the land upon which it is built belongs to them both, and he had the work prohibited because the pl. did not ask his consent to the demolition. Because of certain ambiguities the mayor and aldermen adjourn the proceedings to the quindene; but afterwards the parties agree together.

Fri. 22 May 1338. Henry Darcy, mayor, Gregory de Norton, Richard de Hakenay, John de Causton, Richard de Berkyng, Ralph de Upton [blank], aldermen.

Assize of Nuisance

338. Roger de Forsham, def., v. Stephen de Kettelburgh. [Entry incomplete.]

[m. 51] *Fri. 3 July 1338. Henry Darcy, mayor, Gregory atte Shire, John de Causton, William de Causton, Ralph de Upton, Walter Neel, Richard Berkyng and Richard Costantin, aldermen.*

339. Thomas de Shene complains that for lack of a gutter (guttere) 20 ft. long which Thomas de Polstede and Katherine his wife and John de Waltham and William de Carleton ought to provide, the water from their tenements adjoining his in the par. of St. Peter the Less falls upon his land. The defs. make default, but the sheriff testifies that they were summoned by Walter Gladewyne and Jordan le Shereman. Judgment after view that *within 40 days etc.* they convey their water on to their own land.

Fri. 17 July 1338. [Essoins only.]

Fri. 31 July 1338. Henry Darcy, mayor, Gregory de Norton, John de Causton, John de Oxford, William de Causton, Ralph de Upton, Walter Neel, Richard de Rothyng, John Hamond and Richard de Berkyng.

340. Austin le Waleys and Maud his wife complain that Joan relict of Robert de Algate, 'pottere', and John de Northbrugh have three windows and an aperture (foramen) in one house, and six windows and three apertures in another overlooking their land, and not more than 7 ft. from the ground and unglazed.* The defs. essoin themselves but make default. Judgment after view that they remove the nuisance *within 40 days etc.*
[*Added below:*] The same Austin and Maud also say that for lack of a gutter (gottere) 41 ft. long which the same Joan and John ought to provide, the water from the defs.' houses falls on their land.

341. The same Austin and Maud complain that John de Hadham 'pottere', has two windows in one of his houses overlooking their land only 9 ft. from the ground, four windows in his hall only 4½ ft. from the ground and two apertures 9 ft. from the ground; and in another house two windows and three apertures all unglazed, contrary to the custom of the City.* The def. after essoin makes default. Judgment after view that he remove the nuisances *within 40 days etc.*
[*Added below:*] The same Austin and Maud also say that for lack of a gutter 50½ ft. long which the same John ought to provide, the water from his house falls upon the pls.' land.

Fri. 11 Sep. 1338. Henry Darcy, mayor, Gregory de Norton, Nicholas Crane, Walter Neel, John de Causton, William de Causton, Ralph de Upton.

342. William de Carleton, def., essoins himself against John de Houton by Adam de Heyworth. John, def., appoints Walter Gladewyn his attorney.

[m. 51d.] *Fri. 16 Oct. 1338. Henry Darcy, mayor, Reginald de Conduit,*

Richard le Lacer, John Hamond, Simon Fraunceys, Richard de Rothingg, Richard de Berkyng and William de Causton, aldermen.

342 cont. William de Carleton is summoned to answer John de Houton but the pl. does not prosecute his suit.

Fri. 30 Apr. 1339. Henry Darcy, mayor, Roger de Depham, Andrew Aubrey, Simon Fraunceys, William de Causton, John de Causton, Richard de Berkyng and William de Brykelesworth.

343. The master of St. Thomas the Martyr of Acon complains that for lack of a fillet-gutter (filetti) 16 ft. long, the water from the tenement of Richard de Betoygne adjoining his in the par. of St. Mary de Colcherch falls upon his land. The def. makes default, although the sheriff testifies that he was summoned by John de Cnopwede and Geoffrey le Cotiller. Judgment after view that *within 40 days etc.* he convey the water from his tenement on to his own land by any convenient means, without impediment to the pl.

344. Robert Seymor, 'armurer', and Benedicta his wife complain that for lack of a gutter (stillicidium) 30 ft. long the water from the adjoining tenement of Richard de Betoigne in the same par. falls upon their land. Richard makes default, though summoned by John de Cnopwede and Geoffrey le Cotiller. Judgment after view that *within 40 days etc.* he convey the water from his tenement on to his own land.

Fri. 18 June. 1339. [No entry.]

[m. 52] *Fri. 16 July 1339. Henry Darcy, mayor, Roger de Depham, William de Causton, Simon Fraunceys, Richard Lacer, Ralph de Upton and Richard de Berkyng, aldermen.*

345. Thomas son of Robert de Kelseye essoins himself against William de Carleton by Alan de Gillyngham.

Fri. 30 July 1339. Henry Darcy, mayor, Roger de Depham, John de Grantham, John de Oxford, John de Causton, Richard le Lacer, Roger de Horsham [sic], William de Causton, Richard de Rothyng, Walter Neel and Richard de Berkyng, aldermen.

346. William de Carleton complains that when he hired carpenters and masons to build on a plot of land in the par. of St. Peter de Wodestret, the prior of the new hospital without Bisshopesgate came on Thurs. 1 July and caused the work to be prohibited by the sheriff's serjeant. The prior comes and says that half the stone wall on the north side of his tenement belongs to him and the hospital and in it is a post supporting his timber. Because of certain ambiguities the proceedings are adjourned until the following Wed. [4 Aug.], and again until Sat. 7 Aug. because the mayor and aldermen are not yet fully advised. On that day the proceedings are adjourned until the next Husting.

Assize of Nuisance

347. Precept of the mayor and aldermen to the sheriffs dated 31 Aug. 1339, reciting the judgment in the assize brought by the master of St. Thomas of Acon against Richard de Betoygne on Fri. 30 Apr. [**343**] and the failure of the def. to execute it, and ordering them to put it into effect at his expense, and to exact from him 40s. to their own use for his contempt.

Fri. 15 Oct. 1339. Henry Darcy, mayor, John de Grantham, Roger de Depham, Richard Lacer, Andrew Aubrey, Richard de Hakeneye, William de Causton and Roger de Forsham, aldermen.

348. John de Oxford and Alice his wife complain that when they hired carpenters and other workmen to build a house upon their land in the par. of St. Lawrence in Old Jewry, William de Stratton and Margaret his wife, and William son of William de Hoghtone had the work stopped by the sheriff's serjeants. The defs. make default, although summoned by Nicholas de Reygate and John le Bokeler. The mayor and aldermen, having viewed the premises, find that the pls. have done nothing contrary to the law and custom of the City. Judgment that they complete their work without further impediment. Defs. in mercy.

[m. 52d.] *Fri. 5 Nov. 1339. Andrew Aubrey, mayor, John de Grantham, Roger de Depham, John Hamond, John de Oxford, Richard Lacer, Richard de Berkyng, William de Causton and Roger de Forsham, aldermen.*

349. Austin le Waleys of Woxebregg complains that Stephen son of Stephen de Creye, late citizen, has seven windows and a door (hostium) on the west side of his tenement overlooking the land of the pl. in the par. of St. Martin Orgar, less than 16 ft. from the ground; and that for lack of a gutter (stillicidium) 38 ft. long the water draining from his house falls upon the pl.'s land. The def. after essoin makes default. Judgment after view that he remove the impediments and repair the gutter *within 40 days etc.*

350. The same Austin complains that Christine relict of Thomas de Ware, 'stokfisshemongere', has nine windows and an aperture (foramen) on the east side of her tenement less than 16 ft. from the ground, overlooking his land in the same par.; and for lack of a gutter (stillicidii) 52½ ft long the water draining from her house falls upon his land. The def. after essoin makes default. Judgment after view that *within 40 days etc.* she block up the windows and aperture, and make a gutter 52½ ft. long.

351. The same Austin complains that William de Wetheresfeld ought to provide a gutter (stillicidii) to receive the water draining from his house, according to a deed, which he produces, made between Robert de Merton, dyer, whose estate the def. now holds, and John de Foleham, fishmonger, and Nichola his wife, predecessors of the pl., in which it appears that Robert held a vacant plot of land adjoining the house of John and Nichola on the west, and measuring in width from Robert's land on the south to a stone wall formerly belonging to Thomas Adrian on the north 2¾ ells at the upper end (in superiori parte), and at the lower $3\frac{3}{4}$ ells (in inferiori parte); and the same Robert granted to John and Nichola the free view and light from their house towards the said vacant plot, John undertaking for himself and his heirs always to leave 3 London ft. of ground between them, and to do nothing to obscure the view and light aforesaid. Further, he undertook to provide at his own cost a gutter (stillicidium) to receive the water draining towards the south from the house of John and Nichola and convey it on to his land without claiming any right in the stone wall there except room to place therein five corbels $\frac{1}{4}$ ell 5 ins. long and 6 ins. square. Witnesses:— sir Hugh fitz Otto, then constable of the Tower and warden of the City, Robert de Cornhill and Thomas de Basyng, bailiffs, John Horn, alderman, Edmund Horn, Nicholas Horn, Adam Sutel, Richard Oign', Robert Long, Robert Sutel, Nicholas de Wynton', Robert Lambyn and others [1269–70]. The def. makes default. The mayor and aldermen, having scrutinised the deed and viewed the site, adjudge that *within 40 days etc.* the def. repair the gutter.

[m. 53] *Fri. 5 Nov. 1339. Andrew Aubrey, mayor, and other aldermen.*

352. Margaret relict of John de Bourne, kt., complains that she is unable to build upon a plot of vacant land in Retheresgatelane in the par. of St. Botolph by Billyngesgate because Adam Pykeman, 'fisshemongere', has built opposite her a house $6\frac{5}{8}$ ells long, of which the timbers extend beyond the middle of the lane 14 ins. on the side of the street and 15 ins. on the side of the Thames. The def. comes, but says nothing to delay the assize. Judgment, after the premises have been viewed, that he remove the nuisance *within 40 days etc.*

353. Precept of Andrew Aubrey, mayor, to the sheriffs, 20 Jan. 1340, reciting the failure of Stephen son of Stephen de Creye to execute the judgment given against him on 5 Nov. 1339 in the assize brought by Austin le Waleys [**349**], and ordering them to put it into effect at his expense and fine him 40s. for contempt.

354. Similar precepts sent next day [21 Jan.], ordering the sheriffs to execute the judgments against Christine relict of Thomas de Ware in the assize brought by Austin le Waleys of Wexbregge [**350**]; and against William de Wetheresfeld in the assize brought by the same Austin [**351**].

[m. 53d.] *Fri. 4 Aug. 1340. Andrew Aubrey, mayor, Roger de Depham, John de Causton, Ralph de Upton, William de Causton and Roger de Forsham, aldermen.*

355. Robert de Sutton, 'lorimer', and Ralph de Blythe, saddler, essoin themselves against Thomas de Morle and Idonia his wife by John Trippelowe.

356. Adam Colman and Thomas Colman essoin themselves against the abbot of St. Albans by the same.

Assize of Nuisance

Fri. 17 Nov. 1340. Andrew Aubrey, mayor, Roger de Depham, John de Oxford, Simon Fraunceys, John Hamond, John de Causton, John de Northhall, William Pounfreyt, Richard de Rothyng, John de Refham and Richard de Berkyng, aldermen.

357. William de Fulham, 'pessoner', and Alice his wife complain that William de Braybrok has a pit (puteum) too close to their stone wall, into which the rainwater flows from the def.'s house, and slops and other filth are thrown by his household (familiares), so that their wall is penetrated and the houses and solars built thereon are in danger of ruin. The def., summoned by John de Bixle and John de Refham, makes default. Judgment after view that *within 40 days etc.* he remove the pit and repair the wall damaged by him.

358. John Gysors complains that Henry le Vannere, 'vineter', has built his house extending beyond the middle of the lane (venelle) between their tenements in the par. of St. Martin in Vintry, leading to the Thames, and that he has a gutter (guteram) from which, in rainy weather, the water flows back (redundat) on to the pl.'s tenement. The def. comes in person but says nothing to delay the assize. The mayor and aldermen view the premises and find by oath of the carpenters and masons sworn to the assize that the def.'s house is an inch or more short of the middle of the kennel (canelli) in the lane; but that the water from his gutter falls upon the pl.'s tenement as alleged. Judgment that the pl. be in mercy for a false plaint on the first count; but that *within 40 days etc.* the def. remove or repair the gutter so that it does no further damage to the pl.'s tenement.

[m. 54] *Fri. 1 Dec. 1340. Andrew Aubrey, mayor, Henry Darcy, Roger de Depham, John Hamond, John de Causton, Simon Fraunceys, John de Refham and Richard de Berkyng, aldermen.*

359. John de Hardyngham, clerk, complains that John de London, tanner, and Joan his wife have three windows newly made in the wall of their solar, opposite his chamber and kitchen, and below the height of 16 ft. from the ground, through which they and their household (familiares) can see his private business (secreta). The defs. make default. Judgment after view that *within 40 days etc.* they block up the windows in question.

Fri. 15 June 1341. Andrew Aubrey, mayor, John de Grantham, Henry Darcy, Roger de Depham, Simon Fraunceys, John de Mockyng and Richard Costantyn, aldermen.

360. The abbot of Sautre complains by Thomas de Ware, his attorney, that when he sought to rebuild a ruinous wall adjoining the tenement of Walter de Cheryngton in the par. of St. Nicholas Olof, Walter had the work prohibited by the sheriff's serjeants (servientes). The def. comes in person but says nothing in contradiction of the pl.'s allegations. Judgment that the abbot repair his wall at will. Def. in mercy.

Fri. 13 July 1341. Andrew Aubrey, mayor, Henry Darcy, Roger de Depham,

Assize of Nuisance

John Hamond, William de Causton, Richard Costantyn and Richard de Berkyng, aldermen.

361. The commonalty complain by William de Iford, common serjeant, that the stone wall of William de Cave's house fronting the street on the west side in the par. of St. Antonin is ruinous and on the point of collapse. The def., summoned by William de Henhampsted and Thomas de Ware, makes default. Judgment after view that *within 40 days etc.* he demolish the wall or rebuild it.

362. Isabel relict of John Luter complains that John Trappe, 'skynnere', who has a tenement adjoining her garden in the par. of St. John de Walbrok, has four windows of which the glass is broken, through which he and his servants can see into her garden. The def., summoned by William de Lychebergh and Walter Page, makes default. Judgment after view that he repair the windows *within 40 days etc.*

363. [m. 54d.] The same Isabel complains that John de Thorp, 'skynnere', has seven windows overlooking her adjoining tenement in the par. of St. Stephen de Walbrok, less than 16 ft. from the ground, through which he and his servants can see into the pl.'s tenement. The def., summoned by the same William and Walter makes default. Judgment after view that *within 40 days etc.* he block up the apertures complained of.

364. The same Isabel complains that Henry de Ware has a window and four apertures (foramina) overlooking her adjoining tenement in the par. of St. Antonin, through which the stench from his cess-pit penetrates her tenement. The def., summoned by the same William and Walter, makes default. Judgment after view that he remove the nuisance *within 40 days etc.*

365. The same Isabel complains that John le Leche, fishmonger, has a leaden watch-tower (garritam) upon the wall of his tenement adjoining hers in the same par. upon which he and his household (familiares) stand daily, watching the private affairs of the pl. and her servants. The def., present upon the land before the mayor and aldermen, admits the nuisance, and freely undertakes to remove it within 40 days subject to the customary penalty.

366. The same Isabel complains that Joan relict of Simon Corp has twelve apertures (foramina) overlooking her adjoining tenement in the same par. through which she and her servants can see the private business of the pl. and her servants. The def., summoned by William de Lychebergh and Walter Page, makes default. Judgment after view that she block up the apertures complained of *within 40 days etc.*

367. Precept of the mayor to the sheriffs, Fri. 7 Dec. 1341, ordering them to put in execution the judgment in the assize brought by the above Isabel against John de Thorp [363], and to levy from him 40s. for his contempt.

Assize of Nuisance

368. A like precept for the enforcement of the judgment in the assize brought by the same Isabel against Joan relict of Simon Corp [**366**].

369. The commonalty complain by William de Iford, common serjeant, that the abbot of Redyngges, the prior of the new hospital of St. Mary without Bisshopesgate and William de Causton have neglected to repair the pavement outside their tenements in the par. of St. Benet atte Wodewharf and St. Andrew Castle Baynard, in accordance with the City ordinance; with the result that it is broken and worn down (concavium) and crushed (quassatum) to the danger of both pedestrians and horsemen. The defs. come, but say nothing to delay the assize. Judgment after view that *within 40 days etc.* each of them repair the pavement outside his own tenement.

370. [m. 55] Geoffrey Aleyn and Maud his wife complain that whereas they and their predecessors in their tenement in the par. of St. Stephen de Walebrok have always enjoyed the light and view from their windows and open apertures (foramina) from the foundations to the roof (summitatem), William de Stansfeld, parson of St. Stephen's, William de Hacford and Adam son of Adam de Bury have recently obscured them; and that the same William, William and Adam have two open windows in their tenement, adjoining that of the pls. through which they and their household (familia) have access to the pls.' leaden gutter (guterum plumbeum), breaking it and the tiles of their house, and throwing into it sewage and other refuse which is thus carried through the midst of the pls.' tenement. Further, they say that they have a gutter (guterum) 26 ft. long on the south side of their house into which the water from the defs.' tenement flows; and for lack of a fillet-gutter (filettum) through which the defs. ought to convey the water from their tenement on to their own land or into the street, it falls upon the pls.' land; and, similarly, on the north side of their house is a gutter (guterum) into which the defs.' water flows. The defs. after essoin make default. The mayor and aldermen ask the pls. whether, as regards the first of the alleged nuisances, they can produce any evidence of their right to the light and view through the defs.' tenement. They proffer an indenture in which Walter de Reyglegh, tawyer (allutarius) and Agatha la Rous, whose estate they now enjoy, undertake never to build upon a vacant plot of land lying between the kitchen of William de Hanyton and the stone house of Hamo de Wyndon and Joan his wife, whose estate the defs. now hold; and Hamo and Joan, for their part undertake line for line, to do nothing to impede the light and view of Walter and Agatha. They add that Hamo outlived his wife. It is adjudged that within 40 days the defs. remove the impediment to the pls.' light, and repair their windows with iron or wooden bars; and that they convey the water draining into the gutters on the north and south sides of the pls.' house on to their own land, and make a fillet-gutter (filettum) to receive their own water and convey it on to their land or into the street.

Precept of Simon Fraunceys, mayor, Mon. 13 May 1342, to Richard de Berkyngg, sheriff, to put in execution the judgment against the above William, William and Adam, and levy from them 40s. for their contempt.

Assize of Nuisance

[m. 55d.] *Fri. 30 Nov. 1341. John de Oxford, mayor, Roger de Depham, Ralph de Upton, William de Causton, Richard de Berkyngg, William de Pounfreit, Nicholas Crane and Walter Neel, aldermen.*

371. William de Stanesfeld, parson of St. Stephen de Walbrok, and William de Hacford complain that Geoffrey Aleyn and Maud his wife have two newly-made windows less than 16 ft. from the ground opposite their rent (redditum) in the par. of St. Stephen through which their tenants can see all the private affairs of the pls.' tenants and servants; and that for default of a gutter (guteri) 24 ft. long on the east side of their house, and others respectively 16 ft. and 32 ft. long, their rainwater falls upon the pls.' land; and, further, that they have two latrines (latrinas) so closely adjoining the pls.' tenement that the sewage penetrates and rots their timber and party-walls. Geoffrey comes in person, and Maud by John de Maneweden, her attorney. As far as the latrines and gutters are concerned they offer no defence, but as concerns the two windows they say that the assize does not lie, because in the plea of assize held on Fri. 13 July last [**370**] the defs. produced an indenture in which each of the parties guaranteed to the other, line for line, the light and view of their respective tenements. Having inspected the record of the plea and viewed the premises, the mayor and aldermen adjudge that, as far as concerns the two windows, the pls. take nothing for their plaint, but be in mercy, and the defs. *sine die*; but that *within 40 days etc.* the defs. build a stone wall 2½ ft. thick or an earthen wall 3½ ft. thick between their two latrines and the pls.' tenement, and repair the three gutters.

372. [m. 56] Adam Brabazon, fishmonger, complains that for lack of a gutter (stillicidii) 80 ft. long which Simon le Ussher and Isabel his wife ought to provide in their tenement adjoining his in the par. of St. Augustine[1] in Bredstrete ward, their water falls upon his land, which is flooded in rainy weather; and that they have five windows and six apertures less than 16 ft. from the ground through which they and their servants can see the private business of the pl. and his servants. The defs. come in person, but say nothing to delay the assize. Judgment that *within 40 days etc.* they repair the gutter, and block up the windows and apertures.

Fri. 8 Feb. 1342. John de Oxford, mayor, and the aldermen.

373. William de Causton, senior, mercer, def., essoins himself against Alice daughter of Roger Hosebonde by Adam de Heyworth. All [the parties in **373–4** and **376**] were given a day at the quindene, but the mayor and aldermen could not take the assizes then, because they were summoned to the king at Westminster. Before they left, the pleas were adjourned to the octave.

Fri. 1 Mar. 1342. John de Oxford, mayor, Andrew Aubrey, John Hamond, Roger de Depham, John de Causton, Richard de Hakeneye, William de Thorneye and John de Refham, aldermen.

1. The church is in the ward of Farringdon Within.

Assize of Nuisance

374. Geoffrey Alleyn and Maud his wife, pls., in mercy because they did not prosecute their plaint against William de Stansfeld, parson of St. Stephen de Walebrok, William de Hacford and Adam son of Adam de Bury, defs., who are *sine die*.

375. The commonalty complain by William de Iford, common serjeant, that whereas the rainwater flowing down from the fields behind the hospital of St. Mary without Bisshopesgate used to run thence towards the marsh called la More through a ditch (fossatum) leading through the midst of the royal highway Bisshopesgate in the par. of St. Botolph to the tenement of John de Aulton and Katherine his wife, they and their tenants have obstructed the ditch between the bridge upon the causeway in the high road there (inter pontem super calciam in alto vico ibidem) and their tenement, and impeded the flow of water. The defs. come in person. They deny the charge and put themselves upon their country, and William de Iford likewise. On Thurs. 7 Mar. the jury comes, but because the mayor and aldermen are unable to be present owing to business concerning the City, the proceedings are adjourned until Fri. 22 Mar. On that day the jury and the parties come upon the land in the presence of the mayor and aldermen. The jurors, viz. Godfrey atte Swan, Geoffrey Seriaunt, John le Verneye, Thomas le Barber, Peter de Hakeneye, John de Waltham, Hugh le Skynnere, John Heryng, John le Brewere, William le Bakere, Gilbert le Dyghere and Geoffrey Lythfot say upon oath that the ditch has been obstructed by the defs. and their tenants, adding that the bishops of London for the time being have been accustomed to pay to the tenants of the tenement in question each year at Christmas, for the watercourse running through the midst of their tenements, a half quarter of wheat. Judgment that within 40 days the defs. remove the obstruction from the ditch, under the customary penalty, on the understanding that they may sue the bishop of London for the half quarter of wheat and arrears if they so desire.

376. [m. 56d.] John de Pulteneye, 'chivaler', complains that the water flowing from the adjoining tenement of John de Aulton and Katherine his wife in the par. of St. Botolph without Bisshopesgate falls in rainy weather upon his land for a distance of $3\frac{1}{2}$ perches (perticarum). The defs. come and ask for time to produce their muniments, which are not in the City. On Fri. 15 Mar. the pl. comes by his attorney John de Maneweden, and the defs. likewise appear, but asked by the mayor, John de Oxford, and the recorder, Roger de Depham, to produce their evidence, they can show nothing. For lack of aldermen, the proceedings are adjourned until Fri. 22 Mar., when the parties appear at Guildhall before the mayor, John de Oxford, Roger de Depham, John de Causton, Simon Fraunceys, William de Pontefract and William de Thorneye, aldermen, and the process of the plaint having been recited, it is adjudged that the defs., *within 40 days etc.*, convey their water on to their own land or into the street.

Fri. 25 [*rectius 26*] *April 1342. John de Oxford, mayor, Roger de Depham, John Hamound, Richard de Berkyngg, William de Thorneye, Walter Neel, William de Pountfreyt.*

Assize of Nuisance

377. Nicholas Pyke complains that for lack of a gutter (stillicidii) 200 ft. long the rainwater from the tenement of William de Meldebourne, 'chivaler', and Margery his wife falls upon his adjoining land in the par. of St. Matthew de Fridaystrete; and the defs. have a stone wall 200 ft. long which overhangs the pl.'s land by 1½ ft. so that he cannot build; and further they have two windows overlooking the pl.'s tenement, less than 16 ft. from the ground, through which they and their servants can see the private affairs of the pl.'s tenants. The defs., summoned by John le Mazerer and John de Bentle, make default. After viewing the premises the mayor and aldermen adjudge that the defs. remove the nuisances complained of *within 40 days etc.*

378. Stephen le Mazerer complains that for lack of a gutter 100 ft. long, the rainwater from the tenement of John Gratefige and Thomas his brother falls upon his adjoining tenement in the par. of St. Olave de Colmanstrete; and that the same John and Thomas have a wall [measurements omitted] which overhangs his land by ½ ft. so that he cannot build; and, further, that they have five windows facing his tenement, less than 16 ft. from the ground, through which they and their servants can see the private business of the pl. and his servants. The defs. after essoin make default. Judgment after view that *within 40 days etc.* the defs. remove the nuisances complained of.

[m. 57] *Fri. 28 June 1342. Simon Fraunceys, mayor, William de Causton, Roger de Depham, John de Causton, John de Mockyngg, Richard de Hakeneye, Richard de Berkyngg, Richard Costantyn and John de Refham.*

379. William de Pontefract complains that John atte Pole has five windows, a door and two apertures (foramina) overlooking his tenement in the par. of St. Mary de Wolcherchehawe; and that the water from his house falls, for lack of a gutter (stillicidii) 40 ft. long, upon the pl.'s land; and that his stone wall 14 ft. long overhangs the pl.'s land by 1 ft. The def., summoned by Henry atte Shawe, 'armurer', and Richard de Lyncoln, makes default. Judgment after view that he block up the windows, door and apertures, and repair the gutter and wall *within 40 days etc.*

Fri. 30 Aug. 1342. Simon Fraunceys, mayor, Andrew Aubreye, Roger de Depham, William de Causton, John de Causton, John Hamond, John de Refham and John de Eynesham, aldermen.

380. Edmund de Grymmesby, clerk, complains that John Elys, 'peleter', and Joan his wife have on their land adjoining his in the par. of St. Dunstan West, a ruinous earthen wall 81 ft. long, which is so low that their servants can see over it and watch the private business of the pl.; and that their cesspit is too near his tenement. The defs., summoned by John le Vannere and Thomas de Ware, make default. Judgment after view that *within 40 days etc.* they repair the wall and raise it to a height of 16 ft., and remove the cess-pit 2½ ft. from the pl.'s land if walled in stone, and 3½ ft. if walled in earth.

Assize of Nuisance

Fri. 19 Sep. 1343. Simon Fraunceys, mayor, Roger de Depham, John de Causton, Richard Lacer, William de Causton, Richard de Berkyng and William de Pontefract.

381. Hugh de Brandon, goldsmith, complains that when he sought to rebuild the parcel of a messuage adjoining the tenement of Rose de Farndon in the par. of St. Vedast in Goderomlane, she had the work prohibited by the sheriff. Rose comes and says that the parcel of a messuage in question is a purpresture (purprisa) made upon Goderomlane, and that Hugh has obscured the light to which, according to the custom of the City, she is entitled as the occupant of a tenement abutting on a street or lane, and which she and her predecessors have enjoyed time out of mind. Hugh claims that the land in dispute formerly belonged to Walter Gatewyk, built and enclosed as at present, and that he demised it to Robert de Piphurst, who was succeeded in it by Robert his son and heir, who enfeoffed the pl., and that he sought to rebuild it because it was ruinous. Rose declares that, in the time of Walter, Robert and Robert's son the land was not built upon, but that the light was reserved to her by reason of the lane, as aforesaid. She puts herself upon her country, and the pl. likewise. On Fri. 26 Sep. the parties appear at Guildhall, and the jury comes by Adam Walpol, John de Hynxston, Thomas de Porkele, Alan atte Conduyt, John de Chaumpayne, John de Ideshale, John de Crikkele, Gilbert de (—), Thomas Walisshman, Robert de Herlawe, Robert de Northampton and Richard de (—), who say upon oath that the parcel of land has always, from the time of Walter Gatewyk, been built upon, without reservation of the light to the def. Judgment that the pl. continue his building and that the def. be in mercy.[1]

[m. 57d.] *Fri. 19 Mar. 1344. John Hamond, mayor, Simon Fraunceys, Roger de Depham, Richard Lacer, William Pountfreyt, Richard de Berkyngg and William de Thorneye.*

382. The commonalty complain by William de Iford that David de Kynggeston has narrowed the course of the Walebrok in the par. of St. Margaret de Lothbury by 3 ft. and has built sties for pigs and other animals above the watercourse to the damage of the whole City. The def. comes, but says nothing to delay the assize. Judgment after view that *within 40 days etc.* he remove the nuisance.

383. The commonalty complain by the same William that John de Besseville has narrowed the course of the Walebrok in the same par. by 3 ft. for the whole length of his tenement and has built pig-sties and privies above the watercourse and affixed piles (pilas) in the stream to support them to the damage of the whole City. The def. comes but says nothing to delay the assize. Judgment after view that *within 40 days etc.* he remove the nuisances.

Fri. 26 Mar. 1344. John Hamond, mayor, Roger de Depham, William de Causton, John de Causton, Richard Lacer, Walter Neel, Walter Turk and William de Thorney, aldermen.

1. The foot of this membrane is damaged.

Assize of Nuisance

384. John de Risle and Maud his wife complain that the cess-pit of the privy of Ralph de Ikelyngham called Cressoner and Agnes his wife adjoins too closely their tenement in the par. of St. Margaret Moisi de Fridaistrete, so that the sewage penetrates their wall and defiles their whole premises; and that they have pierced the stone wall on the east side of their tenement and erected a post there as a result of which their tenement is gravely weakened. The defs. come in person but say nothing to delay the assize. Judgment after view that *within 40 days etc.* they build a stone wall $2\frac{1}{2}$ ft. thick or an earthen wall $3\frac{1}{2}$ ft. thick between their latrine and the pls.' tenement, and remove the post they have placed in their wall.

[m. 58] *Fri. 23 July 1344. John Hamond, mayor, Roger de Depham, William de Brykelesworth.*

385. John de Tiffeld, John Sprot, Matthew le Barber and John de Drayton, parishioners of All Hallows de Bredestrete, complain that when, as wardens (custodes) of a tenement in the par. of St. Peter de Wodestrete devised by Faukes de Wakefeld, late citizen and tanner, for the maintenance of the chantry which he founded in the church of All Hallows, they sought to undertake repairs and to place their timber upon half the wall, 11 ft. long, between the same tenement and that of John de Beverly (Beverlaco), John claimed the whole wall as his own. John de Aylesham and John Syward, sheriffs, testify that the def. was summoned by John de Kynggeston and John Makenheued but he makes default. After viewing the premises, the mayor and aldermen adjudge that each of the parties owns half the wall, and that the four wardens may therefore continue to build as they have begun. Def. in mercy.

Fri. 3 Sep. 1344. [Assize adjourned for delivery of Newgate gaol.]

Fri. 24 Sep. 1344. John Hamond, mayor, Roger de Depham, William de Causton, Richard Lacer, Walter Turk, Richard de Rothyng, John de Causton, William de Pomfreyt and John de Aylesham, aldermen.

386. John, prior of the Friars Preachers, complains that, for lack of a gutter (stillicidii) 33 ells long which Richard, prior of Okebourn, ought to provide to carry off the rainwater from his houses and buildings in the par. of St. Andrew Castle Baynard, adjoining those of the pl., it falls upon his land and rots his timber. The def. comes in person and says that his house is an alien priory, and that the temporalities are in the king's hand by reason of the war with France, and he produces as evidence letters patent under the great seal.[1] The mayor and aldermen, wishing to be more fully advised, give the parties a day at Guildhall on Fri. 1 Oct. to hear judgment. On that day the parties come, and the def. asks and is allowed the king's aid. The pl. is recommended to sue before the king if he judges it expedient. Plaint adjourned *sine die*. [m. 58d. Blank.]

[m. 59] *Fri. 14 May 1344. John Hamond, mayor, Roger de Depham, John*

1. *C.P.R. 1334–8*, 483.

Assize of Nuisance

de Causton, Richard Lacer, Walter Turk, John de Northalle, William de Pountfreit and Bartholomew Deumars, aldermen.

387. The commonalty complain by William de Iford that Hugh de Croydon has encroached and built upon the commonalty's soil (de solo communitatis) next the City Wall within Neugate to a length of 16 ft. and to the width of his tenement, and has narrowed the wall by removing stones from it. Hugh appears and says nothing to disprove the first charge, but denies the second, and puts himself upon his country. The mayor and aldermen, after viewing the site, adjudge that he remove the building upon the soil of the City *within 40 days etc.* As regards the second charge, a jury of the venue of Neugate is summoned for the octave.

Fri. 23 Apr. 1344. John Hamond, mayor, Roger de Depham, William de Causton, John de Causton, Richard Lacer, Walter Turk, William de Thorney and William de Pontefract, aldermen.

388. John, prior of the Friars Preachers, complains that Richard, prior of Okebourn, has a stone wall 52 ft. long and 20 ft. high adjoining his land and overhanging it by 1 ft. 3 ins. so that he cannot build.[1] The def. comes but says nothing to delay the assize. The wall is measured by plumb-line (cum perpendiculo) by the masons and carpenters sworn to the assize, from the foundation to the top (summitate), and the allegation of the pl. is found to be correct. Judgment that the def. remove the nuisance *within 40 days etc.*

Fri. 22 July 1345. John Hamond, mayor, Roger de Depham, William de Causton, John de Causton, William de Pountefreyt, Richard de Berkyng and John de Aylesham, aldermen.

389. Benedict de Fulsham and Maud his wife essoin themselves by John de Salesbury against William de Causton, senior, mercer. A day is given the parties at the quindene [5 Aug.], when Benedict and Maud ask for a respite to enable them to produce their muniments, which are not in the City. They are given a day on Fri. 19 Aug. Further adjournments follow, with the consent of the parties, until Fri. 3 Feb. 1346. The parties come on Fri. 10 Mar., but the proceedings are again adjourned because of important business concerning the City. [For love day see below under 19 Aug. 1345.]

390. The commonalty complain by William de Iford that the stone wall of Walter de Eure's house facing the street on the south side in the par. of St. Bartholomew the Less is ruinous and on the point of collapse. Walter, summoned by Ralph and William de Cauntebrigge, makes default. Judgment after view that *within 40 days etc.* he demolish the wall and rebuild it if it seems to him expedient. [The note follows: Quere aliud placitum ad eundem diem inter communitatem et eundem Walterum in dorso ipsius Rotuli . . . **(394)**.]

1. *C.P.M.R. 1323–64*, 209; the prior of Ogbourne is incorrectly calendared as John (Roll A5, m. 22d).

Assize of Nuisance

Precept of Richard Lacer, mayor, to Edmund de Hemenhale and John de Gloucestre, sheriffs, dated Thurs. 16 Feb. 1346, ordering them to put in execution the above judgment. [The note follows: Quia vicecomites nichil fecerunt similis billa missa fuit eisdem vicecomitibus sicut alias die martis proximo ante festum Parasceve (11 Apr.).]

[m. 59d.] *Fri. 5 Aug. 1345. John Hamond, mayor, Roger de Depham, Andrew Aubrey, William de Causton, John de Causton, William de Pountefreyt, Richard de Berkyng and John de Aylesham, aldermen.*

391. Adam de St. Albans brings an assize against William de Hodesdon, 'pessoner', who asks for a respite to enable him to produce his muniments. The parties are given a day at the quindene. Afterwards, with the licence of the mayor and aldermen, they come to an agreement.

Fri. 19 Aug. 1345. John Hamond, mayor, Andrew Aubrey, Roger de Depham, William de Causton, John de Causton, William de Pountefreit, John de Aylesham, Richard de Berkyng, aldermen.

Love day given to the parties [**389**], pending an assize of novel disseisin.

Fri. 26 Aug. 1345. John Hamond, mayor, Roger de Depham, William de Pountefreit, William de Thorneye, John Rokele, Richard de Berkyng and Thomas Leggy, aldermen.

392. Elizabeth de Montacute complains that Master Gilbert de la Brewere, dean of St. Paul's, has begun to build a wharf (kaium) in the Thames to enlarge and improve his property, and has affixed his piles (pilas) opposite her wall, which adjoins his tenement in the par. of St. Benet atte Wodewharf and extends from the river to Thamisestrete, as if claiming half of it as his. The def. comes by Thomas de Ware, his attorney, but says nothing to delay the assize. After viewing the premises the mayor and aldermen find that 18 ft. of the wall is common to the parties, but the rest belongs entirely to the def. It is therefore adjudged that he continue building his wharf as already begun. Pl. in mercy.

Fri. 9 Sep. 1345. John Hamond, mayor, Roger de Depham, Andrew Aubrey, William de Causton, John de Causton, William de Pounfreyt, Richard de Berkyng and John de Aylesham, aldermen.

393. Alice relict of Gregory de Norton complains that the abbot of Stratford has encroached upon her adjoining land in the par. of St. Mary Wolnoth by $2\frac{1}{2}$ St. Paul's ft., so that she cannot repair her stone wall, $22\frac{1}{4}$ St. Paul's ft. long, which is ruinous, or build upon her land. The def. comes by Thomas de Ware, his attorney, but says nothing to delay the assize. The mayor and aldermen find that the pl.'s allegations are correct. Judgment that the def. remove the nuisance *within 40 days etc.*

394. The commonalty complains by William de Iford that Walter de Eure has a vacant plot of land in the par. of St. Bartholomew the Less which is unfenced, so that malefactors and disturbers of the king's peace and robbers lurk there by night and waylay passers-by, attacking, beating and wounding them and stealing their goods. The def., summoned by Ralph and William de Cauntebrigge, makes default. Judgment after view that *within 40 days etc.* he fence the plot of land. [See also **398**; cf. **390**.]

[m. 60] *Fri. 10 Feb. 1346. Richard Lacer, mayor, Roger de Depham, John Hamond, John de Causton, John de Mockyng, John de Northall and Bartholomew Deumars, aldermen.*

395. Hugh le Blount, kt., complains by Thomas de Ware, his attorney, that in rainy weather the water from the tenement of Simon de Wenlok falls upon his adjoining buildings and walls in the par. of St. Mildred the Virgin in Poultry, so that their upper part (in summitate) is rotted; and that the def. and his tenants draw water from his well (fonte), and the water overflowing therefrom, and the sewage and other refuse which they throw outside his tenement rot the foundations of his walls (in profunditate et loco subterraneo). Simon comes in person but says nothing to delay the assize. On viewing the premises the mayor and aldermen find that the pl.'s allegations are correct. Judgment that the def. remove the nuisances *within 40 days etc.*

Fri. 3 Feb. 1346. Richard Lacer, mayor, Henry Darcy, Andrew Aubrey, Simon Fraunceys, John Hamond, Roger de Depham, Walter Turk, William de Causton, John de Causton, John Syward, Thomas Leggy, William de Poumfreyt, Bartholomew Deumars and Richard de Rothyng, aldermen.

396. The commonalty complain by William de Iford that whereas Fisshyngwharf lane leading to the Thames in the par. of St. Mary de Somersete used to be common to all citizens conveying their goods and merchandise to and from the river by horse and cart, William Trig has obstructed it with wooden stalls (trunci), wood and other things so that there is no longer access by it to the Thames. William comes and allows that the lane was formerly common, and declares that it still is, and that he has not obstructed it as alleged; but he says that it is, and always has been, too narrow to be used by carts, which cannot turn in it, and he puts himself upon his country. On Fri. 3 Mar. the parties come and the jury by Stephen de Staneford, Walter le Chaundler, Thomas de Bury, 'cordewaner', Richard le Chaundeler, Thomas Scot, Simon de Turnham, John Tornegold, Hugh le Chaundeler, Ralph de Lenne, John Charryng, Lawrence Albyn and John Lombard, who find for the def. Judgment that William de Iford take nothing for his plaint. William Trig *sine die*.

Fri. 10 Feb. 1346. [Mayor and the aldermen as on 10 Feb. above.]

397. Alice relict of Gregory de Norton complains that the abbot of Stratford has appropriated for building half her stone wall, 6½ ells long, in the par. of St. Mary de Wolnoth. The abbot comes by John de Salisbury

(Sar'), his attorney, and says that the wall is common to him and the pl., and that he was therefore entitled to place his timber upon it. After inspecting the premises, the mayor and aldermen find that the def.'s claim is correct, and it is therefore adjudged that he continue building upon his half of the wall. Pl. in mercy.

398. Precept *sicut alias* of the mayor to the sheriffs, dated at Guildhall Mon. 23 Oct. 1346, ordering them to put in execution the judgment given against Walter de Eure on 9 Sep. 1345 [**394**], or to show cause why they have not done so.

Fri. 15 Dec. 1346. Geoffrey de Wichyngham, mayor, Andrew Aubrey, Reginald de Conduit, Simon Fraunceys, John Hamond, Roger de Depham, John de Causton, William de Causton, Adam Brabazon, Richard de Berkyngg and Richard de Keselyngbury, aldermen.

399. The prior of St. Bartholomew Smethefeld comes in person and complains that John Wroth and Juliana his wife and Thomas son of Bartholomew de Honilane have three doors in their tenement adjoining the property of his church in the par. of All Hallows de Honilane, through which they and their tenants come and go across his land; and they have ten windows less than 16 ft. from the ground, through which they and their tenants can see the private business of his tenants; and in rainy weather the water from their tenement falls upon his premises; [m. 60d.] and they have a jetty (geticium) 38 ft. long and 2½ ft. wide above his land. John and Thomas come by Simon de Kelshull, their attorney, and Juliana in person, and they ask for a respite to enable them to produce their muniments. They are given a day at the quindene [29 Dec.], but are adjourned until Fri. 12 Jan. 1347 at Guildhall, when John Wroth comes in person and Juliana and Thomas by Alan de Gylingham and Simon de Kelshull, their attorneys. Thomas says that he is the tenant of the tenement concerning which the nuisances are alleged, and that from time out of mind he and his predecessors have enjoyed the easement of the doors and windows opening on to the pl.'s land. The pl. contends that John and Juliana are the real tenants, and that Thomas was named in the plaint only as coadjutor. John and Juliana then allege that John de Douegate was formerly seised of the tenement which they now hold, together with half the lane (venelle) between his wall and the prior's houses, and the right of entry and exit by the other half; and that in the reign of Edward I the same John, in his will proved and enrolled in the Husting,[1] devised the tenement and half the lane with the accompanying easement to his daughter Joan and the heirs of her body. The prior declares that neither the defs. nor their predecessors have ever enjoyed, save by his goodwill, any right in the lane, which, as he is prepared to prove, is his sole property in right of his church. After further adjournments the parties come on Fri. 9 Feb. 1347, but because it appears to the court that the custom of the City does not permit of the reference to a jury of the point at issue, the parties are adjudged *sine die*.

1. *Cal. Wills*, i, 155.

Assize of Nuisance

Fri. 14 Dec. 1347 [rectius 15 Dec. 1346]. Mayor and the aldermen as above.

400. Hugh Blount, kt., complains that Thomas de Nottele, parson of St. Mildred the Virgin in Poultry, John de Mimmes, William atte Felde, William Braye, 'peleter', Thomas Canon, 'heumer', and John Scot, 'polter', have caused his building operations on his land adjoining that of the church to be prohibited. The defs. come and ask for time to produce their muniments. On Fri. 12 Jan. 1347 both parties come, but the defs. produce no written evidence. Instead they allege that the plot of land on which the pl. claims to build, and which lies between the church on the west and the tenement of Richard Thurgod and Katherine his wife on the east, and between the street on the south and the pl.'s tenement on the north, is common to the pl. and his tenants on the one hand, and the parson of the church for the time being and his parishioners on the other, and that the latter have always possessed the right of free entry and exit and a right of way (cheminum suum) through it at all times, as well on ferial as on festival days, so that they were fully entitled to put a stop to the pl.'s building operations. Hugh says that the plot of land is solely his, and that the defs.' plea ought not to be admitted because they have not produced the written evidence for which they were granted a respite. The proceedings are adjourned to the quindene so that the mayor and aldermen may be more fully advised. On Fri. 9 Feb. the parties come, but because the court is unable to determine the case either by view or from the pleading, they are adjudged *sine die* and the defence is annulled, with a recommendation that they seek a remedy by another process of law if it seems to them expedient.

[m. 61] *Fri. 31 Aug. 1347. Geoffrey de Wychingham, mayor, Reginald de Conduit, Roger de Depham, John de Northalle, Thomas Leggy, Walter de Mordon, John de Croydon and John de Causton.*

401. Katherine and Agnes, daughters of John de Hales, complain that William de Kelseye, clerk, claims as his own a lane (venella) leading to the Thames between their tenements in the par. of St. Andrew Castle Baynard, which has hitherto been common between them, and has closed it with a bar and a lock and key. William de Iford, on behalf of the commonalty, alleges that the lane is common to the whole community as well as to the parties. The mayor and aldermen order a jury of eighteen of the venue of St. Andrew Castle Baynard, to appear at Guildhall at the quindene to determine the matter.

402. Similar plea between Walter son of Thomas le Ko, pl., and the same William de Kelseye, clerk.

403. John le Yonge complains that Henry le Yonge and John Conyng have a solar above his cellar in the par. of St. Mary de Abbechirche, and the pipe of their latrine is in the same cellar and overflows into it. The defs., summoned by John le Neve and Thomas le Blake, make default. The mayor and aldermen, having viewed the premises, find the nuisance to be as

Assize of Nuisance

alleged. John is given a day on the following Wed. [5 Sep.] to hear judgment, but the defs. do not come. The process having been recited it is adjudged that *within 40 days etc.* they remove the nuisance.

404. Robert le Ro, 'sporier', complains that Alan Gille, warden of London Bridge, has prohibited him from building upon his stone wall 52 ft. long and 2½ ft. wide, adjoining his land in the par. of St. Mary atte Hulle. Alan comes and claims the wall as his. The parties are given a day at the quindene [14 Sep.] at Guildhall to hear judgment. The mayor and aldermen, on viewing the wall, find that 4 ells towards the south are common to the parties, and 13 ells towards the north belong solely to the def. Judgment accordingly, on Fri. 5 Oct.

Fri. 12 Oct. 1347. Geoffrey de Wychyngham, mayor, Richard Lacer, Roger de Depham, William de Pontefract, Adam Brabazon and William de Causton, aldermen.

405. Henry de Causton, mercer, complains that Simon de Bronnesford, spicer, has prohibited him from building on his stone wall, 30 ft. long, adjoining the tenement of the def. Simon comes but says nothing to delay the assize. The mayor and aldermen find that the wall stands wholly on the pl.'s land, and it is accordingly adjudged that he proceed with his building. Def. in mercy.

Fri. 18 Jan. 1348. Thomas Leggy, mayor, Simon Fraunceys, Richard Lacer, Geoffrey de Wychingham, Roger de Depham and John de Causton.

406. Alan Gille complains that Robert le Roo, 'sporiere', has a latrine too closely adjoining the stone wall, 4 ells long and 2 ft. wide, and common to both their tenements in the par. of St. Mary atte Hull, and that the sewage therefrom penetrates his tenement; and that the def. has another stone wall 18 ft. long and 10 ft. high between the pl.'s hall and kitchen, from which in rainy weather the water falls upon his land. The nuisances are found by view to be as alleged. Judgment that *within 40 days etc.* the def. remove the latrine 2½ ft. from the pl.'s wall, and convey the water from the other wall on to his own land or into the street.

[m. 61d.] *Fri. 29 Feb. 1348. Thomas Leggy, mayor, Roger de Depham, Adam Brabazon and Richard de Basyngstok, aldermen.*

407. Simon de Worthstede complains that Robert Bisshop and Roger Madour have six windows and two apertures in their tenement adjoining his in the par. of St. Alban de Wodestrete through which they can see his private business; and his tenants throw sewage and other refuse through the apertures on to his land. The defs. are summoned by Robert de Sutton, 'lorimer', and John de Totenham, 'chaundeler'. Robert makes default. Roger comes but says nothing to delay the assize. The site is viewed but the parties are given a day at Guildhall on Wed. 5 Mar. for lack of aldermen. On that day, there being assembled (congregati sunt) Thomas Leggy,

Assize of Nuisance

mayor, Andrew Aubrey, Richard Lacer, Geoffrey de Wychingham, Roger de Depham, William de Causton, John de Causton, Walter Turk, John Syward, Adam Brabazon and Richard de Basyngstoke, aldermen, Simon and Roger come, and the record and process of the plea having been read, it is adjudged that the nuisance be removed *within 40 days etc.* [See also **409**.]

408. The commonalty complain by William de Iford that Richard de Rittlyng has a house 36 ft. long and 36 ft. wide fronting the street in the par. of St. Sepulchre in Holbourne, which is ruinous and overhanging the street. The def., summoned by John de Blacwell and Peter atte Rededor, makes default. After the premises have been viewed, the assize is adjourned as above, for lack of aldermen, until the Wed. following [5 Mar.], when, there being assembled (congregati sunt) Thomas Leggy, mayor, and [the same aldermen as in **407**], William comes, and the record and process of the plea having been recited, it is adjudged that the house be demolished *within 40 days etc.*

409. Precept [undated] ordering the sheriffs to put in execution the judgment against Robert Bisshop and Roger Madour [**407**].

Fri. 29 Feb. 1348. Continued.

410. Hugh de Huntyngdon complains by Thomas de Ware, his attorney, that in rainy weather the water from the tenement of the abbess of Burnham adjoining his in the par. of St. Andrew Castle Baynard, falls upon his land for the length of 33 ft., and that she has four windows less than 16 ft. from the ground through which her tenants can see the private business of his tenants. The def. after essoin makes default. After the premises have been viewed, the proceedings are adjourned, as above, for lack of aldermen until Wed. 27 Feb. [*rectius* 5 Mar.], when there being assembled at Guildhall Thomas Leggy, mayor, and [the same aldermen as in **407**], Hugh comes by his attorney, and the record and process of the plea having been recited, it is adjudged that *within 40 days etc.* the abbess convey her water on to her own land or into the street, and block up the windows complained of.

Fri. 9 May 1348. Thomas Leggy, mayor, John Hamond, Roger de Depham, William de Causton, Adam Brabazon and Richard Basyngstoke, aldermen.

411. Simon de Worthstede complains that in rainy weather the water from the tenement of Joan relict of Robert Sely and Lawrence Sely adjoining his in the par. of St. Alban de Wodestrete falls upon his land; and that they have two apertures through which their tenants can see the private business of the pl. and his servants. The defs. ask for a respite so that they may produce their muniments but subsequently make default. Judgment after view that *within 40 days etc.* they convey their water on to their own land or into the street and block up the two apertures.

412. [m. 62] John atte Barnet, mercer, complains that the rainwater from

Assize of Nuisance

the tenement of James de Burford, kt., adjoining his in the par. of St. Thomas the Apostle, falls upon his land and rots his timber for the space of $17\frac{1}{4}$ ells. The def. comes by Thomas de Ware, his attorney, but says nothing to delay the assize. Judgment after view that *within 40 days etc.* he make a fillet-gutter (filettum) to convey the water into the street or on to his own land.

413. Adam de Brabazon brings an assize against John Moy, 'Flemyng', concerning a tenement in the par. of St. Matthew de Frydaystrete.

Fri. 1 Aug. 1348. Thomas Leggy, mayor, Simon Fraunceys, John Hamond, Roger de Depham, John de Causton, William de Causton and Richard de Berkyng, aldermen.

414. Ralph de Cauntebrigg complains that the wall dividing the tenement of William Brangweyn, 'vineter' from his in the par. of St. Christopher is not sufficiently thick, so that the sewage from William's latrine penetrates and defiles his whole premises. The def., summoned by Adam Aspal and Simon le Palmere, makes default. Judgment after view that *within 40 days etc.* he build a stone wall $2\frac{1}{2}$ ft. thick or an earthen one $3\frac{1}{2}$ ft. thick between his latrine and the pl.'s tenement.

415. John de Beauchamp, kt., complains by Thomas de Ware, his attorney, that John Sprot, chaplain, claims as his own the stone wall 14 ells 1 ft. 3 ins. long and 1 St. Paul's ft. thick dividing their tenements in the par. of St. Andrew Castle Baynard, and has placed his timber upon it. The def. comes in person but says nothing to delay the assize. Judgment after view that *within 40 days etc.* he remove the timber from the wall, which stands wholly upon the pl.'s land and is his sole property.

[m. 62d.] *Fri. 26 Sep. 1348. Thomas Leggy, mayor, Roger de Depham, Adam Brabazon and Richard de Basyngstoke, aldermen.*

416. Alan Gille and John de Hardyngham, wardens of London Bridge, complain on behalf of the commonalty that whereas Thomas Isoude, rector of St. Margaret Moysy de Fridaistrete, and his predecessors formerly had a gutter (gutero) 40 ft. long lying between his church and the tenement of the Bridge adjoining it on the south side, which used to receive all the water draining from the church and convey it into the street on the west side of the church, he has now torn it up (abradicavit) and built a kitchen where it used to be, and had built two new gutters on the east side of the same kitchen, the one to receive the water from the church, and the other, leading into it, the water and waste from the kitchen; but the water from both falls instead upon the tiles and party walls of the pls.' tenement, so that the foundations and walls and timber are rotted. The def., summoned by Thomas de Tiffeld and William de Aumere, makes default. It is found by view that the nuisances are as alleged, but for lack of aldermen the pls. are given a day at the octave at Guildhall to hear judgment. On that day, viz. 3 Oct., they appear before Thomas Leggy, mayor, Simon Fraunceys,

Richard Lacer, Roger de Depham, John Syward, John de Causton and William de Causton, aldermen, and the record and process having been recited it is adjudged that the def. remove the nuisances complained of *within 40 days etc*.

417. William Peverel, Queen Philippa's tailor, complains that Maud atte Vigne has built a cellar and solar blocking the light of the windows in his tenement in the par. of St. Clement by Candelwykstrete opening on to her land and garden, which he was intending to enlarge. Maud says that she built the cellars and solars on her own land, as she was entitled to do, and that the pl. has no case against her. William replies that her tenement and garden were formerly held by Gilbert de Colcestre, citizen, who granted by deed to Hawyse de Brackele, his predecessor, in perpetuity, the light of the windows overlooking her tenement, with the right to enlarge them at will, and he produces a deed sealed with Gilbert's seal. The def. denies that any such easement as is claimed by the pl. was ever granted by Gilbert, and declares that the deed is not his. The parties are given a day at the next Husting of Common Pleas.

Fri. 29 May 1349. John Lovekyn, mayor, and the aldermen.

418. John de Hardyngham complains that Henry atte Wode and Joan his wife and Alice relict of John Powel, 'pottere', refuse to rebuild a ruinous earthen wall, 80 ft. long, extending from the def.'s garden on the south to the pls.' garden on the north and standing on her land, in the par. of St. Mary atte Naxe. Henry and Joan, summoned by William atte Hurst and John Payn, make default. Alice comes and says that Ralph de Blithe, late saddler and citizen, and Joan his wife, now the wife of Henry atte Wode, formerly held the tenement to which the wall belongs, and in 1332–3 leased it for 20 years at a rent of 36s. 8d. to her and her husband, John Powel, on condition that the lessor should maintain the buildings proof against wind and rain, and should repair the wall when necessary, or, if he failed to do so, should allow the lessees their reasonable expenses from the rent. She produces the relevant indenture in court. Thereupon, the mayor and aldermen, having examined the deed and heard her defence, adjudge that she repair the wall *within 40 days etc.*, recovering her expenses from the rent.

[m. 63] *Fri. 26 Feb. 1350. Walter Turk mayor, Roger de Depham, Simon de Worstede, William de Welde and John Pecche, aldermen.*

419. Adam de Buri, citizen and skinner, and Alice his wife complain that for lack of a fillet-gutter (filetti) 6½ ells 2 ins. long, the rainwater from the tenement of Maud relict of John le Leche, 'pessoner', adjoining theirs in the par. of St. John de Walbrok, falls upon their land; and that she has two windows through which she and her servants can see the private business of the pls. and their servants. Ralph de Lenne, sheriff, testifies that the def. was summoned by John Broun and John de Morton but she makes default. The mayor and aldermen named above, having viewed the

Assize of Nuisance

premises, give the parties a day on the following Mon. [1 Mar.], because their numbers are insufficient. On that day, in full Husting, after recitation of the record and process, it is adjudged that *within 40 days etc.* the def. remove the nuisance.

420. The same Adam and Alice complain that John de Bedeford, skinner, has eleven windows in his tenement adjoining theirs in the same par., through which he and his servants can see the private business of the pls. and their servants. [Then as in **419**. See also **442**.]

421. The same Adam and Alice complain that for lack of a fillet-gutter (filetti) $5\frac{3}{4}$ ells 1 in. long, the rainwater from the tenement of Richard de Essex and Maud his wife adjoining theirs in the same par. falls upon their land; and they have four windows through which they and their servants can see the private business of the pls. and their servants. [Then as in **419**.]

422. The same Adam and Alice complain that the rainwater from the tenement of Robert le Boys, adjoining theirs in the same par. falls upon their land for lack of a fillet-gutter (filetti) $5\frac{1}{4}$ ells 2 ins. long; and that he has five windows through which he and his servants can see the private business of the pls. and their servants. [Then as in **419**.]

423. The same Adam and Alice complain that Nicholas Boylet and Elizabeth his wife have recently made eight windows in their tenement adjoining that of the pls. in the same par., and that they have two gutters (stillicidia) from which, in rainy weather, the water falls upon the pls.' land. [Then as in **419**.]

[m. 63d.] *Fri. 9 Apr. 1350. Walter Turk, mayor, Roger de Depham, Simon Fraunceis, Thomas Leggi, William atte Welde, William de Tedenham, Simon de Worstede, Adam Brabazoun.*

424. William de Sleford, rector of St. Thomas the Apostle, comes in person and complains that James de Burford, kt., has a stone wall $8\frac{3}{4}$ ells long adjoining a vacant plot of land belonging to his church in the par. of St. Thomas, upon which he, the pl., is unable to build, because the said wall, which is 11 ells high in the middle, overhangs the plot of land there by 13 ins., and at the west end, where it is 6 ells high, by 10 ins., and at the east end, where its height is likewise 6 ells, by 8 ins.; and, further, that the rainwater draining from two leaden pipes (pipas) jutting out from the def.'s tenement, falls upon the vacant plot. The sheriffs, Adam de Bury and Ralph de Lenne, testify that the def. was summoned by Thomas de Collesdon, 'brewere', and Robert de St. Albans, but he makes default. Judgment, after view, that *within 40 days etc.* he remove the nuisances.

Fri. 17 June 1351. Richard de Kyslyngbury, mayor, and the aldermen.

425. Thomas son of John de Grantham, def., appears against the dean and chapter of St. Martin le Grand in an assize of nuisance but the pls. do not prosecute their plaint. Therefore they are in mercy and he is *sine die*.

Assize of Nuisance

Fri. 15 July 1351. Richard de Kyslyngbury, mayor, and the aldermen.

426. John de Askham, clerk, complains that the sewage from the latrine of John Barber and Joan his wife penetrates his adjoining tenement in the par. of St. Dunstan de Fletestrete, because the wall between them is not sufficiently thick; and that they have six apertures (foramina) less than 16 feet above the ground, through which their tenants can see the pl.'s private business, and through which they throw filth and other refuse; and that for lack of a fillet-gutter (filetti) 30 ft. long, the water from their tenement falls upon his land. The defs. come but say nothing to delay the assize. The premises having been viewed the parties are given a day on the following Mon. [18 July] to hear judgment. On that day they appear in the Husting of Common Pleas, and the record and process having been recited, it is adjudged that *within 40 days etc.* the defs. remove the nuisances. [See also **428**.]

Fri. 22 July 1351. Richard de Kyslyngbury, mayor, and the aldermen.

427. David le Leche and Juliana his wife complain that they are unable to build upon a plot of land adjoining the tenement of Thomas de Ecton, clerk, in the par. of St. Alphege within Crepelgate because the def.'s timber overhangs it to a length of (—)[1] and a width of $6\frac{1}{2}$ ins. The def. comes but says nothing to delay the assize. Judgment after view that *within 40 days etc.* he remove the nuisance.

428. [m. 64] Precept to the sheriffs [undated] to put in execution the judgment against John Barber and Joan his wife [**426**].

Fri. 9 Mar. 1352. Andrew Aubrey, mayor, Roger de Depham, William de Causton, Simon Dolsaly, John de Gloucestre and Simon de Worstede.

429. John son of Geoffrey le Boteler, draper, complains that the rainwater from a gutter (gutteram) on the house of Gerard Noyl falls upon his land. The def., summoned by John de Swalclive and Richard (? Foven), 'mareschall', makes default. Judgment after view that *within 40 days etc.* he repair the gutter and convey the water on to his own land.
Precept of the mayor, dated Tues. 24 Apr. 1352, to John Wroth and Gilbert de Steyndrop, sheriffs, ordering them to put in execution the judgment in the above assize.

Fri. 2 Mar. 1352. Andrew Aubrey, mayor, Simon Fraunceys, Richard Lacer, Roger de Depham, William de Causton, John de Gloucestre, Richard de Berkyng, William de Welde and Simon de Worstede, aldermen.

430. Thomas B(—) complains that whereas Isabel relict of Nicholas de Basyngge gave by deed, produced in court, to Deodatus de Bedeford, goldsmith, a vacant plot of land in the par. of St. Peter de Westchepe now held by the pl., guaranteeing to him the light into and out of (cum libero

1. Membrane torn.

Assize of Nuisance

introitu et exitu luminis) the windows on the south side thereof, John de Brynchesle, citizen and goldsmith, and Margery his wife, have begun to build a house opposite his cellar and solar, thus blocking his light. The defs. come and say that the pl. is not entitled to the view and light of the said windows, because the tenement from which he claims them is his own, and was formerly a vacant plot of land on which his predecessors built, thus blocking their own light. The pl. makes reply that his whole tenement, in length, height and depth, as far as the vacant plot of land from which he claims the light, was built long ago, and that at the time of building the stones of the windows of the cellar were cut and already in position, and the windows of the solars above were built at the same time. A day is given to the parties at the next Husting of Common Pleas on Mon. [? 5 Mar.] but an adjournment follows at their request until Mon. 19 Mar. Finally the mayor and aldermen, with the masons and carpenters sworn to the assize, come upon the land on Wed. 21 Mar., and find that the pl.'s tenement was built long ago and all at one time. Judgment that the pl. have the light of the windows of his cellar and solars, and that *within 40 days etc.* the building begun by the defs. be demolished.[1]

[m. 64d.] *Fri. 13 July 1352. [No entry.]*

Fri. 15 Feb. 1353. Adam Fraunceys, mayor, and the aldermen.

431. Thomas Gatyn, citizen and fishmonger, and Maud his wife complain that Roger de Leukenore, 'chivaler', refuses to share in the rebuilding of an earthen wall 23½ ells less 1 in. long, common to their tenements in the par. of All Hallows de Graschirche, which has collapsed in ruins. The def., summoned by John de Wasshbourn and Henry Gleam, makes default. After the premises have been viewed, and the nuisance found to be as alleged, a day is given to the parties at Guildhall on the Mon. following [18 Feb.]. The parties appear in the presence of the mayor and aldermen (in congregatione predictorum maioris et aldermannorum), and the record and process having been recited, it is adjudged that *within 40 days etc.* the parties combine to rebuild the wall.

Fri. 14 June 1353. Adam Fraunceys, mayor, and the aldermen.

432. Geoffrey de Wockyngg and Margery his wife complain that the rainwater from two gutters (gutteras) in the tenement of Ralph de Preston and Maud his wife adjoining theirs in the par. of St. Nicholas Hacon, falls upon their buildings (domos), rooms (cameras) and land. The defs., summoned by Robert de Hatfeld and William Fossard, make default. It having been found by view of the mayor and aldermen that the pls.' allegation is correct, the parties appear at Guildhall on Fri. 28 June in the presence of Adam Fraunceys, mayor, Andrew Aubrey, Simon Fraunceys, Richard Lacer, Roger de Depham, Adam de Bury, William de Welde, John de Stodeye, John Peche and Simon de Worstede, aldermen;

---

1. The lower part of the membrane is torn, badly damaged and partly illegible. **430** is followed by a heading, an essoin and another heading, all partly illegible.

and the record and process having been recited, it is adjudged that *within 40 days etc.* the defs. remove the nuisance.

Fri. 12 July 1353. Adam Frаunceys, mayor, Richard Lacer, Roger de Depham, Henry Pycard, Simon Dolsely, Adam Bury, John Pecche and William Welde, aldermen.

433. William de Wyrcestre complains that for lack of a fillet-gutter (filetti) 13¾ ells long, the rainwater from the tenement of Richard de Norton and Alice his wife, adjoining his in the par. of St. Michael de Queenhithe, falls upon his land. The defs., summoned by William de Thame and John Frаunceys, make default. Judgment after view that *within 40 days etc.* they make a gutter of the required length. [See also **439**.]

Fri. 26 July 1353. [Adam Frаunceys], mayor, Roger de Depham, John de Stodeye, William de Welde, Simon de Worstede and [Bartholomew de] Frestlyng, aldermen.

434. Elizabeth de Montacute, prioress of St. John the Baptist of Haliwell, complains by Alan de Horwode her attorney that John son of (? Iter) de Caumpes has two windows overlooking her premises in the par. of St. Michael de Bassyngeshawe, through which his servants throw urine and other refuse, and that the rainwater from his tenement falls upon her land. [Entry largely illegible.]

435. [m. 65] William de Causton, mercer, complains that for lack of a paling (palicii) 23½ ells long between his tenement and that of John de Wyndesore, prior of the new hospital of St. Mary within Crepulgate, in the par. of St. Alphege, the prior's tenants enter his garden and trample down the grass (herbagia) and other things growing there. The def., summoned by Simon de Chykesond and John de Excestre makes default. Judgment after view that *within 40 days etc.* he repair the paling.

436. William de Wyrcestre complains that, for lack of a wall of sufficient thickness, the sewage from the latrine in the adjoining tenement of Philip de Thame, prior of the hospital of St. John of Jerusalem, in the par. of St. Michael Queenhithe, penetrates his land. The def. appears by Alan de Horwode, his attorney, but says nothing to delay the assize. The mayor and aldermen view the premises and give the parties a day at Guildhall on Fri. 2 Aug. to hear judgment. After adjournment until Fri. 16 Aug. the pl. appears in person, and the def. by attorney, and the record and process having been recited, it is adjudged that *within 40 days etc.* the def. build a wall of stone 2½ ft. thick, or of earth 3½ ft. thick, between his latrine and the pl.'s land.

437. Alan de Horwode complains that the rainwater from the house of John Cory, clerk, adjoining his in the same par. falls upon his house for a length of 43 ft. The def., summoned by John Reyner and John Coroner, makes default. Judgment, after view, that *within 40 days etc.* he convey the water into the street or upon his own land.

438. The same Alan complains that the rainwater from the tenement of Thomas son of John de Grantham adjoining his in the same par. is conveyed through a leaden pipe (pipam de plumbo) into his (the pl.'s) gutter (guteram); and that the def. has two gutters (guteros) running through the midst of his tenement, through which, in rainy weather, the water flows into the pl.'s gutter; and that the rainwater draining from the gutters (stillicidiis) of the def.'s buildings (domorum) falls, for a distance of 100 ft. upon his land. The def., summoned by John Reyner and John Coroner, makes default. It having been found by view of the mayor and aldermen that the nuisances are as alleged, the pl. is given a day on Fri. 2 Aug. to hear judgment.

439. Precept to William de Welde and John Lyttle, sheriffs, dated Sat. 26 Oct. 1353, to put in execution the judgment in the assize brought by William de Worcester (Wygornia) against Richard de Norton and Alice his wife [**433**].

[m. 65d.] *Fri. 18 Jan. 1353. Adam Frauncys, mayor, Richard Lacier, Roger de Depham, Adam Brabazoun, William atte Welde, Simon Worstede, aldermen.*

440. Ralph de Brentyngham brings an assize against the prior of the new hospital of St. Mary without Bisshopesgate.

Fri. 25 Jan. 1353. Adam Frauncys, mayor, Andrew Aubrey, Richard Lacer, Roger de Depham, Adam Brabazon, Simon Dolsey, John Stodey and William de Welde, aldermen.

441. John Botiller, 'ropere', and Agnes his wife complain that the timber of John de Hynton, 'vynter', overhangs his land in the par. of All Hallows de Bredestrete for a length of 30 ft. 5 ins., and that in the midst thereof the def. has placed his timber upon the pls.' wall-plate (platam) occupying the pls.' land to a width of $\frac{3}{4}$ in., and it overhangs their land there by $1\frac{1}{2}$ ins., and at the west end by $\frac{3}{4}$ in. The def. comes but says nothing to delay the assize. The mayor and aldermen, having viewed the premises, give the parties a day on the following Mon. [28 Jan.] to hear judgment; but because they are prevented from attending by important business touching the City, the proceedings are adjourned until Sat. 16 Feb., when, the record and process having been recited, it is adjudged that *within 40 days etc.* the def. remove the nuisance.

442. Precept to William de Welde and John Lyttle, sheriffs, to summon John de Beddeford, skinner, before the mayor and aldermen at Guildhall on Fri. 7 June 1353 to show cause why they should not put in execution the judgment in the assize brought against him by Adam de Bury [**420**].

Assize of Nuisance

[m. 66] *Fri. 20 Mar. 1355. Thomas Leggy, mayor, Roger de Depham, John de Stodeye, William de Tudenham, Simon de Worstede, Simon Dolsey, aldermen, and Richard Smelt, sheriff.*

443. Roger de Stratford, rector of St. James de Garlechethe, essoins himself against Simon Fyket and John Baroun, chaplains, by Thomas Rosse.

Fri. 1 May 1355. Thomas Leggy, mayor, and the aldermen.

444. William de Preston, rector of the church of Lambourne, essoins himself against Simon Dolsely, alderman, and the community of the merchants of the Hanse by William de Gilyngham.

Fri. 15 May 1355. Thomas Leggy, mayor, Richard le Lacer, Roger de Depham, Bartholomew de Fristlyngge, Richard de Notyngham, Ralph de Lenne and William de Tudenham, aldermen.

445. Simon de Worstede, mercer, and Alice his wife complain that Richard Lacier, goldsmith, has five open windows in his tenement in the par. of St. Alban de Wodestrete, on the east side, overlooking their garden, through which he and his servants (*servientes*) can see their private affairs, and through which they throw refuse on to the pls.' land. The def., summoned by John de Buksted and John de Kent, 'hanyper', makes default. Judgment, after view by the mayor and aldermen above-named, that *within 40 days etc.* he remove the nuisance.[1]

[m. 66d.] *Fri. 19 June 1355. Thomas Leggy, mayor, Richard le Lacer, Roger de Depham, William de Tudenham, Simon de Worstede and Richard de Notyngham, aldermen, and Richard Smelt, sheriff.*

446. Robert de Thorp complains that because of the ruin of a party-wall 13 ells long and 10 ft. high, standing on a stone foundation on the land of Thomas Pipherst and Joan his wife in the par. of St. Mary de Stanynglane, the defs.' tenants and servants enter his adjoining garden and trample down the grass (*herbagia*) and other things growing there and watch his private business. The defs., summoned by John de Mapelesdene, goldsmith, and Robert Payn, 'fuyster', come in person but say nothing to delay the assize. The mayor and aldermen find by view that the pl.'s allegations are correct and give the parties a day at Guildhall on Fri. 26 June to hear judgment. Since it appears that the wall stands wholly on the defs.' land and was built by their predecessors in the tenement, it is adjudged that *within 40 days etc.* they repair it.[2]

447. Michael de la Pole, kt., complains that the rainwater from the tenement of John de Rokesle, clerk, in the par. of St. Mary Wolnoth, falls, for lack of a gutter (*guttera*) 45 ft. long, upon a stone wall 11 ft. long in the pl.'s adjoining tenement and rots it; and, further, that the def. has a ruinous

1. *C.P.M.R. 1323–64*, 247.
2. *C.P.M.R. 1323–64*, 253.

Assize of Nuisance

chimney (caminum) overhanging his house. The def., summoned by William Doget and Robert de Stratford, makes default. Judgment, after view by the mayor and aldermen above-named, that *within 40 days etc.* he remove the nuisances.[1]

Fri. 23 Oct. 1355. Thomas Leggy, mayor, and the aldermen.

448. John Warender essoins himself against John de Aston, rector of All Hallows Grascherche, by William de Gilyngham.

[m. 67] *Fri. 22 Jan. 1356.* [*Essoin only.*]

Fri. 29 Jan. 1356. Simon Fraunceys, mayor, Adam Fraunceys, Roger de Depham, William atte Welde and Simon de Worstede, aldermen and Walter Forster, sheriff.

449. The commonalty by Adam de Acres bring an assize of nuisance against Roger atte Broke. Adam reports that on Sun. 20 Dec. 1355 a jury of the ward of Chepe presented to Simon Fraunceys, mayor, and the alderman of the ward in wardmote (in wardmote suo), that Roger had obstructed a formerly common way (via communis) through the house (per domum) of Gilott le Fourbour in Ismongereslane [**457**]. Roger, summoned, comes in person, and after view is given a day at Guildhall on Wed. 3 Feb. He pleads that he has no interest in the tenement concerning which the nuisance is alleged save in right of his wife, Agnes, for whose aid he asks. Given a day on the following Thurs. [4 Feb.] to produce her, he makes default. Judgment by Simon Fraunceys, mayor, Adam Fraunceys, Thomas Leggy, Roger de Depham, John de Stodeye, William atte Welde and Simon de Worstede, aldermen, that *within 40 days etc.* he remove the obstruction.

Fri. 5 Feb. 1356. Simon Fraunceys, mayor, Adam Fraunceys, Thomas Leggy, Roger de Depham, William atte Welde, Simon de Worstede and Richard de Notyngham, aldermen, Thomas de Brandon and Walter Forster, sheriffs.

450. The commonalty by the same Adam bring an assize of nuisance against the prior of the hospital of St. Mary within Crepulgate. Adam reports that on Sun. 20 Dec. 1355 a jury of Crepulgate ward presented the said prior to Simon de Worstede, alderman of the ward, in wardmote (wardemoto), as having an earthen wall standing on the soil of the commonalty on the east side of the church of the same hospital. The prior, summoned by John de Layton and William atte Walle, comes in person, but shows no cause why the nuisance should not be removed. Judgment, after view, that he remove it *within 40 days etc.* He is warned accordingly.

451. [m. 67d.] William de Ilkyston, rector of St. Mary le Bow, John de Kynelyngworth, Richard de Welford, James Andrew, William de Essex, William Spark, William de Skelton and John Burgeys, parishioners, complain that John Noyl. [Entry incomplete.]

1. *C.P.M.R. 1323–64*, 252.

Assize of Nuisance

Mon. 8 Feb. 1356. *Common Pleas held in the Husting.*

452. Robert de Thame prays an assize against Brother Thomas de Berkhampsted, master of St. Thomas de Acon concerning a nuisance in the par. of St. Mary le Bow. The sheriff testifies that the def. has been summoned by John Osekyn and William Dyke.

Fri. 10 Feb. [rectius Fri. 12 Feb.] 1356. [Essoin only.]

[m. 68 *No heading.*]

453. The prior of the hospital of St. Mary in the suburb of London[1] was presented to Simon Fraunceys, mayor, on Mon. 11 Aug. 1343, by the men of the venue of Castle Baynard, for building a stone wharf (kayum de muro lapideo) at le Estwatergate in Castle Baynard ward, which encroaches upon the soil of the commonalty beside the Thames by $\frac{3}{4}$ ell, to the nuisance of ships (navium), shouts (shoutarum) and boats (batellorum) putting in there (applicancium).

454. At the wardmote held in the church of St. Alban on Sun. 20 Dec. 1355, John de Horewode, junior, was presented to Simon de Worstede, alderman of Cripulgate ward, for obstructing the common lane (venellam) leading from Phelippeslane to Wodestrete.

455. At the same wardmote it was presented that an earthen wall on the east side of the church of the hospital of St. Mary within Cripulgate stands upon the soil of the commonalty. [See also **450**.]

456. In a wardmote held on the same day John Coke, Richard de Ware, John de Swalclyve and Robert de Ingham were presented to Simon Fraunceys, alderman of the ward of Chepe, for making a purpresture in Ismongerslane.

457. At the same wardmote Roger atte Broke, the present occupant, was presented for obstructing the common way (communis via) through the house of Gilott Fourbour in Ismongerslane. [See also **449**.]

458. At the same wardmote William Pikebou was presented for breaking the sink (puteum) of the conduit by night.

459. On the same day the abbot of Redyng, John Bisshop and Gilbert Botelere were presented to John Costantyn, alderman of Castle Baynard ward, for obstructing a wharf (kayum) at Castle Baynard formerly used by people coming and going to the river to draw water or dispose of dung and other things. [Entry cancelled. m. 68d. Blank.]

[m. 69] Mon. 29 Feb. 1356. *Pleas of land held in the Husting.*

1. St. Mary within Cripplegate (or St. Mary without Bishopsgate?).

Assize of Nuisance

460. John Bernes and Christine his wife pray an assize against John de Fakenham, rector of St. Matthew in Frydaystrete, John Hiltoft, goldsmith, and John Moy, 'armurer', concerning a nuisance in the same par.

Fri. 4 Mar. 1356. [No entry.]

Mon. 28 Mar. 1356. Pleas of land held in the Husting.

461. Simon Dolselly and Joan his wife pray an assize against John son of John atte Pole, late citizen of London, concerning a nuisance in the par. of St. John de Walbrok. The sheriff testifies that the def. has been summoned by William de Carleton and Walter Page. [See **464**.]

Fri. 1 April 1356. [Essoin only.]

[m. 69d.] *Fri. 8 Apr. 1356. Simon Frounceys, mayor, Roger de Depham, William atte Welde, Simon de Worstede, John Costantyn and Richard de Notyngham, aldermen, and Thomas de Brandon, sheriff.*

462. John de London, 'brewere', essoins himself against the prioress of Halywell by John de Ekeheued.

463. John le Bakere essoins himself against Nicholas Hotot by William de Gilyngham.

Fri. 15 Apr. 1356. Simon Frounceys, mayor, Adam Frounceys, Roger de Depham, John de Stodeye, William atte Welde, William de Tudenham and Thomas de Dolsely, aldermen.

464. Simon Dolselly and Joan his wife complain [**461**] that John, son of John atte Pole, late citizen, has two doors, two windows and various other apertures opening on to the alley (alleam) $18\frac{1}{4}$ ells long and $1\frac{3}{8}$ ells wide, adjoining the def.'s tenement in the par. of St. John de Walbrok and leading to their garden; and that the eaves (severunda) of his house overhang the said alley by $\frac{1}{4}$ ell 1 in., so that, for lack of a gutter (stillicidium) $14\frac{7}{8}$ ells long, the water draining from his house falls upon their land. The def. after essoin makes default. The mayor and aldermen find that the nuisances are as alleged. Judgment that *within 40 days etc.* the def. block up the doors, windows and other apertures, and make a gutter of the required length.

Fri. 20 May 1356. Simon Frounceys, mayor, Roger de Depham, William de Tudenham, Adam de Bury, Richard de Notyngham, aldermen, Thomas de Brandon, sheriff.

465. William de Greyngham and Avice his wife, Roger atte Brok, 'felmongere', and Agnes his wife essoin themselves against John Peche, 'draper', senior, by William atte Posse.

466. John de London, 'brewere', essoins himself against Elizabeth, prioress of Halywell, by William atte Rose. [Cf. **462**.]

467. Stephen de Grauntbrugg essoins himself against Robert de Norwych by William atte Grosse.

468. The same Stephen essoins himself against Ralph son of Thomas de Grauntbrugg by the same.

[m. 70] *Fri. 3 June 1356. Simon Franceys, mayor, Adam Franceys, Roger de Depham, William Welde and Adam de Bury, aldermen, and Thomas de Brandon, sheriff.*

469. William de Greyngham and Avice his wife. [Cf. **465**.]

Fri. 10 June 1356. [Respite only.]

[m. 70d.] *Fri. 17 June 1356. Simon Fraunceys, mayor, Roger de Depham, William de Tudenham, Richard de Notyngham and Simon de Worstede, aldermen.*

470. John de London, 'brewere'. [Cf. **466** and **471**.]

Fri. 22 July 1356. Simon Fraunceys, mayor, Adam Fraunceys, Thomas Leggy, Roger de Depham, William Welde and John de Stodeye, aldermen, and Thomas de Brandon and Walter Forster, sheriffs.

471. John de London, 'brewere', essoins himself against Elizabeth de Mountagu, prioress of Halywell, by William atte Posse. [Cf. **462** and **466**.]

472. Robert Leddrede, 'draper', essoins himself against Thomas de Lyllyngston, citizen, by the same. [For amercement of pl. see below under 26 Aug.]

473. William Andrew, 'chaundeler', essoins himself against Thomas de Lyllyngston by the same. [For amercement of pl. see below under 26 Aug.]

Fri. 29 July 1356. [Essoin only.]

[m. 71] *Fri. 5 Aug. 1356. Simon Fraunceys, mayor, Roger de Depham, Simon Dolsely and Thomas Dolsely, aldermen, and Thomas de Brandon, sheriff.*

474. John de Aston, rector of All Hallows de Graschirche, complains that John Warender and Alice his wife have a solar 15 ft. long and 4 ft. wide overhanging the churchyard on the north side, from which the rainwater falls upon the land belonging to the church; and that they have two doors in a stone wall opening on to the churchyard, through which people and the defs.' servants go in and out, day and night, trampling down the grass (herbagia) and other things growing there. Walter Forester, sheriff, testifies that the defs. were summoned by John de Brikelesworth and Adam de Seyntyves. John Warender comes in person and Alice by William de Gillyngham, her attorney, and they ask and are given a day to produce their muniments. On Fri. 2 Sep. the pl. appears against John and Alice in the presence of Simon Fraunceys, mayor, Roger de Depeham, Thomas Leggy, Simon de Wurstede, Richard de Notyngham, Thomas Dolsaly, Bartholomew de Frestlyng and Adam de Bury, aldermen, Thomas de Brandon and Walter Forester, sheriffs; but the defs. make default. Judgment that *within 40 days etc.* the nuisances, which are found to be as alleged, be removed and the doors opening on to the churchyard be blocked up.

475. John de Morton, clerk, complains that the rainwater from a gutter (gutteram) in the adjoining tenement of John Bengeo falls upon his garden in the par. of St. Dunstan Est, and that the def. has a house adjoining the said garden of which the earthen wall on the west side is ruinous; and the wall and part of the house overhang his garden by 2 ft., to his grave danger; further, the def. has dug a cellar 12 ft. long and 8 ft. deep beneath his garden, without a stone foundation or support, so that the earth falls and sinks down into it. Walter Forester, sheriff, testifies that the def. was summoned by Guy Lambyn, 'pessoner', and Robert de Kayton. He comes in person, but says nothing to delay the assize. The proceedings are adjourned until Fri. 12 Aug., when the pl. appears against the def. in the presence of Simon Fraunceys, mayor, Roger de Depeham, Simon Dolsely, Thomas Dolsely, Simon de Wurstede and Richard de Notyngham, aldermen, Thomas de Brandon and Walter Forester, sheriffs, but the def. makes default. Judgment that *within 40 days etc.* the nuisances, which are found to be as alleged, be removed.

[m. 71d.] *Fri. 12 Aug. 1356. Simon Fraunceys, mayor, Roger de Depeham, Simon Dolsely, Thomas Dolsely, Simon de Wurstede and Richard Notyngham, aldermen, and Walter Forster, sheriff.*

476. Thomas son of John de Grantham, citizen and pepperer, complains that Richard Curteys, citizen and fishmonger, refuses to repair a leaden gutter (gutteram plumbeam) lying upon the stone wall 26 ells long situated between their tenements in the par. of St. Michael Queenhithe, and upholding their timber and buildings. Walter Forester, sheriff, testifies that Richard was summoned by Robert de Thame and Richard Shakol. He comes in person and says that he is not bound to receive and convey away the water falling from the roofs (tectis) of the pl.'s buildings upon the wall they hold in common, and that the pl. can show no written evidence in support of his allegation. Thereupon Richard produces a deed, enrolled in the Husting[1] on Mon. 17 Oct. 1328, and dated Sun. 16 Oct. in which Nicholas Maderman, citizen, and Avice his wife, daughter of John de Staneford, citizen and pepperer, the former tenants of the def.'s tenement, undertook in return for certain concessions, to receive and convey away into Thamistrete by a leaden gutter extending the whole length of the wall common to them and

1. H.R. 56 (128).

Assize of Nuisance

John de Grantham, the pl.'s father, the water falling from John's roofs and buildings, and to repair and renew the gutter when necessary. Richard contends that the above deed ought not to prejudice his case, since he alleges that in 1352–3, Alan de Horwode, then tenant of the tenement in question, brought an assize against the pl. concerning the very nuisance of which he now complains, and obtained a judgment in his favour [**438**], and he vouches the record to warranty. On Fri. 26 Aug. the parties come in the presence of Simon Fraunceys, mayor, Roger de Depham, Simon [Dolsely, Simon] de Wurstede, John de Stodeye, William de Tudenham and Thomas Dolsely, aldermen, and Thomas de Brandon, sheriff, but the def. does not produce the record. It is therefore adjudged that *within 40 days etc.* he repair the gutter conveying the water from the pl.'s roofs and buildings into the street in accordance with the terms of the deed.

[m. 72] *Fri. 19 Aug. 1356. Simon Fraunceys, mayor, Roger de Depham, Thomas Dolsely, Simon de Worstede and Richard de Not[ingham], aldermen, and Walter Forster, sheriff.*

477. John de Barton and Beatrice his wife complain that the prior of Holy Cross beside the Tower of London has a door in his garden wall opening on to their garden in the par. of St. Olave by the Tower, which they hold of the mayor and commonalty for the life of the longer liver; and that his servants enter their garden and tread down the grass (*herbagia*) and other things growing there, and see and hear their private business. Walter Forester, sheriff, testifies that the def. was summoned by John atte Walle and John Brademan, but he makes default.

478. Henry de Secheford complains that the prior of the hospital of St. Mary without Bisshoppesgate has three walls (*parietes*) enclosing his tenement in the par. of St. Michael atte Corne, respectively 22 ft. long and 10 ft. high; (—) ft. long and 10 ft. high; and 15 ft. long and (—) ft.[1] high; and these he has always been accustomed to keep in repair; but they are now ruinous and broken down so that men can come and go in the pl.'s close. Thomas de Brandon, sheriff, testifies that the def. was summoned by William de Kelshull and John de Morton, attorney. He comes in person but says nothing to delay the assize. After adjournment that the mayor and aldermen may be more fully advised, the assize comes on Fri. 2 Sep. by Simon Fraunceys, mayor, Roger de Depham, Thomas Leggy, Simon de Wurstede, Richard de Notyngham, Thomas Dolsely, Bartholomew Frestlyng and Adam de Bury, aldermen, Thomas de Brandon and Walter Forester, sheriffs, and the pl. appears but the prior makes default. Judgment that he remove the nuisances, which are found to be as alleged, and repair the wall *within 40 days etc.*

[m. 72d.] *Fri. 26 Aug. 1356. Simon Fraunceis, mayor, Roger de Depeham, Simon de Wurstede, Richard de Notyngham, Thomas Dolsely, Simon Dolsely, William de Tudenham, aldermen, and Thomas de Brandon, sheriff.*

1. Edge of membrane damaged.

Assize of Nuisance

The pls. in mercy for not prosecuting their suits in **472** and **473**.

Fri. 2 Sep. 1356. Simon Fraunceis, mayor, Roger de Depham, Thomas Leggy, Simon de Wurstede, Richard de Notingham, Thomas Dolsely, Bartholomew de Frestlyng and Adam de Bury, aldermen, and Thomas de Brandon and Walter Forster, sheriffs.

479. Assize between Thomas de Lyllyngston, citizen, and Idonia, prioress of St. Mary Clerkenwell, respited by consent of the parties.

480. Thomas de Bakkewell is summoned to answer Simon Dolsely in an assize of nuisance.

Fri. 9 Sep. 1356. Assizes were adjourned owing to the preoccupation of the mayor and aldermen with the affairs of the City and the kingdom.

Fri. 16 Sep. 1356. [Respites only.]

MISC. ROLL FF

[m. 1] *Fri. 18 Nov. 1356. [Essoins only.]*

Fri. 2 Dec. 1356. Henry Pykard, mayor, Thomas Leggy, Roger de Depham, William atte Welde, Simon Dolsely, John Lytle and Bartholomew de Fristlyng, aldermen, and Thomas Dolsely, alderman and sheriff.

481. The prioress of Halywell, def., essoins herself against Walter Doublet, rector of All Hallows de Bredstrete, Thomas Dolsely, John de Brinchesle, John de Mapelesden, John Botyller, Sampson de Swafham and Walter Bacheler, parishioners, by William atte Wodegate.

482. John Bokstede, carpenter, complains that, whereas John Chaundeler and Emma his wife have a tenement adjoining his in the par. of St. Michael de Wodestrete, and a leaden gutter (*guttera*) 60 ft. long lies between them which ought to be maintained at their common charges, he has recently rebuilt his house to a height greatly exceeding that of the defs. and has made a gutter to receive his own water and convey it into the street; but because of the failure of the defs. to repair their portion, the rainwater from their buildings falls into his house and rots his timber to a length of 60 ft. The sheriffs testify that the defs. have been summoned by Richard Brok and John Brown. They come but show no cause why the nuisance should not be removed. The mayor and aldermen, having viewed the premises, adjudge that *within 40 days etc.* the defs. repair the gutter. Defs. in mercy. [*Margin:* Iudicium reddendum in misericordia.]

Fri. 16 Dec. 1356 and [m. 1d.] *Fri. 13 Jan. 1357. [Essoins and respites only.]*

Fri. 27 Jan. 1357. Henry Pycard, mayor, Roger de Depham, Bartholomew de

Assize of Nuisance

Frestlyng, Simon de Worstede, William atte Welde, John le Lyttele, Thomas Perle and Thomas Dolsely, aldermen.

483. Thomas Moryce, common serjeant, complains on behalf of the commonalty that William Stacy and Margery his wife and William Crokhorn have erected a forge (fabricam) in the public street in the same par. greatly narrowing it, and gravely impeding the inhabitants and common people passing by. The sheriffs testify that the defs. have been summoned by John de Boxton and Richard de (? Reve), 'hanyper', but they make default. The mayor and aldermen, having viewed the premises, but wishing to be more fully informed,[1] give the pl. a day on Fri. 11 Aug. to hear judgment. At the assizes held on that day they appoint Simon de Worstede, alderman of Crepulgate, to enquire by a jury of the ward whether the forge is indeed to the nuisance of the common people, and report to them on Fri. 25 Aug. On the appointed day Simon certifies, in the Chamber of Guildhall, that on Tues. 22 Aug. a jury of the venue of Wodestret, viz. John de Kent, 'haneper', Walter Brok, John Broun, Peter de Fikelden, William le Coupere, Nicholas de Harpesfeld, Reginald Pyxlee, William de Aston, Gilbert Spencer, Richard Lacer, goldsmith, John Buntyng and Geoffrey Whyte testified upon oath that the forge in question is to the grave detriment of both inhabitants and passers-by, and William de Greyngham, serjeant of the Chamber, is accordingly ordered to cause the defs. to remove it *within 40 days etc.*

Fri. 10 and 17 Feb. 1357. [Essoins and respites only.]

[m. 2] *Fri. 24 Feb. 1357. Henry Pykard, mayor, Adam Fraunceys, John Lovekyn, Thomas Leggy, Roger de Depham, William atte Welde, and John de Stodeye, aldermen, and Richard de Notyngham, sheriff and alderman.*

484. The assize between Agnes relict of John Hamond, pl., and John de Mapelesden, goldsmith, and Alice his wife respited.

Fri. 17, 24 and 31 Mar. 1357. [Essoins and respites only.]

Fri. 28 April 1357. Assize adjourned because the mayor and aldermen are preoccupied with the king's business.

Fri. 12 May and [m. 2d.] *Fri. 26 May 1357. Assize adjourned.*

Fri. 9 June 1357. Henry Pykard, mayor, Roger de Depham, Simon Dolsely, John Lyttele, Ralph de Lynne, Bartholomew de Frestlyngg and Richard de Notyngham, aldermen.

485. Andrew Pykeman, 'pesshoner', complains that Hugh de Sadelyngstanes and Isabel his wife have, in their tenement adjoining his in the par. of St. Botolph next Billynggesgate, a latrine 12 ft. long and 12 ft. deep, from

---

1. This reason for adjournment has generally not been calendared hereafter as it appears to be common form.

which, for lack of a stone wall 2½ ft. thick or an earthen wall 3½ ft. thick, the sewage penetrates the wall of his tenement and rots it, so that his house built thereon is greatly weakened, and threatens ruin. The sheriffs testify that the defs. have been summoned by John de Pounfreyt and Robert le Gurdlere, but they make default. The mayor and aldermen view the premises and find the nuisance to be as alleged; but wishing to be more fully informed, they give the pl. a day at Guildhall on Fri. 23 June, to hear judgment, and he is instructed, in the meantime, to refer the matter to the carpenters and masons. At the assizes held on Fri. 14 July the pl. appears against the defs., but they again make default. Judgment that *within 40 days etc.* they build a stone wall 2½ ft. thick, or an earthen wall 3½ ft. thick, between their latrine and the wall of the pl.'s tenement.

Fri. 16 June 1357. [Essoins and respites only.]

Fri. 23 June 1357. Assize adjourned because the mayor and aldermen could not attend.

[m. 3] *Fri. 30 June 1357. [Essoins only.]*

Fri. 14 July 1357. Henry Pycard, mayor, Roger de Depham, Adam Fraunceys, William Welde, Simon de Worstede, Bartholomew de Frestlyngg and Thomas Perle, aldermen, and Thomas Dolsely and Richard de Notyngham, aldermen and sheriffs.

486. Stephen de Waltham and Joan his wife complain that the prior of the new hospital of St. Mary within Crepulgate has a tenement adjoining their tenement and land in the par. of St. Alphege, with a gutter (stillicidium) which overhangs their land to a length of 20 ft. and a width of ½ ft.; and the water from his tenement falls upon their land through a leaden pipe (pipam plumbeam) in the middle of the said gutter, so that the foundations of their tenement are rotted. The sheriffs testify that the def. has been summoned by Walter Brok and Alan Ruddok. He comes in person, and says that he has muniments touching his tenement which are not at present to hand. He is given a day to produce them at Guildhall on Fri. 28 July. After adjournments, the parties come on Fri. 25 Aug., and the def. personally acknowledges that the gutter is to the nuisance of the pls. Judgment that *within 40 days etc.* he remove it, and cause the water from his tenement to be conveyed into the street or on to his own land. He is in mercy. [*Margin:* Misericordia.]

487. The commonalty complain by Thomas Moryce, common serjeant, that Ralph, rector of St. Botolph without Aldresgate, has built on the soil of the commonalty, adjoining Houndesdych, a latrine in which all kinds of filth accumulate, to the damage of passers-by, and the nuisance of the commonalty. The sheriffs testify that the def. has been summoned by William de Greyngham and William Beauner, but he does not come. The mayor and aldermen, having viewed the site and found conditions to be as alleged, adjudge that *within 40 days etc.* the def. remove the nuisance.

Assize of Nuisance

488. [m. 3d.] William Heyroun, 'vineter', and Sarah his wife complain that, whereas Thomas de St. Edmunds and Idonea his wife have a plot of ground called le Tytingwowes adjoining their tenement in the par. of St. Michael de la Crokedelane, they and their workmen (homines ipsorum deservientes) come and go by the steps in an alley (allea) running through their (the pls.') tenement, carrying wet cloths, from which the water falls upon the said steps, and runs thence to various parts of the tenement, so that the foundations are rotted. The sheriffs testify that the defs. have been summoned by Richard Bungeye and Giles Pykeman. They come by Alan de Horewode, their attorney, and say that they have muniments bearing on the case which are not at present to hand, and they are given a day on Fri. 28 July to produce them. On that day the pls. appear in person, but Alan de Horwode essoins himself by William atte Posse, who is ordered to produce his warrant at the quindene [Fri. 11 Aug.]. On the appointed day the pls. again appear in person and the defs. by their attorney. They say that the action does not lie, because John Joce, kt., was formerly seised of the tenement now held by the pls., with other tenements and dye-works (tinctoria), together with the right of entry and exit belonging to the same; and by deed dated Mon. 19 Feb. 1303 he granted to William Bussh, citizen and merchant, certain tenements and dye-works, with the right of entry and exit by the steps which are now within the pls.' tenement. William Bussh, by deed dated Fri. 5 May 1307, granted the same to James de St. Edmunds, who was succeeded in turn by his sons John and Thomas. The latter was seised of the premises for a long time; but on Sun. 31 Oct. 1350 he granted them to Richard de Keleshull, kt., who, by deed dated Tues. 9 Nov. 1350 granted them to the defs., who thus, with their ancestors and feoffors have always been peacefully seised of the tenement and dye-works, and have used and enjoyed the right of entry and exit through the pls.' tenement; and they challenge the right of the pls. to bring an assize on their simple word, and without showing any specialty. The pls. say that the entry ought not to be by their steps from le Crokedelane, but by the lane at Estchepe next Candelwykstrete; but the defs. repeat their claim that they and their predecessors have always enjoyed the use of the steps in the pls.' tenement, which, they allege, remained in the possession of John Joce long after his grant to William Bussh, and they put themselves upon their country. It is ordered that a jury of the venue of the par. of St. Michael de Candelwykstrete be summoned for Fri. 25 Aug. 1357. On that day the assize comes by Henry Pycard, mayor, Roger de Depham, William Welde, Simon de Worstede, Bartholomew de Frestlyngg, Adam de Bury, aldermen, Richard de Notyngham and Thomas Dolseley, aldermen and sheriffs, but the pls. do not prosecute their plaint. Therefore they and their pledges are in mercy, and the defs. *sine die*. [*Margin*: Misericordia.]

[m. 4] *Fri. 28 July, 11 and 25 Aug. and 15 Sep. 1357. [Essoins and respites only.]*

Fri. 22 Sep. 1357. Henry Pycard, mayor, Adam Fraunceys, Roger de Depham, Simon de Worstede, William Welde, Bartholomew de Frestlyngg, aldermen, and Richard de Notyngham and Thomas Dolsley, sheriffs.

Assize of Nuisance

489. Henry de Secheford, def., essoins himself against the prior of the hospital of St. Mary without Bisshopesgate by William Posse.

Fri. 20 Oct. 1357. Henry Pycard, mayor, Roger de Depham, William Welde, Simon de Worstede, aldermen.

490. Thomas Pypherst and Joan his wife and William Burdeyn, defs., essoin themselves against the prior of St. Bartholomew de Westsmythefeld by John Rosse.

[m. 4d.] *Fri. 27 Oct. 1357. Henry Pycard, mayor, Roger de Depham, William Welde, Simon de Worstede and William de Tudenham, aldermen, and Stephen Cavendyssh and Bartholomew Frestlyng, sheriffs.*

491. Thomas de Louthe and Joan his wife, defs., essoin themselves against Margaret atte Lee by William de Roussebem.

10 Nov. 1357. John de Stodeye, mayor, Adam Fraunceys, Roger de Depham, William Welde, Simon de Worstede, Richard de Not[ingham], Simon Dolsely and Thomas Dolsely, aldermen, and Bartholomew de Frestlyngg and Stephen Cavendych, sheriffs.

492. The prior of St. Bartholomew de Westsmethefeld complains that Roger Lachebrok and Margaret his wife have two doors in their tenement opening on to his land and that of his church, through which they come and go, and eleven windows less than 16 ft. from the ground, through which they can see all the private business of his tenants; and whereas they ought to convey the rainwater from their tenement on to their own land or into the street, it falls upon his land; and they have a jetty 32 ft. 2 ins. long and 2 ft. wide overhanging his land, and an oven (furnum) 1 ft. 11 ins. wide and 6 ft. long standing upon it. The sheriffs testify that the defs. have been summoned by Walter Parker and John de Nasyngg. Roger comes in person and Margaret by Richard de Olneye, her guardian. They claim that they have muniments touching the tenement in question and are given a day at the quindene to produce them. On Fri. 19 Jan. 1358 both parties come but the defs. do not produce any written evidence. Answering as tenants of the tenement in question, they say that they and all their predecessors have been seised of the door, windows and other easements, with the right of free entry and exit by the land lying between their tenement and that of the pl. The prior, who comes in person, maintains that he and his predecessors, and those whose estate he holds, have been seised, time out of mind, in right of his church, of the land in question, and that the defs. cannot lay claim to any easements thereon, unless they can produce a specialty. After adjournment until Fri. 16 Feb. the assize comes by John de Stodeye, mayor, Roger de Depham, William Holbech, John Pecche, John Malewayn and Richard de Notyngham, aldermen, and the parties appear in person. Having viewed the site, the mayor and aldermen find it impossible to come to any conclusion, since the land in dispute is vacant, and neither party can produce a specialty in support of their claim to it.

It is therefore adjudged that both be *sine die*, and that they seek a remedy by the common law of the City if they so desire.

[m. 5] *Fri. 24 Nov., 8 and 22 Dec. 1357.* [*Essoins and respites only.*]

Fri. 5 Jan. 1358. Assize adjourned on account of the preoccupation of the mayor and aldermen with City affairs.

[m. 5d.] *Fri. 19 Jan. 1358.*

493. Thomas Moryce, common serjeant, complains on behalf of the commonalty that John son of John de Guldeford and Thomas his brother have a great gate in the par. of St. Lawrence in Old Jewry, through which carts and horses with a variety of merchandise come and go upon the soil of the commonalty, so that access by the mayor and aldermen and other citizens to the Guildhall is gravely impeded, and the dung and other refuse which are thrown through the gate are an abomination to the common people passing along the road at night; moreover the defs. have eight windows below the height of 16 ft. from the ground overlooking the soil of the commonalty, and two leaden pipes (pipas plumbi) through which the water from their houses falls upon it, and a jetty (geticium) of two storeys overhanging it by 4 ft. Stephen Cavendyssh and Bartholomew de Frestlyngg, sheriffs, testify that the defs. have been summoned by John de Kayton and Thomas de Neuport. They come by their guardian, John Lucas, and claim to have muniments relating to their tenement. They are given a day on Fri. 2 Feb. to produce them. After adjournment the parties come on Fri. 16 Feb. before the mayor and aldermen [as in **492**] but the defs. show no cause why the nuisances should not be removed. Judgment that *within 40 days etc.* they block up the gate and windows, remove the pipes and jetty, and convey their water on to their own land or into the street.

494. Thomas Moryce, common serjeant, complains on behalf of the commonalty that the master of the scholars of Balliolhalle, Oxford, rector of the church of St. Lawrence in Old Jewry, and his parishioners, have a great gate in a stone wall which opens upon the soil of the commonalty, through which men living in the churchyard throw dung and other refuse, and make their privies, which is an abomination to the mayor and aldermen and the common people passing along the street; and the access of the mayor and aldermen and other citizens is frequently impeded by carts and horses passing through the gate with different kinds of merchandise. Stephen Cavendyssh and Bartholomew Frestlyng, sheriffs, testify by John de Morton, their clerk, that the defs. have been summoned by John de Kayton and Thomas de Neuport. The rector makes default. Richard de Notyngham, mercer, and the other parishioners come but show no cause why they should have the gate complained of. The mayor and aldermen view the site and give the pl. a day on Fri. 16 Feb. to hear judgment. On that day the assize comes and the parties appear. Judgment that the rector and parishioners block up the gate complained of *within 40 days etc.*

Assize of Nuisance

Fri. 23 Feb. 1358. John de Stodeye, mayor, William Welde, Roger de Depham, Simon de Worstede, Richard de Notyngham, Simon Dolsely and William Holbech, aldermen, and Stephen Cavendyssh, sheriff.

495. William Sparke, 'armurer', and Maud his wife, defs., essoin themselves against Walter Salman, 'gurdlere', and Margery his wife by William Russe.

[m. 6] *Fri. 20 Apr. 1358. John de Stodeye, mayor, Roger de Depham, William Welde, John de Chychestre, Simon de Worsted, William Holbech and Richard de Notyngham, aldermen, and Bartholomew de Frestlyngg and Stephen Cavendyssh, sheriffs.*

496. The abbot of Circestre complains by John de Morton, his attorney, that whereas Roger Lestraunge, kt., has a tenement with a garden adjoining his garden in the par. of St. Bride the Virgin, in Fletestret, on the north side of his hall, the def.'s tenants and servants enter his garden and trample down the grass (*herbagia*) and other things growing there, because the earthen wall between them, 43 ells long, is ruinous and broken down, and, since it stands wholly on his land, ought to be repaired by the def. The sheriffs testify that the def. has been summoned by John de Berdene and John Lucas, 'tayllour', but he makes default. The mayor and aldermen find by view that the nuisance is as alleged, and give the pl. a day at Guildhall on Fri. 27 Apr. to hear judgment. On that day he appears by attorney against the def., who again makes default. Judgment that *within 40 days etc.* the def. repair the wall, as he is bound to do.[1]

Fri. 18 May 1358. John de Stodeye, mayor, Roger de Depham, William Welde, Simon de Worstede, John de Chychestre, Thomas Dolsely and William Holbech, aldermen, and Bartholomew de Frestlyngg and Stephen Cavendyssh, sheriffs.

497. Thomas de Bakewell and William de Arraz, defs., essoin themselves against Simon Dolsely by William Posse.

Fri. 1 June 1358. John de Stodeye, mayor, John Lovekyn, Roger de Depham, William Welde, Simon de Worstede, Thomas Dolsely and Thomas Perle, aldermen, and Bartholomew de Frestlyng and Stephen Cavendissh, sheriffs.

498. John de Kyngeston, 'brewere', def., essoins himself against John Forester, chaplain of the chantry in the chapel of St. Nicholas de Berkyngchurche, by John Pusse.

Fri. 22 June 1358. [m. 6d.] *Fri. 29 June, 6 and 13 July 1358.* [*Essoins and respites only.*]

Fri. 20 July 1358. Mayor and the aldermen.

1. Copy in *Cartulary of Cirencester Abbey*, ed. C. D. Ross, i (1964), no. 175.

Assize of Nuisance

499. William atte Nax, def., essoins himself against Henry de Asshebourne, tawyer (*allutarius*), by Walter atte Wall.

500. John de Kyrkeby, draper, complains that the stone wall 18 ft. long of the tenement of Ralph Hattere and Agnes his wife adjoining his in the par. of St. Augustine at St. Paul's gate is so ruinous that it overhangs the pl.'s kitchen by 2 ft. so that it is daily threatened with collapse, to the great danger of all those dwelling in his house; and the water from the def.'s tenement falls, for lack of a gutter (*guttere*) 7 ft. long, upon his wall and rots it. The sheriffs testify that the defs. have been summoned by Henry le Galeys and William Passeware but they do not come. The mayor and aldermen find by view that conditions are as described, and give the pl. a day at the next Husting at Guildhall to hear judgment. Afterwards, at the Husting of Common Pleas held on Mon. 23 July, the pl. appears against the defs., who again make default. After inspecting the record and process, the mayor and aldermen adjudge that *within 40 days etc.* the defs. remove the portion of their wall overhanging the pl.'s kitchen, and erect a gutter 7 ft. long.

501. [m. 7] William Musehacche, William Forester, John Mymmes, John atte Felde, John Bristowe and Joan Mychel complain that whereas Thomas Piphurst, goldsmith, has a messuage adjoining that which they jointly hold in the par. of St. Mary le Bow, and between them the pls. had a gutter (*gutteram*) affixed by nails to their messuage, the def. has removed the same, and built another 23 ft. long and 3 ft. wide near where the pls.' gutter used to be as a result of which the rainwater cannot now make its escape, but enters the pls.' messuage in divers places and rots their timber. The sheriffs testify that the def. has been summoned by Richard de Wrotham and Thomas de Welles. He comes in person and denies the nuisance. The mayor and aldermen, having viewed the premises and taken counsel with the carpenters and masons, find that at the north end of the gutter complained of, the pls.' messuage ought to extend 11 ins. beyond (*extra*) the wooden wall above (*supra*) the stone wall there, over against (*versus*) the def.'s messuage, and at the south end 9 ins. They give the parties a day at the next Husting to hear judgment. At the Husting of Common Pleas held on Mon. 23 July the parties come, and the record and process having been recited in the presence of John de Stodeye, mayor, Roger de Depham, William Welde, William Holbech, John de Chichestre, Simon de Worstede and Thomas Dolsely, aldermen, Bartholomew de Frestlyngg and Stephen de Cavendissh, aldermen and sheriffs, it is adjudged that *within 40 days etc.* the def. restore the gutter to its former state and previous position.

[m. 7d.] *Fri. 3 Aug. 1358. John de Stodeye, mayor, Adam Fraunceys, Roger de Depham, Thomas Perle, Simon de Worstede, Richard de Notyngham and John Malewayn, aldermen, and Bartholomew de Frestlyngg, aldermen and sheriff.*

502. William de Sleford, parson of St. Thomas the Apostle, complains that William Soty and Margery his wife and Thomas son of John Baronet have in their messuage two solars of two storeys, which overhang the churchyard by 4½ ft. on the west and 6 ft. on the east, so that he cannot rebuild his chancel; and that they have a gutter (gutteram) 20 ft. long between the solars, through which the water flows from them on to his land and penetrates the foundations of the stone wall of the chancel to a length of 14 ft. on the east side, so that it threatens ruin and is broken down in divers places; and, further, that they have four windows and a door opening on to the churchyard, through which they and their servants can see and hear the private business of the pl. and his servants. The sheriffs testify that the defs. have been summoned by Robert de Westmelne, 'broydurer', and Thomas atte Cornere, 'brewere'. William and Margery make default but Thomas comes in person and answers as tenant of the tenement in question. He claims to have muniments bearing on the matter and is given a day at the quindene to produce them. On Fri. 31 Aug. the pls. appear against him, but he produces no written evidence, and shows no reason why the nuisances complained of should not be removed. After the premises have been viewed the proceedings are adjourned for lack of aldermen until Fri. 7 Sep., when, the record and process having been recited before John de Stodeye, mayor, Adam Fraunceys, Roger de Depham, William Welde, John Malewayn, Simon de Worstede and Richard de Notyngham, aldermen, Bartholomew de Frestlyngg and Stephen de Cavendyssh, aldermen and sheriffs, it is adjudged that *within 40 days etc.* the defs. remove as much of the solars as overhangs the churchyard, convey their water into the street or on to their own land, and block up the windows and door.

[m. 8] *Fri. 7 June 1359. John Lovekyn, mayor, Hugh de Sadyngstanes, William Welde, Simon de Worstede, William Holbech, John de Chichestre and William de Tudenham, aldermen, and John Bernes and John de Bures sheriffs.*

503. Nicholas Bole, Agnes de Steyndrop and Agnes Carlel, defs., essoin themselves against Raymond Peregryn by William atte Posse.

504. Thomas de Sutton, 'dyghere', def., essoins himself against the prior of St. John of Jerusalem by the same.

Fri. 14 June, 26 July, 9 and 16 Aug. 1359. [*Essoins and respites only.*]

Fri. 6 Sep. 1359. John Lovekyn, mayor, Hugh de Sadelyngstances, John de Stodeye, Simon de Worstede, John de Chychestre, William Holbech, William de Tudenham, aldermen, and John de Bernes and John Bures, sheriffs.

505. Richard de Notyngham and Nicholas Ploket, mercer, complain that Nicholas Marchaunt and Richard de Bradefeld, 'brewere', have broken down their plastered wall (murum plastratum) in the par. of St. Lawrence in Old Jewry, and thrown refuse into two drains (cloace) belonging to their house.

[m. 8d. *Fri. ? 27 Sep. 1359.*]

Assize of Nuisance

506. Stephen de Waltham and Joan his wife complain that John Mychel, 'vynter', and Robert Hamond have inserted three corbels and beams in their stone wall in the par. of St. James de Garlekhethe. John de Bures and John Bernes, sheriffs, testify that the defs. have been summoned by John de Hardyngham and John Dunstaple. They come and claim to have muniments bearing on the matter, and are given a day to produce them. On Fri. 11 Oct. 1359 the pls. come but the defs. make default. Judgment is postponed for lack of aldermen until the following Wed. 16 Oct., when the pls. come.

Fri. 18 Oct. 1359. [Essoins only.]

Fri. 1 Nov. (the feast of All Hallows) 1359. Simon Dolsely, mayor, etc. Assize adjourned on account of the celebration of the aforesaid feast.

507. The assize between Roger Torold and Alice his wife and Roger their son, pls., and John Chaucer, respited.

[m. 9] *Fri. 1 May 1360. Simon Dolsely, mayor, Hugh de Sadelyngstanes, William Welde, Simon de Worstede and John de Chychestre, aldermen, and Simon de Benyngton, sheriff.*

508. The assize between Geoffrey de Godyngton, pl., and William de Nassurton and Alice his wife respited.

Fri. 15 May 1360. [Respites only.]

Fri. 22 May 1360. Simon Dolsely, mayor, Hugh de Sadelyngstanes, Simon Worstede, William Welde and John de Chichestre, aldermen, and Simon de Benyngton, sheriff.

509. William Brangwayn, 'vyneter', def., essoins himself against John prior of St. Bartholomew de Westsmethefeld by William Pusse, and the same John against the same William Brangwayn by William Russe.

510. Nicholas Hotot complains that Thomas de St. Edmunds and Idonea his wife have a latrine (latrinam) with two pipes (pipis) within the bounds of his adjoining tenement in the par. of St. Swithin de Candelwykstret. The sheriffs testify that the defs. have been summoned by John Walsh, goldsmith, and Nicholas Potyn. They come by John Dauncere, their attorney, and say that, by custom, no view ought to be held unless by the mayor and six aldermen, and the number now present is insufficient. They are ordered to make a further answer (ulterius), and thereupon ask judgment concerning the pl.'s bill, on the ground that the plea is properly one of intrusion and not of nuisance. After adjournment the parties come on Fri. 5 June 1360, but the assize is respited by their common consent until Fri. 26 June. The defs.' attorney then appears and claims to have muniments bearing on the case. He is given a day on Fri. 10 July to produce them, but essoins himself by John Purre who is ordered to produce his warrant at the quindene, viz. 24 July. On that day the parties come and the defs. say that the tenement now held by the pl. was formerly held, together with theirs, by Fulk de St. Edmunds, who gave it to William de Wollewercherchehawe and Olive his wife, at which time the privy (garderoba) was already parcel of the tenement which they now hold, and which, on Fulk's death, was inherited by James his son and heir, who devised it to his son John, on whose death it passed to his brother Thomas, the def., who thus with all his predecessors and their feoffees has been seised of the tenement, with the privy as parcel of the same. The pl., protesting, says that he does not acknowledge the privy to be parcel of the defs.' tenement. He maintains that Fulk de St. Edmunds gave the tenement which he now holds to William de Wollercherchehawe and Olive his wife with all rights and appurtenances whatsoever, and produces in court the relevant deed, in which the tenement is described as having been given to Fulk by Roger Loveday, kt., and as comprising a solar, cellar, kitchen, stable and garden situated between the tenements late of John de St. Osiths, John Deumars, and John de Bow (de Arcubus) on the north and the grantor's houses and wall on the south, and between St. Swithin's Lane on the west, and the tenements of William and Olive and of the donor on the east, paying to the abbot and convent of Westminster 2s.8d. at the usual terms, and to the donor a clove at Christmas and a sum of money down as gersum. [m. 9d.] Witnesses: John de Bretoun, kt., warden of the City, John de Storteford and William de Storteford, sheriffs, John de Donestaple, alderman of the ward [of Walbrook], Thomas de Suthfolk, William de Red, Robert Persone, Simon de Brughton, James le Botyller, Hugh de Clopham, Peter de Braghyng, Thomas de Walden, William de Caxton, John de Hatfeld, Roger Foucke, Richard le Barker, serjeant of the ward, Ralph the clerk and others. Dated 16 Mar. 1298. The pl. asks judgment whether the defs. can claim anything in the messuage above described, or within the bounds thereof unless they can show a specialty. The defs. reiterate their claim that the privy in dispute has always been part of the tenement which they hold, and not of that of the pl.; and Nicholas retorts that it is included in the metes and bounds described in Fulk's deed recited above. Both parties ask that the matter be referred to a jury. After adjournment the pl. comes on Fri. 4 Sep. Thomas makes default, but Idonea appears in person and is admitted to plead. She repeats that both the tenements in question were formerly in the possession of Roger Loveday, who enfeoffed therewith Fulk de St. Edmunds, her husband's ancestor, at which time the privy was in the same place as at present, and belonged to the tenement which she and her husband now hold, and she asks judgment whether the assize can be maintained against her without a title. The pl. thereupon declares that in Fulk's time there was no privy in the tenement which he now holds, and asks that the matter be referred to a jury. Idonea, who persists in her claim, makes a similar request. A jury is summoned for Fri. 18 Sep. The parties appear but the jurors do not come. On Fri. 3 Oct. they again fail to appear and the assize is respited until Fri. 16 Oct.

[m. 10] *Fri. 20 Nov. 1360. [Essoins only.]*

Assize of Nuisance

Fri. 4 Dec. 1360. John Wroth, mayor, Hugh de Sadelyngstanes, Simon Dolsely, William Welde, John de Chichestre, Simon de Worstede, William Tudenham, aldermen, and John Dynes, sheriff.

511. Thomas Cheyner, 'mercier', son and heir of Henry Cheyner, complains that Alice relict of John de Staunton, kt., has built a house upon her land interfering with his free access by a right of way, guaranteed by deed, from St. Laurence's Lane in Jewry, within the def.'s gate, to his tenement. Walter de Berneye and John Dynes, sheriffs, testify that the def. has been summoned by John de Bedyngton, mercer, and Nicholas de Horwoode, but she makes default. Because the mayor and aldermen wish to be more fully informed concerning the truth of the pl.'s allegations, William de Grenyngham, serjeant of the Chamber, is ordered to cause 24 lawful men of St. Laurence Lane to appear before them on Fri. 18 Dec. to enquire concerning the truth of the pl.'s allegations. After adjournment the pl. comes in person on Fri. 29 Jan. 1361, but the def. again makes default. The jury comes by Richard Russell, Roger Reygate, Thomas atte Shoppe, Stephen Edulf, Richard Wayte, William Gorel, Adam Sprot, William Stoke, John Abraham, Thomas Charlewod, Robert Foundour and Robert le Chaundeler, who say upon oath that the pl. is entitled to a right of way through the gate of the def.'s tenement from St. Laurence Lane to his tenement, and that the def. has impeded him by building a house. Judgment that *within 40 days etc.* the nuisance be removed. [*Margin:* Recuperacio.]

512. John Fraunceys, tawyer, and Emma his wife complain that the rainwater from the adjoining tenement of Bartholomew Guydo, 'chaungeour', falls through a gutter (gutteram) upon their vacant plot of land, 14 ft. long, in the par. of St. Clement by Candelwykestret. John Deynes and Walter de Berneye, sheriffs, testify that the def. has been summoned by John de Thame and John Tiryngton. He appears but the proceedings are adjourned at the request of the parties until the quindene. [*Margin:* Dies amoris.]

[m. 10d.] *Fri. 19 Feb. 1361. John Wroth, mayor, the aldermen and sheriffs.*

513. John Lytle, 'pessoner', complains that the tenement of Thomas Clenche and Goda his wife in the par. of St. Magnus de Bruggestret is ruinous and broken down with age, and without a roof (coopertura discoopertum), and is on the point of collapsing into the king's highway, to the grave danger of the passers-by; and it is sinking down (succumbit) upon the pl.'s tenement to which it is affixed with iron nails, so that it rots the party-walls and threatens to overthrow the said tenement because of its ruinous state. Walter de Berneye and John Deynes, sheriffs, testify that the def. has been summoned by Richard Greylond and William de Olneye, but they do not come. The mayor and aldermen view the premises and give the pl. a day on Fri. 26 Feb. to hear judgment. On that day, the record and process having been recited in the presence of John Wroth, mayor, and the aldermen, it is adjudged that *within 40 days etc.* the nuisances be removed. The sheriffs are ordered to warn the defs. accordingly.

Assize of Nuisance

[m. 11] *Fri. 18 Mar. 1362. [Essoins only.]*

Fri. 1 Apr. 1362. John Pecche, mayor, Thomas Lodelowe, John Lytle, Walter Forester, William de Tudenham, Simon de Worstede and Thomas de Pykenham, aldermen, and William Holbech and James de Thame, aldermen and sheriffs.

514. Roger Newe and Agnes his wife complain that Richard de Worstede, mercer, and Margaret his wife have made six windows in their adjoining tenement in the par. of St. Alphege, less than 16 ft. from the ground and overlooking their land, so that the defs. and their tenants can see all their private business, and through which they throw refuse into their garden. The sheriffs testify that the defs. have been summoned by Henry de Bradele and John de Walden, but they make default. After viewing the premises the mayor and aldermen adjudge that *within 40 days etc.* the defs. block up the windows. They are in mercy. [*Margin:* Misericordia.]

Fri. 20 May 1362. John Pecche, mayor, the aldermen and sheriffs.

515. Thomas de Kendale, clerk, def., essoins himself against John Coraunt, goldsmith, by Robert Rose.

Fri. 22 July 1362. Mayor, the aldermen and sheriffs.

516. Richard Lacer, goldsmith, def., essoins himself against Simon de Worstede, mercer, by William Russe.

517. Richard de Norton of Chesthunte and Alice his wife, defs., essoin themselves against John de Morton, clerk, by William Buresse. [m. 11d. Blank.]

[m. 12] *Fri. 24 Feb. 1363. Stephen de Cavendyssh, mayor, John Lovekyn, Thomas de Lodelowe, Adam Fraunceys, William Welde, William de Tudenham, Bartholomew de Frestlyng, aldermen, and John de St. Albans and James Andrew, aldermen and sheriffs.*

518. Henry Godchep and Agnes his wife complain that whereas they and the prior of the hospital of St. Mary without Bisshopesgate have a number of adjoining tenements in the par. of St. Mary le Bow, between which is a stone wall 85 ft. long and 3 ft. wide belonging wholly to the pls., the def. has placed on it his timber for building. The sheriffs testify that the def. has been summoned by William atte Wode and John Russe. He comes in person, but although he can show no specialty in support of his claim to build upon the wall, he asks that the mayor and aldermen view the site in the presence of the masons and carpenters. It is found that the wall, as alleged, belongs entirely to the pls., and it is therefore adjudged that they have and hold it as appurtenant to their tenement, and that *within 40 days etc.* the def. must remove his timber, and all other nuisances, and rebuild the wall as it was formerly.

Assize of Nuisance

Fri. 23 June 1363. [Essoins only.]

Fri. 30 June 1363. Mayor, the aldermen and sheriffs.

519. Margery de Honylane, prioress of St. Helen's, complains by Robert de Watlyngton, her attorney, that the earthen wall 20 ft. long between her garden and that of Thomas Hore, smith, in the par. of St. Ethelburga the Virgin, which stands upon her land, is ruinous and broken down, so that strange men and animals enter her garden and trample down the grass (*herbagia*) and other things growing there, and carry off the fruit, and see the private business of the pl. and her servants. The def. who had essoined himself, makes default. The mayor and aldermen, having viewed the premises, find that the pl.'s allegations are correct. Judgment that *within 40 days etc.* the def. repair the wall, as he is bound to do.

520. The same Margery complains by her attorney that the earthen wall 25 ft. long between her garden and that of Simon le Spycer 'lombard', in the par. of St. Peter de Cornhull, and built upon her land, is ruinous, [etc. as in **519**. Judgment as in **519**.]

[m. 12d.] *Fri. 16 Feb. 1364. John Nott, mayor, Thomas de Lodelowe, William Welde, William de Tudenham, Simon de Worstede, James de Thame, James Andrew and Walter Forester, aldermen, etc.*

521. Amaury de Shyrlond, clerk, complains that Thomas Chauntecler has a tenement adjoining his land on the west side in the par. of St. Bride de Fletestret, and for lack of a fillet-gutter (*filetti*) 86 ft. long the rainwater from the chambers on the west side of his tenement and likewise, for lack of a similar gutter 25 ft. long, from another chamber on the south side, falls upon the pl.'s land; and, further, from two other gutters (*stillicidia*) the water in rainy weather falls upon his land; and he has six windows in a stone wall of his tenement, and sundry other windows and apertures (*foramina*) in other plastered walls (*muris plastratis*) looking on to the pl.'s land, through which he and strangers visiting (*perhendinantes*) and staying (*morantes*) there can see the private business of the pl. John Hyltoft and Richard de Croydon, sheriffs, testify that the def. has been summoned by Robert de York and Andrew Grauncourt, but he does not come. Upon viewing the premises the mayor and aldermen find that the nuisances are as alleged. Judgment that *within 40 days etc.* the def. make a fillet-gutter (*filettum*) 86 ft. long upon the chambers on the west side of his tenement, and on the chamber on the south side another 25 ft. long, and that he turn (*declinata*) the two other gutters (*stillicidia*) so that the rainwater can flow on to his own land or into the street, and block up the windows and apertures of which the pl. complains.

[m. 13] *Fri. 10 Nov. 1363. John Nott, mayor, Thomas de Lodelowe, John Lovekyn, John de Stodeye, John Litle, James de Thame, William de Tudenham and Walter Forester, aldermen, and Richard de Croydon, sheriff.*

Assize of Nuisance

522. Adam Lovekyn and Katherine his wife complain that the tenement of Elias Catesby, chaplain, John Brewere, John Olyver, senior, John Oliver, junior,[1] Henry Cancy, Richard Haslemere, Richard Kene, Brian Tannere, Thomas de Benchesham, John Story, senior, Robert Lenard, Robert Dunvill and John Totyng adjoining theirs on the west side in the par. of St. Michael upon Cornhull, is so ruinous that it is on the point of collapse, because of the weakness and decay of the timber, and it leans against the pls.' tenement, so that their wall on the west side, measuring $19\frac{1}{2}$ ells in length, is broken down by the heavy weight. Richard de Croydon and John Hyltoft, sheriffs, testify that the defs. have been summoned by Stephen Daubeneye and Andrew Pyebakere, but they make default. The mayor and aldermen, having viewed the premises, and wishing to take counsel with the carpenters and masons concerning the judgment to be given, give the pls. a day on Mon. 25 Nov. On that day the pls. appear in person, and the record and process having been recited and full information obtained from the carpenters and masons, it is adjudged that the nuisances be removed *within 40 days etc.* [m. 13d. Blank.]

[m. 14] *Fri. 9, 30 May, 13, 20 June, 4 July and 17 Oct. 1365.* [*Essoins and respites only.*]

[m. 14d.] *Fri. 24 Oct. 1365. Adam de Bury, mayor, John Lovekyn, Adam Fraunceys, William Halden, William Welde, John de St. Albans, John Lytle and Simon de Worstede, aldermen, and John de Briclesworth and Thomas de Irlond, sheriffs.*

523. William de Tudenham, mercer, def., essoins himself against Stephen Bradele by William Russe.

524. Simon de Worsted, mercer, complains that Gilbert Lyrp, 'bakere', who has a tenement adjoining his in the par. of St. Alphege within Crepulgate, has built up a stack (staccum) of large wood called 'wodefyn' next the party wall of his tenement, and in rainy weather the drips fall from it on to the wall and rot all the timber. Further, Gilbert has various animals —viz. oxen, cows and pigs, which constantly break down the walls of his house, and their excrement rots the foundations. The sheriffs testify that the def. has been summoned by William Kyng, 'tymbermongere', and William Whelpele, tawyer, but he does not come. The mayor and aldermen, after viewing the premises, give the pl. a day on Fri. 7 Nov. to hear judgment. On that day he appears against the def. at the pleas of assize held before Adam de Bury, mayor, Adam Fraunceys, William Haldene, William Welde, Thomas Pykenham, and James Andrew, aldermen, but Gilbert makes default. Judgment that he remove the nuisances *within 40 days etc.*

[m. 15] *Fri. 24 Oct. 1365. Adam de Bury, mayor, and the aldermen.*

525. John Pecche, John Moy, John Blaunche, William Passeware, Richard

1. *Margin:* Beaumond.

Assize of Nuisance

de Knoesle, Walter Bacheler, Thomas de Thornton, John de Mytford, Richard de Stokes, Thomas de Same, Robert Box, John de Pakenham, Thomas Fourneux, Hugh le Walssh, Adam Carlel, John de Redyng, John de Levendale, Michael de Cornewayll, Robert de Somersete, John de Kyrkeby, Thomas de Essex, Andrew de Cornewayll, John de Waudene and Adam de Chyppenham, chaplain, complain by John de Peruch, their attorney, that in rainy weather, for lack of a fillet-gutter (filettum) 68 ft. long, on the east side, the water from the adjoining tenement of William de Coloygne, clerk, in the par. of St. Peter upon Cornhull falls upon their land; and that he has seven windows in the party-wall of his tenement opening thereon, through which his tenants and servants throw out refuse and other scandalous things (facinora); and that he has a house adjoining their garden in which are five gutters (guttere), from which all the water falls upon their land, and there are twelve windows opening upon the same garden through which the def.'s tenants throw urine and other filth, and see the private business of the pls.' tenants. The def. comes in person and claims to have muniments bearing on the case. He is given a day on Fri. 6 Nov. [? *rectius* 1 or 7 Nov.] to produce them. On that day the def. essoins himself by William Russe, who is ordered to produce his warrant at the quindene. On 20 Nov. [? *rectius* 14 or 21 Nov.] the pls. again appear by their attorney against the def., who does not come. The mayor and aldermen find the nuisances to be as alleged and give the pl. a day on Fri. 28 Nov. at Guildhall to hear judgment. The assize then comes by Adam de Bury, mayor, John Lovekyn, Adam Fraunceys, William de Halden, William Welde, Thomas Pykenham and James Andrew, aldermen, and the sheriffs, and the record and process having been recited, it is adjudged that the nuisances be removed *within 40 days etc.* The sheriffs are ordered to warn William de Coloygne accordingly.

526. [m. 15d.] At the Husting of Pleas of Land held on Mon. 16 Nov. 1366, John de Totenham, Richard atte Cherche and Richard de Shrobshire delivered a bill [French] to the mayor and aldermen, certifying that the wall between William Stokes and Richart Storteford running from east to west is partible between them unless William can produce an enrolled deed in his favour. The arches of the wall are of the same depth on either side, and the old wall-plate and beams of William's tenement do not occupy a full half of its width.
Et predicti Willelmus Stokes et Ricardus Storteford petunt quod predicta billa irrotulatur in rotulis assisarum nocumentorum etc. Et ista billa irrotulata fuit die veneris in festo Sancti Edmundi Regis et martiris anno quadragesimo supradicto de assensu parcium predictarum [20 Nov. 1366]. [See also **591**.]

527. [*Margin:* Ex'. recordum carpentariorum inter Thomam atte Noket querentem et Gilbertum de Hoo.]
Certificate of John de Totenham, Richard de Salyng, Richard de Schropschire and Richard atte Cherche, carpenters and masons [French]. They report that Thomas atte Noket, citizen and draper, who has a tenement in the par. of Our Lady of Wolnoth in Lombardstrete, situated between the

tenement of Gilbert de Hoo, formerly belonging to Thomas de Ware, 'pelliter', and called 'la Cardenaleshatte' on the east, and that of Cecily de Bosenham on the west, is entitled to 12¾ ins. of the stone wall, between his tenement and Gilbert's, and extending northwards for 10 ells 1 in. to his kitchen. Further, he is entitled to 9½ ins. of the wall running north for 13¼ ells from his same kitchen, in which, moreover, there is a chimney which overhangs his tenement, to his great inconvenience, and which ought to be demolished. Also, there is a leaden gutter (une gotiere de plombe, guttysoun) 7½ ells long on la Cardenaleshat, from which the water overflows on to Thomas's land (place), and which Gilbert ought to turn away from his tenement (droit est qe le dit Gilbert de Hoo face turner la dite guttysoun hors del tenement le dit Thomas). Finally, the stone wall between Thomas's hall (sale) and the tenement of Cecily de Bosenham, extending northwards to the tenement of Thomas de Irland, is declared to be partible between Thomas and Cecily.

Istud recordum intratur hic tempore Johannis Lovekyn maioris anno regni regis Edwardi tercii post conquestum quadragesimo [1366–7] ad rogatum et assensum predictorum Thome atte Noket et Gilberti de Hoo ad testificandum de premissis tempore futuro.

[m. 16. ? *Nov. 1365*.]

528. The prior of St. Bartholomew de Westsmethefeld complains that the water from the houses of Roger Lachebrok and Margaret his wife adjoining his in the par. of All Hallows de Honylane, falls in rainy weather upon his land to a length of 167 ft., and that they have two doors and twenty windows below the height of 16 ft. from the ground, opening on to his land, through which they and their tenants see the private business of his tenants, and a solar of which the jetties overhang his land to a length of 32 ft. 2 ins. and a width of 2 ft. Simon de Mordon and John de Mitford, formerly sheriffs, returned elsewhere that the defs. had been summoned by John Herewardstok' and Simon de Leuesham. They come, and ask that the prior's declaration (declaracionis) be read. Having heard it, they say that they have muniments relating to their tenements which are not at present to hand, and they are given a day to produce them on Fri. 21 Nov. 1365. On that day the parties come. The defs. produce no documents, but answer as tenants of the tenement in question. They say, protesting, that they do not acknowledge the nuisances of which the prior complains, and cite an assize brought against them by his predecessor, John, during the mayoralty of John Stodeye, when the number of windows complained of was eleven and not twenty, and the mayor and aldermen, having viewed the premises, were unable to reach a conclusion, and so, on Fri. 19 Jan. 1358, declared both parties to be *sine die* [**492**]. They ask judgment whether, in consequence, the present pl. should be allowed an assize. The prior reaffirms that there are now twenty windows, and asks that the additional nine be viewed by the mayor and aldermen, with the masons and carpenters. He maintains that the previous judgment ought not to exclude him from an assize as regards the remaining nuisances, since it was not in conformity with the plea of either party (eo quod in se totaliter extitit repugnans et non

Assize of Nuisance

referebatur nec extitit conformis placito alicuius partis parcium predictarum, set predicto placito totaliter impertinens fuit et aliena). Moreover, in the earlier proceedings, Prior John, in challenging the right of way of the defs. on the land between their tenements, had expressly and without contradiction claimed it as his own, so that they were not entitled to any easements thereon unless they could show a specialty. [m. 16d.] He argues further, that in any judgment rendered in accordance with right and reason, by which a person is finally excluded from an action, either the pl. must acquire or recover something, and the def. be in mercy for an unjust defence, or the def. must retain what he holds and the pl. be in mercy for a false plaint (quia in omni iudicio secundum formam iuris et racionis reddito per quod aliquis ab accione sua finaliter excluderetur, requiritur ut pars conquerens aliquid adquirat sive recuperet per suam querelam et defendens pro iniusta defencione in misericordia, aut quod defendens teneat pacifice quod prius tenuit et idem conquerens pro iniusta prosecucione sive querela in misericordia), and since in the previous proceedings this principle was not observed, the judgment (consideracio) amounted to no more than an adjournment (discontinuacio) until the mayor and aldermen should have deliberated more fully on the matter. He therefore asks that a view be now made with the assistance of the masons and carpenters. After adjournment until Mon. 1 Dec. 1365 that the mayor and aldermen may be more fully advised, the prior comes. Roger de Lachebrok makes default, but Margaret is admitted to plead. She says that John Douuegate, late citizen, formerly held the tenements concerning which the nuisances are alleged, with all the appurtenant easements, and that she is his kinswoman and heiress, viz. the daughter of Thomas, the son of Joan, the daughter of John, to whom John devised the tenements in fee tail. The pl., protesting, refuses to acknowledge the entail or to recognise the def.'s claim to the easements unless she can produce a specialty, and demands that, since the action is one of nuisance, in which no free tenement is in question, an assize be held and the nuisances removed. After further adjournments the parties come on Sat. 13 Dec. 1365. Margaret refuses to admit the nuisances, but says that the land between her tenements and those of the pl. is a lane (venella), which has existed from time out of mind, and by which she and her ancestors and those whose estate she holds have always enjoyed free access to Chepe, and to her kitchen, which opens upon the lane; and in it all the other tenants and lessees dwelling there, and merchants buying and selling their wares have enjoyed a like easement. She says further that the doors and windows complained of open upon the lane, and the rainwater from her tenements flows through it into Chepe, and her jetties extend into the middle of it, and that rebuilding and repairs are undertaken by tenants when necessary. She asks judgment whether the pl. is entitled to an assize. [m. 17] The prior, protesting, maintains that what Margaret calls a lane in common use is in fact parcel of his own land, which, as his deeds clearly show, and as she does not deny, adjoins immediately her own, and declares that, according to the law and custom of the City, easements which cause a nuisance to another, even if in existence long before the purchase of a tenement, or continuously enjoyed from time out of mind, are void unless a specialty can be shown. He therefore demands that the nuisances of which he complains be viewed and removed. The def. denies that the lane is parcel of the pl.'s tenement, and that the custom of the City is as alleged, and asks judgment since the pl. does not deny that she, her ancestors and those whose estate she holds have enjoyed the use of the lane and the other easements time out of mind. The proceedings are adjourned until Mon. 19 Jan. 1366 that the court may be more fully advised. [m. 17d.] There follow numerous other adjournments until Fri. 16 Oct. 1366, when Richard de Olneye, the def.'s attorney, reports that she has died. It is therefore adjudged that the pl. take nothing for his plaint, and be *sine die*.

[m. 18] *Fri. 22 Jan. 1367. John Lovekyn, mayor, Adam Fraunceys, William Halden, William Welde, Stephen Cavendyssh, John de St. Albans, William de Tudenham, aldermen, and John Warde and Thomas atte Leye, sheriffs.*

529. Assizes between the prior of St. Bartholomew de Westsmythefeld, pl., and John atte Harpe, 'brewere', and between the same John, pl., and the same prior, respited. [*Margin:* Concordati sunt.]

530. Assizes between Simon de Pystoye and Emma his wife, pls., and the prioress of St. Helen's, and the same prioress, pl., and Simon Lumbard, spicer, and Emma his wife, respited.

Fri. 29 Jan. 1367. John Lovekyn, mayor, Adam Fraunceys, Stephen Cavendyssh, William Halden, William Welde, William de Tudenham and John de St. Albans, aldermen, and John Warde and Thomas atte Leye, sheriffs.

531. Thomas, prior of the hospital of St. Mary without Bysshopesgate, def., essoins himself against William de Sandford, clerk, by William atte Purre. Robert de Wachyngton, pl.'s attorney. [*Margin:* Concord'.]

532. William Bedel, cordwainer, and Joan his wife, defs., essoin themselves against William de Sandford, clerk, by William atte Purre.

533. John Limare, William Stodle, rector of St. Benet beside Pauleswharf, Thomas de Morle, John de Somerton and Stephen Stanard, parishioners, defs., essoin themselves against Robert de Draycote, prior of the new hospital of St. Mary within Crepulgate, by William atte Polle.

Wed. 31 Mar. 1367. John Lovekyn, mayor, Adam Fraunceys, William de Halden, John Pecche, John de Mitford, Simon de Mordon, William Welde and Bartholomew Frestlyng, aldermen.

534. Report [French] to the mayor and aldermen by Richard atte Celer and John Cook, appointed arbitrators (nounpiers) in a dispute between Robert Gille and John Lyterworth concerning a gutter (gotere) leading from a well (fountaigne) which they share and are jointly bound to repair, in accordance with an indenture made between them. The parties agree that Robert shall make the outlet (fra le issue) and undertake the repair of the gutter leading (issant) from the well on to John's land and into the street in the par. of St. Andrew upon Cornhull, carrying out the work well and competently (convenablement) in all respects at his own expense, whenever necessary, so that in future John shall suffer no damage or inconvenience (greve) through his default. The agreement is enrolled at the request of the parties and the arbitrators.

[m. 18d.] *Fri. 26 Nov. 1367. James Andrew, mayor, Adam Frauncey, William de Halden, William Welde, Stephen de Cavendyssh, John de Bernes, William de Tudenham and Simon de Mordone, aldermen.*

535. James de Thame essoins himself against Bartholomew de Castre, goldsmith, by William Russe.

Fri. 3 Dec. 1367. James Andrew, mayor, John Lovekyn, Adam Frauncey, John Wroth, William de Halden, Simon de Mordon, John Lytle and William de Tudenham, aldermen, etc.

536. The commonalty complain by John de Wentebrigg, common serjeant, that Agnes relict of William de Leyre has a solar in the par. of All Hallows the Less in Douuegate ward which overhangs the king's highway by 23 ft. in length and 10 ft. in width, gravely impeding the people living there, and the common folk passing along the street, and preventing the neighbours from carting hay and straw and other victuals to their tenements. The sheriffs testify that the def. has been summoned by Nicholas de Snypston and William Cavel, but she makes default. The mayor and aldermen, having viewed the premises, give the pl. a day at Guildhall on Sat. 11 Dec. to hear judgment. On that day he appears in the Chamber, in the presence of James Andrew, mayor, William de Halden, John de Stodeye, Stephen de Cavendyssh, Bartholomew de Frestlyngg, Simon de Mordon, Walter Forster, John Chychestre, William de Tudenham, John de St. Albans, John Lyttle and Richard de Croydon, aldermen, John de Tornegold, alderman and sheriff, and William Dykeman, sheriff, and the record and process having been read, it is adjudged that *within 40 days etc.* the nuisance be wholly removed, according to the terms of the statute of buildings (iuxta formam statuti editi de edificiis). The sheriffs are ordered to warn the def. accordingly.
Afterwards, on 17 Feb. 1368, they reported that they had caused the nuisance to be removed in accordance with a mandate directed to them. [*Margin:* Amocio nocumenti per vicecomites.]

537. [m. 19] Thomas Whytcherch and William Whetele, tawyers, complain that the same Agnes has a solar in the same par. which overhangs their land to a length of 16 ft. and a width of 7 ins. so that they cannot build their house upright (linialiter in altitudine). The sheriffs testify that the def. has been solemnly summoned upon the land where the nuisances are alleged to be, by Nicholas de Snypston and William Cavell, but she makes default. The mayor and aldermen, having viewed the premises, give the pls. a day at Guildhall on Sat. 11 Dec. to hear judgment. On that day, in the presence of the mayor and aldermen [as in 536] they appear, and it is

Assize of Nuisance

adjudged that *within 40 days etc.* the nuisance be wholly removed. The sheriffs are ordered to warn the def. accordingly.

Afterwards, on 17 Feb. 1368, they reported, as above, that they had caused the nuisance to be removed. [*Margin:* Amocio nocumenti per vicecomites.]

[m. 19d.] *Fri. 28 Apr. 1368. James Andrew, mayor, the aldermen and sheriffs.*

538. The abbot of Cirencester, def., essoins himself against John atte Seler and Alice his wife by William atte Polle.

539. William la Zouche of Haryngworth, kt., def., essoins himself against Richard de Penbrigg, kt., by William Russe.[1]

Fri. 5 May 1368. James Andrew, mayor, the aldermen and sheriffs.

540. John de Cornewayll, 'glovere', and Collecta his wife, defs., essoin themselves against John de Dunton by William Posse.

541. William Bonet, 'wodemongere', and Christine his wife, defs., essoin themselves against Alice relict of Simon de Worstede by the same.

Fri. 16 June 1368. James Andrew, mayor, and the aldermen.

542. Emma relict of Simon le Spicer, lumbard, def., essoins herself against Margery de Honylane, prioress of St. Helen's, by William Posse.

543. Assize between Edward Sende, 'smyth', pl., and John Kempeseye, chaplain, respited.

Fri. 30 June 1368. [No entry.]

544. Thurs. 27 July 1368, Adam Chippenham, parson of St. Clement Candelwykstrete, presented a bill in the following terms: As mair et Recordour de la Citee de Londres monstrent Adam Chippenham persone del esglise de Seint Clement ioust Candelwykstrete en Londres et les parochiens de mesme lesglise, que come Roger de Depham devisa certains tenementz en la dite paroche as mair aldermans et commonalte de la dite Citee a eux et a lour successours a touz iours, queux tenementz sont edifiez od ij gettez chescun parmont altre, pendantz outre la esglise et le cymiter de mesme la esglise a graunt anoysaunce de les persone et parochiens avantditz, dont pur dieu et en amendement de le alme avantdit Roger ils prient remedie.

After the mayor and aldermen had viewed the premises, and taken counsel among themselves and discussed the matter (habito . . . colloquio) with the complainants, the latter agreed that the tenement should remain in perpetuity as at present, and released and quit-claimed, for themselves and their successors, all actions, plaints and demands concerning it. The mayor,

1. For plaint see *C.P.M.R. 1364–81*, 88.

Assize of Nuisance

aldermen and commonalty in their turn undertook to provide the parson and parishioners yearly from the Chamber, by the hands of the chamberlain, with two torches (torcheas) of new wax, weighing 24 lbs., on the vigil of the Assumption, to burn at the elevation of the Body of Christ, and on appropriate occasions (temporibus opportunis) when the Lord's Body is carried (pro baiulacione) through the parish, as long as the tenement remains in their hands.

[m. 20] *Fri. 6 Oct. 1368. [Essoins only.]*

Fri. 20 Oct. 1368. James Andrew, mayor, and the aldermen and sheriffs.

545. Alice relict of John Deynes complains that William Dykeman, 'ismongere', and Idonea his wife have a tenement in the par. of St. Olave in Old Jewry, in Lovelane, over against (erga) hers on the north side, consisting of two storeys, of which the second, in front, on the west side of the lane extends for a width of 5 ins. beyond the middle of the lane and continues, gradually diminishing (particulariter dimuendo) for 21 ft. towards the east side, so that the pl. cannot build her tenement on the south side of the lane by reason of the overhang. The defs. come in person and say that they have muniments bearing upon the matter, and are given a day to produce them on Fri. 3 Nov. After adjournment the assize comes on the land on Fri. 17 Nov. by Simon de Mordon, mayor, William de Halden, John de Stodeye, James Andreu, William Welde, William de Tudenham and John de Mitford, aldermen, and Adam de Wymondham and Robert Gurdlere, sheriffs. The pl. appears by her attorney, Robert Creswyk. William Dykeman makes default. Idonea comes prepared to answer and is admitted to plead in defence of her right, but she says nothing to delay the assize. After viewing the premises the mayor and aldermen find that the allegations of the pl. are correct, and it is adjudged that the nuisance be removed *within 40 days etc*. The sheriffs are ordered to warn the defs. accordingly.

Fri. 27 Oct. 1368. [Essoin only.]

[m. 20d.] *Fri. 3 Nov. 1368. Simon de Mordon, mayor, Adam Fraunceys, William de Halden, James Andrew, William Welde, aldermen, and Adam Wymondham and Robert Gurdlere, sheriffs.*

546. Adam Chipenham, parson of St. Clement in Estchepe, Thomas Clench and John Pope, parishioners, complain that Christine Pekham has a house with a jetty which overhangs the churchyard for a length of 15 ft. and a width of 2 ft., with two gutters (stillicidia) projecting for $2\frac{1}{2}$ ft. beyond the jetty (pendent ultra predictum geticium in cemiterio predicto) from which the rainwater falls upon the churchyard. The sheriffs testify that the def. has been summoned by Thomas de Same, 'taillour', and William atte Watere, 'bocher', but she makes default. The mayor and aldermen view the premises, but wishing to be more fully advised, give the pls. a day at Guildhall on Fri. 17 Nov. On that day the assize comes by the

Assize of Nuisance

mayor, aldermen and sheriffs [as in **545**] and it is adjudged that *within 40 days etc.* the nuisances be removed. The sheriffs are ordered to warn the def. accordingly.

Fri. 10 Nov. 1368. [Respite only.]

Fri. 24 Nov. 1368. [No entry.]

[m. 21] *Fri. 22 Dec. 1368 and Fri. 5 Jan. 1369. [Essoins only.]*

Fri. 19 Jan. 1369. Simon de Mordon, mayor, William Halden, William Welde, William de Tudenham, John de St. Albans and John Mitford, aldermen, Adam Wymondham and Robert Gurdler, sheriffs.

547. John de Wentbrigge, common serjeant, complains on behalf of the commonalty that Geoffrey Marchal has built a forge (fabricam) in the par. of St. Michael de Hoggenlane in Wodstret in the public highway, which is greatly narrowed thereby, and a pentice above it, so that laden horses and carts and horsemen and persons carrying burdens cannot pass without difficulty, as they were formerly accustomed to do. The def. comes in person, but says nothing to delay the assize. The mayor and aldermen, having viewed the site, adjourn the proceedings until Mon. 22 Jan. On that day the def. makes default, but the record and process having been read in the presence of the mayor, William Halden, recorder, William Welde, John Lytle, William Tudenham, John Tornegold, Bartholomew Frestlyng and John Mitford, aldermen, it is adjudged that *within 40 days etc.* the nuisance be removed. The sheriffs are ordered to warn the def. accordingly.

548. [m. 21d.] John Beaufront, 'wolmongere', and Margery his wife complain that the same Geoffrey Mareschal of Wodestret has built a forge in the public highway with a pentice above, so that scarcely any daylight can penetrate their shop, and the craftsmen (artifices) who used to carry on their trade and craft (artificum et misterum) there can no longer see to do so. The def. comes in person. [Remainder as in **547**.]

549. John Haukyn complains that the rainwater from the house of Alice relict of William de Bury, late citizen and draper, in the par. of St. Botolph without Algate, falls upon his garden, so that the vines (vites) and other plants (herbe) there, which used to grow and bear fruit, are withered (arescunt) and barren (fructum proferre nequeunt); and she has six windows below the height of 16 ft. from the ground opening on to his garden, through which her tenants can see his private business and that of his tenants. The def. comes and claims to have muniments bearing on the matter, and is given a day on Fri. 16 Feb. when the def. essoins herself by James Posse, who is ordered to produce his warrant at the quindene [Fri. 2 Mar.]. After further adjournment until Fri. 16 Mar. the parties come, but the def. says nothing to delay the assize. Since the mayor and aldermen find by view that the pl.'s allegations are correct, it is adjudged that the nuisances be removed *within 40 days etc.* and the sheriffs are ordered to warn the def. to block up the windows, and to make a fillet-gutter (filettum) to carry off the rainwater on to her own land or into the street.

Fri. 2 Feb. 1369. Assize adjourned.

[m. 22] *Fri. 16 Feb. 1369. Simon de Mordon, mayor, and the aldermen.*

550. Emma relict of Simon de Pistoye, def., essoins herself against William la Souche, kt., and lord of Harryngworth, by William Gill. [For loveday, see under 9 Mar.]

Fri. 2 Mar. 1369. Assize adjourned.

Fri. 9 Mar. 1369. Simon de Mordon, mayor, and the aldermen.

551. John Boterwyke, Richard Stonham and Margery his wife, defs., essoin themselves against William de Bristowe, grocer, by Richard Forster.

Loveday given to the parties in **550**.

Fri. 20 Apr. 1369. Simon de Mordon, mayor, and the aldermen.

552. John Hore, def., essoins himself against Alice relict of Simon de Worstede by William Greyngham.

553. John de Ratforde, def., essoins himself against the same by the same.

554. The assize between Thomas Frowyk, pl., and Walter Walden, spicer, adjourned by consent of the parties.

[m. 22d.] *Fri. 4 May 1369. [Respites only.]*

Fri. 18 May 1369. Assize adjourned.

Fri. 1, 15 and 29 June 1369. [Respites only.]

Fri. 13 July 1369. Simon de Mordon, mayor, and the aldermen.

555. Gilbert atte Stone, 'bocher', def., essoins himself against Alice relict of John Deynes, 'ismongere', by Gilbert Meldebourne.

556. The abbot of Fécamp (Feskampe), def., essoins himself against Roger Holm, canon of St. Paul's, by William Greyngham.

[m. 23] *Fri. 27 July 1369. Simon de Mordon, mayor, and the aldermen.*

557. Thomas Hanhampstede, citizen and grocer, def., essoins himself

Assize of Nuisance

against Geoffrey Puppe, citizen and 'stokfishmongere', by Adam Pylk. [See below under 14 Dec.]

Fri. 10 and 24 Aug. 1369. Assize adjourned.

Fri. 31 Aug. 1369. Simon de Mordon, mayor, and the aldermen.

558. John de Bampton, def., essoins himself against William, abbot of St. Mary Graces beside the Tower, represented by Gilbert de Meldebourne, by William Hockele.

Fri. 7 Sep. 1369. Assize adjourned on account of the preoccupation of the mayor and aldermen with City affairs.

[m. 23d.] *Fri. 14 Sep. 1369. Assize adjourned.*

Fri. 21 Sep. 1369. [Essoins and respites only.]

Fri. 28 Sep. 1369. Simon de Mordon, mayor, and the aldermen.

559. Isabel wife of William Chyvele, 'taillour', def., essoins herself against Richard de Chelmersford, carpenter, by John Tyrp. The same William appears. [See below under 1 Feb. 1370.]

Fri. 5 Oct. 1369. Simon de Mordon, mayor, Adam Fraunceys, William Halden, John Stodeye, Stephen Cavendissh, William Welde, John de Chichestre and John Mitford, aldermen.

560. Robert de Watlyngton is summoned to answer Thomas de Saham, 'taillour', who does not prosecute his suit (non prosecutus). [See below under 19 Oct.]

[m. 24] *Fri. 5 Oct. continued, and 12 Oct. 1369. [Respites only.]*

Fri. 19 Oct. 1369. Simon de Mordon, mayor, and the aldermen, and John Pyel and Hugh Holbech, sheriffs.

561. Gilbert Lyrp, baker, def., essoins himself against John Mayn, baker, and Christine his wife by Ralph Coo.

562. Edward de Kendale, kt., def., essoins himself against John de Wycoumbe by William Sewale.

563. Reginald Love, citizen, def., essoins himself against John Buris, prior of Crutched Friars beside the Tower, by Gilbert Meldebourne.

Pl. and his pledges in mercy for not prosecuting his suit [560].

Fri. 26 Oct. 1369. [Essoins and respites only.]

Assize of Nuisance

Fri. 2 Nov. 1369, [m. 24d.] *Fri. 9 Nov. 1369. Assize adjourned.*

Fri. 16 Nov. 1369. John de Chychestre, mayor, William Halden, recorder, Simon de Mordon, William Welde, John Tornegold and John Pyel, aldermen, and the same John and Hugh Holbech, sheriffs.

564. Joan wife of John Hende, draper, def., essoins herself against Edmund Cheyne, kt., and Katherine his wife by Richard Postek.

565. Thomas de Sallowe, master of St. Thomas Dacon, def., essoins himself against Edmund Cheyne, kt., and Katherine his wife by the same.

566. Thomas Whitcherch, tawyer, complains that Maud Frembaud has an open window in her tenement in the par. of St. Michael at Corne, opening upon his, and that her tenants constantly come out of it into his gutter (gutter'), into which they throw excrement and other refuse, so that it is stopped up, and the rainwater cannot escape, but overflows and floods his wall and rots the timber; and she has another tenement adjoining his, with a plastered wall (murum plastratum), broken down and open on the east side, through which her tenants go in and out, and see his private business; and the rainwater from her tenement, and the water which her tenants draw from her well falls upon his land, and flows through a gutter in the midst of another tenement belonging to him. The def. comes in person and says that she has muniments bearing on the matter, and is given a day on Fri. 30 Nov. to produce them. She then essoins herself by Robert Watlyngton, who is ordered to produce his warrant at the quindene. After further adjournment the mayor and aldermen come on Fri. 8 Feb. 1370 and give the parties a day at Guildhall on Mon. 11 Feb. to hear judgment. It is adjudged that *within 40 days etc.* the nuisances be removed and the broken plastered wall repaired. The sheriffs are ordered to warn the def. accordingly.

Certificate [French] of Richard de Shropshire and Thomas Fant, carpenters, Richard atte Chirche and Thomas atte Barnet, master masons, to the effect that the tenements of Thomas Whitcherche and Maud Frembaud were formerly one (dune frame), and built together (faitz ensemble), and that the couple beams (les couples bemes) of Thomas's tenement form the reason[1] (resun) of the party-wall between them, but that another of Maud's party-walls rests upon the reason of Thomas's tenement, and is affixed to it by nails. It therefore seems that the first party-wall ought to belong to Thomas.

[m. 25] *Fri. 23 Nov. 1369. Assize adjourned.*

Fri. 30 Nov. 1369. [Essoins and respites only.]

Fri. 7 Dec. 1369. John de Chychestre, mayor, and the aldermen.

1. Reason, or wall-plate (O.E.D. *sb.* 2; Salzman, Building in England, 203).

Assize of Nuisance

567. Agnes relict of William de Glendale complains of Michael de Cornewaill and Fredeswyde his wife who say that they have nothing in the tenement concerning which the nuisance is alleged save for a term of years and that the fee belongs to the dean and chapter of St. Paul's. Therefore the pl. is in mercy and the defs. *sine die.*

568. The assize between John Asshwell and Parnel his wife, pls., and John de Ware, 'chaundeler', and Christine his wife respited.

Fri. 14 Dec. 1369. John Chychestre, mayor, and the aldermen.

Pl. and his pledges in mercy for not prosecuting his bill of assize [**557**].

Fri. 21 Dec. 1369. Assize adjourned on account of the preoccupation of the mayor and aldermen with City affairs.

[m. 25d.] *Fri. 28 Dec. 1369, 4, 11, 18 and 25 Jan. 1370. Assize adjourned.*

Fri. 1 Feb. 1370. John de Chichestre, mayor, and the aldermen.

Pl. and his pledges in mercy for not prosecuting his suit [**559**].

Fri. 8 Feb. 1370. [Respites only.]

[m. 26] *Fri. 15 Feb. 1370. John Chychestre, mayor, William de Halden, recorder, Stephen Cavendyssh, James Andreu, Walter Forster, John Mitford and John Piel, aldermen.*

569. Brother Robert de Madyngton, guardian of the Friars Minor, complains by Robert de Watlyngton, his attorney, that Richard Bayser, 'bocher', and Emma his wife have built a 'skaldynghous' in their tenement in Pentecostlane in the par. of St. Nicholas Shambles, in which they slaughter pigs and many other animals, and the water mixed with the blood and hair of the slaughtered animals, and with other filth from the washing (lotura) [of the carcases], flows into the ditch or kennel in the street, through which it is carried into the friars' garden, causing a stench in many places there. The defs. come, but show no cause why the assize should be delayed. The mayor and aldermen, having viewed the premises, give the parties a day to hear judgment.

570. Adam, abbot of Rewley (de loco regali) near Oxford, complains by William Hockelee, his attorney, that in rainy weather the water from the tenement of Thomas de Salesbury, kt., which is 20 ft. long, and adjoins his in the par. of St. Stephen de Colmanstret falls upon his land, for lack of a fillet-gutter (filettum); and also that the def. has an earthen wall 200 ft. long standing upon the pl.'s land, and adjoining his garden, which is ruinous in various places, and because the def. does not repair it as he is bound to do, men and dogs and other animals enter and tread down and destroy the plants (herbas) growing in the garden. The def. comes by

Robert de Watlyngton, his attorney, and says that he has muniments bearing on the matter. He is given a day at the quindene to produce them.

571. [m. 26d.] William son of Robert de Thame and Juliana his wife bring an assize against Robert de Draycote, prior of the hospital of St. Mary de Elsyngespitle within Crepulgate.

572. Agnes relict of William de Glendale complains by Robert de Watlyngton, her attorney, that the dean and chapter of St. Paul's have a house adjoining her tenement in the par. of St. Matthew de Frydaystret, from which in rainy weather, for lack of a leaden fillet-gutter (filetti plumbi) 18½ ft. long, the water falls upon her land; and whereas she has in her garden a soakaway (voragine) 6 ft. long and 2 ft. wide to receive the water from her house, which from time out of mind used to flow thence through a gutter (gutter') in the wall of the defs.' tenement, they have now obstructed it so that the water flows back (refluit) and floods the walls and floors (areas) of the buildings (domorum) in her tenement. John Piel and Hugh Holbech, sheriffs, testify that the defs. have been summoned by William Passeware and Thomas Skremyn of Frydaystret, but they do not come. After viewing the premises, the mayor and aldermen give the parties a day at the quindene to hear judgment. Afterwards, on Fri. 26 Apr. 1370, Agnes appears by her attorney against the defs. who make default, and the record and process having been recited, it is adjudged that *within 40 days etc.* the defs. repair the fillet-gutter (filettum) and clear the other gutter (gutter') so that the water from the pl.'s soakaway may flow freely as it used to do.

Fri. 22 Feb. 1370. John de Chychestre, mayor, and the aldermen.

573. John Sely, 'skynnere', def., essoins himself against Hugh de Badewe, kt., John Aubrey and John Philipot by Alan Post.

Fri. 1 Mar. 1370. Assize adjourned.

[m. 27. *No heading.*]

574. On Mon. 11 Mar. 1370 Geoffrey de la Launde, parson of St. Leonard de Estchepe, Walter Hervyll, 'peutrer', and the other parishioners, presented to the mayor and recorder a bill [French] in the following terms: the above-named parson and Walter Hervyll, William Ivory, Robert Boydon, Robert Lyndewyk, Thomas Spicer, John Bronnesbury, Henry atte Beche, Richard atte Suyte, William Gylet and the other parishioners, complain that Walter Doget claims a window in the party-wall of the church, to the nuisance and disherison of the parson and parishioners and of a house which they have bought in honour of God, his Blessed Mother, and all Saints for the enlargement and repair of the same church; and that the pentice of a room and a garret (gareyte) in his house overhang the churchyard; and, further, that he holds by deed (feat) a plot of land in the churchyard for an annual rent of 8s., on condition of building there upon four posts, but has

Assize of Nuisance

done nothing. John Chamberleyn, serjeant, is ordered to cause the parties to appear before the mayor and aldermen on Fri. 15 Mar. Both come in person, and the def., having heard the bill read, says that he has muniments bearing on the matter. He is given a day on Fri. 22 Mar. to produce them. On that day both parties again appear and the def. maintains his claim to the window as the son and heir of Thomas Doget, who was seised of the same and of the view through it into the chapel, and had enjoyed for a long time the overhang (iactesia) and the light, both high and low (luminaria alta et yma) in his buildings (domibus) next the church and churchyard, having given a portion of his house, in honour of God and the Blessed Virgin, for the enlargement of the said chapel. He produces an indenture between Richard de Godwyneston, late rector, Thomas de Burgh, William Knyth, John Odyerne, Boydin Fader, Adam de Canefeld, John atte Gate, Geoffrey Fairher, John Blod, John Leman, John Edward, Richard Casse and Gilbert atte Forde, parishioners, and the above-named Thomas Doget, 'vynter', reciting his gift to the church of a portion of his house, and guaranteeing in return to him and his heirs enjoyment in perpetuity of the overhang and light, with the right to insert a wooden plate 5 ft. long and 6 ins. wide on the west side of the chapel to support that side of his house, and to enjoy the view through a small window built in the corner of the chapel wall during Mass (tempore missalis servicili). Dated Fri. 15 Aug. 1337. As to the pentice and garret, the def. says that, as a parishioner, he is entitled to the easement, and that they were not built to the nuisance of the pls. Concerning the plot of land in the churchyard, he produces an indenture between himself, citizen and vintner, and Thomas Archer, late rector, William Ivory, Robert Boydon, Walter Hervill, 'peuatrer', Robert Lyndewyk, John Fairher and John Bronnesbury, parishioners, in which the rector and parishioners lease to him for 99 years, as from the following 24 June, a vacant plot of land between his own tenement on the north, and that of Robert Furneux on the south, and between the tenement of Roger Shipbrok on the west and the churchyard on the east, for an annual rent of 8s., the lessors retaining the right to distrain for arrears, with permission to build there on four sufficient posts measuring 8 or 9 ft. from the ground to the joists (gistas). Dated 22 May 1364. Witnesses: John Lytle, Richard de Croydon, William Cherchegate and others. He declares that he has duly paid the rent and that the rector and parishioners have no right to molest (occasionare) him. [m. 27d.] On Fri. 29 Mar. 1370 the assize comes upon the site (super placeam predictam) by John Chichestre, mayor, Adam Fraunceys, William Halden, recorder, John Pecche, Stephen Cavendisshe, Simon de Mordon, William Welde, Bartholomew Frestlyng, John Warde and John Pyel, aldermen, and Hugh Holbech, sheriff, who find by view that the pls. have suffered no nuisance. It is therefore adjudged that the def. retain the window and view into the chapel, and the pentice and garret and plot of land with all the other easements enjoyed hitherto. Thereupon, in the presence of the mayor and aldermen, the parties agree that Walter shall cause a new window to be built in the corner of the new stone wall, in the same place as before, and shall continue to enjoy, without challenge, all the other easements to which he lays claim, and they ask that the agreement be enrolled in the above form.

Assize of Nuisance

[m. 28] *Fri. 8 Mar. 1370. John de Chychestre, mayor, and the aldermen.*

575. John Thorneye, pl., essoins himself against Richard Nortbury and Ymanya his wife by Adam Post.

Fri. 15, 22, 29 Mar., 5 Apr., 5 July (after the feast of St. Leo, pope), 8 Mar. (before the feast of St. Gregory)[1] *1370. Assize adjourned.*

Fri. 26 Apr. 1370. [Respites only.]

[m. 28d.] *Fri. 3 May 1370. Mayor and the aldermen.*

576. Assize between John Cook, brewer, pl., and William Hordele, 'sherman', and Thomas Byrche, 'haberdassher', respited by consent of the parties. [*Margin:* Vac'.]

Fri. 10, 17, 24, 31 May, and 7 June 1370. [Essoins and respites only.]

Fri. 14 June 1370. Assize adjourned.

[m. 29] *Fri. 15 Nov. 1370. John Bernes, mayor, William de Halden, recorder, Stephen Cavendyssh, John Stodeye, William Welde, John Piel, aldermen, and Robert de Kayton, sheriff.*

577. William de Ufford, earl of Suffolk, and Joan his wife complain by Robert de Watlyngton, their attorney, that whereas they have a messuage in the par. of St. Mary de Somersete, extending from Tamisestret to the river, and adjoining on the east side Disebourlane, John Tornegold, citizen and fishmonger, has a messuage on the west side of the lane, likewise extending from the street to the Thames, and he holds the said lane, which is 215 ft. long, 7 ft. wide at the end next the street, and 1 ell wide at the end next the river, and there used to be, in the midst of the same lane, a kennel (canellum) deep and wide enough to receive and carry off all the water flowing from all the City streets into the river, but the def. has raised with stones and timber the level of the lane adjoining his messuage, and has dug out the soil adjoining that of the pls., and has made a gutter (gutteram) across (extransverso) the end (capud) of the lane next the Thames, by which the flow of water is held back and cannot escape, so that all the water flowing from the street, and the water, both hot and cold, thrown out by the tenants-at-will (tenentes per voluntatem) of the def., flows back (refluit) on to the pls.' party-walls and rots and penetrates them, and enters their messuage with such force and in such quantity that they and their tenants cannot remain (comorari) there. Further, the def. has built across the lane at the end next the street an iron grating (cratam ferream), which holds back the water which used to flow out through the lane so that it flows back on to the end of the pls.' house which abuts upon the street, and the walls are rotted, and the pls. and their tenants cannot enter by the door there. The def. comes in person, and says that John de Gildesburgh, citizen and fishmonger, formerly held the tenement which he

1. ? Fictitious dates for 12 and 19 Apr., Good Friday and the Friday following.

now holds, and the present king, by his letters patent,[1] produced in court (? quas ostendit), confirmed him in possession, and therefore the assize does not lie. The pls. contend that he has shown no cause why they should be excluded from the assize, and since he makes no further defence, the proceedings continue. The mayor and aldermen, having viewed the premises, give the parties a day on Sat. 16 Nov. After adjournment until Mon. 10 Mar. 1371 the pls. come by their attorney, and the def. in person, and the premises having been recited it is adjudged that the nuisances be removed *within 40 days etc.*

[m. 29d.] *Fri. 14 Mar. 1371. John Bernes, mayor, and the aldermen.*

578. Mariota relict of Adam Carlille, draper, essoins herself against John de Mitford, draper, and Joan his wife by William Post.

Fri. 28 Mar. and (? 28 [sic] June, the feast of St. Leo, pope)[2] 1371. Assize adjourned.

Fri. 27 June 1371. John Bernes, mayor, and the aldermen.

579. John Merden, 'bocher', and Alice his wife, John de Cressyngham and Richard le Coupere, defs., essoin themselves against the dean and chapter of St. Paul's by Adam Potelle.

Fri. 4 July 1371. John Bernes, mayor, and the aldermen.

580. Henry atte Hale, fishmonger, and Joan his wife, defs., essoin themselves against John Broun of Grantesdene by Thomas Post.

[m. 30. *16 Jan. 1372.*]

581. Certificate [French] of Richard Sropshire and Thomas Fant, carpenters, Thomas atte Barnet and Richard atte Chirche, masons, to the mayor, recorder, and aldermen, touching the tenements of 'les bones gentz de la Fraternite des Haberdassheres' in St. Laurence Lane, Old Jewry, joined to the timber of a chamber called 'haltepas' held by William Waleys, 'gurdeler'. They report that a door (huys) of the haberdashers' tenement is hung on hinges (crokes) affixed to the timber of William's tenement, and that it ought to be removed and re-hung upon hinges in the haberdashers' tenement.
Thomas Botulston, John Grafton and Henry Northfolke appear on behalf of the fraternity, but can show no cause why the door of their tenement should hang on hinges (cardines) on William's timber. It is therefore adjudged that it be removed and re-hung on their own timber, and that they enter and leave by it as formerly.

[*Fri. 28 May 1372.*]

1. ? *C.P.R.* 1361–4, 225.
2. ? Fictitious date for 4 Apr., Good Friday.

Assize of Nuisance

582. Certificate [French] of the same carpenters and masons concerning the quay of Oystregate and the land of the prior and convent of St. Mary de Overee to the following effect:— 'vous plese savoir que nous avoms vieu le wharf de Oystregate et la terre le Priour et covent de nostre dame de Overee quel est parentre le Wharf William Byce envers le West dune part et la venelle de Oystregate susdit envers le est. Sur quel vew nous vous dioms qe le dit priour et covent ont fyche lour pyle sur la commune en laure au poynt de lour auncien place sur Thamise al est bout de lour wharf iouste Oystregate par ij pees et iij pouces et le quart dune pouce, et issint le dit wharf contient dilloeque tanque a le Wharf William Byce xv pies, et le coyn del mure a de piere du dit priour et covent a la cornere iouste Oystregate susdit adiugge bon et qelle estera as touz iours.'

[*Fri. 30 Sep. 1373.*]

583. Certificate [French] of the same carpenters and masons concerning the fixtures (choses nient remuables) in the tenement held for life by Philip Draper, cook, in the par. of St. Michael atte Corne. They report that they viewed the premises in the presence of Henry Yuele, William Fraunceys, Richard Godchild, William Twyford and John Simond, 'chaundeler', and found that Thomas Bermysygham [*sic*] had removed (arace) two leaden vessels (plumb') in a stone oven (ffurneys de pere), a leaden 'tappetrowe', and a 'maltbynne' affixed by nails to the timber of the tenement, and two 'ovenemouthes', the which articles are the property of William Burdeyn and Isabel his wife, daughter and heiress of the above-named Philip, and, according to the custom of the City, ought not to have been removed.
Thereupon William Burdeyn appears in person against Thomas Bermyngham [*sic*], who makes default, and because he had previously put himself upon the view of the masons and carpenters, it is ordered that he be distrained to appear on Fri. 7 Oct. to hear judgment, and the same day is given to the pl.[1] [m. 30d. Blank.]

[m. 31] *Fri. 10 Dec. 1372. John Pyel, mayor, Adam Fraunceys, William Haldene, John Stodey, Adam Stable, John Philipot and Nicholas Bremble, aldermen.*

584. John Schalyngford, 'taillour', complains that John Prentys, draper, has in his tenement in the par. of St. Nicholas Shambles a soakaway (varaginem) next his stone wall, the foundation of which is rotted by the water and filth from it; and in rainy weather the water penetrates the wall and flows into a cellar in his tenement, and settles on his land. The sheriffs testify that the def. has been summoned by Walter atte Grene and Richard Bayser, 'bocher', but he makes default. The mayor and aldermen, having viewed the premises, and found conditions to be as alleged, give the pl. a day at Guildhall to hear judgment on Mon. 13 Dec. On that day, at the Husting of Common Pleas, it is adjudged that the nuisances be removed *within 40 days etc.*

1. Cf. *C.P.M.R. 1364–81*, 150.

Assize of Nuisance

585. Thomas Kendale, rector of St. Augustine by St. Paul's Gate, and Richard Pykebourne, chaplain, complain that there is a wooden roof (coopertura de ligno) called a 'pentys' affixed to the party-wall of the house of William Kentoys and Alice his wife adjoining theirs in the above-named par., and in rainy weather the water falling upon it lies upon their walls and rots them. They complain further that whereas they have a stable (stabulum) situated above a vault (valtam), with a high chamber (cameram altam) above part of the stable, the aforesaid Thomas and Richard [? *rectius* William and Alice] have a latrine below the said chamber and above part of the stable, and the party-walls at its back and sides are affixed to the beams (trabibus) of the same chamber in such wise that the beams cannot sustain their weight but are forced out of position (unde parietes predicte tali modo fixe tam ponderantes super trabes predictas, ita quod trabe ille sustentare non poterunt pondus nec onus predictum, et per quod trabe predicte detracte sunt extra naturalem gradum suum), so that the chamber is in danger of collapse. Also, beneath the latrine is a cess-pit (puteus), the bottom (fundus) of which is level with the aforesaid vault (equalis in profunditate valte predicte), so that the ordure therefrom stops it up, and emits so great a stench that the pls. can have no profit from their stable, and the beams of the vault are rotted.

[m. 31d. *? 10 Dec. 1372.*]

586. William Stodeye, 'vynter', complains that a solar in the tenement of Thomas Kynwardesle above the alley leading to the entrance (aleiam introitus) of the pl.'s tenement in the par. of St. Martin in Vintry is broken down and the roof thereof demolished (prostratus), so that it stands open, and in rainy weather the water falls from it on to his land, and flows into his cellar, and rots his timber and party-walls; and the def. has a stone wall beneath the same solar, extending along the east side of the alley, which, on account of its insecurity (propter debilitatem) leans so heavily upon the pl.'s buildings and so weighs them down (super illas iacet eas opprimendo) that their party-walls are broken, and the joists (giste), planks (planchie), and beams (trabes) are thrust out of position (a proprio situ suo expelluntur); and the buildings are on the point of collapse; also, the wall itself is so insecure, and so far out of the perpendicular (tam debilis et ruinosus et declinans est versus tenementi predicti Willelmi) that it is a grave danger to all passing along the alley. Further, the water from the def.'s houses built upon the same wall falls in rainy weather, for lack of a fillet-gutter (filettum) running the length of his tenement, upon the pl.'s land in the alley aforesaid. John Philipot and Nicholas Bremble, sheriffs, testify that the def. has been summoned by Geoffrey Neuton and John Aas, but he makes default. The mayor and aldermen, having viewed the premises, give the pl. a day at Guildhall on Mon. 13 Dec. 1372 to hear judgment. He comes in person, and the premises having been recited, it is adjudged that *within 40 days etc.* the def. repair the solar and stone wall and make a fillet-gutter to receive and carry off the water. The sheriffs are ordered to warn him accordingly.

[*Dec. 1372.*]

Assize of Nuisance

587. John de Wentebrigg complains that whereas all the water falling within his close (clauso) used to flow through a gutter (gutterum) in the midst of the adjoining tenement of John Froile and Edmund Daunvers in the par. of St. Peter by Oldefisshstret, into the street, the defs. have now stopped up the gutter and prevented (pertubarunt) the flow of water, so that as well in rainy weather as at other times it remains standing on the ground in his close, and often flows into his cellar and rots both the foundations and the timber of his party-walls. John Philippot and Nicholas Brembre, sheriffs, testify that the defs. have been summoned by William Kelshull, 'pessoner', and William Carlill, 'botiller', but they make default. The mayor and aldermen, having viewed the premises and found the nuisances to be as alleged, give the pl. a day at Guildhall on Fri. 7 Jan. 1373 to hear judgment, when, the premises having been recited in the presence of John Pyel, mayor, William Halden, recorder, John Wroth, John Stodeye, John Little, Adam Stable, William Walworth and John Philippot, aldermen, it is adjudged that *within 40 days etc.* the nuisances be removed, and that the defs. clear the gutter so that the water from the pl.'s close can flow as formerly into the street through their tenement.

[m. 32 *No heading*.]

588. Memorandum that Thomas de Newenham, clerk, lately sued out a bill of assize of nuisance against William Herland, carpenter, because he refused to give 1½ ft. of his land towards the building of a stone wall between their gardens in the pars. of St. Benet at le Wodewharf, and St. Peter the Less by Pauleswharf. Afterwards, on Fri. 1 Apr. 1373, the parties appeared before John Pyel, mayor, at Guildhall, and agreed together to build a new stone wall upon their common land and at their common charges, in accordance with the custom of the City, the same to remain in common to them and their heirs and assigns in perpetuity. This agreement and grant the mayor recorded and reported to the recorder and aldermen, and ordered it to be enrolled in the above form. [Cf. **590**.]

Fri. 6 May 1373. John Pyel, mayor, William Halden, John Stodeye, John Chichestre, Bartholomew Fristlyng, John Warde, John Tornegold, Adam Stable, John Aubrey and Nicholas Brembre aldermen.

589. William Schirbourne and Isabel his wife complain that Edmund Cheyne, kt., and Katherine his wife, who have a tenement in the par. of St. Swithin 14 ells less 6 ins. wide, including a building which used to be a tenter-yard (tentorium), have removed the roof thereof and torn up and carried away a leaden gutter (gutteram plumbiam) annexed to the pls.' tenement, through which their rainwater used to flow, so that the water now falls on their timber and the party-walls of their tenement and rots them; and the defs.' timber has collapsed (ruit), and leans against the pls.' buildings, which are on the point of falling to the ground by reason of the weight. John Philippot and Nicholas Brembre, sheriffs, testify that the defs. have been summoned by John Hende and Robert Watlyngton, but they make default. The mayor and aldermen, having viewed the premises, give the pls. a day at Guildhall at the next Husting to hear judgment. Afterwards, at the Husting of Common Pleas held on Mon. 25 July 1373, the pls. appear in person against the defs., who again make default. Judgment that *within 40 days etc.* they re-roof the building in their tenement which was formerly a tenter-yard, replace the gutter through which the pls.' water used to flow, and remove the timber which has collapsed and leans against the pls.' buildings. The sheriffs are ordered to warn them accordingly.

[m. 32d.] *Fri. 13 May 1373. John Pyel, mayor, Adam Fraunceys, William Halden, John Stodeye, John Chichestre, John Litle, William Walworth, Walter Forster, John Mitford, John Tornegold, Nicholas Brembre and John Philippot, aldermen.*

590. Thomas de Newenham, clerk, complains that William Herland, carpenter, has a tenement and garden in the par. of St. Benet at le Wodwharf, adjoining his in the par. of St. Peter the Less by Pouleswharf, but refuses to participate in the building of a wall between them, so that the pl.'s garden lies open and the plants growing there are trodden down and destroyed. The def. appears, but shows no cause why a wall should not be built in accordance with the assize. The mayor and aldermen, having viewed the premises, give the parties a day at Guildhall on Mon. 16 May to hear judgment. On that day they both appear in person, and the premises having been recited, and the parties having agreed together to build a stone wall 60 ft. long between their tenements, it is adjudged that *within 40 days etc.* each shall give 1½ ft. of his land for the building of a wall 3 ft. wide and 16 ft. high, the same to remain to them in common. [Cf. **588**.]

[m. 33 *No heading.*]

591. On Thurs. 11 Aug. 1373 Richard de Stortford, 'letherseller', delivered to the mayor and aldermen a bill [French] complaining that William de Stoke and Margery his wife had sued out a bill of assize of nuisance against him in Nov. 1366 [**526**] concerning their tenement in the par. of St. Lawrence in old Juerye, and by their common consent and order of the mayor and aldermen for the time being, the master carpenters and masons had viewed the alleged nuisance, which concerned a stone wall running from east to west between the tenements of the parties, and had certified that it was partible between them, and that the arches on either side of it were the same depth, and the old plate and beams (bemes) of William's tenement occupied less than half of its width. The certificate was duly enrolled at the request of the parties, but later, the pl. wishing to build on his portion of the wall, and having long made ready his timber (et long temps passe eit fait son meryn), William maliciously refused to allow him to carry out his intention.

The certificate having been inspected, William de Greyngham, serjeant, was ordered to warn both parties to appear on the following Sat. 13 Aug. The defs. appear in person, and, asked whether they could show any cause why the pl. should not build upon his portion of the wall, declare that they do not acknowledge (intendunt) the wall to be partible, as certified by the carpenters and masons, but claim it as their exclusive property and they ask that the same carpenters and masons view it, and certify the mayor and aldermen of their findings. The pl. asks likewise that judgment be given in accordance with their report, as the law and custom of the City require. The parties are given a day on Wed. 31 Aug., and the carpenters and masons, present in court, are ordered to make their return on the same day. They, i.e. Thomas Fant, Richard Schropsshire, Richard atte Chirche and Thomas atte Barnet, then certify in writing [French] that the wall extending from west to east between the two tenements is partible between Thomas and William and Margery, unless the latter can show any ancient deed enrolled to the contrary. They say also that the arches on both sides of the wall are of equal depth, and that the beams and plate of William's tenement do not occupy a full half of the wall. Further, there is on Richard's side an old cupboard (almorye), and the joists (gistes) of his tenement were affixed to the said wall, as is shown by the 'pertuces'[1] of an old house which formerly stood there.

The above having been recited in the presence of John Piel, mayor, Adam Fraunceys, William Haldene, recorder, John Stodeye, James Andrew, John Chichestre, John Bernes, John Warde, Adam Stable, John Aubrey and John Philipott, aldermen, and the same sheriff, it is adjudged that Richard may build upon one half and the defs. upon the other, from end to end, and that *within 40 days etc.* the latter are to demolish anything they have built beyond their half to the nuisance of the pl.

[m. 33d.] *Fri. 19 Aug. 1373. John Pyel, mayor, and the aldermen.*

592. William Dykeman, 'ismongere', complains that Brother Henry, master of the hospital of St. Thomas the Martyr, Suthewerk, has twelve apertures (foramina) below the height of 16 ft. in his tenement in the par. of St. Edmund de Lumbardstret opening on to the pl.'s garden, through which the tenants of the def. see the private business of the pl.'s tenants, and throw refuse into his garden. Nicholas Brembre and John Philipot, sheriffs, testify that the def. has been summoned by John Cok, 'chaundeler', and Andrew Smyth, 'pyebakere', but he makes default. The mayor and aldermen view the premises, and give the pl. a day at Guildhall on Mon. 22 Aug. to hear judgment. After adjournment until the Husting of Pleas of Land on Mon. 24 Oct. the pl. appears in person before John Pyel, mayor, William Haldeyn, recorder, John Lytile, John Aubrey and the sheriffs and aldermen [*sic*] and it is adjudged that the sheriffs be ordered to warn the def. to block up the apertures *within 40 days etc.*

593. On Fri. 25 Nov. 1373 the mayor and aldermen, because of pressing business touching the City, are unable to hold the assize between Nicholas, abbot of Cirencester, pl., and William Sallowe and Alice his wife, which is adjourned until Fri. 9 Dec. On Mon. 21 Nov. at the Husting of Pleas of Land, Nicholas, abbot of Cirencester, presented a bill of assize of nuisance against William Sallowe and Alice his wife concerning a tenement in the par. of St. Bride in Fletstret. Afterwards, on Fri. 9 Dec. the pl. appears by

1. ? Holes bored for posts.

Assize of Nuisance

Henry Berdefeld, his attorney, and William Sallowe comes in person, and they freely put themselves upon the view and ordinance of the master masons and carpenters, who are accordingly ordered to make the view and certify the result to the mayor and aldermen. On Tues. 20 Dec. they report that a broken-down earthen wall between the tenement of the def. on the west and that of the pl. on the east, measures in length from north to south between the privy (garderoba) of the def. and the tenement of the earl of Lincoln, 22 ells $2\frac{1}{2}$ ft., and since it stands on the abbot's land, they are of opinion that William Sallowe is bound to repair it. The parties are warned to appear on Thurs. 22 Dec. to hear judgment, when, the premises having been recited, William is ordered to rebuild the wall to the same length, breadth and height as formerly, *within 40 days etc.*[1]

[m. 34] *Fri. 25 Nov. 1373. Assize adjourned.*

Fri. 27 Jan. 1374. Adam de Bury, mayor, and the aldermen.

594. John Curson and Alice his wife and Thomas son of David, capper, defs., essoin themselves against Walter de Aldebury, canon and stagiary of St. Paul's, by John Cappe. [*Margin:* Concordati sunt.]

Fri. 23 Dec. 1373 and 27 Jan. 1374. [*Essoins only.*]

Fri. 3 Feb. 1374. Adam de Bury, mayor, and the aldermen, viz. William Halden, John Bernes, Adam Stable and John Aubrey.

595. Philip de Crumpton and Alice his wife complain that the wall of plastered wood (murum ligno plastratum) measuring $23\frac{1}{2}$ ells in length and 1 ft. in width, between a stone wall of the pls.' tenement and the tenement of Robert Savage, and dividing his garden from theirs in the par. of St. John Zakarie, is ruinous and fallen to the ground, because Robert refuses to repair it, as he is bound to do; and the pls.' garden consequently lies open, so that men and animals destroy and trample down the plants growing there. The sheriffs testify that the def. has been summoned by Peter Fykelden and Robert Lucas, but he makes default. The mayor and aldermen, having viewed the premises and found the nuisance to be as alleged, give the pls. a day to hear judgment at Guildhall on Fri. 10 Feb. On that day the pls. appear, and the premises having been recited in the presence of Adam de Bury, mayor, William Halden, recorder, John Lytle, John Mitford, William Waleworth and Adam Stable, aldermen, it is adjudged that *within 40 days etc.* the def. build a wall of plastered wood of the same length, breadth and height as that which it is to replace; and the sheriffs are ordered to warn him accordingly.

[m. 34d.] *Fri. 10 Feb. 1374. Adam de Bury, mayor, and the aldermen.*

596. Edmund Penerege, rector of St. Edmund in Lombardstrete, Thomas atte Barnet, 'hosteler', and John Leycestre, cordwainer, churchwardens,

1. Copy in *Cartulary of Cirencester Abbey*, ed. C. D. Ross, i (1964), nos. 176-7.

pls., and their pledges in mercy for not prosecuting their plaint against William de Sleford, dean, and the chapter of St. Stephen Westminster.

Fri. 17 Feb. 1374. [Respite only.]

Fri. 3 Mar. 1374. Adam de Bury, mayor, William Halden, recorder, Adam Fraunceys, John Stodeye, John Chychestre, John Bernes, John Lytle, Adam Stable and John Phylipot.

597. William Walworth, citizen and alderman, complains that whereas there is an old stone wall 12 ells less 7 ins. in length between the tenement of William de Wotton and his garden in the par. of St. Michael de Crokydlane, and he has in it two arches (archeas), each 1 ft. deep, in virtue of which he is entitled to affix his wall-plate (panam) thereto to a width of 1 ft. for the whole length of the wall, the def. has built the solar of his tenement across the entire width of the wall, so that the pl. is prevented from building on his wall-plate. John Aubrey and John Fyfhede, sheriffs, testify that the def. has been summoned by John de War' and Richard Edward, but he makes default. The mayor and aldermen, having viewed the premises, give the pl. a day at Guildhall on Mon. 6 Mar. to hear judgment. After numerous adjournments because the court is not fully advised, the pl. appears at the Husting of Pleas of Land on Mon. 17 July, and the premises having been recited in the presence of the mayor, recorder, John Bernes, Bartholomew Fristlyng and Adam Stable, aldermen, it is adjudged that *within 40 days etc.* the def. remove the nuisance. He is in mercy.

Fri. 28 Apr. 1374. Adam de Bury, mayor, William Halden, recorder, Simon de Mordon, John Chichestre, John Bernes, John Mitford, Adam Stable and John Aubrey, aldermen.

598. John Bakewell complains that in rainy weather the water from the tenement of John Semer of Gyldeford in the par. of St. Lawrence in Old Jewry, falls upon his adjoining stone wall, 32 ft. long by 12 ft. high, so that it is rotted and has become ruinous and broken down for lack of a fillet-gutter (filetti) which the def. is bound to affix to it to carry off the rainwater aforesaid. John Aubrey and John Fyfhede, sheriffs, testify that the def. has been summoned by John Hook and Adam Sprot, but he makes default. The mayor and aldermen, having viewed the premises, and found the nuisance to be as alleged, give the pl. a day at Guildhall on Thurs. 4 May to hear judgment. On that day he comes in person, and the premises having been recited in the presence of the mayor, recorder, Adam Fraunceys, Simon de Mordon, John Chichestre, John Pyel, Bartholomew Frestlyng, John Aubrey and Richard Lyons, aldermen, it is adjudged that *within 40 days etc.* John Semer build at his own expense a fillet-gutter the length of the wall in question, to carry off the water from his tenement on to his own land or into the street. He is to be warned accordingly.

[m. 35] *Fri. 5 May 1374. Adam de Bury, mayor, William Halden, John Wroth, John Pyel and William Waleworth, aldermen.*

Assize of Nuisance

599. William Chevelee, 'taylour', and Isabel his wife and William's daughter Emma complain that the rainwater from the buildings (domibus) of John Turk, clerk, and Alexander Turk, falls upon their adjoining house and garden in the par. of St. Andrew upon Cornhull for a distance of 84 ft., for lack of leaden gutters (gutterarum de plumbo) which the defs. ought to provide to convey the water on to their own land or into the street. As a result, the greater part of the pl.'s house is decayed and ruinous, and the plants (herbe) in their garden are destroyed (adnullate). John Turk appears by John Asshwell, his attorney, and Alexander by Richard Forster. John says that he holds a plot of land 50 ft. long and 1 ft. wide for a term of 293 years, in virtue of a lease by Isabel Gloucestre, late prioress of St. Helen's, and her convent, to Richard Baldewyne, whose estate he now holds, and that the free tenement belongs to the prioress and convent for the time being, and he asks judgment concerning the bill. Against this the pls. affirm that the defs. have the free tenement of the land in question, as stated in the bill, and they ask that the question be referred to a jury. John and Alexander concur. It is ordered that a jury be summoned for Fri. 2 June. The proceedings are twice respited by consent until Fri. 30 June. [See also **608**.]

[m. 35d.] *Fri. 12 May 1374. Adam de Bury, mayor, and the aldermen.*

600. Philip Forster, John atte Felde, William Kyriel, John Mymmes, Gilbert Chelchethe and Richard Mosehach, defs., essoin themselves against Robert, prior of the hospital of St. Mary de Elsyng within Crepulgate, by John Plot.

601. The same defs. essoin themselves against Simon Bristowe, chaplain, by the same.

602. The same defs. essoin themselves against Henry de Frowyk, mercer, and William Burdeyn, goldsmith, by the same.

603. The same defs. essoin themselves against Robert Parys, 'ismongere', by the same.

Fri. 16 June 1374. Adam de Bury, mayor, and the aldermen.

604. Robert de Denton, chaplain, essoins himself against John Leycestre and Henry Spark, by Ralph Coo in an assize of nuisance. Ralph is ordered to produce his warrant at the quindene [30 June]. On that day the parties appear in person, and voluntarily submit to the view and report of the master carpenters and masons. On Fri. 14 July, Thomas Fant and Richard Schropshire, carpenters, and Thomas atte Barnet and Richard atte Chirche, masons, having made the view and considered it, present to the mayor and aldermen their certificate, which is filed among the bills of assize of nuisance for the current year. They report that in Robert's wall, between his tenement and that of John Leycestre and Henry Spark, there are fifteen windows and apertures below the height of 16 ft., opening on to the pls.'

garden, contrary to the City ordinance, and, further, that he has a fillet-gutter (filettum) 12 yards (virgas) 2 ft. (? 1½ ins.) long, from which in rainy weather the water falls into the pls.' garden. The pls. come but the def. makes default, and is ordered to appear on Mon. July 17 to hear judgment. On that day, at the Husting of Pleas of Land, John Baldok, serjeant, testifies that the def. has been duly summoned by John and Hamo Lumbard, but he again makes default. Thereupon, the process having been recited in the presence of the mayor, recorder, John Bernes, Bartholomew Frestlyng, William Waleworth and Adam Stable, aldermen, it is adjudged that Robert block up all the windows and apertures complained of, and repair the fillet-gutter so as to convey his water on to his own land. The same to be done *within 40 days etc.* He is warned accordingly.

[m. 36] *Fri. 4 Aug. 1374. Adam de Bury, mayor, William Halden, recorder, John Stodeye, John Litle, Adam Stable and John Aubrey, aldermen.*

605. Robert Savage and Joan his wife complain that the earthen wall between their garden and that of Philip de Broumpton and Alice his wife in the par. of St. Anne within Aldresgate, is ruinous and broken down in divers places, so that men and animals enter, and destroy (consumunt) and trample down their plants (herbas); and they are bound by the custom of the City to repair it, because it stands upon the pls.' land. John Aubrey and John Fifhide, sheriffs, have testified elsewhere (alias testati fuerunt) that the defs. have been summoned by Thomas Hay and Robert Watlyngton, but they make default. The mayor and aldermen, having viewed the premises, but wishing to be more fully informed as to the land upon which the wall is built, order the carpenters and masons, present in court, to make diligent enquiry and report to them on Mon. 7 Aug. at Guildhall. On that day the pls. appear by their attorney, Robert Watlyngton, and the carpenters and masons report that the wall in question is 14 ells long and 3 ft. wide, and stands on the pls.' land except at the east and next the defs.' tenement, where 1½ ft. 3 ins. stand on the pls.' land and the rest on the defs.' The mayor and aldermen, in order to have time for further consultation, give the pls. a day on Fri. 11 Aug. to hear judgment. They appear by attorney, and the premises having been recited, it is adjudged that, in accordance with the custom of the City, the defs. shall *within 40 days etc.* repair as much of the wall as stands on the land of the pls.

Fri. 23 Nov. 1375. John Ward, mayor, William de Halden, William Waleworth, John Pyel, John Aubrey and Adam Stable, aldermen.

606. Adam Fraunceys and Margaret his wife complain that Thomas, parson of St. Michael de Bassyeshawe, William Willesdon and John Sandon, parishioners, have built a stile (scaleram) across the path (viam) leading from the street to their tenement in the churchyard, by which they and all the tenants of their same tenement have had free passage, time out of mind, for themselves, their servants, horses, carts and all manner of transport (cariagio), with every kind of merchandise (mercandizus) and goods (rebus). John Haddele and William Neuport, sheriffs, have testified elsewhere that the defs. have been summoned by John Hoke and Robert Cog, but they make default. The mayor and aldermen view the premises, and because the nuisance caused to the pls. by the stile is manifest, it is adjudged that *within 40 days etc.* the defs. remove it. The sheriffs are ordered to warn them accordingly.

[m. 36d.] *Fri. 29 June (after the feast of St. Leo, pope) 1375. William Waleworth, mayor, William Halden, recorder, John Mitford, John Tornegold, Adam Stable, John Fyfhide and John Hadele, aldermen.*

607. John de Wentebrigg and John de Wakfeld complain that whereas all the water in their close (clausam), as well in rainy weather as at other times, used to flow through a gutter (gutterum) running from their close through the midst of the tenement of Edmund Daunvers adjoining theirs in the par. of St. Peter [Paul's Wharf] in St. Peter's Lane, and so into the street, and this easement was enjoyed by all their predecessors, the def. has now obstructed the gutter and checked the flow of water, so that it remains standing on the pls.' land and often flows into their cellar, rotting the timber and foundations of their party walls. Moreover, a plastered wall (murus plastratus) next their close is broken down in sundry places, so that their fowls (volatilia) escape through the apertures and are lost. Richard Lyouns and William Wodehouse, sheriffs, testify that the def. has been summoned by Thomas Welford and John Queldryk, but he makes default. The pls. are given a day to hear judgment at Guildhall on Fri. [? 2 May 1376] (before the feast of St. John before the Latin Gate, prox' futur'). On that day the pls. appear, and since the mayor and aldermen had found by view that the nuisances were as alleged, it is adjudged that *within 40 days etc.* the gutter be cleared and the plastered wall repaired and rebuilt.

Fri. 27 June 1376. John Warde, mayor, William de Halden, John Wroth, John Tornegold, John Phelipot and [John Haddele].

608. William Chevelee, 'taillour', Isabel his wife, Richard Irlonde and Emma his wife, William's daughter, complain that the rainwater from the buildings (domibus) of John Turk, clerk, falls upon their adjoining tenement and garden, 84 ft. long, in the par. of St. Andrew upon Cornhull, for lack of the construction and repair by the def. of leaden gutters (gutterarum de plumbo) to receive it and convey it away, so that the greater part of the pls.' house is decayed and ruinous, and the plants in their garden are totally destroyed (consumpte, destructe et adnullate). The sheriffs have testified elsewhere that the def. was summoned by John Lylye 'chaundeler', and John Cok, 'chaundeler'. He appears by Ralph Coo, his attorney, who says that he has muniments bearing on the matter. He is given a day at Guildhall on Fri. 11 July to produce them. On that day the pls. appear in person, and the def., as before, by his attorney, who produces no written evidence, but says that the def. holds the tenement concerning which the nuisance is alleged for a term of 200 years from the prioress and convent of St. Helen's, to whom the reversion belongs. The pls. say that he is not the lessee but the free tenant of the tenement in question. They ask that the matter be referred to a jury, and the def. likewise. William Sewale, serjeant of the Chamber, is ordered to summon twelve men of the venue to appear before the mayor and aldermen on Fri. 26 Sep. [Cf. **599**.]

[m. 37] *Fri. 22 Feb. 1376. John Warde, mayor, William Waleworth, Nicholas Brembre, John Aubrey, John Tornegold, Adam Stable, Nicholas Twyford and John Norhampton, aldermen.*

609. William Chaloner and Felicia his wife complain that the earthen wall, 120 ft. long, on the east side of their garden, dividing their tenement called Eveshammesyn in Faytereslane in the par. of St. Dunstan in Fletestret from that of William Pountefreyt, citizen and skinner, is broken down and ruinous, so that men and animals enter their garden and tread down and destroy the grass (herbagia) and other things growing there and carry off the fruit, and see the private business of the pls. and their servants, and they claim that the def. is bound by the custom of the City to repair the wall, which stands upon their land. John Haddele and William Neuport, sheriffs, have testified elsewhere that the def. has been summoned by Richard Stacy and Henry Traynel, but he does not come. And because it is manifest to the view of the mayor and aldermen that the wall complained of stands on the pls.' land, it is adjudged that *within 40 days etc.* the def. build there a new earthen wall 120 ft. long. The sheriffs are ordered to warn him accordingly.

610. The same William and Felicia complain that the earthen wall, 50 ft. long, between their same tenement and that of William Yoman, 'ferour', and Margery his wife is likewise ruinous. The defs., summoned [as in **609**], come in person and freely acknowledge that they are bound to build and repair the wall in question as the pls. claim. Judgment that they do so *within 40 days etc.*

[m. 37d.] *Fri. 27 June 1376. John Warde, mayor, William de Halden, recorder, John Wroth, John Tornegold, John Phelipot and John Haddele, aldermen.*

611. Robert Knolles and Constance his wife complain that in rainy weather the water from the tenement of Henry Colle and Margery his wife adjoining their tenement and garden in the pars. of All Hallows de Berkynge and St. Olave next the Crutched Friars falls upon their land for lack of a leaden fillet-gutter (filetti) which the defs. ought to provide; and the defs.' tenement overhangs theirs so that they cannot complete the stone wall which they had begun to build. John Haddele and William Neuport, sheriffs, have testified elsewhere that the defs. have been summoned by Richard Fulsham and Gilbert Meldebourne, but they make default. The mayor and aldermen, having viewed the alleged nuisances, order the master carpenters and masons, present in court, to view the premises and report to them at Guildhall on Wed. 2 July. On that day the pls. come by their attorney, and the four viewers certify that the water from the defs.' house falls upon their

Assize of Nuisance

land for a length of 34 yards (virg') 1 in., and that it overhangs their land by 1½ ins. at the corner of the tenement on the east, and further along the wall of the same tenement by 3 ins., and in the middle of the wall by 5 ins., and in the corner on the west by 3½ ins., and for a total length of 12 ells 2 ft.

612. On 8 May 1377 John Coraunt, goldsmith, and Thomas Farndon appear before Nicholas Brembre, mayor, in a dispute concerning two stone walls in the pars. of St. Michael and St. Peter de Wodestrete in which both claim a share. They agree to submit the matter to the arbitration and judgment of the masons and carpenters, who thereupon, by order of the mayor, view the walls in question, and, that same day, certify upon oath that the wall in the par. of St. Michael, which extends as far as Wodestrete and of which Thomas claims half, belongs wholly to John Coraunt; but the stone wall in the par. of St. Peter, in which John claims to have corbels, belongs wholly to Thomas Farndon, and John ought not to have any corbels in it unless he can show a specialty. The parties agree to abide by this judgment from now on.

[m. 38] *Fri. 5 Dec. 1376. Adam Stable, mayor, William Cheyne, recorder, John Pyel, William Waleworth, John Tornegold, John Aubrey, John Fyfide, John Haddele, John Orgon, Adam de St. Ives (Sancto Ivone), John Norhampton and Robert Launde, aldermen.*

613. Margery, prioress of St. Helen within Bisshopesgate, complains that Richard atte Felde, rector of St. Michael upon Cornhull, has built a stone step (gradum lapideum) and a (? bench) (scanile) across the lane (venellam) by which she and all the tenants of her capital messuage situated on the north side of the churchyard have always had access to and from Cornhull for pedestrians, horsemen, carts and other transport carrying their merchandise, victuals and other things; and further, that he has narrowed the entry by the door of her messuage by affixing a piece of timber opposite to it, so that whereas she used to be able to let the property for 100s. per annum, it is now worth only 10s. John Norhampton and Robert Launde, sheriffs, have testified elsewhere that the def. has been summoned by William Badby and John Myte to appear in the Chamber of Guildhall on Fri. 21 Nov., but on that day he essoins himself by Richard Ruer. On Fri. 5 Dec. the pl. comes upon the land by Gilbert de Meldebourne and Richard Galeys, her attorneys, but the def. makes default. The mayor and aldermen, having viewed the premises, give the pl. a day at Guildhall on Fri. 16 Jan. 1377. After various adjournments she appears by her attorneys on Fri. 2 Feb. in the presence of the mayor, recorder, John Pyel, *John Chichestre* [deleted], William Waleworth, John Aubrey, John Fiffide, John Tornegold, Thomas Cornewaleys, Andrew Pykeman and Robert Launde, aldermen, and the record and process having been recited it is adjudged, in accordance with the view already made upon the land, that the step and bench and the piece of timber complained of be removed *within 40 days etc.*

Fri. 11 Dec. 1377. Nicholas Brembre, mayor, William Cheyne, recorder,

John Boseham, William Wodehous, William Neuport, Adam Lovekyn, John Bryan, and Thomas Welford, aldermen.

614. William Waryn, 'chaundeler', complains that Robert atte Haye, 'ferour', and Alice his wife have stopped up an underground gutter (gutteram subterraneam) on their land adjoining his in the par. of St. Dunstan West in Fletestrete, into which the water from his tenement always used to flow from a similar underground gutter in his messuage, and thence into Fletestret, and the defs. and all other tenants of their tenement have always hitherto maintained and kept clear (purgare) the gutter in their tenement at their own expense, but since it was stopped up the water in rainy weather flows back into and floods the pl.'s buildings, so that the party walls and timber are rotted, and he can have no profit or easement from them. Andrew Pykeman and Nicholas Twyford, sheriffs, have testified elsewhere that the defs. were summoned by William Persshore and Jordan Barton to appear before the mayor and aldermen on Fri. 11 Dec. 1377. On that day they come upon the land and claim to have muniments bearing on the matter, and are ordered to produce them in a month's time, in order to avoid Christmas Day. On Fri. 8 Jan. 1378 the parties appear, but because of important business touching the City, the proceedings are adjourned until Fri. 22 Jan., when the pl. essoins himself by Robert Watlyngton. At the quindene [5 Feb.] the pl. appears, but Robert atte Haye makes default. Alice his wife, who appears in person, is admitted to plead, the pl. raising no objection. [m. 38d.] She says that she and her husband are seised of a tenement on the east side of that of the pl., and that they have a receptacle (receptaculum) for the water falling from their own buildings, and an underground gutter which they and all the tenants of their messuage repair at their convenience (pro voluntate sua). She denies the pl.'s allegations and puts herself upon her country. The pl. reiterates his claim and likewise asks that the matter be referred to a jury. William Wircestre, serjeant of the Chamber, is accordingly ordered to summon a jury for Thurs. 25 Feb.

Fri. 15 Jan. 1378. Nicholas Brembre, mayor, William Cheyne, recorder, William Wodehous, Thomas Noket, John Southam, Adam Karlill and Walter Sibyle, aldermen, and Nicholas Twyford, sheriff.

615. Robert Willyngham complains that Patrick Byker, Isabel relict of Boniface Byker and William Arblaster have two gutters (gutteras) on their tenement adjoining his in the par. of St. Katherine de Cricherche, one 34 ft. and the other 23 ft. long, which receive the water falling from their tenement and convey it thence into the pl.'s gutter; but in rainy weather the volume of water is so great that his gutter cannot contain it, and it falls upon his buildings and land so that his timber is decayed and ruined and his house flooded and its party walls rotted, and he can have no profit therefrom. John Norhampton and Robert Launde, sheriffs, have testified elsewhere that the defs. have been summoned by Robert Otery and Walter Morton. They come upon the land by Richard Forster, their attorney, and claim to have muniments bearing on the case. Given a day on Fri. 29 Jan.

they again appear by attorney, but Robert Willyngham makes default. Therefore he and his pledges are in mercy, and the defs. *sine die*.

[m. 39] *Fri. 19 Mar. 1378. Nicholas Brembre, mayor, William Cheyne, recorder, John Haddele, John Orgon, John Rote, John Clevele, Geoffrey Neuton, John Eston, John Vyne and Richard Preston, aldermen, and Nicholas Twyford, sheriff.*

616. Geoffrey Chadenesfeld, rector of St. Margaret Fridaystret, Walter Selsham, chaplain, and William Whetele, citizen and tawyer (allutarius), complain that Thomas Yonge and Alice his wife have built a concave leaden gutter (filacium plumbeum concavatum) upon the eaves of their solar and house adjoining on the east side the tenement of the pls. in the par. of St. Augustine by Paul's Gate, to receive the rain, hail and snow and all the water falling upon their house and convey it into a leaden underground channel (fistula) annexed to their tenement, but in bad weather it flows thence into a gutter (guttero) and similar underground channel belonging to the pls., and overflows on to their land and floods their houses, destroying the property (res diversa) of their tenants, so that they can have no profit from their houses. Nicholas Twyford and Andrew Pykeman, sheriffs, have testified elsewhere that the defs. have been summoned by Henry Traynell and Robert Markes. They come in person and claim to have muniments bearing on the case, and are given a day at Guildhall on Fri. 2 Apr. to produce them. On that day they appear by Richard Forster, their attorney, who essoins himself. Both parties are given a day at the quindene [16 Apr.].

617. [m. 39d.] Thomas Yonge and Alice his wife complain by Richard Forster, their attorney, that the above-named Geoffrey Chadenesfeld, Walter and William with Stephen atte Fryth, 'armurer', on Mon. 5 Oct. 1377 built a forge (fabricam) of earth and timber, 40 ft. from the road, in the close of their tenement adjoining the pls.' messuage in the par. of St. Augustine by Paul's Gate, on the south side of Watlyngstrate, of which the chimney (tuellus) is lower by 12 ft. than it should be, and not built of plaster and stone as the custom of the City requires; and the blows of the sledge-hammers (grossis malleis) when the great pieces of iron called 'Osmond' are being wrought into 'brestplates', 'quysers', 'jambers' and other pieces of armour, shake the stone and earthen party-walls of the pls.' house so that they are in danger of collapsing, and disturb the rest of the pls. and their servants, day and night, and spoil the wine and ale in their cellar, and the stench of the smoke from the sea-coal used in the forge, penetrates their hall and chambers, so that whereas formerly they could let the premises for 10 marks a year, they are now worth only 40s. Andrew Pykeman and Nicholas Twyford, sheriffs, have testified elsewhere that the defs. have been summoned by John Little, 'taillour', and Andrew Cornewaille. They come in person but Stephen Fryth says that he has no interest in the tenement in dispute. Geoffrey, Walter and William answer as tenants. They deny the pls.' contention that chimneys ought to be built of stone and plaster, and high enough to cause no nuisance to the neighbouring tenements, and declare

Assize of Nuisance

that good and honest men of any craft, viz. goldsmiths, smiths, pewterers, goldbeaters, grocers, pelters, marshals and armourers are at liberty to carry on their trade anywhere in the City, adapting their premises as is most convenient for their work, and that according to ancient custom any feoffor may give, bequeath or lease his property as well to craftsmen using great hammers as to others. They add that they have let the premises against which the nuisance is alleged to Stephen Fryth for a term of years which has not yet expired, and that he has set up his anvil in what was formerly the kitchen at a sufficient distance from the pls.' messuage, and strengthened the chimney with mortar and clay and raised it by 6 ft. or more. They maintain that the pls. cannot in any case complain of the chimney or of the noise of the hammers or the smoke, because their messuage was built as recently as 1349–50, and is much higher than the house it replaced, and has windows facing the forge, which its predecessors had not.

[m. 40] *Fri. 2 Oct. 1377. Nicholas Brembre, mayor, William Cheyne, recorder, William Neuport, Adam Karlill, William Baret, Robert Boxford, Robert Lucas, Walter Sibyle and Thomas atte Noket, aldermen, Nicholas Twyford and Andrew Pykeman, sheriffs.*

618. John Norhampton, draper, and Parnel his wife complain that whereas they have built five messuages on the west side of Pentecostlane in the par. of St. Nicholas Shambles, and two on the east side, and from time out of mind the rain, sleet and snow from their gutters (stillicidiis et gutteris) and the water thrown out of their houses has flowed into the kennel in the same lane through the midst of the garden of the Friars Minor, and out by way of an aperture in the City Wall into Houndesdych, William Newe, guardian of the same friars, has caused a stone wall to be built across the lane, near the convent garden and the pls.' messuages, in which is a narrow aperture partially blocked (obstrusum) by an iron grating (ferrimenta), and has obstructed the kennel itself, with the result that in bad weather the water from the pls.' messuages cannot reach the Houndesdych by its accustomed route, but overflows (refluit) so that the inhabitants and the children of the tenants are often drowned, and their goods and chattels are submerged and destroyed, and the timber and party-walls of their messuages are rotted, so that the pls. can get no profit from their houses or maintain them in adequate repair. The sheriffs have testified elsewhere that the def. has been summoned by Simon Mazerer and Nicholas Thame. He comes in person upon the land in the presence of the mayor, recorder and aldermen and claims to have documents bearing upon the case. He is given a day at Guildhall at the quindene [16 Oct.], but the court being unable to attend (vacare) because of important business touching the plea, the proceedings are adjourned until Fri. 30 Oct. Finally, on Fri. 23 July 1378 the guardian again appears upon the land in the presence of the mayor, recorder, John Pyel, Adam Stable, John Haddele, John Organ, Robert Launde, William Knyghtcote, John Eston, John Vyne, John Hoo, Nicholas Twyford, Thomas Reynham, John Kirketon, William Badeby, John Clivele, John Rote and Adam de St. Ives, aldermen, and expressly acknowledges that the pls.' water used to flow from the kennel in the lane through the midst of his garden, by way of an underground gutter (gutteram subterraneam), and that he had torn up (abracadasse) part of the same gutter and obstructed the rest and narrowed the outlet by an iron grating. And because the interests of the City are involved, and the parties are suspected of fraud and trickery, John Baldok, the mayor's serjeant, is ordered to summon a jury of twelve of the most trustworthy and senior men of the venue that the truth may be ascertained. They come by Elias de Weston, William Horwode, Nicholas Jurdon, John Thurkild, John Dorsete, senior, Thomas Soneman, Nicholas Thame, Robert atte Grene, John atte Shoppe, Thomas Martyn, John Curson and Henry Asshelyn, and corroborate on oath the statements of the parties, who are given a day at Guildhall on 2 Aug. to hear judgment. They appear in the presence of the mayor and aldermen, and it is adjudged that *within 40 days etc*. William Newe clear and repair the gutter, and restore it to its former state.

[m. 40d.] *Fri. 7 May 1378. Nicholas Brembre, mayor, William Cheyne, recorder, Adam Stable, Adam de St. Ives, Andrew Pykeman, John Hoo, John Eston, John Vyne, Thomas de Reynham and John Rote, aldermen, and the same Andrew Pykeman, sheriff.*

619. Roger Dunster, rector of St. Martin in Vintry, complains by Gilbert de Meldebourne, his attorney, that John Desterny and Philippa his wife have a house with a jetty overhanging the churchyard for a length of 14 yards (virgas) 16 ins., and a width of 21½ ins. so that he cannot build there. Andrew Pykeman and Nicholas Twyford, sheriffs, have testified elsewhere that the defs. have been summoned by Sampson Soham and Thomas Langeford. They come in person and claim to have muniments bearing on the case. They are given a day to produce them at Guildhall on Fri. 21 May, but then essoin themselves. On Fri. 4 June they appoint Richard Forster their attorney, and the pl. also appears by his attorney. The defs. produce in court letters patent of Edward III,[1] dated 8 June 1377, reciting a grant for life on 16 July 1369 to John Desterny for services rendered, of a messuage in the par. of St. Martin formerly belonging to Henry de Hereford, which came into the king's hand by way of escheat, and a later grant on 6 July 1372 of two cellars, three solars and three houses built thereon in the same par., which belonged to Thomas Swanlond, and were taken into the king's hand because Thomas died indebted to him, to hold as long as they so remain; and conceding, at the request of the said John, that the aforesaid messuage, with the cellars, solars and houses, as long as they remain in the king's hand, may be held by John and Philippa his wife, and their heirs male, lawfully begotten, with reversion to the crown in failure of such issue. The defs. therefore contend that the plea ought not to proceed without consultation with the king, to whom the reversion of the messuage, concerning which the nuisance is alleged, belongs. The pl. argues that John and Philippa held the messuage jointly at the time of suing out of the bill, but that in the letters patent shown in court Philippa is not named as tenant, although no evidence has been produced that the original grant was quashed or altered. The defs. ask judgment as above whether the

1. *C.P.R. 1374–7*, 478.

assize should proceed. The parties are given a day on Fri. 18 June. They come by their attorneys, but the proceedings are adjourned until Fri. 2 July, when permission is given to the defs. to have recourse to the king's aid. Finally, on Fri. 23 July, the parties come, and Roger's attorney is told that he may proceed against the king if he so desires.

MISC. ROLL II

[m. 1] *Mayoralty of John Philipot 1378–9*

620. Certificate [French] of Thomas Fant, Thomas Mallyng, Richard atte Cherche and Stephen Warde, masons and carpenters, to the effect that Henry Frowyk of the county of Middlesex, is bound to rebuild the earthen wall (pareie de terre) between his tenement and that of the earl of Suffolk in the par. of St. Giles without Crepulgate, and to maintain it in repair at all times at his own expense, unless he can produce a specialty discharging him of the obligation.

621. The like to the effect that the houses in the tenement held by John Laufare, 'masson', of the parishioners of St. Benet Paules Wharfe, are in such poor condition (si fiebles) as regards chimneys, privies (garderobes) and floors (flores), that they cannot long remain without extensive repairs.

Fri. 9 Dec. 1379. John Haddele, mayor, William Cheyne, recorder, John Bosham, Adam Karlill, John Sely, Roger Elys, Thomas Irland and Thomas Welford, aldermen.

622. Richard Widden, 'coupere', complains that Lawrence Bloseworth or de Ware, has an old tenement in the par. of St. Ethelburga within Bisshopesgate adjoining his own, in which there are two newly-built houses, one 59 ft. 1 in. and the other 34 ft. 3 ins. long; and the def.'s rainwater falls upon the first named house for lack of a leaden gutter (gutteri plumbei) of the required length which he ought to provide; and the pl. has built a leaden gutter (gutteram plumbeam) between his other house and that of the def., who refuses to pay his share of the cost as he is bound to do. As a result of his neglect a great part of the pl.'s houses and a newly-built cellar in the front of his tenement (in parte anteriori) next the street are rotted. The sheriffs have testified that Lawrence has been summoned by William atte Chapel and William Herlawe. He comes in person, but says nothing to delay the assize. The court, wishing for further information, orders the masons and carpenters, with the consent of the parties, to enquire into the alleged nuisance, and report their findings at Guildhall on Fri. 16 Dec. They certify [French] that the def. is bound to receive his own rainwater for a distance of 59 ft. 1 in., measuring from Bisshopesgatestret on the east westwards, without detriment to the pl.'s tenement, but that the gutter 34 ft. 3 ins. long built between their houses by the pl. is partible between them, so that the def. is bound to pay half the cost of its construction. After adjournment until Tues. 31 Jan. 1380, Richard comes in person, and

Assize of Nuisance

the def. by Richard Forster, his attorney, in the presence of the mayor and recorder, John Heylesdon and William Baret, sheriffs, Walter Sibyle, Adam Karlill, John Horn, Hervey Begge, Thomas Irlond, Robert Boxford, Thomas Welford and John Southam, aldermen, and the record and process having been recited, it is adjudged that since as well by view of the mayor and aldermen as by report of the four viewers, the nuisances are as alleged by the pl. the def. amend them *within 40 days etc.* The sheriffs are ordered to warn him accordingly.

[m. 1d.] *Fri. 20 Apr. 1380. John Hadele, mayor, William Cheyne, recorder, Adam Stable, Nicholas Brembre, William Neuport, John Eston, John Bryan, Robert Launde, Andrew Pykeman, William Badby, John Horn and Walter Doget, aldermen, and John Heylesdon, sheriff.*

623. Robert Sprotburgh, rector of St. Margaret de Briggestrete, complains that Arnold Ingelbright, 'armurer', has a tenement adjoining his churchyard in the wall of which is a door in the form of a window (ad modum fenestre) less than 16 ft. from the ground, and barred with iron, the bars hanging on hooks (gumphos) and hinges (vertivellas), so that it can be opened and closed at will by the def. and others living or coming there, both men and women, who enter the churchyard and see his private business, and trample the churchyard down and defile it (sordidant). John Heylesdon and William Baret, sheriffs, have testified elsewhere that Arnold has been summoned by William Ivory and John Smart. He comes in person and in the presence of the mayor, recorder, aldermen and sheriffs the parties voluntarily agree, the rector for himself and his successors and Arnold for himself, his heirs and assigns, that Arnold shall enclose the said door or window with iron bars so deeply embedded in the stone wall of his tenement that no one shall in future be able to enter or leave thereby, and they ask that this agreement be entered so that it may remain in perpetuity. At their request it was entered in the above form.

Fri. 27 Sep. 1381. William Waleworth, mayor, William Cheyne, recorder, John Bosham, William Knyghtcote, John Horn, Robert Lucas and William Kyng, aldermen, and the same William Knyghtcote, sheriff.

624. Thomas Barton, citizen and goldsmith, complains that the rainwater from the tenement of John Humber adjoining his in the par. of St. Bartholomew the Less falls upon his soil for a length of 10 [blank] and 1 ft. for lack of a leaden fillet-gutter (filetti plumbei), and that his earthen wall overhangs his land for a length of [blank] by 3 ins. so that he cannot build. William Knyghtcote and Walter Doget, sheriffs, have testified elsewhere that the def. has been summoned by William atte Castell and Richard Gregory to come upon the land to answer the plaint, but he makes default. The mayor, recorder and aldermen view the premises, but for their further information refer the matter to the masons and carpenters, present in court. The pl. is given a day in the Chamber of Guildhall on Thurs. 3 Oct. to hear judgment. He comes in person, and because it appears to the view of the masons and carpenters as well as to that of the mayor and aldermen

Assize of Nuisance

that the nuisances are as alleged by the pl., it is adjudged that the def. remove and amend them *within 40 days etc.*

Mayoralty of John Norhampton, 1381–2.

625. Memorandum that on 8 May 1382, with the consent of John Ive, rector of St. Michael de Wodestret, Adam Bamme and John Forster, goldsmiths, attorneys of Robert Launde, kt., and of John Loveye, mercer, and John Fraunceys, goldsmith, the four masons and carpenters were authorised by the mayor and aldermen to investigate the claim of the same John Loveye, and John Fraunceys to a watercourse through the tenement of Robert Launde. They report on 10 May [French] that they have measured the land of Sir Robert in Chepe, and that it is 2 yards 2½ ft. long 'de cler soyl plus ou meynz', and that the water from the tenements of John Fraunceys and John Loveye ought to flow through it into Chepe, according to custom, unless Sir Robert can produce evidence under seal prohibiting it (evidence enseale a ice forbarrer).

[m. 2] *Fri. 11 July 1382. John Norhampton, mayor, William Cheyne, recorder, John Rote, John Eston, John More, Thomas Karleton and Simon Wynchecoumbe, aldermen, and John [blank], sheriff.*

626. Geoffrey Crymelford and Alice his wife complain that whereas they are possessed in her right of a vacant plot of land in the par. of St. Stephen de Walbrok, inside the gate leading from Bukeleresbury to the said church, and they and their predecessors in their tenement have always enjoyed freedom of access by the same to their houses for the carriage of victuals and other goods, Richard Aylesbury has recently made in his tenement a door with four stone steps by which he can descend to the vacant land, and see the private business of the pls. and their tenants. Moreover, he has so narrowed the path (viam) that the pls. can no longer use it for the transport of goods as formerly. John Rote and John Hende, sheriffs, have testified elsewhere that the def. has been summoned by John Cook and John Dadyngton, but he makes default. The pls. are given a day at Guildhall to hear judgment on Mon. 28 July. They come in person, and because it is manifest to the view of both the mayor and aldermen and the four masons and carpenters that the nuisances are as alleged, the def. is ordered to remove them *within 40 days etc.* [*Margin:* Amocio nocumentorum. *In a later hand:* Nota pour le barge in bokelesbury.]

Fri. 21 Nov. 1382. John Norhampton, [mayor], William Cheyne, recorder, William Neuport, Simon Wynchecombe, John Sely and Gilbert Maunfeld, aldermen.

627. Juliana Bidyk complains that Thomas Lyle, 'pyebaker', whose tenement adjoins hers in the par. of St. Mary the Virgin de Fanchirche, has made a gutter (gutteram) running through her house, into which his rainwater falls and overflows on to her land. John Sely and Adam Bamme, sheriffs, have testified elsewhere that the def. has been summoned by

Assize of Nuisance

Thomas Bonaunter and William Rook, but he makes default. The pl. is given a day at Guildhall on Wed. 26 Nov. to hear judgment. She comes, and because the nuisance is manifest to both the mayor and aldermen and the four viewers, it is adjudged that the def. remove it *within 40 days etc.* [*Margin:* Amocio nocumenti.]

628. Note that on 20 May 1383 the four masons and carpenters presented to John Norhampton, mayor, and the aldermen, a bill [French] to the effect that the stone wall on the west side of the church of St. Duns Bakechirch 'cest a dire passant en lungure auxi avant come le bem illeoqz gisant en laeur en la dite eglise' is partible between the parishioners and Bakewell.

[m. 2d.] *Fri. 9 Oct. 1383. John Norhampton, mayor, William Cheyne, recorder, John Bosham, Thomas Cornwaleys, William Staundon, Richard Norbury, William Kyng and William Olyver, aldermen, and Simon Wynchecombe, sheriff.*

629. John Wade, fishmonger, complains that in the tenement of Agnes Bever, adjoining his garden in the par. of St. Botolph without Aldrichesgate, there is a chimney (camynam) built upon a corbel (corbellum) which overhangs his land by 15 ins., and that the rainwater from her tenement falls upon it for a length of 20 ells less 3 ins. The sheriffs have testified elsewhere that the def. has been summoned by Thomas Waryner and Walter Hopere. She appears in person and claims to have muniments bearing on the matter, and is given a day to produce them in the Chamber of Guildhall at the quindene [23 Oct.]. The mayor and aldermen being unable to attend that day because they have to appear before the king's council at Westminster, the proceedings are again adjourned until the quindene. Finally, after further adjournments for the same and other causes, on Fri. 4 Dec. the pl. appears by Richard Forster, his attorney, and the def. by Henry Hamwode, and since by view of John Norhampton, mayor, and the recorder and aldermen, as well as by report of the masons and carpenters, the nuisances are found to be as alleged, Simon Wynchecombe, sheriff, is ordered to warn the def. to remove them *within 40 days etc.*

[m. 3] *Fri. 4 Nov. 1384. Nicholas Brembre, kt., mayor, William Cheyne, recorder, John Organ, John Rote, John Eston, Thomas Welford, William Ancroft and Geoffrey Crymelford, aldermen, Nicholas Extone and John Fresshe, sheriffs.*

630. Thomas Asshebourne, prior of the Austin Friars, complains that Robert Dyngele and Margaret his wife have made nine windows below the height of 16 ft. in their tenement in the par. of St. Peter in Bradstret ward, adjoining his churchyard, through which they and their servants, lessees (firmarii) and tenants can see the private business of the prior and his brethren and servants. Further, the rainwater from their houses, measuring respectively 40 ft. and 24 ft. in length, falls upon the soil of the churchyard. The sheriffs have testified elsewhere that the defs. have been summoned by John Olescombe and William Wetenhale to come here upon the land to

Assize of Nuisance

answer the prior's plaint, but they make default. But because the assize was sought (impetrata) long since (adiu est), and has been long adjourned (continuata) so that the defs. had not been warned to come on that particular day, John Bockysham, mayor's serjeant, is ordered to summon them to appear in the Chamber of Guildhall on Wed. 2 Nov. [sic]. On that day he reports that they have been duly summoned, but again they fail to come or to show cause why the assize should not proceed. The prior appears by Gilbert de Meldebourne, his attorney, and is given a day on Mon. 21 Nov. to hear judgment; and since both by view of the mayor and aldermen upon the land, and by report of the masons and carpenters, the nuisances are found to be as alleged, it is adjudged that the defs. remove them *within 40 days etc.*

Fri. 5 Aug. 1384. Nicholas Brembre, kt., mayor, William Cheyne, recorder, Robert Warburton, John Organ, John Estone, William Staundon, William Anecroft, Roger Elys, John Sely, Henry Vanner, John Fraunceys and Thomas Welford, aldermen, and Simon Wynchecoumbe and John More, sheriffs.

631. Adam Fraunceys, kt., and Margaret his wife complain by Richard Forster, their attorney, that whereas, in Margaret's right, they hold a tenement within (infra) the churchyard of St. Michael de Bassyeshawe, to which they and all Margaret's ancestors, and those whose estate they now hold, and their tenants, have from time out of mind, enjoyed as appertaining to the same tenement, a path (viam) extending in breadth from a post (stulpa) standing on the west side of the door of their tenement (. . . parte ostii eiusdem tenementi sui occident' fixa) transversely to the old wall of the churchyard (extransverso [? versus] antiquum murum cimiterii eiusdem ecclesie), and thence in length and breadth directly and in a straight line (linealiter) to the street called Bassyeshawe, and from the same street to the aforesaid post, and thence (? to the door) of their tenement on the west side (et ab eodem vico regio usque ad predictam stulpam et ultra usque . . . tenementi sui predicti ex parte occidentale), with freedom of access for their servants, horses and carts, and transport (cariagio) for all kinds of merchandise and other goods, until William, parson of St. Michael, William Hawe, Simon Worstede, William Lyncolne, John Seymore, John Vyne, mercer, William Willesdon and John Toller, parishioners, dug a ditch (fossatum) from the street in length (–).[1] [m. 3d.] William the parson, William Hawe, Simon, William Lyncolne and John Seymour come in person. The other defs. named do not appear and the assize proceeds without them. The parson, William, Simon, William and John say that the assize does not lie, because the path which the pls. claim as appurtenant to their tenement is held by them only at the will and by the licence of the defs. The pls. contend that they are not bound to answer the objections of the parishioners, who are merely participants in the nuisance (coadjutores) but only that of the parson who is sole tenant of the free tenement. Their contention is accepted. As far as the parson is concerned, they say that he ought not to be admitted to contest their title, since on 23 Nov. 1375 they

1. The rest of the membrane is much damaged so that the abstract is incomplete at this point.

brought an assize [606] against Thomas, his predecessor, concerning the building of a stile across the path in question, and obtained a judgment against him, as appears by the record remaining in the custody of the court. The def. none the less asks for verification of the pls.' title, and the mayor and aldermen, wishing to be more fully advised before giving judgment, give the parties a day on Wed. 12 Oct. in the Chamber of Guildhall. It is adjudged that the def. withdraw his demand for verification (abiudicetur a verificacione predicta . . . contra recordum predictum pretensa). A day is then given to the parties on Sat. 12 Nov. on the land in order that the mayor and aldermen may personally survey the tenement and the place in which the nuisance is alleged to have been caused (pro meliori avisamento inde habendo et ad melius supervidendum tam tenementam predictum ad quod nocumentum predictum supponitur fore factum, quam eciam locum in quo nocumentum predictum supponitur esse levatum etc.). The parties come to the messuage and place on the appointed day, but the proceedings are adjourned until Fri. 27 Jan. 1385 that the court may deliberate further. On that day the parties duly appear in the Chamber, but the court is unable to meet because of important business concerning the king and the City, and there is a further adjournment until Fri. 10 Mar. The mayor and aldermen, having been given to understand that a house had formerly been built on the north side of the path, within the precincts of the churchyard, order the four masons and carpenters to dig there and attempt to uncover the foundations, so that the breadth (largitatem) of the path at that time may be ascertained and further evidence and information obtained. On 24 Mar. the pls. appear by their attorney and the def. in person at the messuage and on the site of the alleged nuisance, in the presence of the mayor, recorder, John Hadle, John Bosham, John Hende, Robert Warburton, Henry Vannere, Simon Wynchecoumbe, John Organ, William Standon, Adam de St. Ives, Thomas Welford, John Fraunceys, aldermen, and Nicholas de Exton and John Fressh, aldermen and sheriffs, and the masons and carpenters report that their digging has revealed no new evidence. It is therefore adjudged that the pls. have their path, extending from their tenement to Bassieshawe and back; as appurtenant to their tenement.[1] (—domus predicte ex transverso versus boriam per tres ulnas ferreas domini [regis]—a plata prope terram shoparum que se extendunt a dicto tenemento usque vicum [regium]—per largitatem trium ulnarum usque in vicum regium etc. Et quod predictus [Willelmus persona]—cimiterium predictum per quod via predicta artatur, per quam artationem—trium ulnarum a plata predicta versus boriam linealiter usque in viam—) *within 40 days etc.*

[m. 4] *Record of an assize taken before Nicholas Brembre, kt., mayor, and the aldermen and sheriffs, between John Marchal and John Bentele, pls., and Thomas Blount, 1384.*

632. Memorandum that in a congregation of the mayor and aldermen in the Chamber of Guildhall on Mon. 11 July 1384, John Marchal and John Bentele brought an assize against Thomas Blount of Essex concerning a

1. The dimensions follow but the membrane is so damaged that only the following fragments can be deciphered.

nuisance in the par. of St. Mildred in Poultry. On Fri. 29 July, in the presence of Nicholas Brembre, kt., mayor, William Cheyne, recorder, John Hende, Adam de St. Ives, William Ancroft, John Eston, Geoffrey Crymelford, aldermen, and Simon Wynchecoumbe, sheriff, the pls. appeared by Henry Herbury, vintner, their attorney, upon the land, and the def. came in person. The pls. complained that the def. has a flight of steps (gradus) called 'steire' leading up to the house formerly belonging to John de St. Albans, which stand upon their land. After the premises had been viewed by the mayor and aldermen, the parties voluntarily submitted to the arbitration of four men, two to be chosen by the pls., and two by the defs., together with the four masons and carpenters; but the arbitrators were not then named, nor was anything decided between the parties. They therefore came before the mayor and aldermen in the Chamber on Sat. 6 Aug., and Henry Herbury, attorney of the pls., chose Walter Sibyle and Thomas Girdelere, and the def. chose William Baret and William Cressewyk to act as arbitrators with the four viewers, on the understanding that they should reach an agreement between Sat. 3 and Mon. 5 Sep., and that if either party failed to produce its chosen arbitrators, or refused to carry out the agreement reached, the other should arbitrate, with the help of the four viewers, without any objection being raised by the defaulters. Afterwards, on Mon. 24 Oct., the pls.' attorney came into court and reported that one John Pigeon, 'piebaker', had come to him on 12 Sep. at the tenement in connection with which the nuisance is alleged, claiming to be the lessee (firmarium) of the def., and to have been appointed by him as his attorney, with full power (plenam potestatem) to reach a final agreement (finalem concordiam) concerning the matters in dispute, and to commit the findings to writing. With the mediation of friends of both the parties an agreement was reached, and the document [French] was duly presented in court. It recited that certain tenements within the gate (porte) of the 'Scaldynghous' in the par. of St. Mildred had been partitioned between John Blount of Beveresbroke and Thomas Blount, those which had belonged to John de Seint Albon being allotted to Thomas, and those adjoining to John Blount, from whom they were afterwards purchased by John Marchal and John Bentele. Since, however, certain points in the relevant documents were obscure, disputes subsequently arose, the purchasers alleging, in particular, that a 'steire' leading to the hall (sale) of Thomas Blount's house, stood on their land. To settle the dispute the parties have now agreed that the 'steire' shall remain in perpetuity as at present, but that the cellar beneath the house built in the eastern part of the tenements, which belongs to the pls., shall be kept in repair by the def., while the pls. in turn shall be bound to roof (coverer) and maintain the solar built above it, which belongs to the def. The pls. are in addition to be granted a piece of land for the building of a new house.[1] [m. 4d.] The pls. maintain, through Henry Herbury, their attorney, that John Pigeon promised on his master's behalf, that the schedule containing the terms agreed upon between them should be indented and sealed by Thomas, or else enrolled, on his next visit to London; but

1. The right-hand half of the foot of the membrane is completely indecipherable. It appears to contain the remainder of the agreement and the first part of a bill in French, brought by the pls.

although he has often been in the City since the agreement was reached, the document has never been sealed, nor has anything been placed on record, to their damage £40.[1] It is therefore adjudged that John Pigeon be summoned to appear on Fri. 18 Nov. to answer their complaint. On that day he comes, with the pls.' attorney, and fully acknowledges the agreement and promise, adding that he had been empowered to make them by the def., Thomas Blount. Thomas is accordingly summoned (premuniatur) for Fri. 2 Dec. to show cause why he should not recognise and carry out the agreement. He comes in person, and denies that he empowered John Pigeon to act as his attorney and come to an agreement with the pls., and declares that he never consented to it or promised to abide by it. John Pigeon calls Stephen, who had been in Thomas's confidence at the time, to witness to the truth of his allegation. Thereupon Stephen, in the presence of both parties, testifies upon oath that Thomas made John his attorney, as alleged, to draw up the agreement, but that he had always insisted that it should not be embodied in an indenture or other sealed deed, but should simply be acknowledged before the mayor and aldermen, and enrolled, Henry having meanwhile undertaken on behalf of his masters that whatever Stephen declared on oath in court to be the truth, they would accept and carry out. It is accordingly adjudged that the agreement should be enrolled and put on record between the parties and their heirs, in accordance with the oath and testimony of Stephen, and with the consent of the parties.

[m. 5] *Fri. 2 Aug. 1387. Nicholas Exton, mayor, William Cheyne, recorder, William More and William Staundon, sheriffs and aldermen, John Rote, Thomas Wilford, Adam de St. Ives, aldermen.*

633. Joan Bohun, countess of Hereford, complains by Richard Forster, her attorney, that the wall or other fence (murus vel alia claustura) 2 ells long, between her tenement in the par. of All Hallows de Stanynge and that of Ralph Parles and Mary his wife, ought to be built and maintained by the said Ralph and any other tenant of the said tenement at their own expense, but through their neglect it is now broken down and ruinous, so that men and servants and unknown persons enter and carry off divers goods and chattels, and see the private business of the countess and her servants; moreover the pl. complains that she and the defs. and a certain William Wythome share a well (unum puteum vel fontem), which for lack of a cover, and of cleaning and repair is so stopped up with filth that she can get no clean water (aquam claram) or other profit from it, and the defs. refuse to take their share in its covering (cooperturam) and repair. The sheriffs have testified elsewhere that the defs. have been summoned by Richard Morell and Thomas Evesham, but they make default. The parties are given a day in the Chamber of Guildhall on Fri. 9 Aug., and John Harewell, the mayor's serjeant, is instructed to order the four masons and carpenters to inspect the nuisances and certify the mayor and aldermen concerning them. On the appointed day, the pl. appears by her attorney, and the four viewers report that the defs. are bound to repair the wall complained of at their own expense, and to pay a third of the cost of the repair

1. End of the bill brought by the pls.

of the well. Judgment is given accordingly that the nuisances be repaired *within 40 days etc.*

634. The same Joan complains that William Badby has neglected to repair the earthen wall 12 ells long on the south side of her tenement in the same par., as he is bound to do. [Then as in **633**.] The def., summoned by Richard Morell and Thomas Evesham, comes and asks that the four masons and carpenters be required to inspect the premises, and undertakes to abide by their report, the pl., by her attorney, consenting. John Harewell, the mayor's serjeant, instructs them accordingly, and on Fri. 16 Aug. the parties appear at Guildhall, and the four viewers certify that the def. is bound to repair the wall. It is adjudged that he do so *within 40 days etc.*

Fri. 21 May 1389. Nicholas Twyford, kt., mayor, William Cheyne, recorder, Hugh Fastolf, John Fraunceys, John Loveye and Thomas Austyn, aldermen, and the same Thomas and Adam Karlill, sheriffs.

635. William Baret, citizen, complains that John Serieaunt, Robert Lyndeseye and John Louthe, tailors, have made in their tenements seven windows less than 16 ft. from the ground, opening upon his adjoining tenement and garden in the par. of All Hallows de Bredstret, through which they, their servants and household (familiares) and their lessees (firmarii) and tenants can see the private business of the pl., his tenants and servants. The sheriffs have testified elsewhere that the def. has been summoned by Robert Riseby and William Rotewell, but he does not come. His default is recorded. The mayor and aldermen adjourn the proceedings from quindene to quindene. Finally, on Fri. 2 July the parties come upon the land in the presence of the mayor, the recorder, Thomas Austyn, Adam Bamme, John Hende, William Sheryngham and Henry Bamme, aldermen. Judgment that the windows less than 16 ft. from the ground be stopped up *within 40 days etc.*

[m. 5d.] *Fri. 2 July 1389. Nicholas Twyford, kt., mayor, William Cheyne, recorder, Thomas Austyn, Adam Bamme, Henry Bamme, John Hende and William Sheryngham, aldermen.*

636. The same William Baret complains that William, prior of St. Bartholomew de Westsmythefeld, has made fifteen apertures (foramina) in his tenements in the same par. adjoining the tenement and garden of the pl. [See above, **635**.] The def. makes default. Judgment, after view, that all nuisances under the height of 16 ft. from the ground be stopped up *within 40 days etc.*

Fri. 25 June 1389. Nicholas Twyford, kt., mayor, John Hadle, William Cheyne, recorder, William More, Adam Bamme, Thomas Austyn, William Watton and John Walcote, aldermen, and the same Thomas and Adam Karlill, sheriffs.

637. Richard Preston complains that whereas he has certain tenements and a plot of land with a quay (kayo) adjoining in Thames Street (vico Tamisie) in the par. of St. Dunstan Est, and John Chastilon, 'chivaler', has tenements adjoining his plot of land and quay for a length of 28½ ells, the rainwater from his tenements falls upon the pl.'s soil. Moreover, the def. has two tenements adjoining his from which in rainy weather, the water flowing through a great gutter (*magnam gutteram*) falls upon the pl.'s tenements and rots them, so that they threaten ruin. Further, the def. has a door and six [blank] windows through which his tenants and servants have access to the pl.'s property, and can see his private business and that of his servants and tenants. The sheriffs have testified elsewhere that the def. has been summoned by John Scut and Reginald Pay, but he makes default. His default is recorded, and a day is given to the pl. in the Chamber of Guildhall on Fri. 9 July to hear judgment. Richard appears by Gilbert de Meldebourne, his attorney, but the proceedings are adjourned until Sat. 24 July. It is then adjudged that all the above nuisances be removed *within 40 days etc.*

Fri. 29 July 1390. William Venour, mayor, John Hadle, John Tremayn, recorder, William More, Adam Bamme, John Shadworth, Adam Karlill, William Brampton, aldermen, and John Loveye, alderman and sheriff.

638. Bernard Brocas, kt., complains by Richard Forster, his attorney, that in rainy weather the water from the tenement of Thomas Brampton, 'squyer', and William Sallowe of Fletestrete and Joan his wife in the par. of St. Bride de Fletestrete falls upon his adjoining tenement and garden for lack of a leaden fillet-gutter (*filetti plumbei*). [John Loveye] and John Walcote, sheriffs, have testified elsewhere that the defs. have been summoned by (—) and Walter Dunmowe, but they do not come. Their default is recorded. [Remainder of entry illegible.]

[m. 6. *No heading.*]

639. A dispute having arisen between the parishioners of St. Margaret in Frydaystret and Stephen Hamme, citizen and tailor, concerning the claim of the former to a processional way on festival days on the latter's land at the east end of the church, the parties appeared before John Hadle, mayor, and the aldermen, on Fri. 22 May 1394 and put themselves upon the view and sentence of the master masons and carpenters, viz. Simon Hooke and Henry Gerard, masons, and Richard Burnham and William Wiltshire, carpenters, who are instructed by the mayor accordingly on Fri. 29 May. On 5 June they reported [French] that they have found that Stephen's tenement extends westward in length from Bredstret for 21 yards 11½ ins. as far as the wall of the church, and that the parishioners can therefore claim no right to a processional way without his assent and goodwill, unless they can show sufficient written evidence to the contrary. They say further that Stephen ought not to have a door in the wall of the church unless on to his own land, and ask that the mayor and aldermen provide a remedy (*item diont qe le dit Estephen navera nulle huys pendaunt sur le mure du dit esglise mes pur soun propre terre. Pur quoy vous please ent ordeigner remedye.*).

640. [m. 6d.] William Middelton, citizen and grocer, complains that John

Assize of Nuisance

Crosseby has placed his timber and built upon 11¾ ins. of a stone wall 35 ft. 9½ ins. long and 1 ft. [blank] ins. wide between their tenements in the par. of St. Margaret Briggestret.

[m. 7] *Fri. 16 Mar. 1397. Adam Bamme, mayor, John Cokayn, recorder, John Hadlee, William Staundon, Thomas Knolles, William Brampton, John Wade and William Askham, aldermen, Thomas Wilford and William Parker, sheriffs.*

641. Richard Abberbury, junior, kt., complains that the abbot of Bittelesden has placed his timber for building upon the whole width of the east end of the stone wall, 33 ft. long and 17 ins. wide between their tenements in the par. of St. Nicholas Coldeabbey in Dystaflane, half of which belongs of right to the pl. The sheriffs testify that the def. has been summoned by Richard Giffard and Walter Torgold to appear upon the land, but he makes default. The pl. comes in person, and the mayor and aldermen having viewed the site and found that the nuisance is as alleged, give judgment that the def. remove it *within 40 days etc.*

Fri. 8 Feb. 1398.[1] *Adam Bamme, mayor, Thomas Wilford and William Parker, sheriffs, John Hadlee, William Staundon, William Brampton, Thomas Knolles, John Hende, John Shadworth, John Wade and William Askham, aldermen.*

642. John Moot, abbot of St. Alban the Martyr in the county of Hertford, complains that whereas John Wakelee, 'vynter', has a garden in the par. of St. Peter the Less in Bradstret adjoining his, the stone wall between them, running from east to west for 29 ft. and standing on the pl.'s land, so that the def. is bound to repair it, is broken down and ruinous, and the def.'s tenants and servants enter his garden, and tread down the grass (herbagia) there, and they see and hear his private business and that of his tenants and servants through the windows and other apertures (foramina) which overlook his garden. Moreover, the water from the def.'s premises falls upon his land for a length of 36 ft. The sheriffs testify that the def. has been summoned by Richard Daneler and Roger Stokton, but he makes default. Judgment, after view, that the nuisances complained of are expressly contrary to the custom of the City, and that *within 40 days etc.* the def. repair the wall and gutter (stillicidia) and block up the windows and apertures.

[m. 7d.] *Fri. 4 June 1400. Thomas Knolles, mayor, William Walderne and William Hyde, sheriffs, William Brampton, William Askham, Thomas Wilford, William Evote, William Venour and John Wakelee, aldermen.*

643. John Sybille complains that Juliana Purbyk has affixed her tenting-frames (tentoria) to certain stone walls, 21½ yds. long, belonging to his tenement in the par. of St. Martin Orgar, which are gravely weighed down thereby (graviter opprimere nititur), and the rainwater which floods her land flows through the midst of them, so that within a short time they are

1. An incorrect date; Wilford and Parker were sheriffs, 1396–7.

Assize of Nuisance

like to be ruined. The sheriffs have testified elsewhere that the def. has been summoned by John Drew and John Pope to appear upon the land to answer the pl., but she makes default. Judgment after view by both the mayor and aldermen and the four masons and carpenters that, since the nuisances complained of are expressly contrary to the custom of the City, the def. must remedy and remove them *within 40 days etc.*

644. Robert Asshecombe, citizen and 'brouderer', complains that Gilbert Accon, citizen, and Mazera his wife have divers lights (luminaria), windows, broken-down walls and openings to latrines (foramina latrinarum) in their tenement adjoining his in the pars. of St. Alban the Martyr in Wodestrete and St. Mary de Stanynglane, and they, their tenants and lessees (firmarii) and the members of their household (familiares) can see and hear the private business of the pl., his tenants, lessees and the members of his household. Moreover they throw filth and rubbish into his close, and evil odours come from their latrines. The sheriffs have testified elsewhere that the defs. have been summoned by Henry Payn and Thomas Bristowe to appear upon the land to answer the pl., but they make default. After view by both the mayor and aldermen and the masons and carpenters, it is adjudged that, since the nuisances alleged are expressly contrary to the custom of the City, they be removed and remedied *within 40 days etc.*

[m. 8] *Mon. [sic] 4 May 1405. John Hende, mayor, Thomas Thorneburgh, recorder, William de Louthe and Stephen Speleman, sheriffs, William Askham, John Warner, William Venour, Thomas Fauconer, William Crowmere and Henry Pomfreyt, aldermen.*

645. Nicholas Wotton, citizen and merchant (mercatori), complains that Henry Boseworth, citizen and mercer (mercerus), has an old and ruinous wharf on the east side of his, which adjoins his tenement in the par. of St. Magnus the Martyr, and that for lack of repairs to the def.'s wharf (wharvam) his own is on the point of collapsing into the Thames. The sheriffs testify that the def. has been summoned for the following Friday by Richard Honyman and John Ferers, but he essoins himself. A day is then given to the parties on Fri. 5 June, when the mayor and sheriffs, taking with them the six aldermen named above to go to the site. The pl. appears in person, but the def. makes default. Thereupon the mayor, sheriffs and aldermen instruct the four viewers—viz. John Wolfey and Richard Style, masons, and Robert Lardyner and John Petit, carpenters, to inspect the premises and report as soon as possible. In a bill remaining in the file of nuisances they certify that the def.'s wharf measures from east to west 13 ft. 11 ins., and is very ruinous, and that he ought to repair and maintain it so that the wharves on either side do not suffer damage through his neglect. They certify further that the pl.'s wharf is 12 ft. 1 in. high, and overhangs that of the def. by $7\frac{1}{2}$ ins. through the latter's fault. On Tues. 16 June, it is accordingly adjudged that *within 40 days etc.* the def. repair, correct and amend his wharf so that it causes no further damage to that of the pl.

[*No heading.*]

Assize of Nuisance

646. A dispute having occurred between Nicholas Hamme, citizen and mercer, and Margaret relict of Stephen Hamme, late citizen, concerning the removal of various leaden utensils (plumborum utenciliorum) and vessels (vasorum) and household goods (hostilmentorum) and necessaries (necessariorum) from Nicholas's brewhouse (bracinee) called 'le glene on the Hope' in the par. of St. Mildred in Bredstrete, and claimed by Nicholas as his property, the parties appeared on 22 Dec. 1407 before William Staundone, mayor, and the aldermen, and agreed to abide by the findings of the four master masons and carpenters. Accordingly, on 23 Dec. the mayor instructed the four viewers to inspect the premises and certify the court of their findings. On 17 Jan. 1408 they—viz. John Wolphey, Richard Style, Robert Lardyner and John Petyt, reported [French] to the mayor and aldermen [m. 8d.] that the two leads (plumbes), two leaden 'taptrogh' with all their appurtenances (apparaille), two 'masshtonnes', three quernes in a 'bynne' in the brewhouse (brwerne), and two 'ȝiletonnes' in the cellar (celer) belong to the free tenement of Nicholas, with all the benches, 'speres', 'entreclosewalles', the cellar (celour) beneath the parlour, the door, windows, 'steyres', a great press of two floors (j graunt presse de deux flores) in the 'pavynge chambre', the pavement in the hall (sale) and the chambers there and all the 'crestes' in the hall and parlour; but the other household goods in the tenement, viz. vats (fattes), kimnels (kymylyns), 'tubbes', 'tynes', 'clensyngsyvis', 'barellys', 'fourmes', 'bordes', tables and other moveables are claimed by him contrary to the custom of the City and belong to the administrators of the goods of the late Stephen. They therefore ask that a remedy be provided in accordance with their findings, unless either party can show a specialty.

647. An indenture [French] drawn up on 25 Sep. 1406, between John Wolfey, Robert Lardyner, carpenters [*sic*], Richard Stile and John Petyt, masons [*sic*], with Thomas Clynan, Thomas Somerton, Henry Hert, drapers, and John Shawe 'vynter', citizens, with the consent of the prior of St. Mary Overey in Southwerk, William Weston, draper, John Megre, 'peautrer', John Sotherey, 'tapicer', John Gentyll and Richard Lyes, drapers, and sworn to before John Wodecok, mayor and the aldermen, apportioning between the prior and the others named with him the £10 annual rent, comprising £9 13s. 4d. for the maintenance of two chaplains celebrating in the church of St. Mary Wolnoth in Lumbardstrete, and 6s. 8d. payable to the prioress and convent of St. Mary Clerkenwell, in accordance with the provisions of the testament[1] of Thomas Noket, late citizen and draper, viz.:— from the tenements of John Megre in Lumbardstrete £4 9s. 11d. towards the maintenance of the two chaplains, and 3s. 1d. to the prioress of Clerkenwell; from the tenements of John Gentyll and Richard Lyes in Shitebournelane and Abbechirch lane 41s. 10¾d., and 17¼d.; from a tenement in Cornhull belonging to the prior and convent of St. Mary Overy 21s. 2¾d., and 9¼d.; from the tenement of William Weston, draper, in Cornhull 20s. 1¾d., and 8¼d.; from a tenement belonging to John Sothereye and Cecily his wife in Cornhull 20s. 1¾d., and 8¼d.

1. *Cal. Wills*, ii, 322–3.

Assize of Nuisance

[m. 9. *1431.*]

648. Robert Ottele, citizen and grocer, complains by John Stafford, his attorney, that the rainwater from the tenement of William Warde, citizen and draper (pannarius), Joan his wife and John Fan, citizen and skinner, falls upon his garden in the par. of St. Stephen in Walbrooke for a length of 41 ft. 1½ ins., and so floods it that the plants (herbe) wither and decay; and they have two large windows overlooking his same garden, above the height of 16 ft. from the ground, but neither glazed nor shuttered (fenestrare), through which their tenants and their servants can see the private business of the pl., his servants and tenants. Robert Large and Walter Cherteseye, sheriffs, testify that the defs. have been summoned by John Lemman and John Harry to appear upon the land to answer the plaint, but they make default. The mayor and aldermen view the premises, but wishing to be more fully advised, give the pl. a day at Guildhall on Fri. 29 June to hear judgment; and because it is evident to the mayor and aldermen, as well by their own view as by the report of the masons and carpenters, that the nuisances complained of are expressly contrary to the custom of the City, it is adjudged that the defs. amend and remove them *within 40 days etc.*

649. The same Robert Ottele, by his same attorney, brings a similar plaint against Richard Spicer, esquire (armiger), Richard Denton and William Beverley, in respect of rainwater falling from their tenements, upon his garden for a length of 18 ft. and of five windows and five apertures called 'wikettes' opening on to his land. The sheriffs testify that the defs. have been summoned by John Chadde and John Lurchon, but they make default. The pl. is given a day and judgment is given [as in **648.**]

650. [m. 9d.] The same Robert, by the same attorney, brings a like plaint against John Middelton and John Ray, concerning rainwater falling on his garden for a length of 30 ft. 2 ins., and seven windows and two apertures opening on to his land. The defs., summoned as above, make default. The pl. is given a day and judgment is given [as in **648**].

[m. 10] *Fri. 23 May 1427. John Reynwell, mayor, John Symond, recorder, William Cauntbrigge, John Michell, Nicholas James, Richard Gosselyn. Simon Seman, John Perveys and Robert Arnold, sheriff.*

651. Walter de la Pole, 'chivaler', William Alyngton, John Burgoyne, Nicholas Caltecote, Clement Liffyn, citizen and draper, John Reyner and Thomas Parys complain that the rainwater from the tenement of Robert Broun, skinner, and William Prest, 'talughchaundeler', falls upon their garden for a length of 69 ft., flooding it and destroying the plants (herbe) there; and that they have five windows less than 16 ft. from the ground opening on to it, through which their tenants and servants can see the private business of the pls., their servants and tenants. Robert Arnold and John Hyham, sheriffs, testify that the defs. have been summoned by John Joly and John Briklesworth to appear to answer the plaint, but they make default. The mayor and aldermen view the premises, and give the pl. a day at Guildhall on Fri. 6 June to hear judgment; and because it is evident that the nuisances complained of are expressly contrary to the custom of the City, it is adjudged that the defs. remove and amend them *within 40 days etc.*

Fri. [5 Sep. 1427 (Fri. after the feast of St. Giles, 5 Henry VI, rectius 6 Henry VI)]. John Reinwell, mayor, and the aldermen.

652. William Kylshyll, fishmonger, complains that the rainwater from the tenement of Alice Gayton, widow, falls upon his tenement for a length of 36 ft., and rots his timber, so that it threatens ruin, and that she has three windows less than 16 ft. from the ground overlooking his premises, through which her servants and tenants can see the private business of the pl., his tenants and servants. The def. comes by John Stafford, her attorney, and says that, as regards the fall of water, the assize does not lie, because the tenement she holds formerly belonged to Christine relict of John Steynour and on her death without heirs it escheated[1] to the crown in the time of Edward III, who granted it by his letters patent[2] to John Kyngeston, whose estate she now holds, and from time out of mind the rainwater from the same has been received by the pl. and his predecessors and conveyed through a gutter (gutteram) into the street. As regards the windows, she claims that, according to the custom of the City, it has always been permissible for them to overlook a neighbouring tenement, provided they are more than the height of a man, viz. 8 ft. or more, from the ground and glazed with thick glass or barred with iron (cum vitro spisso vel fermentis ferreis includere), and the windows in her messuage fulfil those requirements; wherefore she asks judgment. The pl. by John Crowton, his attorney, denies her allegations, and claims that he is not bound in law to answer her (ad placita predicta modo in forma superius placitata non tenetur nec necesse habet par legem terre respondere); to which the def. replies that her plaint is sufficient in law and asks that the pl. be excluded from the assize if he refuses to answer (dicit ex quo ipsa placitavit placita sufficientia in lege ad que predictus Willelmus nichil respondit ne replicat in lege petit judicium, et quod predictus Willelmus ab assisa sua predicta precludatur). The court gives the parties a day at the assizes to be held at Guildhall on Fri. 30 Jan. 1428, and the record having been read, heard and understood, it is then adjudged that *within 40 days etc.* the def. remove the nuisances complained of, viz. that in accordance with custom of the City she block up the windows and receive upon her own land or convey into the street the rainwater falling on her tenement. [m. 10d. Blank.]

[m. 11] *Fri. 13 July 1425. John Michell, mayor, John Fray, recorder, Ralph Barton, John Coventre, John Welles, William Estfeld, Simon Seman, John Bithewater and Henry Frowyk, aldermen.*

653. John Frank, clerk, warden (custos) of the House of Converts and Master of the Rolls (custos rotulorum cancellarie) complains that an earthen wall between the great tenement or inn (hospicium) called 'le

1. *C.I.P.M.*, xiv, no. 205.
2. *C.P.R. 1374–7*, 173.

Converse' with its gardens and other appurtenances and the tenement and garden of William de Haryngton, kt., Christopher de Morisby, William del Garth, Thomas Romondby, clerk, and Thomas Skirwith, called 'Cliffordesyngardyn' in the par. of St. Dunstan West in Fletestrete, is broken down and ruinous on both the east and north sides of the defs.' garden for a length of 120 ft., so that men and animals enter the pl.'s gardens and trample down the plants (herbe) growing there, and destroy and carry off the fruit, and see his private business and that of his servants; and since the wall stands upon the pl.'s land the defs. are bound to repair it. Simon Seman and John Bithewater, sheriffs, have testified elsewhere that the defs. have been summoned by Geoffrey Gybon and Henry Gernoun to appear upon the land and answer the plaint, but they make default. The mayor and aldermen, having viewed the site, give the pl. a day at Guildhall on Fri. 24 Aug. He comes by John Crowton, his attorney, but the court adjourns the proceedings until Fri. 19 Oct. After further adjournments, the mayor and aldermen, wishing to view the site again before giving judgment, give the pl. a day upon the land on Fri. 14 June 1426. On that day he duly appears by his attorney before John Coventre, mayor, John Fray, recorder, Thomas Fauconer, Ralph Barton, Robert Tatersall, John Bithewater, Henry Frowyk and John Brokle, aldermen, and is given a day at Guildhall on Fri. 28 June, when, since it appears as well by inspection by the mayor and aldermen as by report of the four masons and carpenters that the wall stands upon the pl.'s land, it is adjudged that *within 40 days etc.* the defs. rebuild and repair it. Defs. in mercy.[1] [*Margin:* Misericordia.]

[m. 11d.] *Fri. 15 Nov. 1426. John Reynwell, mayor, John Symound, recorder, William Cauntbrigge, John Coventre, Ralph Barton, John Wellis, Robert Tatersall, John Bythewater, Henry Frowyk and both sheriffs.*

654. Margaret Curteys complains by John Hethingham, her attorney, that she holds a tenement in the par. of All Hallows de Honylane, adjoining that of John Sargere, warden of the college of St. Mary Otery, co. Devon, and John Stone of London, 'hosteller', in the par. of St. Lawrence in Old Jewry and the two tenements were formerly one, until Elias de Honylane granted the portion which is now held by the pl., to William Joynour and his heirs, by a deed, dated and sealed, which is produced in court, on the express understanding that all the water from it should be received by the donor and conveyed by an underground gutter (receptaculum, guttera subterranea) through the midst of his tenement into Seintlaurenslane, and that nothing should be done to obstruct the light of the three windows facing in his direction; but the defs. have now blocked the light of the same by building a new 'shedde' opposite to them, and have stopped up the gutter with stones and other material so that the water cannot escape, but flows back into the pl.'s tenement and floods it. Robert Arnold and John Higham, sheriffs, have testified elsewhere that the defs. have been summoned by John Joynour and John Trethewe to appear upon the land to answer the plaint, but they make default. The mayor and aldermen, having viewed the premises give the pl. a day on Fri. 29 Nov. upon the land. She

1. For plaint, see *C.P.M.R. 1413–37*, 177.

Assize of Nuisance

appears by attorney before the mayor and recorder, John Coventre, John Welles, Robert Tatersall, Ralph Barton, Richard Gossellyn, John Perveys, Nicholas James, John Bithewater and Henry Frowyk, aldermen, and John Higham, sheriff. Judgment that the defs. remove the nuisances *within 40 days etc.*, and that they be in mercy.[1] [*Margin:* Misericordia.]

655. [m. 12] Memorandum that on Tues. 4 May 1423, Thomas Cradok, clerk, John Carpenter and Richard Osbarn appeared with William Tristour, William Coldwell, Henry Gernoun, John Ballarde and Robert Graunger, tenants of adjoining tenements in Goterlane and Wodestrete before William Walderne, mayor, and the aldermen, in a dispute concerning chimneys and other buildings which the latter, and those whose estate they hold, have built upon the walls enclosing a messuage belonging to the former in Wodestrete, in the par. of St. Peter de Westchepe, now occupied by John Bethewater, and occasioning, as they declare, a grave nuisance. The parties pledge themselves to abide by the judgment of the mayor and aldermen, and the report of the four masons and carpenters. On Fri. 7 May, the mayor and aldermen, accompanied by the four viewers go to the site, the parties appearing in person; but because they wish for further information before giving judgment, they instruct the four viewers to inspect and measure the walls and buildings concerned, and report to them in the king's court in the Chamber of Guildhall on Fri. 21 May. On that day the parties appear in person, and Walter Milton, William Coupere, William Serle and Esmond Werlowe, the four master masons and carpenters, come and certify [French] that there is a stone wall running for 72 ft. $8\frac{1}{2}$ ins. from east to west on the south side which belongs wholly to the demandants, and on it are a double chimney (chymnye) on the south side and a little building (meason) at the west end belonging to the defs. which ought to be removed; and at the east end of the same wall is another running for 23 ft. 10 ins. from west to east which for its whole length belongs to the defs.; and at the west end of the first wall is another running for 3 ft. 1 in. from south to north on which are built the tenements of the defs., 11 ins. of its width belonging to them and the remainder to the demandants; and from that end from east to west on the north (et a celle fin de est en west par la north partie) is another stone wall beneath the same tenements 33 ft. $7\frac{1}{2}$ ins. long, of which a width of 11 ins. belongs to the defs., and the remainder to the demandants; and on the north side of the east as far as Goterlane (en la north partie del est tanque en Goterlane) is a stone wall 22 ft. 11 ins. long enclosing the said messuage, which belongs wholly to the demandants. They therefore ask that a remedy be provided in accordance with their findings, unless either party can show a specialty. Judgment that the defs. remove the chimney and building (edificium), and that in future both parties, their heirs and assigns, hold the said walls quietly and peaceably, according to the metes and bounds set out in the above bill. [m. 12d. Blank.]

656. [m. 13] On 15 Nov. 1417 the prior of St. Mary Royston (Roiston) and Robert Cawode, citizen and glazier, appear before Richard Merlawe, mayor, and the aldermen, and for the removal of doubt and ambiguity concerning

1. For plaint, see *C.P.M.R. 1413–37*, 200.

the boundaries of their adjoining tenements in the par. of St. Dunstan West in Fletestrete, agree to refer the matter to the four masons and carpenters and to abide by their report. After taking careful measurements and hearing the evidence of the parties and the arguments of their counsel (consiliorum) and friends, the four viewers, viz. Walter Walton, William Wiltshire, Walter Milton and Richard Hemmyngburgh, present to the mayor and aldermen, in the presence of the parties, a certificate [French] to the effect that the stone wall which runs for 37 ft. from the king's highway to Robert's door belongs to the prior; and of the same wall running for 21 ft. from the said door to a crack (fracture) and 'relese' in the same, a width of 7 ins. belongs to Robert; and for 16 ft. from the same crack to a corner-stone (coigne) next (vers) the street, the land and also the skew (la scuwe) belong to him, but the cornerstone itself with the wall there belongs to the prior and convent. In the wall is a privy built contrary to the custom of the City, which Robert ought to remove at his own expense. Further, on the south side of the above-mentioned door is a wall 37 ft. 10 ins. long, in which for a length of 24 ft. he is entitled to a width of 8 ins. at the beginning and end thereof; but he has possessed himself of and built upon 11 ins., without the consent of the prior and convent to whom the wall belongs. The above bill having been read and heard, it is adjudged by the mayor and aldermen that each of the parties observe the metes and bounds therein contained, and that Robert remove the privy. The parties leave the court agreeing to execute the judgment. [m. 13d. Blank.]

657. [m. 14] On 3 Aug. 1413, John Frenssh, citizen and goldsmith, and John, prior of St. Andrew, Rochester, appear in person before William Crowmere, mayor, and the aldermen upon a vacant plot of land in the tenement of John Frenssh in the par. of St. Bride in Fletestrete, which the prior claims as his free tenement in right of his church, by an assize of novel disseisin[1] held before John Sely and Adam Bamme, sheriffs, and Richard Wellesborn, coroner, on Sat. 29 Nov. 1382. On 4 Aug. the four viewers, Walter Walton, William Wiltshire, Walter Milton and Richard Hemmingburgh, masons and carpenters, are ordered to inspect and measure the site to see whether the metes and bounds correspond with those claimed by the prior. On 17 Aug., in the Chamber, in the presence of the parties, they report [French] that the disputed plot of land measures from south to north 46 ft., and from west to east 24 ft. according to the measurements given in the assize of novel disseisin aforesaid. Their report having been read and understood, it is adjudged by the mayor and aldermen that the prior have, hold and enjoy the said vacant plot of land in accordance with the metes and bounds given above, without any further disturbance or molestation by John Frenssh or his executors.

658. [m. 14d.] Memorandum that in a congregation of the mayor and aldermen in the Chamber on Mon. 15 Apr. 1415 Brother Walter Grendon, prior of the hospital of St. John of Jerusalem, sought an assize of nuisance against Richard Burne and Juliana his wife, John Gamboun and William

1. *London possessory assizes*, no. 167.

Merlyn, concerning his tenement in the par. of St. Michael at Queenhithe.[1] The sheriffs, ordered to summon the defs. for the following Fri., 19 Apr., testify that they have been summoned by John Woxbregge and Robert Brendwode, The prior appears by John Carpenter, his attorney, but the defs. essoin themselves. On Fri. 11 Oct., Thomas Fauconer, mayor, John Barton, recorder, Thomas Knolles, Richard Merlawe, Robert Chichele, William Crowmer, William Norton, William Chichele and Thomas Aleyn, aldermen, come to the site of the alleged nuisance, and the prior appears by his attorney and complains that the upper part (summum edificium) of the defs.' tenement opposite his messuage in Bredstrete overhangs the street so far that the light of his tenement is obscured, and his tenants cannot see to carry on their crafts (artificia) and business (negocia), but often leave the premises, so that the prior loses his profit and rent from the same; and they have a chimney so badly built that it often causes fires in the houses of the prior and those living nearby. The defs. make default. Thereupon the mayor and aldermen order the four viewers, viz. Walter Walton, William Wiltshire, Walter Milton and Richard Hemmyngburgh, to inspect the premises and report to them. On 20 Mar. [1416] they present a bill [French] to the effect that the topmost jetty (le plus haut gette) of the defs.' tenement overhangs the street contrary to right and reason, so that the light of the windows in the prior's messuage is obstructed, and it ought to be set back (estre retreet); and that their chimney is a great nuisance and danger to the prior and all the neighbours, and should be amended at the discretion of the masons and carpenters. The mayor and aldermen, having heard and understood the report adjudge that the defs. remove the nuisances *within 40 days etc.* [*Below:* Assise de tempore Riccardi Merlawe.]

659. Memorandum that in a congregation of the mayor and aldermen in the Chamber on Mon. 3 Oct. 1412, John Dyne, rector of St. Leonard in Estchepe, and William Beverych, Edmund Twyn, John Furner and Richard Gynne, churchwardens, sought an assize of nuisance against John Cornewaleys, John Weston, John Wade, John Proffyt, Henry Shelford, Robert Fitzhugh and William Bailly, citizen and linendraper, their feoffor, in respect of a tenement in the same par. The sheriffs, ordered to summon the defs. to appear before John Chichele, mayor, and the aldermen in the Chamber on the Fri. following, return that they have been summoned by John Sadiller and William Ivory. The pls. appear by John Carpenter, their attorney. The defs. do not appear, but are essoined, and the proceedings are adjourned from quindene to quindene. On Fri. 18 Nov. William Waldern, mayor, John Preston, recorder, Richard Whityngton, William Crowmer, Henry Barton, William Norton, William Chichele, Walter Cotton, aldermen, and Ralph Lobenham, alderman and sheriff, come upon the land, and the pls. appear by their attorney, and complain that the defs. have a tenement adjoining the churchyard which overhangs it for a length of 27 ft., and a width of 5 ft. at the eastern corner and of 4 ft. 4 ins. at the western corner. The defs. make default. Thereupon the mayor, aldermen and sheriff instruct the four viewers, viz. Walter Wylton [*sic*], Walter

1. *C.P.M.R. 1413–37*, 35.

Milton, William Wyltshire and Robert Lardener, master masons and carpenters, to inspect the premises and report to them. On 22 Nov. they present a bill [French] corroborating the pls.' allegations, and asking that a remedy be provided unless either party can show a specialty. On Fri. 3 Mar. 1413 the mayor and aldermen adjudge that the defs. remove the nuisance *within 40 days etc.* [m. 15d. Blank. m. 16 Entry as on m. 15. m. 16d. Blank.]

[m. 17] *In a congregation of the mayor and aldermen in the Chamber on Mon. 10 Oct. 1407.*

660. John Eynesham seeks an assize of nuisance against Thomas Pyrye, prior of New Place near Gyldeford in Surrey, concerning his tenement in the par. of St. Giles without Crepulgate. The sheriffs are ordered to summon the def. to appear before Richard Whityngton, mayor, and the aldermen in the Chamber on the Fri. following [14 Oct.]. They return that he has been summoned by Thomas Wegge and Robert Edmond. The pl. comes by William Kyngeston, his attorney. The def. does not appear, but is essoined by Thomas Locke, and a day is given to the parties on Fri. 21 Oct. On that day both parties appear by their attorneys, but because the mayor and aldermen cannot come to the site on account of business concerning the City, the proceedings are adjourned until Fri. 4 Nov. Further adjournments follow until Fri. 20 Jan. 1408, when the parties come by their attorneys before John Staundon, mayor, and the aldermen in the Chamber, and are given a day to appear on the land in the presence of the mayor, John Preston, recorder, Thomas Knolles, William Askham, John Warner, Thomas Polle, William Norton, aldermen, and Henry Halton and Henry Pountfreyt, sheriffs. They come in person, and the pl. complains that the prior has built a roof on his adjoining messuage which overhangs his garden for a length of 87 ft. and a width of 2 ft., so that the rainwater therefrom falls upon his land and totally destroys the plants growing there. The mayor, aldermen and sheriffs ask the def. whether he has anything to say in his defence, and he answers that the assize does not lie, because at the time of the building of the roof the pl.'s garden was his own free tenement, and still is, as he is prepared to prove. The pl. denies his allegation, and asks that the assize proceed. Thereupon a jury is summoned, comprising John Arnold, Nicholas Stratton, Stephen Toppesfeld, Henry Payn, Alan Brette, Thomas Osbarn, John Em, John Mapisden, Stephen Roberd, John Stombelhole, Roger Loundres and John Cosham, who say upon oath that the garden is, and was at the time of the bringing of the assize, the free tenement of the pl., as far as the foundation of the prior's messuage, and that the overhanging roof was built long since by his predecessors and demolished and rebuilt by him. They add that the fall of rainwater is contrary to the custom of the City, and is to the pl.'s damage £3. Asked by the court whether the roof was built with the consent and licence of the pl. or his ancestors or merely by his sufferance, and whether it was rebuilt longer and wider than before, they say that it was built by his sufferance, and neither longer nor wider than at present. The parties are given a day on Fri. 3 Feb. Adjournments follow until Fri. 14 June 1409, when the pl.

appears in person in the Chamber before Drew Barantyn, mayor, the recorder and aldermen, and judgment is given, in accordance with the findings of the jury, that the def. remove the nuisance *within 40 days etc.*

[m. 17d. *No heading.*]

661. At the Husting of Pleas of Land held on Mon. 28 Jan. 1409 (10 Henry V, *rectius* 10 Henry IV), William Middelton, citizen and grocer, sought an assize of nuisance against John Crosseby, citizen, concerning a tenement in the par. of St. Margaret de Bruggestrete. The sheriffs are ordered to summon the def. to appear before Drew Barentyn, mayor, and the aldermen in the Chamber on the Fri. following [1 Feb.], and they return that he has been summoned by Thomas Duffehous and Roger Crouche. On that day the pl. appears in person, but the def. essoins himself, and the proceedings are adjourned from quindene to quindene until Fri. 1 Mar., when Drew Barentyn, mayor, Thomas Knolles, William Louthe, Stephen Spelman, Henry Pountfreit, William Chichele and William Norton, aldermen, come upon the land. The pl. appears in person and complains that whereas he has within his tenement and upon his own soil a stone wall 35 ft. $9\frac{1}{2}$ ins. long, the def. has built upon it to a width of $11\frac{3}{4}$ ins. The def. makes default. The mayor and aldermen instruct the four viewers, viz. John Wolfey, Richard Style, Richard Lardyner and John Petyt, master masons and carpenters, to inspect the premises and report to them. On 20 Mar. they present a bill [French] corroborating the allegation of the pl. The mayor and aldermen, having heard and understood their report, adjudge that *within 40 days etc.* the def. remove the nuisance.

INDEX

References in Roman numerals are to the pages of the Introduction; Arabic numerals denote entries in the calendar (and not pages) unless printed in Italics when they refer to the heading of an entry in the calendar. For other points concerning the Index, see p. xxxiv.

Aas, John, 586
Abberbury, Richard, junior, kt., 641
Abchurch Lane (Abbechirch lane), 647
Abel
  John, 331–2
  William, butcher, & Joan his wife, 309
Abraham, John, 511
Absolon, Adam, 85
Abyndon(e)
  Simon de, alderman, *230–59*; def., 164, 248; sheriff, *244*
  Stephen de, 119; alderman, *185*; mayor, *223–8*; sheriff, *221*
Accon, Gilbert & Mazera his wife, 644
Acres (Acre)
  Adam de, common serjeant, xxix; commonalty's attorney, 449–50
  John de, 256
Adrien (Adrian)
  John, 169
  Peter, 154
  Thomas, 351
Albyn (Aubyn)
  John (son of Lawrence), 209, 217
  Lawrence, 396
Aldebury, Walter de, canon of St. Paul's, 594
Aldermen: on assizes, x–xi, xiii; jurors in pleas of intrusion, xi; pls. while on assize, xxxi; two adjourn assize, xvi; *see also* Mayor & aldermen
Ale, 617; -tuns (ʒiletonnes), 646
Aleyn (Alleyn)
  Geoffrey & Maud his wife, 370–1, 374
  Thomas, alderman, 658
Algate, Joan relict of Robert de, potter, 340
Alien priory, 386; *see also* Fécamp
All Hallows Barking (St. Mary de Berkyngechapel): chantry chaplain of the chapel of St. Nicholas, *see* Forster, John; church, 125; par., 146, 251, 259, 611; parishioners (named), 259; parson, Walter, 259; rector, *see* Gatewyk, William de

All Hallows Bread Street: chantry in church, 385; par., 28, 304–5, 441, 635–6; parishioners (named), 385, 481; rector, *see* Doublet, Walter; wardens of a tenement in, 385
All Hallows Honeylane: church, 399; par., 528, 654
All Hallows Lombard Street (Garscherche, Grascherche): church, 260; churchyard, 260, 474; par., 77, 184, 212, 431; parishioners (named), 260; parson, Roger, 260; rector, *see* Aston, John de
All Hallows London Wall, par., 188, 293
All Hallows Staining, par., 633–4
All Hallows the Great (at Hay, atte Heywharf, *etc.*), par., 37, 118–19, 244, 253, 265
All Hallows the Less: par., 50, 164, 536–7; parishioners, 50; rector, *see* Egemere, Master John de
Alleyn, *see* Aleyn
Alleys, 464, 488, 586
Alms, gift in, 34
Alure, *see* Buildings
Alyngton, William, 651
Amoundesham, Henry de, 145
Ampney, Nicholas de, abbot of Cirencester, 593
Amys (Amizs)
  John, 74
  William, 149
Ancroft (Anecroft), William, alderman, 632, *630–1*
Andrew (Andreu)
  James, 451; alderman, 524–5, 591, *518–69*; mayor, 536, 545, *535–45*; sheriff, *518*
  Richard, 258
  William, chandler, 473
Animals, 63, 66, 218, 519, 524, 570, 595, 605, 609, 653; slaughtered, 569; *see also* Cows; Dogs; Fowls; Horses; Oxen; Pigs
Anvil, 617

184

Index

Arblaster, William, 615
Archer, Thomas, rector of St. Leonard Eastcheap, 574
Arches, *see* Buildings
Arcubus, *see* Bow
Armenters (Darmenters), John de, 326; alderman, *19–54*; Joan his relict, xxxii, 316, 323, 325–6, 328
Armour, 617
Armourer, *see* Trades
Arnold
    John, 660
    Robert, sheriff, 651, 654, *651*
Arondel, William de, 79
Arraz
    Alice de, 236
    Robert de, sheriff, 318
    William de, 497
Askham
    John de, clerk, 426
    William, alderman, 660, *641–5*
Aspal, Adam, 414
Asshe, Robert de, cordwainer, 199
Asshebourne
    Henry de, tawyer, 499
    Thomas, prior of Austin Friars, 630
Assheby, John de, 306
Asshecombe, Robert, broderer, 644
Asshelyn, Henry, 618
Asshendon
    Alan de, & Margery his wife, 261
    Gilbert de, 47, 80, 102–3
Asshwell
    John & Parnel his wife, 568
    John, attorney, 599
Asshwy, Isabel relict of Stephen, 171
Assize of buildings (fitz Ailwin's assize), ix–xi, xii–xxxii *passim*; cited in pleading, xv
Aston
    John de, rector of All Hallows Lombard Street, 448, 474
    William de, 483
Attorneys, xv
Aubrey (Aubre)
    Andrew, alderman, 319, 407, 432, *334–441*; def., xxxii, 316, 323–4, 326; mayor, 353, *349–61, 429–30*; pl., 304–5, 325, 328; Joan his wife, 316, 322–6, 328
    John, alderman, 591–2, 598, 613, *589–613*; pl., 573; sheriff, 597–8, 605
Aubyn, *see* Albyn
Aulton, John de, & Katherine his wife, 375–6
Aumere, William de, 416
Austin Friars, priory: garden, 188, 293; prior, 133, 293, Elias, 113, *see also* Asshebourne, Thomas; prior & brethren, 188, 630

Austyn, Thomas, alderman, 635, *635–7*; sheriff, *635–7*
Aveynes, Thomas de, Isolde his wife & Lucy their daughter, 69
Aylesbury, Richard, 626
Aylesham (Eynesham), John de, alderman, *380–93*; sheriff, 385

Bacheler
    Denise relict of John (le), 125, 259
    Walter, 481, 525
Badby (Badeby), William, 613; alderman, 618, *623*; def., 634
Badewe, Hugh de, kt., 573
Bailiff, Philip son of John le, 14
Bailiffs, City, xi; *see also* Basing, Thomas de
Bailly, William, linendraper, 659
Bakehouse, *see* Buildings
Baker, *see* Trades
Bakere
    John le, 463
    William le, 375
Bakewell (Bakkewell)
    ——, 628
    John, 598
    Thomas de, 480, 497
Balauncer, Ralph le, def., 127; sheriff, *230*
Baldewyne, Richard, 599
Baldok, John, (mayor's) serjeant, 604, 618
Balesham, Roger de, 115, 122; Isabel his wife, 115
Ballard
    John, 655
    Nicholas son of Alan, *see* Sutton
Balle, Ranulph, 85, 104; Isabel his wife, 104
Balliol Hall, *see* Oxford
Bamme
    Adam, alderman, 635, *636–8*; goldsmith, attorney, 625; mayor, *641–2*; sheriff, 627, 657
    Henry, alderman, 635, *636*
Bampton, John de, 558
Bannebury, Thomas de, & Joan his wife, 4
Barage, Arnold & Christine his wife, 6, 8
Barantyn (Barentyn), Drew, mayor, 660–1
Barber (Barbier, Barbour)
    Geoffrey le, 78
    John & Joan his wife, 426, 428
    Matthew le, 385
    Peter le, 234
    Richard le, of Bread Street, 111
    Robert le, 77, 260
    Simon le, 292
    Thomas le, 305, 375
Barber, *see* Trades
Bardeneye, Walter de, 85, 100
Barentyn, *see* Barantyn
Baret, William, alderman, *618*; arbitrator, 632; pl., 635–6; sheriff, 622–3

Index

Barge, le, tenement called, [St. Stephen Walbrook par.], 626
Barker, Richard le, serjeant of Walbrook ward, 510
Barkeworthe, Walter de, 234
Barnet (Barnette)
  John atte, mercer, 412
  John de la, 168, 177
  Thomas atte, hosteler, 596
  Thomas atte, mason, 566, 581–3, 591, 604
Baronet, Thomas son of John, 502
Baroun
  J., essoiner, 224
  John, chaplain, 443
Barre, John de la, ward-beadle, 312
Barrels, 646
Bars: for closing a lane, 401; iron, 623; *see also* Buildings, windows
Barsham, Robert de, 312
Barton
  Henry, alderman, 659
  John, recorder, 658
  John de, & Beatrice his wife, 477
  Jordan, 614
  Ralph, alderman, 653–4, *653–4*
  Thomas, goldsmith, 624
Basing (Basingg, *etc.*)
  Gregory de, 161
  Isabel relict of Nicholas de, 430
  Margery de, 196
  Reginald son of Margery de, 196
  Solomon de, 124
  Thomas de, bailiff of the City, 351
  William de, & Richolda his wife, 160, 163
Basset, Thomas & Isabel his wife, 40
Bassishaw: street, 641; ward, 261
Basyngstoke, Richard de, alderman, 407, *407–16*
Bataille, Ralph, 305
Batour, Peter le, 109
Bauquelle, John de, 103; Cecily his wife, 103, 129, 227, 235
Bavente, Alice, executors of, 41
Baynard's Castle, *see* Castle Baynard
Bayser, Richard, butcher, 569, 584; Emma his wife, 569
Beams, *see* Buildings
Beauchamp, John de, kt., 415
Beauflur (Beauflour)
  Geoffrey son of Geoffrey, 312
  James, 296
Beaufront, John, woolmonger, & Margery his wife, 548
Beaumond, 522n
Beauner, William, 487
Beauveys, Philip son of Philip de, 240
Beche, Henry atte, 574
Bedeford (Bedeforth)
  Deodatus de, goldsmith, 430; *see also* Deodonatus
  John de, skinner, 420, 442
  Richard de, & Isabel his wife, 58
Bedel, William, cordwainer, & Joan his wife, 532
Bedyngton, John de, mercer, 511
Begge, Hervey, alderman, 622
Bekenesfeld, *alias* Fulham, Adam de, & Alice his wife, 327
Bekles, John de, 271
Bell-tower, *see* Buildings
Benches, 613, 646
Benchesham, Thomas de, 522
Benere
  John le, warden of London Bridge, 51–2, 59
  Walter le, 213
Bengeo, John, 475
Benstede, Robert de, 329
Bentele
  John, 632
  John de, 377
  Maud de, 219
Benyngton, Simon de, sheriff, *508–9*
Berdefeld
  Henry, attorney, 593
  Richard de, 234
Berdene, John de, 496
Berkhampsted, Thomas de, master of St. Thomas of Acon, 452
Berkyng (Berkyngge)
  Richard (de), alderman, *331–430*; sheriff, 370
  Thomas de, goldsmith, 255
Bermyngham (Bermysygham), Thomas, 583
Bernard, William, 85, 111
Bernes, John (de), alderman, 591, 597, 604, *535–98*; mayor, *577–80*; pl., 460; sheriff, 506, *503–5*; Christine his wife, 460
Berneval, Peter & Maud his wife, 45
Berneye, Walter de, sheriff, 511–13
Beryng, Richard, tanner, 187
Besseville, John de, 383
Bethewater, *see* Bithewater
Betoyne (Béthune, Betoygne, *etc.*)
  Richard de, alderman, 312, *293–325*; def., 343–4, 347; mayor, xiii, 286
  William de, alderman, 2–3, 26, 37, *6–72*
Bever, Agnes, 629
Beverly (Beverlaco, Beverle, *etc.*)
  Adam de, skinner, 261
  John de, 385
  John de, tailor, 203
  Walter de, 305
  William, 649
  William de, chaplain, 189
Beversbrook (Beveresbroke), Wilts., *see*

Index

Blund, John
Beverych, William, 659
Biddlesden (Bittelesden), Bucks., abbot, 641
Bidyk (Bydik)
  Juliana, 627
  William de, 85
Billingesgate, Ralph de, taverner, 139
Billingsgate ward, 312
Bin (bynne), 646
Bird, Richard, essoiner, 210
Birdene, John de, 193
Bishopsgate (Bisshopesgate), 292, 375; street, 622
Bisshop
  John, 459
  Robert, 407, 409
Bithewater (Bethewater, Bythewater), John, 655; alderman, 653–4, *653–4*; sheriff, 653
Bittelesden, *see* Biddlesden
Bixle, John de, 357
Black Death, xxx
Black Friars, *see* Friars Preachers
Blackmore (Blakemore), Essex, prior, 244
Blacwell, John de, 408
Blake, Thomas le, 403
Blakeneye
  Adam de, executors of, 99
  Peter de, 125
  Thomas de, draper, 292
Blakethorn, John de la, 255
Blaunche, John, 525
Blith (Blythe)
  Geoffrey de, & Cecily his wife, 212
  Ralph de, saddler, 355, 418; Joan his wife, 418
Blod, John, 574
Blood, animals', 569
Bloseworth, *alias* de Ware, Lawrence, 622
Blund (Blount, *etc.*)
  Hugh (le), kt., 5, 135, 395, 400
  Hugh le, 46
  Idonia la, *see* Hagham, Robert de
  John, of Beversbrook, 632
  John le, alderman, 6, 205; mayor, 26, 37, 85, *10–131*
  John le, goldsmith, 255
  John son of Walter le, 25
  Peter le, parson of St. Stephen Walbrook, 169, 174
  Ralph le, 255
  Ralph le, goldsmith, 203
  Simon le, baker, 205
  Thomas, of Essex, 632
  Thomas le, 78
Bluntesdon, Henry de, 136
Boards (bordes), moveable, 646; *see also* Buildings, planks
Boats, 453

Bockysham, John, mayor's serjeant, 630
Bocton
  Adam de, 218
  Ralph son of John de, 262
Bohun, Joan, countess of Hereford, xxxi, 633–4
Bokbyndere, John le, 295
Bokeler, John le, 348
Bokerel, *see* Bukerel
Bokstede, John, carpenter, 482
Bole
  Nicholas, 503
  William le, 38
Bolet, Simon, alderman, 154, *120–85*
Bolyngton, John de, & Isabel his wife, 221
Bonaunter, Thomas, 627
Bonde, John le, & Joan his wife, 26, 35
Bonet, William, woodmonger, & Christine his wife, 541
Bordeslee, Geoffrey de, & Albreda his wife, 172
Borgard, Ralph, [sheriff's] serjeant, 269
Bosenham
  Cecily de, 527
  Peter, sheriff, 205
Boseworth, Henry, mercer, 645
Bosham (Boseham), John, alderman, 631, *614–29*
Boteler (Botyller, *etc*)
  Geoffrey le, draper, 290–1
  Gilbert, 459
  James le, 510
  John, 481; roper, 441; Agnes his wife, 441
  John son of Geoffrey le, draper, 429
Boterwyke, John, 551
Botoner (Botonner)
  Gregory le, 36
  John le, 85, 168, 177, 202, 206
  John le, tanner, 187
Botulston, Thomas, haberdasher, 581
Bouden, Henry de, 154, 236
Bourne, Margaret relict of John de, kt., 352
Bow (Arcubus), John de, 510
Bow Lane (Cordewanerstret), 317
Box
  Martin, alderman, *4*
  Robert, 525
Boxford, Robert, alderman, 622, *618*
Boxton, John de, 483
Boydon, Robert, 574
Boylet, Nicholas & Elizabeth his wife, 423
Boys, Robert le, 422
Brabazon (Brabazoun), Adam, alderman, 407, *399–441*; pl., (fishmonger), 372, 413
Brace, *see* Buildings
Brackele (Brakkele, *etc.*)
  Hawyse de, 417

Index

Brackele, *continued*
  John de, essoiner, 71, 137, 161
  Thomas de, 244, 253
  Thomas de, & Alice his wife, 272
Brackelelane [unidentified; ?All Hallows the Great par.], 114
Bracton, Henry de, xii, xxxii
Bradefeld, Richard de, brewer, 505
Bradele
  Henry de, 514
  Stephen, 523
Brademan, John, 477
Brainford (Brainforth, *etc.*), William de, essoiner, xvi, 6–8, 22, 40, 42, 47, 49, 65, 79, 88, 127–8, 134–5, 168, 177–8
Brampton
  Thomas, esquire, 638
  William, alderman, *638–43*
Brandon
  Hugh de, goldsmith, 381
  Thomas de, sheriff, 474–6, 478, *450–79*
Brangweyn
  Thomas, 225
  William, vintner, 414, 509
Brauhing (Braughyng, *etc.*)
  Bartholomew de, essoiner, 76
  Henry de, 298
  John de, 305
  John son of Peter de, 76
  Peter de, 76, 510
Brauncestre
  Imanya (Ymane) de, 14, 70
  Thomas de, 43, 318
Bray
  Adam & Tiffany his wife, 127
  Adam de, 308
  Edmund son of Joan de, 313
  Joan relict of John de, 313
  John, 287
  Osbert de, & Isabel his wife, 54, 61, 233–4, 239
  Robert de, 109, 298
  William, skinner, 400
Braybrok, William de, 357
Bread Street (Bredstrete): 233–4, 639, 658, *see also* Barber, Richard le; Cergere, William le *and* Keu, Albert le; ward, 205, 372, 630
Breast-plates, 617
'Breggehouse, le', *see* Bridge House, tenement called
Bregges, Robert de, 300
Brembre (Bremble), Nicholas, (kt.), alderman, *584–623*; mayor, 612, 632, *614–19*, *630–2*; sheriff, 586–7, 589, 592
Brendwode, Robert, 658
Brentyngham, Ralph de, 440
Bret (Brette)
  Alan, 660
  Robert le, alderman, *312–25*

Walter le, & Juliana his wife, 300
William le, 193
Bretoun, John de, kt., warden of the City, 510
Brewer, *see* Trades
Brewere
  Gilbert de la, dean of St. Paul's, 392
  Henry le, 183
  John, 522
  John le, 375
Brewhouse, *see* Buildings
Bridge, over causeway, 375
Bridge House, property, *see* London Bridge, land, *etc.*
Bridge House (le Breggehouse), tenement called, [St. Botolph Bishopsgate par.], 292
Briklesworth (Bricklesworth, Brykelesworth)
  John, 651
  John de, 474; sheriff, *523*
  William de, alderman, *343-85*
Brinchesle (Brynchesle)
  John de, 481
  John de, goldsmith, & Margery his wife, 430
Bristoll (Bristowe)
  John, 501
  Peter de, goldsmith, 70
  Simon, chaplain, 601
  Thomas, 644
  William de, & Denise his wife, 173
  William de, grocer, 551
Brocas, Bernard, kt., 638
Broderer, *see* Trades
Broke (Brok)
  Philip, 317
  Richard, 482
  Robert, hosier, 317
  Roger atte, (fellmonger), 449, 457, 465; Agnes his wife, 449, 465
  Thomas, 317
  Walter, 483, 486
Brokhampton, Geoffrey de, 101
Brokle, John, alderman, 653
Bromyerd, Richard de, 317, 330; Cecily his wife, 317
Bronnesbury, John, 574
Bronnesford, Simon de, spicer, 405
Brother, Isabel relict of John, senior, 312
Broumpton, Philip de, & Alice his wife, 605
Brounford, Juliana de, 231
Brounyng, Oliver, 221
Broutone (Brughton), Simon de, 88, 510
Brouwe, Raymond de la, 131
Brown (Broun, Brun, *etc.*)
  Andrew, 169
  Giles son of Nicholas, 145
  John, 419, 482–3

188

Index

John, of Gransden, 580
Nicholas le, 85
Richard le, 145
Robert, skinner, 651
Roger de, attorney, 227
Thomas, 132
Brughton, *see* Broutone
Bryan, John, alderman, *614–23*
Brycheford, John de, 318; Alice his wife, 314, 318
Brye, Alice relict of Gerard de, 151
Bucklersbury, 626
Bucr', *see* Bukerel
Buildings & parts thereof
  alure, 95
  arches, xxi, 308, 323, 526, 591, 597
  bakehouse, 140–1
  beams, 37–646 *passim*; couple, 566; reason, 566; summers, 92, 283; transoms, 193
  bell-tower, 308
  brace, 204
  brewhouse, 646
  cellars, 2–646 *passim*; dimensions of, 475
  chambers, high, 585; paving, 646
  chimneys, xxii, 77, 205, 265, 331, 447, 527, 617, 621, 629, 655, 658
  cisterns, 43, 277, 318
  closes, 478, 587, 607, 617, 644
  corbels, xxi, 37, 90, 92, 235, 272, 323, 351, 506, 612, 629
  corner-stones, 656
  courtyards, 30, 318
  'crestes', 646
  cupboards, xxi, 323, 591
  doors, 77, 163, 234, 323, 379, 492, 581, 613, 626; in the form of a window, 623
  drains, channels, 266, 505, 616; *see also* gutters; privies; sinks; *and* Ditches; Kennels
  eaves, 54, 61, 95, 257, 261, 464, 527, 616
  fences, xxii & n
  fillet-gutters, xxiii
  floors, 572, 621
  forges, 483, 547–8, 617
  foundations, search for, 631; stone, 446; *see also* wall-plates
  frame, 566
  gables, 283, 312; stone, 119; *see also* skew
  garret, 574
  gates, 36, 125, 175, 219, 259, 626; great, 493–4
  gutters, xxii–xxiv; underground, 214, 614, 616, 618, 654
  halls, 164, 183, 341, 406, 527, 617, 632; great, 219; of a brewhouse, 646
  hautpas (haltepas), a room raised on pillars extending into the street, xxviii, 581
  hinges, 581, 623
  hooks, iron, 206, 623
  jetties, xxviii, 77, 399, 492–3, 528, 544, 546, 619, 658
  joists, 203, 206, 282–3, 295, 309, 323, 325, 574, 586, 591
  kitchens, 61, 71, 156, 203, 215, 261, 359, 370, 406, 416, 500, 510, 527–8, 617
  mortar, 617
  nails, 54, 61, 501, 566, 583; iron, 513
  paling, 276, 335, 435; wattle & daub, 278–9
  parlours, 311, 646
  pentices, xxviii, 234, 547–8, 574, 585
  pipes, leaden, 283, 424, 438, 486, 493; wooden, 214
  place (placea), 95
  planks, boards, 203, 206, 325, 586
  posts, 76, 156, 204, 206, 211–12, 221, 269–71, 283, 295, 384, 574, 631; holes for, 591
  privies, latrines, cess-pits, xi, xxiv–xxv, xxx
  puncheons, 283, 295
  'relese', 656
  ridge-tile, 298
  roofs, xi & n, 95, 222, 282, 323, 325, 476, 513, 586, 589, 632, 660; wooden, 325, 585; *see also* tiles
  scalding houses, 569, 632
  seld, 187
  sheds, 293, 654
  shops, goldsmith's, 70; woolmonger's, 548
  shutters, 206, 648
  sinks, soakaways, 222, 277, 572, 584; of a conduit, 458
  skew, 656
  solars, xxviii, 206–632 *passim*; of two storeys, 502
  stables, 71, 183, 510, 585
  staples, 335
  steps, stairs, 234, 488, 613, 626, 632, 646
  storeys, two or three, 206, 502; *see also* solars
  tiles, 61, 184, 298, 370, 416
  turret, 31
  vault, 585
  wall-plates, 146, 204, 206, 236, 253, 282–3, 319, 323, 441, 526, 591, 597
  walls, stone, x, xx–xxii; of other materials, xxii; rabbet of, 272
  watch-tower, 365
  windows, apertures, *etc.*, xxv–xxvi, barred, 312, 370, 623, 652; called 'wikettes', 649; glazed, 81, 255, 362, 652; in a church, 574; stone frame, 312
  see also Dye-works; Pavements; Pigsties; Wells; Wharves

Index

Bukerel (Bokerel, Bucr')
  Andrew, mayor, 272
  Stephen, alderman, 255
Buksted, John de, 445
Bungeye, Richard, 488
Buntyng, John, 483
Buntyngs, Anastasia, 233
Burdeyn
  Robert, goldsmith, 219; sheriff, 206, *201–15*
  William, 490, 583; goldsmith, 602; Isabel his wife, 583
Bures, John de, sheriff, 506, *503–5*
Buresse, William, essoiner [? fictitious], 517
Burford (Bureford)
  James de, kt., 412, 424
  John de, sheriff, 37, 62, *62–9*
Burgeys, John, 451
Burgh (Burgo)
  Thomas de, 574
  William de, *282–7*
Burgoyne
  Adam de, 306
  John, 651
Buris, John, prior of Crutched Friars, 563
Burne, Richard & Juliana his wife, 658
Burnham, Bucks., abbess, 410
Burnham, Richard, carpenter, 639
Burreforth, John de, 85; sheriff, *65–7*
Burton
  Adam de, 147
  John de, clerk of the Chamber, xxxiii, p. 63
Bury
  Adam (de), alderman, 432, 474, 478, 488, *433–79*; mayor, 524–5, 595, *523–5, 594–605*; sheriff, 424; skinner, pl., *419–23*, 442; Alice his wife, *419–23*
  Adam son of Adam de, 370, 374
  Alice relict of William de, draper, 549
  Thomas de, attorney, 323
  Thomas de, cordwainer, 396
Bury St. Edmunds, Suffolk, xii n
Bussh(e)
  William, 160, 163
  William, merchant, 488
Butcher, *see* Trades
Butler, *see* Trades
Byce, William, wharf of, [near Oystergate], 582
Bykele, William de, 111
Byker
  Isabel relict of Boniface, 615
  Patrick, 615
Byrche, Thomas, haberdasher, 576

Callere (Kallere)
  Henry le, tanner, 187
  Robert le, 220; sheriff, 205
Caltecote, Nicholas, 651
Cambridge (Cauntebrigge)
  Idonea de, 131
  Ralph de, 390, 394, 414
  William, alderman, *651, 654*
  William de, 390, 394
  see also Grauntbrugg
Camera, *see* Chambre
Campes (Caumpes)
  John son of (? Iter), 434
  Richard de, 85
  Thomas de, 167
Campete Wharf, le [unidentified; ? St. Magnus par.], 327
Cancy, Henry, 522
Candles, used for soldering, xxii
Candlewick Street, *see* Cannon Street
Canefeld
  Adam de, 574
  William de, 252, 289
Cannon Street (Candlewick Street), 488
Canon, Thomas, armourer, 400
Canterbury, Kent, xii n
Canterbury
  John de, alderman, 6, *1–58*
  Michael de, mason, 205
  Simon de, carpenter, 205, 304
Cappe, John, essoiner [? fictitious], 594
Capper, *see* Trades
Cardinal's Hat, tenement called, 527
Carleton (Karleton)
  John de, prior of St. Bartholomew, 509, 528
  Thomas, alderman, *626*
  William de, 339, 342, 345–6, 461
Carlille (Carlel, Karlill)
  Adam, alderman, 622, *615–38*; pl., 525; sheriff, *635–7*
  Agnes, 503
  Mariota relict of Adam, draper, 578
  William, butler, 587
Carpenter, John, 655; attorney, 658–9
Carpenter, *see* Trades
Cartere, Roger le, & Juliana his wife, 336
Carts, 219, 396, 493–4, 536, 547, 606, 613, 631
Casse, Richard, 574
Castelacre, John de, & Isabel his wife, 304–5
Castell, William atte, 624
Castle Baynard, 85, 459; ward, 288, 453, 459; ward-alderman, *see* Costantyn, John
Castre, Bartholomew de, goldsmith, 535
Catesby, Elias, chaplain, 522
Caumpes, *see* Campes
Cauntebrigge, *see* Cambridge
Causeway, 375
Causton

190

Index

Henry de, mercer, 405
John de, alderman, 272, 286, 312–13, 318–19, 327, 333, 376, 407, 416, *289–414*; sheriff, *273–7*
William de, alderman, 319, 407, 416, *313–430*; def., 43, 369; (mercer), pl., 314, 318, 435; sheriff, 230; Denise his wife, 43, 314, 318
William de, senior, mercer, 373, 389
Cave, William de, 361
Cavel (Cavell), William, 536–7
Cavendissh (Cavendyssh, *etc.*), Stephen (de), alderman, 536, 574, *529–77*; mayor, *518*; sheriff, 493–4, 501–2, *491–8*
Cawode, Robert, glazier, 656
Caxton, William de, 84, 510; Maud his wife, 84
Celer, Richard atte, 534
Celeseye, *see* Kelseye
Cellars, *see* Buildings
Cergere, William le, of Bread Street, 234
Cess-pits, *see* Buildings, privies, *etc.*
Chadde, John, 649
Chadenesfeld, Geoffrey, rector of St. Margaret Moses Friday Street, 616–17
Chalk-pit, 251
Chaloner, William & Felicia his wife, 609–10
Chamber of London: clerk of, *see* Burton, John de; king's court in, 655; serjeants of, xvii, xviii, *see also* Greyngham, William de; Sewale, William; Worcester, William
Chamberlain, City: xix; makes extent of debt, 289; pleads on behalf of City, xxix; to provide wax torches, 544; *see also* Dode, John; Havering, Luke de; Mazerer, John le
Chamberleyn, John, serjeant, 574
Chambers, *see* Buildings
Chambre (Camera, Chaumbre)
John de (la), alderman, *223–36*
John son of John de la, 303
Chandler, *see* Trades
Changer, *see* Trades
Channels, *see* Buildings, drains
Chantries, xxi, 385, 498, 647
Chapel, William atte, 622
Chapel, view into, 574
Chaplain, Robert the, warden of London Bridge, 51–2, 59
Charleton, John de, 306
Charlewod, Thomas, 511
Charryng, John, 396
Chastilon, John, chivaler, 637
Chaucer
Elias le, 90
John, 507

Chaumpayne, John de, 381
Chaundeler
Arnold le, 260
Hugh le, 396
John & Emma his wife, 482
John le, of Coleman Street, 107
Nicholas le, & Alice his wife, 270–1
Richard le, 396
Robert le, 511
Walter le, 145, 396
William le, 219, 238, 241; Christine his wife, 219
Chauntecler
Roger, 134
Thomas, 521
Cheap ward: alderman, *see* Fraunceys, Simon; jury, 449; wardmote, 449, 456–8
Cheapside (Chepe, forum, Westchep), xi, 11, 201, 206, 282–3, 305, 318, 528, 625
Chelchethe (Chelchehethe)
Geoffrey de, tanner, 187
Gilbert, 600–3
Chelmersford, Richard de, carpenter, 559
Cherche (Chirche), Richard atte, mason, 526–7, 566, 581–3, 591, 604, 620
Cherchegate, William, 574
Cherleton, John de, kt., 294
Cherteseye, Walter, sheriff, 648
Cheryngton, Walter de, 360
Cheshunt (Chesthunte), Herts., 517
Chesthonte, John de, 194
Chevelee (Chyvele)
Emma daughter of William, 599, 608
William, tailor, & Isabel his wife, 559, 599, 608
Cheyne
Edmund, kt., & Katherine his wife, 564–5, 589
William, recorder, 632, *613–37*
Cheyner
Henry le, mercer, 319
Thomas son of Henry, 511
Chibenherst, John de, 186
Chichele, William, alderman, 658–9, 661; mayor, 659
Chichestre (Chychestre), John (de), alderman, 501, 536, 591, 598, 613, *496–598*; mayor, 574, *564–75*
Chigwell (Chiggewelle, *etc.*)
Hamo de, alderman, 233, *223–308*; mayor, 272, *244*, *255–302*; mayor's *locum tenens*, xxiii, 286–7; pl., 288; sheriff, *221*
Richard de, 11, 14; alderman, *89*
Robert de, 162, 165
Children, 293, 618
Chimneys, *see* Buildings
Chingeford, Richard de, 138

191

Index

Chippenham (Chyppenham), Adam (de), chaplain, 525; parson of St. Clement Eastcheap, xxix, 544, 546
Chipstede
  Roger de, tanner, 187
  Walter de, tanner, 187
Chirche, *see* Cherche
Churchyards, xxxi
Chykesond, Simon de, 435
Chyvele, *see* Chevelee
Ciltre, Daniel de, 85, 109
Cirencester (Circestre), Glos., abbot, 496, 538, *see also* Ampney, Nicholas de
Cirugien, *see* Surgeon
Cisterns, *see* Buildings
City Wall, xxix, 85, 387; hole in, at Houndsditch, 618
Clare
  Gilbert de, earl of Gloucester, bailiff & house of, xxxi, 64
  Nicholas de, kt., 299
  Thomas de, kt., 302
Clay, 617
Clench, Thomas, 513, 546; Goda his wife, 513
Clerk
  William, 146
  William le, attorney, 125
Clerkenwell
  hospital of St. John of Jerusalem, prior, 504, *see also* Grendon, Walter; Thame, Philip de
  priory of St. Mary, prioress, 647, *see also* Let, Idonia
Clevele, *see* Clivele
Cleymunt, John, 41
Clifford's Inn, garden, 653
Clivele (Clevele), John, alderman, 618, *616*
Clopham, Hugh de, 510
Closes, *see* Buildings
Cloths, wet, 488
Clouton, Ellen de, 180–1
Clynan, Thomas, draper, 647
Cnopwede, John de, 343–4
Cobham (Cobeham)
  Adam de, & Agnes his wife, 138
  Henry de, kt., 313
  Thomas de, (woodmonger), 244, 253
Codestone, John de, 234
Coffrer, Alexander le, 85
Cog, Robert, 606
Cokayn, John, recorder, *641*
Coke (Cok), *see* Cook
Cokfeld, Robert de, kt., 146
Colcestre (Colecestre)
  Gilbert de, 32, 417
  John de, attorney, 102
  Walter de, 78
Colchester, archdeacon of, *see* Meleford, William de

Coldwell, William, 655
Coleman Street, 107; ward, 261
Colle, Henry & Margery his wife, 611
Collesdon, Thomas de, brewer, 424
Colman
  Adam, 356
  Thomas, 356
Cologne (Coloygne)
  John de, 337
  William de, clerk, 525
Combe (Coumbe)
  Adam de, & Alice his wife, 44
  Peter de, 312
Combemartin (Coumbemartin, Cumbemartyn, *etc*.)
  Henry de, alderman, 272, 314, 318, *289–335*; sheriff, *304–6*
  William (de), alderman, 85, 154, *80–185*; def., 178; sheriff, *56–87*; Margery his wife (relict), 178, 251
Common clerk, xiv, *see also* Waltham, Hugh de
Common serjeant, xxix, *see also* Iford, William de; Morice, Thomas; Norton, Gregory de; Pecok, Ralph; Wentebrigg, John de; Wolleward, Reginald
Common soil, xxviii–xxix
Commonalty of London: as pl., xxvii–xxx, 15, 28, 97, 166–7, 179, 188, 259–60, 264, 292, 299–300, 302–3, 334–5, 361, 369, 375, 382–3, 387, 390, 394, 396, 401, 408, 416, 449–50, 483, 487, 493–4, 536, 547; attorney of, *see* Pecok, Ralph *and* Wolleward, Reginald; bill presented against, 544; comes with the assize, xiv; judgment against, 396
Compton, Christine de, 146
Conduit (Conduyt)
  Alan atte, 381
  Geoffrey de, alderman, *125–61*; def., 14
  Reginald de, alderman, 272, 284, 286–7, 313, 318–19, 327, *288–401*; mayor, 333, *331–4*; pl., 229; sheriff, *255*
Conduit in Cheap ward, 458
Congregation, *see* Mayor & aldermen
Convers, Robert le, goldsmith, 85
Converts, house of (le Converse), 653
Conyng, John, 403
Coo, Ralph, attorney, 608; essoiner, xvi, 561, 604
Cook (Cok, Coke)
  John, 456, 534, 626
  John, brewer, 576
  John, chandler, 592, 608
Cook, *see* Trades
Cooper, *see* Trades
Coraunt, John, goldsmith, 515, 612
Corbels, *see* Buildings
Corder, *see* Trades

192

Index

Cordewanerstret, *see* Bow Lane
Cordwainer, *see* Trades
Cordwaner (Cordewaner)
   Alan le, & Joan his wife, 150, 153
   Richard le, 78, 223, 260
Cornere, Thomas atte, brewer, 502
Corner-stones, *see* Buildings
Cornhill, 613, 647
Cornhill (Cornehulle, *etc.*)
   Robert de, bailiff of the City, 351
   William de, parson of St. Mary Aldermanbury, 204, 226
Cornwaleys (Cornewaleyes)
   John, 659
   Thomas, alderman, 613, *629*
Cornwall (Cornewayll, *etc.*)
   Andrew (de), 525, 617
   John de, 169, 174
   John de, glover, & Collecta his wife, 540
   Michael de, 525, 567; Fredeswyde his wife, 567
Coroner
   John, 437–8
   John le, alderman, *see* Vintry
Corp, Simon (de), alderman, 206, *215–23*; pl., 154, 236; sheriff, 174, *168–77*; Joan his relict, 366, 368
Cory, John, clerk, 437
Cosham, John, 660
Cosin (Cosyn)
   Peter, 336
   William, alderman, *126–38*; sheriff, 85, *98–101*
Costantyn (Costentyn)
   John, alderman (of Castle Baynard ward), 459, *462*
   Richard, alderman, *277–379*
Coteler (Cotiller)
   Geoffrey le, 343–4
   Solomon le, alderman, 26, 37, *1–125*; pl., 29–30, 66
Cotes, John de, 100
Cotton (Coton, *etc.*)
   John (de), alderman, *277–305*; def., 169, 174, 196; sheriff, *280*
   Walter, alderman, 659
Coudres, John de, 272
Coumbe, *see* Combe
Coumbemartin, *see* Combemartin
Coupere (Cuver)
   Ralph le, & Celestria his wife, 92, 98, 126
   Richard le, 579
   William, (viewer), 655
   William le, 483
Courtyards, *see* Buildings
Coventre
   John, alderman, 654, *653–4*; mayor, 653
   Rose de, 93
Cows, 524

Cradok, Thomas, clerk, 655
Crane, Nicholas, alderman, *335–71*
Cranle, Nicholas de, essoiner, 296
Craye (Creye)
   Stephen son of Stephen de, 349, 353
   William de, 99
Crenellation, 158n
Crepulgate, *see* Cripplegate
Crepyn
   Richard, 208–9
   Walter, 208–9, 217
Cressewyk, *see* Creswyk
Cressingham (Cressyngham, Kressyngham)
   John de, 579
   John de, joiner, 228
Cressoner, Ralph de, *see* Ikelyngham
'Crestes', *see* Buildings
Creswyk (Cressewyk)
   Robert, attorney, 545
   William, arbitrator, 632
Creye, *see* Craye
Crikkele, John de, 381
Cripplegate hermitage, 333
Cripplegate (Crepulgate) ward: 255n, *267*; jury, 450, 483; wardmote, 450, 454–5
Crispin, Baldewyn, 305
Crofton, Richard de, [? sheriff's] clerk, 170
Crokhorn, William, 483
Crooked Lane, 488
Cross (Cros)
   Gilbert, 312
   Walter, 148
   William, 143
Crosseby, John, 640, 661
Crouche
   John atte, 234
   Roger, 661
Crowmer, William, alderman, 659, *645*; mayor, 657
Crowton, John, attorney, 652–3
Croydon
   Hugh de, 387
   John de, alderman, *401*
   Richard de, 574; alderman, 536; sheriff, 521–2, *522*
Crumpton, Philip de, & Alice his wife, 595
Crutched Friars (Holy Cross beside the Tower), prior, 111, 477, *see also* Buris, John
Crymelford, Geoffrey, alderman, 632, *630*; pl., 626; Alice his wife, 626
Cumbemartyn, *see* Combemartin
Cupboards, *see* Buildings
Curson, John, 594, 618; Alice his wife, 594
Curteys
   Margaret, 654
   Richard, fishmonger, 476
Cutler, *see* Trades
Cuver, *see* Coupere

Index

Dadyngton, John, 626
Dalby, William de, 261
Dallyng, John de, (mercer), 167, 318; sheriff, 253, *234–45*; his serjeant, *see* Pikeman, William
Dalstone, Alan de, potter, 41
Daneler, Richard, 642
Darcy (Darci), Henry, alderman, 333, *309–96*; mayor, *336–48*; sheriff, *288–302*
Darmenters, *see* Armenters
Dask, Richard, 193
Dates: early use of day & month, *288*; possibly fictitious, p. 145n, p. 146n, *607*; *see also* Legal matters, *dies non*
Daubeneye, Stephen, 522
Dauncere, John, attorney, 510
Daunvers, Edmund, 587, 607
David, Thomas son of, capper, 594
Delle, William atte, 65
Denecombe, Henry de, 266
Denton
    Richard, 649
    Robert de, chaplain, 604
Deodonatus, goldsmith, 305; *see also* Bedeford, Deodatus de
Depeden', Hugh de, 234
Depham (Depeham), Roger de, alderman (& recorder), 376, 407, 416, 432, 449, 474–6, 478, 488, 492, 501–2, 544, *343–502*; pl., 298; Margaret his wife, 298
Derby, Hugh de, rector of St. Leonard Eastcheap, 99
Derteford, William de, 21
Desborne Lane (Disebourlane), 577
Desterny, John & Philippa his wife, 619
Deumars
    Bartholomew, alderman, *387–96*
    John, 510
    Reginald & Isabel his wife, 148
Devineys, John, 196
Dew (Dieu), Thomas, 114, 118
Deynes (Dyne, Dynes)
    John, rector of St. Leonard Eastcheap, 659
    John, (ironmonger), sheriff, 511–13, *511*; Alice his relict, 545, 555
Dieu, *see* Dew
Disebourlane, *see* Desborne Lane
Distaff Lane (Dystaflane), 641
Ditches, 99, 109, 188, 292, 375, 631
Dode, John, 85, 167; City chamberlain, 213–14
Dodeford, Robert de, 147
Doget
    John, 269
    Thomas, vintner, 574
    Thomas son of John, 269
    Walter, alderman, *623*; sheriff, 624
    Walter son of Thomas, 574
    William, 447
Dogs, 66, 293, 570
Dolsely (Dolsaly, *etc*.)
    Simon, alderman, 444, 475–6, *429–511*; mayor, *507–9*; pl., 461, 464, 480, 497; Joan his wife, 461, 464
    Thomas (de), 481; alderman, 474–6, 478, 501, *464–98*; sheriff, 488, *481–9*
Donestaple, *see* Dunstaple
Doors, *see* Buildings
Dorgoyl, Gerard, 6
Dorsete, John, senior, 618
Doublet, Walter, rector of All Hallows Bread Street, 481
Dowgate (Douegate, Douuegate)
    Joan daughter of John, 528
    John, 528
    John de, 399
    Thomas son of John, 528
Dowgate (Douegate) ward, 253, 536
Drains, *see* Buildings
Draper
    Isabel daughter of Philip, 583
    Philip, cook, 583
Draper, *see* Trades
Draycote, Robert de, prior of Elsing Spital, 533, 571, 600
Drayton, John de, 385
Drew, John, 643
Drie, Geoffrey, tanner, 187
Drury (Druri), Nigel, alderman, 145, *124–85*; sheriff, *129*
Duffehous, Thomas, 661
Duket
    Christine, 22
    John son of Lawrence, 22
    Sybil relict of Lawrence, 22
Duly, John, kt., 19
Dung, 493–4; disposal of, 459
Dunholm', *see* Durham
Dunmowe
    Robert de, 266
    Walter, 638
Dunstaple (Donestaple)
    John, 506
    John de, alderman, 6, 37, 85, 510, *1–111*
Dunster, Roger, rector of St. Martin Vintry, 619
Dunton, John de, 540
Dunvill, Robert, 522
Durham (Dunholm', Durem), Henry de, alderman, 149, 151, 206, *125–204*; pl., 137
Dyer, *see* Trades
Dye-works, 488
Dyghere, Gilbert le, 375
Dyke, William, 452
Dykeman, William, ironmonger, 545, 592; sheriff, 536; Idonea his wife, 545
Dyne(s), *see* Deynes

194

Index

Dyngele, Robert & Margaret his wife, 630

East Cheap (Estchepe), 269, 488
East Watergate (Estwatergate), Castle Baynard ward, 453
Eaves, *see* Buildings
Ecton, Thomas de, clerk, 427
Edelmeton(e)
  Peter de, 78
  Roger de, tanner, 187
Edmond, Robert, 660
Edulf, Stephen, 511
Edward
  John, 574
  Richard, 597
Egemere, Master John de, rector of All Hallows the Less, 50
Ekeheued, John de, essoiner, 462
Elsing Spital (St. Mary Within Cripplegate): church, 450, 455; prior, 450, 453, 486, *see also* Draycote, Robert de; Wyndesore, John de
Ely
  Robert de, alderman, 312, 328, *307–23*; sheriff, *309*
  Roger de, (fishmonger), 115, 169, 308; Margery his wife, 115
Elys
  John, skinner, & Joan his wife, 380
  Roger, alderman, *622–31*
Em, John, 660
Enclosed order, attorney of, 80
Enefeld
  David de, goldsmith, 70
  John de, kt., 306
Entreclosewalls, ? substantial screens, 646
Essex, *see* Blund, Thomas
Essex
  John son of Roger de, 182
  Matthew de, 267, 317
  Richard de, & Maud his wife, 421
  Thomas de, 525
  William de, 451
Est, *see* East
Estfeld, William, alderman, *653*
Eston, John, alderman, 618, 632, *616–31*
Estre, Isabel de, 23
Eure (Euere)
  Roger de, 63, 198
  Walter de, 390, 394, 398
Evesham, Thomas, 633–4
Evesham Inn (Eveshammesyn), [in Fetter Lane], 609
Evil-doers, 260; *see also* Robbers
Evote, William, alderman, *643*
Exchequer, xiii
Exeter (Excestre, Exon')
  Henry de, essoiner, 115–16, 159
  John de, 435
Exton, Nicholas de, alderman, 631; mayor, *633*; sheriff, 631, *630*
Eynesham
  John, 660
  John de, 147; *see also* Aylesham
Eyre of London (1321), xxvii, 254

Fader, Boydin, 574
Fairhed, John, 78
Fairher, Geoffrey, 574
Fakenham, John de, rector of St. Matthew Friday Street, 460
Fan, John, skinner, 648
Fant, Thomas, carpenter, 566, 581–3, 591, 604, 620
Farndon (Farendon)
  Nicholas de, alderman, 37, 85, 205, 233, 236, 313, 318–19, 327, *10–328*; mayor, 145, 193, 206, 312, *132–45, 161, 193–215, 267*
  Rose de, 381
  Thomas, 612
  Thomas de, 85
Farringdon ward, 372n
Farweberwe, Robert de, 100
Fastolf, Hugh, alderman, *635*
Fauconer, Thomas, alderman, 653, *645*; mayor, 658
Faytereslane, *see* Fetter Lane
Fécamp (Feskampe), Seine-Maritime, abbot, 556
Felde
  John atte, 501, 600–3
  Richard atte, rector of St. Michael Cornhill, 613
  William atte, 400
Fellmonger, *see* Trades
Fences, *see* Buildings
Ferers, John, 645
Feskampe, *see* Fécamp
Fetter Lane (Faytereslane), 609
Feure, Ralph le, sheriff, 318
Fifhide, *see* Fyfhide
Fikelden (Fykelden) Peter (de), 483, 595
Fillet-gutters, *see* Buildings
Finchingfeld (Fynchyngfeld)
  Walter de, (junior), alderman, 26, 37, 85, 205, *1–120*; arbitrator, 61; pl., 67
  William de, 125
Fire, obligation to rebuild after, 206; risk of, 77, 141, 658
Fires in London, ix & n, xi
Firewood, xxx, 16, 55, 60, 183, 199, 312
Fish Wharf Lane (Fisshyngwharf lane), 396
Fishmonger, *see* Trades
Fitz Ailwin, Henry, regulations of (1212), xi; *see also* Assize of buildings
Fitz Herves', Philip, tanner, 187
Fitz Hugh, Robert, 659
Fitz Isabel, William, 305

Index

Fitz Otto, Hugh, constable of the Tower, warden of the City, 351
Fitz Robert, Simon, (son of Robert le Pesshoner), & Agnes his wife, 26, 35
Fitz Stephen, Henry, 318
Fitz Thomas, Thomas, mayor, 255
Fixtures, view of, 583
Fleet, xxiii
Fleet Street (Fletestret), 614; *see also* Sallowe, William
Fleming, *see* Moy, John
Flete, Amice relict of Walter de, 134
Floors, *see* Buildings
Foleham, *see* Fulham
Folk, James, *see* St. Edmunds, James
Food, *see* Victuals
Forbour, *see* Fourbour
Forde
   Gilbert atte, 574
   Thomas de la, sheriff, 255
Fordwick, Kent, xii n
Forester, *see* Forster
Forges, *see* Buildings
Forms (fourmes), benches, 613, 646
Forsham
   Roger de (Horsham), alderman, *346–55*; def., 338
   William de, tanner, 187
Forster (Forester)
   John, chaplain, 498
   John, goldsmith, attorney, 625
   Philip, 600–3
   Richard, attorney, 599, 615–16, 619, 622, 629, 631, 633, 638; essoiner, 551
   Walter, alderman, 536, *514–90*; sheriff, 474–8, *449–79*
   William, 501
Fossard, William, 432
Foucke, Roger, 510
Foundations, *see* Buildings
Foundour (Fundour)
   Margery la, 191
   Robert, 511
Fourbour (Forbour)
   Adam le, 145
   Gilott (le), alderman, 449, 457
   Henry le, 147
Fourneux, Fourneys, *see* Furneux
Foven, Richard, marshal, 429
Fowls (cocks & hens), 293, 607
Frame, *see* Buildings
Frank, John, clerk, warden of the House of Converts & Master of the Rolls, 653
Fraunceys (Fraunceis, *etc.*)
   Adam, alderman, 449, 502, 524–5, 574, 591, 598, *449–597*; mayor, 432, *431–41*
   Adam, (kt.), & Margaret his wife, 606, 631

John, 433
John, alderman, 631, *631–5*; goldsmith, pl., 625
John, tawyer, & Emma his wife, 512
Simon, alderman (of Cheap ward), 376, 416, 432, 449, 456, *334–430*; mayor, 370, 449, 453, 474–6, 478, *379–81*, *449–79*; sheriff, *304*
William, 583
Fray, John, recorder, 653, *653*
Frembaud
   Maud, 566
   Thomas & Joan his wife, 264
Frenssh, John, goldsmith, 657
Fressh, John, alderman, 631; sheriff, 631, *630*
Frestlyng (Fristlyng, *etc.*), Bartholomew (de), alderman, 474, 478, 488, 536, 547, 574, 597–8, 604, *434–589*; sheriff, 493–4, 501–2, *491–502*
Friars, *see* Austin Frairs; Crutched Friars
Friars Minor: garden, 34, 618; guardian, 189, *see also* Madyngton, Robert de; Newe, William; Sutton, Henry de
Friars Preachers (Black Friars): prior John, 386, 388; prior & brethren, xxix, 85
Friday Street (Frydaystret), *see* Skremyn, Thomas
Fristlyng, *see* Frestlyng
Froile, John, 587
Frowyk (Frowik, *etc.*)
   Henry, alderman, 653–4, *653–4*; mercer, 602
   Henry, of Middlesex, 620
   Henry de, 255
   Roger de, 111, 162; alderman, *187–221*
   Thomas, 554
Fruit, 34, 218, 519, 549, 609, 653; *see also* Vines
Fryth, Stephen atte, armourer, 617
Fulbert (Fulberd), Cambin (son of), 212, 260
Fulham (Foleham)
   Adam de, *see* Bekenesfeld, Adam de
   Adam de, *6–87*; def., 52
   John de, fishmonger, & Nichola his wife, 351
   Robert de, & Albreda his wife, 53
   William de, fishmonger, & Alice his wife, 357
Fulmere, John de, 312
Fulsham
   Benedict de, alderman, 313, 318, 327, *293–328*; sheriff, *273*, *277*
   Benedict de, & Maud his wife, 389
   Richard, 611
   Robert de, 167
Fundour, *see* Foundour
Furbisher, *see* Trades

Index

Furner, John, 659
Furneux (Fourneux, Fourneys, *etc.*)
   Robert, 574
   Thomas, 525
   William de, 200; sheriff, 240, *237*
Fuster, *see* Trades
Fyfhide (Fifhide, *etc.*), John, alderman, 613, *607–13*; sheriff, 597–8, 605
Fyket, Simon, chaplain, 443
Fykeys, Thomas, essoiner, 113
Fylin, Rose daughter of Clarekin, 38

Gables, *see* Buildings
Galeys, *see* Waleys
Gamboun, John, 658
Gardens: xxii, 34–660 *passim*; cellar dug beneath, 475; hedge & ditch around, 188; *see also* Fruit; Trees; Vines
Garret, *see* Buildings
Garth, William del, 653
Garton
   Hugh (de), alderman, 284, 287; def., 230; pl., 232; sheriff, 206, *213–15*
   William de, 1–2
Gate, John atte, 106, 574; Avice his wife, 106
Gates, *see* Buildings
Gatewyk
   Walter, 381
   William de, rector of All Hallows Barking, 125
Gatyn, Thomas, fishmonger, & Maud his wife, 431
Gaunt, John of, earl of Lincoln, 593
Gayton, Alice, widow, 652
Gedney, William, prior of St. Bartholomew, 636
Gentyll, John, draper, 647
Gerard, Henry, mason, 639
Gernoun
   Henry, 653, 655
   Master Thomas, 222
   Walter, 305
Giffard, Richard, 641
Gildeford, *see* Guildford
Gildere, Ralph le, & Amice his wife, 246
Gildesburgh, John de, fishmonger, 577
Gill
   Alan, warden of London Bridge, 404, 406, 416
   Robert, 534
   William, 320; essoiner, 550
Gillyngham (Gilyngham)
   Alan de, attorney, 399; essoiner, 345
   William de, attorney, 474; essoiner, 444, 448, 463
Girdelere (Gurdlere)
   Robert, sheriff, 545, *546–7*
   Robert le, 485
   Thomas, 632

Girdler, *see* Trades
Gisors (Gysorcio, Gysors, *etc.*)
   Anketin (de), alderman, 233, 236, 274, 286–7, 329, *182–325*; def., 15; pl., 37; son of Margery de, 55
   Henry de, alderman, 313, *325*
   John (de), 276, 329, 358
   John de, alderman, xxix, 206, 233, 236, *107–236*; mayor, 186, *182–7, 221–2*; pl., 179; son of Margery de, 55; tenement of, 205
   Margery relict of John de, 55
   Thomas, 156
Gladewyn(e), Walter, attorney, 342; summoner, 339
Glanvill (*De Legibus*), xii
Glazier, *see* Trades
Gleam, Henry, 431
Glean on the Hoop (le Glene on the Hope), brewhouse, 646
Glendale, Agnes relict of William de, 567, 572
Gloucester, earl of, *see* Clare, Gilbert de
Gloucestre (Glowcestre)
   Henry de, 335
   Henry de, alderman, 37, 85, 145, 205, *10–232*
   Isabel, prioress of St. Helen's, 599
   John de, alderman, *429–30*; sheriff, 390
   Richard de, alderman, 26, 37, 154, 205, 236, *17–236*; pl., 210
   Robert de, goldsmith, 151
Glover, *see* Trades
Godchep
   Hamo, alderman, 286, *232–77*; Isabel his relict, 312
   Henry & Agnes his wife, 518
   Ralph & Margery his wife, 79
   Richard & Margery his wife, 235
Godchild, Richard, 583
Goderomlane, *see* Gutter Lane
Godeston, John de, & Lucy his wife, 315; *see also* Codestone
Godwyneston, Richard de, rector of St. Leonard Eastcheap, 574
Godyngton, Geoffrey de, 508
Goldbeater, *see* Trades
Golde
   Richard, 33
   Thomas, essoiner, 67
Goldsmith, *see* Trades
Goldsmithery, 70
Gorel, William, 511
Gossellyn, Richard, alderman, 654, *651*
Goterlane, *see* Gutter Lane
Gracechurch (Grascherch), *see* Taillour, John le
Grafton(e)
   John, haberdasher, 581
   William de, essoiner, 103

197

Gransden (Grantesdene), *see* Brown, John
Grantham
  John de, alderman, 313, 318, 327, *288–360*; pl., 301; tenement of, 476
  Thomas son of John de, (pepperer), 425, 438, 476
Grapefige, Walter, 85, 109
Grascherche, Peter de, 218, 224
Gratefige
  John, 378
  Thomas, 378
Grating, iron, 577, 618
Grauncourt, Andrew, 521
Graunger, Robert, 655
Grauntbrugg
  Ralph son of Thomas de, 468
  Stephen de, 467–8
Gregory, William, 624
Grendon, Walter, prior of St. John of Jerusalem, 658
Grene
  Boydin atte, 99
  Robert atte, 618
  Walter atte, 584
Grenstede, William de, attorney, 294
Greylond, Richard, 513
Greyngham (Grenyngham), William de, 465, 469; essoiner, 552–3, 556; serjeant of the Chamber, 483, 511, 591; summoner, 487; Avice his wife, 465, 469
Grocer, *see* Trades
Grosse, William atte, essoiner [? fictitious], 467–8
Grymmesby, Edmund de, clerk, 380
Gubbe
  John, 298
  Richard, 298
Guildford (Gyldeford), Surrey, *see* Newark; Semer, John
Guildford (Gildeford, Guldeford)
  Henry de, 41
  John de, 39
  John son of John de, 493
  Thomas son of John de, 493
Guildhall: xxviii, xxx; access to, impeded, 493; judgment given at, xvii; middle & outer gate, 213; *see also* Chamber of London; Husting
Gurdlere, *see* Girdelere
Gut, Simon, 85
Gutter Lane (Goderomlane, Goterlane), 381, 655
Gutters, *see* Buildings
Guydo (Guydicio)
  Bartholomew, changer, 512
  Thomas son of, 12
Gybon, Geoffrey, 653
Gylet, William, 574
Gynne, Richard, 659

Haberdasher, *see* Trades
Haberdashers, fraternity, 581
Hackford (Hakford, *etc*)
  Walter son of William de, 149
  William de, 370–1, 374
  William de, & Avice his wife, 150, 153, 175, 215
Hadham
  John de, potter, 341
  Lawrence de, tanner, 187
  Stephen de, tanner, 187
  Walter de, tanner, 187
Hadle (Haddele), John, alderman, 618, 631, *607–42*; mayor, 639, *622–3*; sheriff, 606, 609, 611
Hagham, Robert de, & Idonia la Blunde his wife, 194
Hakeneye
  Peter de, 375
  Richard de, alderman, 286–7, 327, 333, *277–379*; def., 249
  Simon de, 229
  Walter de, 78
  William de, tanner, 187
Hakford, *see* Hackford
Halden, William (de), alderman (& recorder), 524–5, 536, 545, 547, 574, 587, 591–2, 595, *523–611*
Hale, Henry atte, fishmonger, & Joan his wife, 580
Hales
  Agnes daughter of John de, 401
  Geoffrey de, 78
  Katherine daughter of John de, 401
  Thomas de, 78
Halghford, John de, 205
Haliwell, Middx., priory of St. John the Baptist, prioress, 92, 98, 128, 195, 462, 481, *see also* Montacute, Elizabeth de
Hallingbury (Hallyngburi, *etc*.)
  Adam de, 21, 54, 61
  Bartholomew de, 54, 268
  William de, 243
Halls, *see* Buildings
'Haltepas', *see* Buildings, hautpas
Halton, Henry, sheriff, 660
Hamme
  Margaret relict of Stephen, 646
  Nicholas, mercer, 646
  Stephen, tailor, 639
Hamond (Hamound, *etc*.)
  Agnes relict of John, 484
  John, alderman, 333, *334–414*; mayor, *382–93*; sheriff, 318
  Robert, 506
Hamwode, Henry, 629
Hanaper, *see* Trades
Hanhampstede (Henhampsted)
  Thomas, grocer, 557

Index

William de, 361
Hanisard, William, sheriff, 318
Hanningtone (Hanyngton, Hanyton), William de, (skinner), 48, 147, 169, 174, 370
Hanse, community of merchants, 444
Hardel
 John, 211
 Ralph, 7
Hardyngham, John de, (sheriff's) clerk, 292; pl., 359, 416, 418; summoner, 506; warden of London Bridge, 416
Harewe
 John de, 298
 Walter de, 86
Harewebrewe, Adam de, 169
Harewell, John, mayor's serjeant, 633–4
Harewold, Thomas (de), sheriff, 312, *309*
Harpe
 John atte, brewer, 529
 Roger atte, 22
Harpesfeld, Nicholas de, 483
Harringworth (Haryngworth), Northants, *see* Zouche, William la
Harry, John, 648
Haryngton, William de, kt., 653
Haslemere, Richard, 522
Hatfeld
 John de, 510
 Peter de, & Juliana his wife, 105
 Robert de, 432
Hattere, Ralph & Agnes his wife, 500
Haukyn, John, 549
Hauteyn (Hautayn)
 Henry, 42
 John, alderman, *280–315*; pl., 267–8; sheriff, *294*
Hautpas, *see* Buildings
Haverhull, Peter de, clerk, 255
Havering (Haveryng)
 John de, 281
 Luke de, City chamberlain, 166–7; sheriff, *4*
Hawe, William, 631
Hay, 356
Haye
 Robert atte, smith, & Alice his wife, 614
 Thomas, 605
Heaumer, Maud relict of John le, 160, 163
Hedersete, William de, & Joan his wife, 73–4, 115, 216
Helvetone, William de, 85
Hemenhale
 Edmund de, sheriff, 390
 John de, 280–1
Hemmyngburgh, Richard, (viewer), 656–8
Hende, John, alderman, 631–2, 635, *636*, *642*; mayor, *645*; sheriff, 626; summoner, 589; Joan his wife, 564
Henhampsted, *see* Hanhampstede

Herbury, Henry, vintner, attorney, 632
Hereford
 bishop of, *see* Swinfield, Richard
 countess of, *see* Bohun, Joan
Hereford
 Henry de, 619
 Robert de, 265
Heresseye, Robert de, essoiner, 95
Herewardstok', John, 528
Herland, William, carpenter, 588, 590
Herlawe
 Robert de, 381
 William, 622
Herlyng (*alias* le Taverner), Peter de, taverner, 203, 260
Herst, *see* Hurst
Hert
 Henry, draper, 647
 Rose relict of Walter le, 263
Hervyll, Walter, pewterer, 574
Heryng, John, 375
Heston, Geoffrey de, 272
Hetherent (? *rectius* Hethereve), Robert le, 252
Hethingham, John, attorney, 654
Heylesdon, John, sheriff, 622–3, *623*
Heyron (Heyroun)
 John, 110, 136
 Thomas, 325
 William, vintner, & Sarah his wife, 488
Heyworth, Adam de, essoiner, 342, 373
Hierst, *see* Hurst
Higham
 Isabel relict of Roger de, 166
 John, sheriff, 651, 654
Hiltoft (Hyltoft), John, goldsmith, 460; sheriff, 521–2
Hinges, *see* Buildings
Hirreys, Peter le, tailor, 161
Hithe, *see* Queenhithe
Hockele, William, attorney, 570; essoiner, 558; another, pl., 242
Hodesdon
 Warin de, 293
 William de, fishmonger, 391
Hoggenlane, par., *see* St. Michael Wood Street
Hoghtone, *see* Houghton
Hoke, John, 606
Holbech
 Hugh, sheriff, 572, 574, *561–4*
 William, alderman, 492, 501, *495–514*; sheriff, *514*
Holm, Roger, canon of St. Paul's, 556
Holte, Stephen atte, 270–1
Holy Cross, *see* Crutched Friars
Holy Trinity Aldgate, prior, ix n, 57, 112, 218, 276; prior & convent, 329
Holy Trinity the Less, par., 129, 205, 336

Index

Honylane (Honilane)
  Elias de, 654
  Margery de, prioress of St. Helen's, 519–20, 542, 613
  Ralph de, alderman, 205, *36–92*
  Thomas son of Bartholomew de, 399
Honyman, Richard, 645
Hoo
  Gilbert de, 527
  John, alderman, 618, *619*
Hook
  John, 598
  Simon, mason, 639
Hooks, *see* Buildings
Hopere, Walter, 629
Hordele, William, shearman, 576
Hore
  John, 552
  Thomas, smith, 519
Horemade, Isabel relict of Richard de, 184
Horewode, *see* Horwode
Hormede, Alan de, essoiner, 328; *see also* Horwode, Alan de
Horn
  Amice, 9, 31
  Andrew, ix
  Edmund, 203, 351
  John (I), alderman, 351
  John (II), alderman, 622, *623–4*
  Nicholas, 351
Horsemen, 260, 300, 369, 547, 613
Horses, xxviii, 219, 396, 493–4, 606, 631; laden, 547; *see also* Buildings, stables; Carts
Horsham
  Adam de, 62, 82–3
  Roger de, *see* Forsham
Hortone, Roger de, attorney, 211
Horwode (Horewode)
  Alan de, attorney, 434, 436, 488; pl., 437–8, 476, *see also* Hormede, Alan de
  John de, attorney, 304, 313; pl., 336; Maud his wife, 336
  John de, junior, 454
  Nicholas de, 511
  William, 618
Hosebonde (Husebonde)
  Alice daughter of Roger, 373
  John, sheriff, *322–5*
  Roger, 43, 85; Maud his wife, 43
Hosier, *see* Trades
Hosteler, *see* Trades
Hotot, Nicholas, 463, 510
Hottokeshathere, William de, 34
Houghton (Hoghtone, Houthtone, Houton)
  Fremond de, & Margery his wife, 118
  John de, 342
  William son of William de, 348
Houndesdiche (Hundesdich)
  Gervase de, tanner, 187
  Philip de, tanner, 187
  William de, 85
Houndsditch, xxiii, 487, 618
Household goods, 646
Houthtone, Houton, *see* Houghton
Huggin (Hoggen) Lane, par., *see* St. Michael Wood Street
Humber, John, 624
Hundesdich, *see* Houndesdiche
Hundeslowe, Richard de, 109
Hunteman, Adam, 178, 251
Huntyngdon, Hugh de, 410
Hurst (Herst, Hierst)
  Gilbert atte, 169, 174
  William atte, 329, 418
Husebonde, *see* Hosebonde
Husting: aldermen chosen for assize in, x–xi; bills of complaint in, xiii; complaint in, re non-execution of judgment, xix; enquiry in, 43; judgment in, xvii; quorum in, xiii n; re-summons of assize in, xvi
Hyde, William, sheriff, *643*
Hyngeston (Hynxston)
  John de, 381
  John de, alderman, 319
Hynton, John de, vintner, 441

Ideshale, John de, 381
Iford, William de, common serjeant, **334–5**, 361, 369, 375, 382–3, 387, 390, 394, 396, 401, 408
Ikelyngham, *alias* Cressoner, Ralph de, & Agnes his wife, 384
Ilkyston, William de, rector of St. Mary le Bow, 451
Ingelbright, Arnold, armourer, 623
Ingham, Robert de, 456
Ipswich, Suffolk, xii n
Ireys, Peter le, tailor, 13, 144
Irland (Irlonde)
  Richard & Emma his wife, 608
  Thomas (de), alderman, 622, *622*; sheriff, *523*; tenement of, 527
Ironmonger, *see* Trades
Ironmonger Lane (Ismongereslane), 449, 456–7
Isoude, Thomas, rector of St. Margaret Moses, 416
Ispania, *see* Spain
Italian merchant, 12
Ive, John, rector of St. Michael Wood Street, 625
Ivory, William, 574, 623, 659

Jambers, 617
James, Nicholas, alderman, 654, *651*
Jetties, *see* Buildings
Joce, John, kt., 488

Index

Joiner, *see* Trades
Joists, *see* Buildings
Joly, John, 651
Jordan (Jurdon)
  Nicholas, 618
  Richard, 111
Joynour
  John, 654
  William, 654
Justices itinerant, xxvii, 254

Kaleys, Francis de, 157
Kallere, *see* Callere
Karleton, *see* Carleton
Karlill, *see* Carlille
Kary, Amice relict of Thomas, 17
Kayton
  John de, 493–4
  Robert de, 475; sheriff, *577*
Kele, Henry de, 85
Kellshull (Keleshull, Kylshyll, *etc.*)
  Richard de, kt., 488
  Simon de, attorney, 317, 323, 399
  William, fishmonger, 587, 652
  William de, 478
Kelseye (Celeseye, Kelseie, *etc.*)
  Robert de, alderman, 233, 236, *228–36*; pl., 127, 306; tenement of, 201
  Thomas son of Robert de, 345
  William de, clerk, 401–2
Kempeseye, John, chaplain, 543
Kendale
  Edward de, kt., 562
  Thomas de, clerk, 515; rector of St. Augustine Watling Street, 585
Kene, Richard, 522
Kennels (i.e. gutters), xxiii, 358, 577, 618
Kensington, John de, prior of St. Bartholomew, 93
Kent
  Henry de, 317
  John de, hanaper, 445, 483
  Robert de, 78
  Thomas de, essoiner, 107; serjeant, 151
  Thomas de, tailor, & Juliana his wife, 99
Kentoys, William & Alice his wife, 585
Keselyngbury, *see* Kyslyngbury
Kettelburgh, Stephen de, 338
Keu (Ku)
  Albert le, of Bread Street, 305
  Henry le, painter, 65, 68, 71
  P. le, essoiner, 157
Kilwardby, Robert, archbishop, 85
Kimnels, 646
King's court in the Chamber, 655
King's gift, xiv & n, 314
Kirketon, John, alderman, 618
Kissere, Hugh le, 109
Kitchens, *see* Buildings
Knoesle, Richard de, 525

Knolles
  Robert & Constance his wife, 611
  Thomas, alderman, 658, 660–1, *641–2*; mayor, *643*
Knyght, John, tailor, 186
Knyghtcote, William, alderman, 618, *624*; sheriff, 624, *624*
Knyth, William, 574
Ko, Walter son of Thomas le, 402
Kressyngham, *see* Cressingham
Ku, *see* Keu
Kydemenstre, Robert de, 317
Kylshyll, *see* Kellshull
Kynelyngworth, John de, 451
Kyng
  William, alderman, *624–29*
  William, timbermonger, 524
  William le, 109
Kyngeston (Kynggeston)
  Adam de, fishmonger, 331–2
  David de, 382
  John, 652
  John de, 257, 385; Sabine his wife, 257
  John de, brewer, 498
  William, attorney, 660
Kynwardesle, Thomas, 586
Kyriel, William, 600–3
Kyrkeby
  John de, 525
  John de, draper, 500
Kyslyngbury (Keselyngbury), Richard de, alderman, *399*; pl., (hosier), 317, 330; mayor, *425–7*

Lacer (Lacier)
  Richard (le), alderman, 333, 407, 416, 432, *335–446*; mayor, 390, *395–6*; sheriff, *307*
  Richard, goldsmith, 445, 483, 516
Lachebrok, Roger & Margaret his wife, 492, 528
Lambourne, Essex, rector, *see* Preston, William de
Lambyn
  Edmund, alderman, *259*
  Guy, fishmonger, 475
  John, alderman, 233, 236, *185*; sheriff, *185*
  Robert, 351
Lane, Richard in the, 272
Lanende, William atte, 298
Lanes, blocked or obstructed, 85, 327, 358, 401, 449, 454, 457, 577, 613, 618; disputed ownership, 528; grant of, 85; narrowed (allegedly), 97, 396; timbers extend beyond middle of, 352, 358
Langbourn ward, xxx n
Langeford, Thomas, 619
Langeleye (Langgele)
  John de, 95–6

Index

Langeleye, *continued*
  Jordan de, 237
Lardener (Lardyner), Robert, carpenter, 645–7, 659, 661
Large, Robert, sheriff, 648
Latrines, *see* Buildings, privies etc.
Laufare
  John, mason, 621
  John de, 185
  John de, cordwainer, 58
  John de, cutler, 109
Launde
  Geoffrey de la, parson of St. Leonard Eastcheap, 574
  Robert, alderman, 613, 618, *613–23*; kt., 625; sheriff, 613, 615
Layton, John de, 450
Leather hides, 251
Leatherseller, *see* Trades
Leche
  David le, & Juliana his wife, 427
  John le, fishmonger, 365; Maud his relict, 419
Leddrede, Robert, draper, 472
Lee
  Margaret atte, 491
  Walter atte, clerk, & Sabine his wife, 220
Legal matters
  adjournments & respites, xiii, xvi–xvii, xxxiii–xxxiv
  agreement between parties, xviii
  amercement, xviii–xix; def. puts himself in mercy, 193; pardoned, 312
  arbitration, xviii
  attorneys, xv & n
  bills of complaint, xiv, 574, 591, 604, 644
  building permission, 310
  common land, 43
  common soil, xxviii–xxix
  courtesy of England, xiv, 14, 333
  damages, xvii & n
  death, of def., 528; of pl., 317
  declaration by pl., 528
  dies non, xvi & n
  distraint for rent prevented, 289
  dower, xx, 160, 298
  escheat to crown, 313, 619, 652
  essoins, xv–xvi, xxxiii–xxxiv
  extent of debt, 289
  false plaints, xviii
  fees for bills, xxxi
  file of nuisances, 645
  fines, xix
  forshard, 269 & n
  fraud & trickery suspected, 618
  freeehold, defs. deny having, xiv
  friends, arguments of, 656; mediation of, 632
  gavelet, 269
  imprisonment, xiii
  inquest on doubtful points of assize, xvii–xviii, 145
  inquisition held in a church, 309
  intrusion, xi; alleged, xv, 510; pleas of, xiv n, 240; *see also* novel disseisin
  judgment, xviii–xix
  juries, xi, xvii
  king's aid, 386, 619
  leases, for 99 years, 574; for 293 years, 599; repairing, 418
  licence to agree, xviii
  licence to crenellate, 158 n
  light & view, xxvi
  limitation, period of, xi, xiv–xv
  love days, 139, 389, 550
  malice, xxxii
  minors, xv
  non prosecution of suits, xviii
  novel disseisin, assize of, 389 (p. 96), 657; *see also* intrusion
  ordinance concerning windows, 604
  partition (among co-heirs), 160, 233, 632
  penalty clause in agreement, 193
  pledges to prosecute, xviii
  protection, letters of, 158
  purprestures, xxvii–xxx
  quit-rent, repudiated, 20
  quorum, at assizes, x; in Husting, x n
  record & process recited, xvii
  remedy by another process advised, xix
  respites, *see* adjournments
  rights of way, xxxii
  rolls of assize, xxxiii–xxxiv; in custody of clerk of the Chamber, *282*; inspected, 272, 302, 371
  seisin, length of, pleaded, xv
  shartfort, 269 n
  statute of Westminster II, xiv n
  summons, xiii–xiv, xvi
  trespass, xv
  wills, vouched to warranty, xv
  writs, xii; *de rectis serviciis*, 269; *fieri facias*, 223, 239
  see also Aldermen; Assize of buildings; Commonalty; Husting; Mayor, *etc.*; Sheriffs; Wardmote
Leggy (Leggi), Thomas, alderman, 449, 474, *392–484*; mayor, 407–8, 410, 416, *406–16, 443–8*
Leicester (Leicestre, Leycestre)
  John, 604
  John, cordwainer, 596
  Robert de, essoiner, 12, 23, 112, 124, 133, 135, 138
Leire (Leyre)
  Idonea daughter of William de, 197, 205
  Thomas de, alderman, *293–309*
  William de, alderman, 6, 37, 61, 85, 149, 206, 233, 236, *4–236*; arbitrator, 61; def., 13, 120; pl., 50, 164, 237;

Index

Idonea his wife, 120
William son of William de, 319; Agnes his relict, 536–7
Leman (Lemman), John, 574; another, 648
Lenard, Robert, 522
Lenne, *see* Lynne
Lesnes, Gilbert de, 89
Lestraunge, Roger, kt., 496
Let, Idonia, prioress of St. Mary Clerkenwell, 479
Leuesham, Simon de, 528
Leukenore
  Lucy relict of Thomas de, 27
  Roger de, 310–11; chivaler, 431
  Thomas de, 41
Leuter (Leutour, Luter), John le, 25, 115, 165, 190, 195; Isabel his wife (relict), 190, 195, 308, 362–8
Levendale, John de, 525
Levesone, Walter, 145
Leye, Thomas atte, sheriff, *529–31*
Leyre, *see* Leire
Liffyn, Clement, draper, 651
Lifton, John de, 306
Liger, Robert, 147
Limare, John, 533
Lincoln, earl of, *see* Gaunt, John of
Lincoln (Lyncoln)
  Alice de, 197, 205
  John (de), 205; alderman, 154, 206, 236, *147–236*; sheriff, *70–83*
  Richard de, 379
  William, 631
Lindesseye (Lyndeseye)
  Adam de, & Christine his wife, 60
  Robert, tailor, 635
Linendraper, *see* Trades
Lintone, Roger de, 85
Lisson
  Henry, 135
  Robert brother of Henry, 135
Littelton, Richard de, clerk, 128
Little (Litle, Lytle, *etc.*)
  John (le), alderman, 536, 547, 587, 592, 595, *481–605*; fishmonger, 513; sheriff, 439, 442; witness, 574
  John, tailor, 617
Lobenham, Ralph, alderman, 659; sheriff, 659
Lock & key, 401
Locke, Thomas, essoiner, 660
Lodelowe, Thomas, alderman [& recorder], *514–22*
Lombard (Lumbard)
  Hamo, 604
  John, 396, 604
  Simon, *see* Spicer, Simon le
  see also Trades
Lombard Street, 527, 647

London, bishops of, 375
London
  John de, brewer, 462, 466, 470–1
  John de, tanner, & Joan his wife, 359
London Bridge: houses on, 52; land & tenements, xxix, 51–2, 416; wardens, 87, *see also* Benere, John le; Chaplain, Robert the; Gill, Alan; Hardyngham, John de
London Wall, *see* City Wall
Long, Robert, 351
Lorence, John, 47
Loriner, *see* Trades
Loundres, Roger, 660
Louthe
  John, tailor, 635
  Thomas de, & Joan his wife, 491
  William (de), alderman, 661; sheriff, *645*
Love, Richard, 563
Love Lane [off Coleman Street], 545
Loveday, Roger, kt., 510
Lovekyn
  Adam, alderman, *614*; pl., 522; Katherine his wife, 522
  John, 298
  John, alderman, 525, *484–536*; mayor, 527, *418, 503–5, 529–34*
Loveye, John, alderman, *635, 638*; mercer, pl., 625; sheriff, 638, *638*
Lucas
  Adam, 327
  John, 493
  John, tailor, 496
  Robert, 595
  Robert, alderman, *618–24*
Lucca, Italy, society of the Ricardi, 12
Luco
  Francis de, 226
  John de, 226
  John son of John de, 226
Luda, Thomas de, tanner, 187
Ludekyn, Adam, 139; sheriff, *187*
Ludgate, xxix n
Ludgershale, John son of John de, 333
Ludlow, Salop, xii n
Lumbard, *see* Lombard
Lung
  John le, & Agnes his wife, 110
  John son of Roger le, 33
  Robert le, 298
Lurchon, John, 649
Luter, *see* Leuter
Lychebergh, William de, 362–4, 366
Lyes, Richard, draper, 647
Lyle, Thomas, pie-baker, 627
Lyllyngston, Thomas de, 472–3, 479
Lylye, John, chandler, 608
Lyndewode, John de, 322
Lyndewyk, Robert, 574

203

Index

Lynne (Lenne) Ralph de, alderman, *445–85*; juror, 396; sheriff, 419, 424
Lyons (Lyouns)
 Richard, alderman, 598; sheriff, 607
 William de, hermit, 333
Lyrp, Gilbert, baker, 524, 561
Lyterworth, John, 534
Lythfot, Geoffrey, 375

Mabely
 Ralph son of William, surgeon, 185
 William, 225
 William de, & Alice his wife, 27
Macchyng, Edward de, 185
Maderman
 Nicholas & Avice his wife, 476
 Robert le, 125
Madour, Roger, 407, 409
Madyngton, Robert de, guardian of the Friars Minor, 569
Makenheued, John, 385
Malewayn, John, alderman, 492, 502, *502*
Mallyng, Thomas, mason, 620
Malt-bin, 583
Maneweden, John de, attorney, 371, 376
Mapelesden, John de, (goldsmith), 446, 481, 484; Alice his wife, 484
Mapisden, John, 660
March
 Robert de la, tailor, 169, 190, 195
 Thomas de la, 275, 278, 307
Marchal (Mareschal)
 Geoffrey, of Wood Street, 547–8
 Gilbert le, 32, 120; Amice his wife, 120
 Henry le, 234
 John, 632
 John le, 147
 John le, of Walbrook, 88
 William le, 72, 77, 237, 293; Margaret his wife, 293
Marchaunt, Nicholas, 505
Marezerer, *see* Mazerer
Mariner, Elias le, 146
Markes, Robert, 616
Martyn, Thomas, 618
Mash-tubs (masshtonnes), 646
Mason, *see* Trades
Mass, celebration of, xxxi, 574
Maunchier, Richard le, 109
Maunfeld, Gilbert, alderman, *627*
Maupyn, Peter, 193
Mayn, John, baker, & Christine his wife, 561
Mayor: *locum tenens*, xiii, 286–7; pl., 9; presides over assizes, x, xiii; serjeant of, xvi, 151, *see also* Baldok, John; Bockysham, John; Harewell, John
Mayor & aldermen: congregation of, xiii, xvi, xix; perambulations of, xxix–xxx
Mayor & citizens, 189

Mayor & commonalty, 477, 544; pls., 170–1, 213–14
Mayor's court, xxiv
Mazerer (Marezerer, Mazeliner)
 John le, 377
 John le, City chamberlain, 188
 John le, goldsmith, 111
 Simon, 618
 Stephen le, 378
 William le, alderman, *1*
Mede Lane, 97
Megre, John, pewterer, 647
Megucer
 John le, 109
 Richard le, 109
Meldebourne
 Gilbert (de), attorney, 558, 613, 619, 630, 637; essoiner, xvi, 555, 563; summoner, 611
 Reginald de, & Gunnilda his wife, 222
 Richard de, 24
 Thomas de, 24
 William de, chivaler, & Margery his wife, 377
Meleford, William de, archdeacon of Colchester, 185
Meleward, *see* Milward
Melf, John, nakerer, & Joan his wife, 309
Meltone, William de, dean of St. Martin le Grand, 189
Mercer, *see* Trades
Merchandise, 493–4, 606, 613, 631
Merchant, *see* Trades
Merden, John, butcher, & Alice his wife, 579
Mereworth, Simon de, 182
Merlawe, Richard, alderman, 658; mayor, 656
Merlyn, William, 658
Merre
 Adam son of Geoffrey, 297
 William son of Geoffrey, 297
Merton, Surrey, prior, 149
Merton, Robert de, dyer, 351
Michel (Mychel, *etc.*)
 Joan, 501
 John, alderman, *651*; mayor, *653*
 John, loriner, 246
 John, vintner, 506
Middelton
 John, 650
 William, grocer, 640, 661
Middlesex, *see* Frowyk, Henry
Milk Street, 319
Milton, Walter, (viewer), 655–9
Milward (Meleward)
 Walter le, 259
 William le, tanner, 187
Mimmes (Mymmes)
 John (de), 400, 501, 600–3

Index

William de, tanner, 187
Mineter, Roger le, 144, 161
Minoresses, *see* St. Clare without Aldgate
Miter(e)
    Richard le, 249
    William le, 87
Mitford, John (de), alderman, 545, 547, 595, *534–607*; draper, 578; pl., 525; sheriff, 528; Joan his wife, 578
Mockyng, John de, alderman, *360–95*; sheriff, 313, *313*
Molers (la Molere), Alice (de), 159, 192
Molgas, Adam, tailor, 20
Molling, William, 99
Molton (Multone), Robert de, tailor, & Agnes his wife, 12, 17, 49
Mompesson, Richard de, 131
Montacute (Mountagu), Elizabeth de, 392; prioress of Haliwell, 434, 466, 471
Montfichet (Munfichet), tower, 85
Monthermer, Ralph de, 250
Montquoy, Henry de, 97
Moor (la Moore, More), xxiii, 266, 292, 375
Moot, John, abbot of St. Albans, 642
Mordon (Moredon)
    Gilbert de, sheriff, 282–3, *280*
    Simon de, alderman, 536, 574, 598, *534–98*; mayor, 545, *546–61*; sheriff, 528
    Walter de, alderman, *331–401*; def., 298; sheriff, 331
More
    Beatrice daughter of Ralph de la, 255
    Cecily atte, 91
    Henry atte, goldsmith, 255
    John, alderman, *626*; sheriff, *631*
    Maud atte, daughter of Ralph de la, 255
    Ralph de la, 255
    William, alderman, *637–8*; sheriff, *633*
    William atte, 109
Moredon, *see* Mordon
Morell, Richard, 633–4
Morice (Moryce)
    Thomas, common serjeant, 483, 487, 493–4
    Walter & Sarah his wife, 117
Morisby, Christopher de, 653
Morle
    Thomas de, 533
    Thomas de, & Idonia his wife, 355
    Thomas de, sheriff's clerk, 287
Mortar, *see* Buildings
Morton
    John de, attorney, 478, 496; clerk, 475, 517; sheriff's clerk, 494; summoner, 419, 478
    Walter, 615
Mosehach (Musehacche)

Richard, 600–3
William, 501
Moun, James de, 67
Mounby, William de, essoiner, 226
Mounde, John, baker, & Avice his wife, 257
Mountagu, *see* Montacute
Moy, John, 525; armourer, 460; Fleming, 413
Moyne, Henry le, 36
Multone, *see* Molton
Munfichet, *see* Montfichet
Musehacche, *see* Mosehach
Mustrel, Robert, of Tonbridge, 273, 277
Mynot (Myngihot), Michael, 321, 335
Myte, John, 613

Nails, *see* Buildings
Nakerer, *see* Trades
Nassurton, William de, & Alice his wife, 508
Nasyngg, John de, 492
Nax, William atte, 499
Neel, Walter, alderman, *339–84*
Nettlestede (Netlestede), Roger de, 169, 174
Neuberi, Christine relict of Alan de, 209
Neuelon, Adam son of Peter son of, 97
Neugate, *see* Newgate
Neuport
    Thomas de, 493–4
    William, alderman, *614–27*; sheriff, 606, 609, 611
Neusom, Thomas de, clerk of Ralph de Monthermer, 250
Neuton, Geoffrey, alderman, *616*; summoner, 586
Neve
    John le, 403
    William le, furbisher, 233–4
New Hospital, *see* St. Mary without Bishopsgate
New Place without Aldgate, *see* St. Clare
Newark (New Place near Guildford), Surrey, prior, *see* Pyrye, Thomas
Newcastle, Peter de, 169, 308
Newe
    Roger & Agnes his wife, 514
    William, guardian of the Friars Minor, 618
Newenham, Thomas de, clerk, 588, 590
Newenton, Henry de, rector of St. Mary Magdalen Milk Street, 306
Newgate (Neugate), xxix, 387; gaol delivery, xvi, 313, 323, *386*
Noket, Thomas (atte), alderman, *615*, *618*; draper, 527, 647
Norbury (Nortbury), Richard, alderman, *629*; def., 575; Ymanya his wife, 575
Noreys, Thomas le, 15

Index

Northall (Northhalle), John de, alderman, *357–401*
Northampton, xii
Northampton (Norhampton)
  John, alderman, *609–13*; draper, 618; mayor, 628–9, *625–9*; sheriff, 613, 615; Parnel his wife, 618
  Robert, carpenter, 205
  Robert de, 381
Northbrugh, John de, 340
Northfolke, Henry, haberdasher, 581
Northwyc, Walter de, & Cecily his wife, 12
Norton
  Geoffrey de, alderman [& recorder], 26, *1–34*
  Gregory de (*alias* Gregory atte Shire), alderman, 312–13, 318–19, 327, 333, *288–342*; common serjeant, xxix, 260, 264; essoiner, 245; recorder, 272, 319, *294*; Alice his relict, 393, 397
  Richard de, & Alice his wife, 433, 439
  Richard de, of Cheshunt, & Alice his wife, 517
  William, alderman, 659–61
Notingham (Notyngham), Richard de, alderman, 474–5, 478, 492, 502, *445–502*; mercer, def., 494; pl., 505; sheriff, 488, *484–9*
Nott, John, mayor, *521–2*
Nottele, Thomas de, parson of St. Mildred Poultry, 400
Nottingham, xiii
Noyl
  Gerard, 429
  John, 451
  William, 290–1

Odyerne, John, 574
Ogbourne (Okebourn), Wilts., prior Richard, 386, 388
Oign', Richard, 351
Oistergate, Alice relict of Stephen de, 327
Okebourn, *see* Ogbourne
Olescombe, John, 630
Oliver (Olyver)
  John, junior, 522
  John, senior, 522
  William, 331
  William, alderman, *629*
Olneye
  Richard de, attorney, 528; guardian, 492
  William de, 513
Order of Preachers, *see* Friars Preachers
Organ (Orgon), John, alderman, 618, 631, *613–31*
Orpedeman, Thomas, essoiner, 242, 246
Osbarn
  Richard, 655
  Thomas, 660

Osekin (Osekyn)
  John, 452
  Robert, carpenter, 53
'Osmond', iron called, 617
Otery, Robert, 615
Ottele, Robert, grocer, 648–50
Ottery (Otery), Devon, college of St. Mary, warden, *see* Sargere, John
Oven, 492; stone, 583
Ovesseye, John de, 42
Oxen, 524
Oxford, Balliol Hall, master of, 494
Oxford
  Hugh de, tailor, & Maud his wife, 69, 86
  John de, alderman, 286–7, *322–57*; mayor, 376, *371–7*; pl., 348; Alice his wife, 348
  Katherine & Lucy, daughters of Hugh de, 69
Oystergate, 582

Paas, Isabel relict of John, 315
Pabenham (Pakenham), Simon de, mason, 205, 233, 304
Page, Walter, 362–4, 366, 461
Painter (Peyntour)
  Adam, 109
  John le, 292
Painter, *see* Trades
Pakenham
  John de, 525
  Simon de, *see* Pabenham, Simon de
Paling, *see* Buildings
Palmer (Paumer)
  Henry le, 243
  Philip the, of Wood Street, 219
  Roger le, 156, 205; alderman, *280*
  Simon le, 414
  Thomas le, 145
Pancrich, Stephen de, 85
Paris (Parys)
  John de, saddler, 110, 200; Alice his wife, 110
  Robert, ironmonger, 603
  Robert de, mercer, 261
  Roger de, alderman, 206, *185–235*; mercer, def., 236; sheriff, *70–84*
  Simon de, alderman, 6, 26, 37, 85, 145, 154, 236, *1–236*; guardian, 25; sheriff, *36–54*
  Thomas, 651
  William de, draper, & Maud his wife, 233
Parker
  Walter, 492
  William, sheriff, *641–2*
Parles, Ralph & Mary his wife, 633
Parlours, *see* Buildings
Passenham, Henry de, attorney, 158, 174; essoiner, 172

Index

Passeware, William, 500, 525, 572
Paths: allegedly dedicated, 125; narrowed, 64, 626; obstructed, 43, 125, 260, 606, 631
Paumer, *see* Palmer
Pavements, xi, xxx & n, 140–2, 175–6, 186, 206, 249, 369
Paviour, *see* Trades
Pay, Reginald, 637
Payn
  Henry, 644, 660
  John, 418
  Robert, fuster, 446
Pecche (Peche)
  John, alderman, 432, 492, 574, *419–534*; mayor, *514–15*; pl., 525
  John, draper, senior, 465
Pecok, Ralph, commonalty's attorney, 15; common serjeant, xxix
Pekham, Christine, 546
Pelham, John de, 155, 158
Pembroke, earl of, *see* Valence, Aymer de
Penbrigg, Richard de, kt., 539
Penerege, Edmund, rector of St. Edmund King & Martyr, 596
Penne, Ralph de la, 151
Pentecost Lane, 569, 618
Pentices, *see* Buildings
Pepperer, *see* Trades
Perambulations, *see* Mayor & aldermen
Perceval, Thomas, 170
Peregryn, Raymond, 503
Perle, Thomas, alderman, *483–502*
Perndon, Nicholas de, 266
Person
  Robert, 147, 510
  Robert, skinner, 173
Persshore, William, 614
Peruch, John de, attorney, 525
Perveys, John, alderman, 654, *651*
Pesshoner, Robert le, *see* Fitz Robert, Simon
Peterborough, abbot, 141
Petit, John, (viewer), 645–6, 647, 661
Peu, William atte, 109
Peverel, William, Queen Philippa's tailor, xxxi, 417
Pewterer, *see* Trades
Peyntour, *see* Painter
Philip Lane (Phelippeslane), 454
Philipot (Phelipot, *etc.*), John, alderman, 587, 591, *584–611*; mayor, *620*; pl., 573; sheriff, 586–7, 589, 591–2
Philippa, queen [of Edward III], tailor of, *see* Peverel, William
Picard (Pycard, Pykard)
  Henry, alderman, *433*; mayor, *481–91*
  Hugh & Sabine his wife, 172
Picot (Pikot, Pycot)
  John son of Nicholas, 262

  Nicholas, alderman, 26, 37, 149, 154, *1–182*; def., 94; pl., 100; sheriff, *125–7*; Alice his wife, 94, 100
Pie-baker, *see* Trades
Piel (Pyel), John, alderman, 574, 598, 613, 618, *564–613*; mayor, 587–8, 591–2, *584–92*; sheriff, 572, *561–4*
Pigeon, John, pie-baker, 632
Pigs, 63, 293, 524; slaughtered, 569
Pig-sties, xxx, 263, 332, 382–3
Pikebou, William, 458
Pikeman (Pykeman)
  Adam, fishmonger, 352
  Andrew, alderman, 613, *619–23*; fishmonger, 485; sheriff, 614, 616–17, 619, *618–19*
  Giles, 488
  John, rector of Wickham, 10
  Robert, 312
  Stephen, 312
  Thomas brother of John, 10
  William, 108, 312; sheriff's serjeant, 253
Pikenham (Pykenham)
  John de, 238, 241; Emma his wife, 241
  Thomas de, alderman, 524–5, *514*
Pikot, *see* Picot
Piles: in Thames, 392, 582; in Walbrook, 383
Pipehirst (Pipherst, Piphurst)
  Robert de, 85, 381
  Robert son of Robert de, 381
  Thomas & Joan his wife, 446, 490
  Thomas, goldsmith, 501
Pipes, *see* Buildings
Pit: for tanning hides, 251; *see also* Buildings, privies; Chalk-pit
Place, *see* Buildings
Planks, *see* Buildings
Plates, *see* Buildings, wall-plates
Ploket, Nicholas, mercer, 505
Plot, John, essoiner [? fictitious], 600–3
Plumb-line, 76, 84, 89, 271, 295, 301, 388
Podeo, Orlandino de, 12
Pole
  John son of John atte, 461, 464
  Michael de la, kt., 447
  Richard atte, 310–11
  Walter de la, chivaler, 651
  William atte, 379
Polle
  Thomas, alderman, 660
  William atte, essoiner, 533, 538
Polstede, Thomas de, & Katherine his wife, 339
Polteneye, *see* Pulteneye
Pontefract (Pomfreyt, Pountfreit, *etc.*)
  Henry, alderman, 661, *645*; sheriff, 660
  John de, 485
  John de, goldsmith, 255
  William, skinner, 609

Pontefract, *continued*
   William (de), alderman, 376, *357–405*; def., 306; pl., 379
Pope, John, 546, 643
Porkele, Thomas de, 381
Posse, James & William (atte), essoiners [? fictitious], xvi, 465, 471–3, 488–9, 497, 503–4, 540–2, 549; *see also* Pusse
Post, Adam, Alan, Thomas & William, essoiners [? fictitious], xvi, 573, 575, 578, 580
Postek, Richard, essoiner [? fictitious], xvi, 564–5
Posts, *see* Buildings
Potelle, Adam, essoiner [? fictitious], xvi, 579
Poteman, Henry & Denise his wife, 10, 51, 59
Potter, Paul le, 124
Potter, *see* Trades
Potyn, Nicholas, 510
Poulter, *see* Trades
Pountfreit, *see* Pontefract
Pountoyse, John de, & Alice his wife, 304
Pourte, Hugh, alderman, 37, *1–104*; pl., 53; sheriff, *36–49*; Margaret his wife, 53
Powel, John, potter, & Joan his wife, 418
Poyntel
   John, alderman, 286–7, *277–306*
   Roger, 180
   William, 85
Prat
   Adam, essoiner, 179
   Robert, essoiner, 321
Pre, Adam, essoiner, 225
Prentys (Prentiz)
   John, draper, 584
   Thomas, 249
Press, great, in brewhouse, 646
Prest
   Andrew, essoiner, 322
   William, tallow-chandler, 651
Preston
   John, corder, 265
   John, recorder, 659–60
   John de, 272; alderman, 312, *259–312*; mayor, 318, 327, *314–28*; sheriff, *244*
   John de, girdler, 191
   Ralph de, & Maud his wife, 432
   Richard, alderman, *616*; pl., 637
   Stephen de, 258
   William de, rector of Lambourne, Essex, 444
Pride, J., essoiner, 220
Priour (Priur), John, alderman, 312, (senior) 314, 318, *277–323*; def., 259; sheriff, 233, 236, 240, *235–7*
Privies, *see* Buildings
Processions, parochial, 43, 544, 639

Prodhomme
   Henry, 269
   William, sheriff, 255, *255*
Proffyt, John, 659
Pudding Lane (Retheresgatelane), 352
Pulteneye (Polteneye), John de, alderman, 272, *289–325*; chivaler, 376; mayor, 313, *309–35*
Puncheons, *see* Buildings
Pung, Alexander, 85
Puppe, Geoffrey, stockfishmonger, 557
Purbyk, Juliana, 643
Purre, John & William atte, essoiners [? fictitious], 510, 531–2
Purtreor, Robert le, 147
Pusse, John & William, essoiners [? fictitious], 498, 509; *see also* Posse
Pye, Adam, essoiner, 152
Pyebakere, Andrew, 522
Pyk(e), Nicholas, 377; sheriff, *322–5*
Pykard, *see* Picard
Pykebourne, Richard, chaplain, 585
Pykerel, William, 309
Pylk, Adam, essoiner, 557
Pynnote, Gilbert, 23
Pyrye, Thomas, prior of Newark, 660
Pyrynton, Robert de, essoiner, 330
Pystoye, Simon de, 530; Emma his wife, 530, 550
Pyxlee, Reginald, 483

Queenhithe (Hithe), xxv, 214
Queldryk, John, 607
Querns, 646
'Quysers' [i.e. cuisses], 617

Rabbet, *see* Buildings, walls
Rabot, William, 327; Juliana his wife, 242
Ralph, clerk, 510
Rameseye, John de, 146
Rasne
   John de, essoiner, 320
   William de, attorney, 319
Ratforde, John de, 553
Ray, John, 650
Reading (Redyng, Redyngges), Berks., abbot, 369, 459
Realle, *see* Reyle
Reason, *see* Buildings, beams
Recorder, xiii–xiv, *see also* Barton, John; Cheyne, William; Cokayn, John; Depham, Roger de; Fray, John; Halden, William; Lodelowe, Thomas; Norton, Geoffrey de; Norton, Gregory de; Preston, John; Simond, John; Swalclive, Robert de; Thorneburgh, Thomas; Tremayn, John; Wengrave, John de
Red, William de, 510
Rededor

Index

Peter atte, 408
Thomas atte, brewer, 320
Redyng, Redyngges, *see* Reading
Redyng (Redign), John de, 287, 525
Refham
   John de, alderman, *357–80*; son of Richer de, 283–4, 286–7; summoner, 357
   Richer de, (kt.), alderman, 37, 85, *19–120*; arbitrator, 61; def., 95, 282, 285–6; house, 100; mayor, *163–77*; petitions on behalf of Minoresses, 80; pl., (mercer), 96, 104, 202, 206–7, 245; sheriff, 312
Reille, *see* Reyle
'Relese', *see* Buildings
Retheresgatelane, *see* Pudding Lane
Reve ?, Richard de, hanaper, 483
Rewley, near Oxford, abbot, *see* Stanley, Adam de
Reygate
   Nicholas de, 348
   Roger, 511
Reyglegh, Walter de, tawyer, 370
Reyle (Realle, Reille, *etc.*)
   Agatha relict of Walter de, 100
   William de, attorney, 256; essoiner, xvi, 37, 39, 41, 46, 51, 56, 58–9, 82, 136, 149–50, 153, 162, 166, 169, 173, 182, 194, 241
Reyner
   Benedict & his wife, 288
   John, 437–8, 651
Reynham, Thomas (de), alderman, 618, *619*
Reynwell, John, mayor, *651–4*
Ricardi, society of, *see* Lucca
Richard, Avice his daughter & Thomas her brother, 146
Riche
   John le, & Rose his wife, 19
   John son of John le, 240
Ridge-tile, *see* Buildings
Riseby, Robert, 635
Risle, John de, & Maud his wife, 384
Rittlyng, Richard de, 408
Ro (Roo), Robert le, spurrier, 404, 406
Roads & streets: gutters in, xxiii; narrowed, 188, 483
Robbers, 394
Roberd, Stephen, 660
Robert, William, essoiner, 227
Roche, William atte, 234
Rochester, Kent, priory of St. Andrew, prior, *see* Sheppey, John de
Rokesle (Rokele)
   Adam de, alderman, *70–124*
   Gregory de, mayor, 85, 318; sheriff, 255
   Gregory son of Robert de, 117
   John, alderman, *392*

John de, clerk, 447
Roger de, 143
Rokyngham, Hugh de, goldsmith, 318
Rolls, Master of, *see* Frank, John
Romeyn (Romayn, Romein, *etc.*)
   Juliana, 224
   Thomas, alderman, 6, *1–168*; mayor, 149, 154, *146–56*; pl., 39
Romondby, Thomas, clerk, 653
Roofs, *see* Buildings
Rook, William, 627
Roper, *see* Trades
Ropery, 119
Rosse (Rose)
   Adam, potter, 28, 81; his wife, 28
   John, Robert, Thomas & William atte, essoiners [? fictitious], xvi, 443, 466, 490, 515; *see also* Russe
Rote, John, alderman, 618, *616–33*; sheriff, 626
Rotewell, William, 635
Rothing (Rothyng)
   Adam de, 274–5; Katherine his relict, 279
   Adam de, carpenter, 233
   Hawyse de, 71
   R. de, essoiner, 237–8
   Richard de, alderman, *334–96*; pl., 294; sheriff, 286–7; his clerk, 287; Joan his wife, 294
Rous, Agatha la, 370
Roussebem, William de, essoiner [? fictitious], 491
Routon, Richard de, 57
Royston, Herts., priory of St. Mary, prior, 656
Ruddok
   Alan, 486
   John, 312
Ruer, Richard, essoiner [? fictitious], 613
Ruffini, Laude, attorney, 12
Russe
   John, 518
   William, essoiner [? fictitious], xvi, 495, 509, 516, 523, 525, 535, 539
Russel(l)
   Elias, alderman, 312, *17–47*; mayor, 6, 205, *1–6*; pl., 9, 44
   Gilbert, essoiner, 108
   Richard, 269; (? another), 511
Ry, John le, sheriff's serjeant, 293

Sabrichesworth, John de, junior, 215
Sachere
   Adam le, 234
   Avice la, 129
Saddler, *see* Trades
Sadelyngstanes (Sadlyngstanes, *etc.*), Hugh de, alderman, *503–11*; def., 485; Isabel his wife, 485

Index

Sadiller, John, 659
Saham, Thomas de, tailor, 560
St. Alban Wood Street: church, 454; par., 36, 407, 411, 445, 644
St. Albans, Herts., abbot, xxxi, 356, *see also* Moot, John
St. Albans (Seint Albon)
  Adam de, 391
  Adam de, & Isabel his wife, 104
  Isabel de, 283
  John de, alderman, 536, *518–47*; house of, 632
  Richard son of Adam de, 104
  Robert de, 424
St. Alphege London Wall (beside Crepelgate), par., 110, 222, 427, 435, 486, 514, 524
St. Andrew by the Wardrobe (Castle Baynard): jury of the venue, 401; par., 369, 386, 401, 410, 415
St. Andrew Rochester, *see* Rochester
St. Andrew Undershaft (de Cornhulle), par., 307, 534, 599, 608
St. Anne within Aldersgate, par., 605
St. Antonin, par., 25, 323, 361, 364–6
St. Augustine Watling Street (at the east door of St. Paul's): par., 303, 372, 500, 585, 616–17; rector, *see* Kendale, Thomas de
St. Bartholomew (Smethefeld), priory: church, 492; prior, 97, 130, 399, 490, 492, 528–9, *see also* Carleton, John de; Gedney, William; Kensington, John de
St. Bartholomew by the Exchange (the Less), par., xxviii, 262, 390, 394, 624
St. Benet Fink: churchyard, 63; par., 185; parson, Luke, 63
St. Benet Gracechurch, par., 203
St. Benet Paul's Wharf (atte Wodewharf): par., 369, 392, 588, 590, 621; parishioners (named), 533; rector, *see* Stodle, William
St. Botolph Aldersgate: par., 272, 487, 629; rector, Ralph, 487
St. Botolph Aldgate, par., 218, 549
St. Botolph Billingsgate, par., 312, 352, 485
St. Botolph Bishopsgate, par., 292, 375–6
St. Bride Fleet Street (St. Brigid beyond Flete Bridge), par., 117, 295, 496, 521, 593, 638, 657
St. Christopher, par., 414
St. Clare without Aldgate (Minoresses, Our Lady of the New Place), abbess (& sisters), xv, 45, 80, 102, 211, 296
St. Clement Eastcheap (by Candelwykstret): churchyard, 546; par., 417, 512, 544; parishioners, 544, (named) 546; parson, *see* Chippenham, Adam; processions through, 544

St. Dionis Backchurch (St. Duns Bakechurch), church, 628
St. Dunstan in the East (by the Tower): par., xxx, 160, 163, 208–9, 217, 250, 313, 475, 637; parson, John, 208
St. Dunstan in the West (Fleet Street), par., 183, 380, 426, 609, 614, 653, 656
St. Edmund King & Martyr (in Lombard Street): churchwardens (named), 596; par., 32, 592; rector, *see* Penerege, Edmund
St. Edmunds
  Fulk de, 75–6, 84, 105, 298, 510; Agnes his wife, 76
  James son of Fulk de (*alias* James Folk), 75, 298, 488; sheriff, 149, *150–6*; Margaret his wife, 298
  John son of James de, 488
  Juliana daughter of Fulk de, 105
  Thomas de, & Idonia his wife, 488, 510
  Thomas son of James de, 488
St. Ethelburga Bishopsgate, par., 281, 519, 622
St. Gabriel Fenchurch (St. Mary de Fancherche), par., 229, 627
St. Giles Cripplegate, par., 620, 660
St. Helen's (within Bishopsgate), priory: prioress, 233, 530, *see also* Gloucestre, Isabel, *and* Honylane, Margery de; prioress & convent, 307, 310, 599, 608
St. Ives (Seyntyves), Adam de, alderman, 618, 631–2, *613–33*; summoner, 474
St. James Garlickhithe: par., 93, 193, 506; rector, *see* Stratford, Roger de
St. James Westminster, hospital, *see* Westminster
St. John of Jerusalem, hospital, *see* Clerkenwell
St. John the Baptist, *see* Haliwell
St. John the Evangelist (St. Werburgh Friday Street): par., xxxiii n; parson, William, 81
St. John Walbrook: par., xxx, 101, 362, 419–23, 461, 464; parishioners (named), 147; rector, John, 147
St. John Zachary (Zacharie), par., 165, 595
St. Katherine Cree (Cricherche), par., 615
St. Laurence Lane (Seintlaurenslane, in Jewry), 511, 581, 654
St. Lawrence (Old) Jewry: churchyard, 494; par., xxx, 13, 62, 83, 191, 213, 319, 348, 493, 505, 591, 598, 654; parishioners, 494; rector, *see* Oxford, Balliol Hall, master of
St. Lawrence Pountney (Candlewick Street), par., 105
St. Leonard Eastcheap: chapel, 574; church, xxxi, 99, 269, 574; churchwardens (named), 659; churchyard, 574, 659; par., 99, 269; parishioners

210

(named), 99, 475; parson, *see* Launde, Geoffrey de la; rectors, *see* Archer, Thomas; Derby, Hugh de; Deynes, John; Godwyneston, Richard de
St. Magnus the Martyr (de Bruggestret), par., 51–3, 327, 513, 645
St. Margaret Fish Street Hill (Briggestret): churchyard, 623; par., 623, 640, 661; rector, *see* Sprotburgh, Robert
St. Margaret Lothbury: lane leading to church, 175; par., 382–3; rector, Ranulph, 198
St. Margaret Moses Friday Street: church, 416, 639; par., 384, 416, 639; parishioners, 639; processional way, 639; rectors, *see* Chadenesfeld, Geoffrey; Isoude, Thomas
St. Martin le Grand: canons (named), 34; dean, *see* Meltone, William de; dean & chapter, 34, 112, 189, 425; vicars choral, 34
St. Martin Ludgate, church, 85
St. Martin Orgar (in Candilwickestrete), par., 44, 349–50, 643
St. Martin Vintry: churchyard, 619; par., xxx, 6, 15–16, 18, 55, 211, 358, 586, 619; rector, *see* Dunster, Roger
St. Mary Abchurch, par., 403
St. Mary Aldermanbury: churchyard, 181; par., 335; parishioners, 181; parson, *see* Cornhill, William de
St. Mary Aldermary (Aldermaricherche), par., 240, 324, 334
St. Mary at Hill, par., 87, 248–9, 404, 406
St. Mary Axe (atte Nax): par., 57, 276, 418; street, 276
St. Mary Bothaw, par., 290–1
St. Mary Clerkenwell, *see* Clerkenwell
St. Mary Colechurch, par., 100, 104, 201, 282–7, 343–4
St. Mary de Berkyngechapel, *see* All Hallows Barking
St. Mary Fancherche, *see* St. Gabriel Fenchurch
St. Mary Graces, abbot, *see* Warden, William de
St. Mary le Bow (de Arcubus): par., 89–90, 187, 235, 317, 452, 501, 518; parishioners (named), 451; rector, *see* Ilkyston, William de
St. Mary Magdalen Milk Street: par., 131; parishioners (named), 306; rector, *see* Newenton, Henry de
St. Mary Otery, *see* Ottery
St. Mary Overey, *see* Southwark
St. Mary Royston, *see* Royston
St. Mary Somerset, par., 396, 577
St. Mary Staining, par., 446, 644
St. Mary within Cripplegate, (new) hospital, *see* Elsing Spital

St. Mary without Bishopsgate (new) hospital: fields behind, 292, 375; prior, 37, 55, 86, 235, 346, 369, 440, ?453, 478, 488, 518; prior Thomas, 531
St. Mary Woolchurch: churchyard, 64, 302; par., 289, 299–300, 302, 379; rector & parishioners, 64
St. Mary Woolnoth (in Lombard Street): chaplains, 647; par., 60, 92, 98, 126, 393, 397, 447, 527, 647
St. Matthew Friday Street: church, 318; par., 14, 43, 264, 377, 413, 460, 572; procession, 43; rector, *see* Fakenham, John de; rector & parishioners, 43
St. Michael Bassishaw: churchyard, 606, 631; par., 434; parishioners (named), 606, 631; parsons, Thomas, 606, 631, William, 631
St. Michael Cornhill: churchyard, 311, 613; par., 94, 262, 270–1, 310, 522; rector, *see* Felde, Richard atte
St. Michael Crooked Lane (Candelwykstrete): churchyard, 298; par., 9, 31, 38, 298, 331, 488, 597; parson, Ralph, 298; rector & parishioners (named), 298
St. Michael le Querne (atte Corne), par., 69, 478, 566, 583
St. Michael Paternoster, par., 74, 95–6, 243
St. Michael Queenhithe, par., xxx, 214, 252, 301, 433, 436–8, 476, 658
St. Michael Wood Street (Hoggenlane): par., 54, 61, 219, 255, 482–3, 547, 612, 625, *267*; rector, *see* Ive, John
St. Mildred Bread Street: church, 156; par., 109, 156, 240, 646
St. Mildred Poultry: church, 400; par., 29–30, 66, 395, 632; parishioners (named), 400; parson, *see* Nottele, Thomas de
St. Nicholas Acon (Hacon), par., 432
St. Nicholas Cole Abbey (Coldeabbey), par., 221, 641
St. Nicholas de Berkyngchurche, *see* All Hallows Barking
St. Nicholas Olave (Olof), par., 360
St. Nicholas Shambles: church, 309; par., xxxi, 19, 309, 569, 584, 618
St. Olave Colmanstrete [?Old Jewry], par., 378
St. Olave Hart Street (by the Tower, next the Crutched Friars), par., 111, 477, 611
St. Olave Old Jewry, par., 545; *see also* St. Olave Colmanstrete
St. Olave Silver Street, par., 24, 158
St. Osiths, John de, 510
St. Pancras Soper Lane, par., 236

Index

St. Paul's: bakehouse, master of, xxvii, 140–1; canons, *see* Aldebury, Walter de; Holm, Roger, *and* Thorp, Walter de; close, 141; dean, *see* Brewere, Gilbert de la; dean & canons, xxvii, 141; dean & chapter, 69, 228, 250, 567, 572, 579

St. Paul's Wharf, 140

St. Peter Cornhill, par., 337, 520, 525

St. Peter le Poor (St. Peter the Less in Bradestrete): churchyard, 630; par., 230–2, 339, 630, 642

St. Peter Paul's Wharf (by Old Fish Street, the Less by St. Paul's Wharf, *etc.*), par., 288, 587–8, 590, 607

St. Peter Westcheap (Wodestrete), par., 14, 70, 346, 385, 430, 612, 655

St. Peter's Lane, 607

St. Sepulchre Newgate (in Holbourne), par., 132, 186, 294, 408

St. Stephen Coleman Street, par., 175, 215, 570

St. Stephen Walbrook: altar of B.V.M., 169; bell-tower, 308; church-wall, 174; par., xxx, 25, 363, 370–1, 626, 648–50; parishioners (named), 169, 174, 308; parson, *see* Blund, Peter le *and* Stanesfeld, William de; rector, William, 308

St. Stephen Westminster, *see* Westminster

St. Swithin (Swythun in Candelwikstrete), par., 76, 84, 510, 589

St. Swithin's Lane, 510

St. Thomas (the Martyr) of Acon (Dacon), master, 343, 347, *see also* Berkhampsted, Thomas de; Sallowe, Thomas de

St. Thomas the Apostle: chancel, 502; churchyard, 502; par., 216, 412, 424; rector, *see* Sleford, William de

St. Thomas the Martyr, hospital, *see* Southwark

St. Vedast, par., 381

St. Werburgh Friday Street, *see* St. John the Evangelist

Salisbury (Salesbury, Sar')
 John de, attorney, 397; essoiner, 315, 319, 389
 John de, barber, & Margery his wife, 22
 Thomas de, kt., 570
 William de, clerk, 204

Sallowe
 Thomas de, master of St. Thomas of Acon, 565
 William & Alice his wife, 593
 William, of Fleet Street, & Joan his wife, 638

Salman, Walter, girdler, & Margery his wife, 495

Salyng, Richard de, (viewer), 527

Same

Thomas de, 525
Thomas de, tailor, 546
Sandford, William de, clerk, 531–2
Sandon, John, 606
Sar', *see* Salisbury
Sargere, John, warden of St. Mary Ottery, 654
Sautreour, Guillotin le, 110
Savage (Sauvage)
 Robert, 595, 605; Joan his wife, 605
 Roger, kt., 194
Sawtry (Sautre), Hunts., abbot, 360
Sayssello, Charleto de, attorney, 34
Scalding houses, *see* Buildings
Scantling, measurement by, 156
Schalyngford, John, tailor, 584
Schirbourne, William & Isabel his wife, 589
Schrobshire, *see* Shropshire
Scot
 Geoffrey, junior, 152
 John, 260; essoiner, 195
 John, poulter, 400
 Richard, essoiner, 120, 280
 Thomas, 396
Screens, *see* Entreclosewalls; Speers
Scullard, John, essoiner, 313
Scut, John, 637
Sea-coal, 617
Seccheford (Sechford, Sescheford, *etc.*)
 Henry de, 478, 489
 Henry de, alderman, 272, 286, 312–13, 318–19, 328, *259–315*
Seint Albon, *see* St. Albans
Seintlaurenslane, *see* St. Laurence Lane
Seld, *see* Buildings
Seler, John atte, & Alice his wife, 538
Selsham, Walter, chaplain, 616–17
Sely (Seely)
 John, alderman, *622–31*; sheriff, 627, 657; skinner, 573
 Lawrence, 411
 Robert, alderman, *259*; son of Thomas, 115–16; Joan his wife (relict), 115–16, 411
 Thomas, alderman, 37, 145, 154, *65–177*; sheriff, 312
Seman, Simon, alderman, *651, 653*; sheriff, 653
Semer, John, of Guildford, 598
Sende, Edward, smith, 543
Seriaunt (Serieaunt)
 Geoffrey, 375
 John, tailor, 635
Serjeant of the Chamber, *see* Chamber of London
Serle, William, (viewer), 655
Servat (Servad), William (le), alderman, 149, 154, 158n, *135–236*; def., 29
Sescheford, *see* Seccheford

Index

Settere
  Alexander le, 317
  Joan daughter of Clement le, 279
Sewage, *etc.*, xxiv–xxv; *see also* Buildings, privies; Dung; Stench
Sewale
  John, fishmonger, 78
  William, essoiner, xvi, 562; serjeant of the Chamber, 608
Seymor(e)
  John, 631
  Robert, armourer, & Benedicta his wife, 344
Seyntyves, *see* St. Ives
Shadworth, John, alderman, *638*, *642*
Shakol, Richard, 476
Sharp
  John, 99
  Richard, 99, 312
Shawe
  Henry atte, armourer, 379
  John, vintner, 647
Shearman, *see* Trades
Sheds, *see* Buildings
Shelford, Henry, 659
Shenche, Martin, 62, 82
Shene, Thomas de, 339
Shenefeld, Walter de, tanner, 187
Sheppey, John de, prior of Rochester, 657
Sherborne Lane (Shitebournelane), 647
Shereman, Jordan le, 339
Sheriffs: amercements levied to use of, xix; on assizes, xiv; prohibit building, xviii; summon defs., xiv; summon juries, xvii, 43; to execute judgment, xviii
Sheryngham, William, alderman, 635, *636*
Shipbrok, Roger, 574
Ships, 453
Shire, Gregory atte, *see* Norton, Gregory de
Shitebournelane, *see* Sherborne Lane
Shoppe
  John atte, 618
  Thomas atte, 511
Shops, *see* Buildings
Shordich, Peter de, attorney, 45
Shorne
  Benedict, 289
  Henry de, 128
Shouts, 453
Shropshire (Salop, Schrobshire, *etc.*)
  Geoffrey de, 169, 174
  Richard de, carpenter, 526–7, 566, 581–3, 591, 604
Shrovesbery, Geoffrey de, 300
Shutters, *see* Buildings
Shyrlond, Amaury de, clerk, 521
Sibyle (Sybille)
  John, 643

Walter, alderman, 622, *615–18*; arbitrator, 632
Sieves (clensyng syvis), 646
Silverstone, Master John de, 140
Simond (Symond, Symound)
  John, chandler, 583
  John, recorder, *651*, *654*
Sinks, *see* Buildings
Skelton, William de, 451
Skew, *see* Buildings
Skinner, *see* Trades
Skirwith, Thomas, 653
Skremyn, Thomas, of Friday Street, 572
Skynnere, Hugh le, 375
Sledge-hammers, 617
Sleford, William de, dean of St. Stephen Westminster, 596; rector of St. Thomas the Apostle, 424, 502
Slomo, William, ? essoiner, 103
Smalebregge, Simon atte, tanner, 187
Smart, John, 623
Smelt, Richard, sheriff, *443–6*
Smith, *see* Trades
Smithfield, 151
Smoke, 617
Smyth, Andrew, pie-baker, 592
Snypston, Nicholas de, 536–7
Soakaways, *see* Buildings, sinks
Sodingtone (Sodyngton, Sudington), Master John de, 113, 133, 230–2
Soham, Sampson, 619
Solars, *see* Buildings
Somersete
  Henry de, 78
  Robert de, 525
Somerton
  John de, 533
  Thomas, draper, 647
Somery, John, 21; Margery his wife, 21, 219
Soneman, Thomas, 618
Soper Lane (Soperelane, Soperislane), 154, 206
Sotherey, John, tapicer, & Cecily his wife, 647
Soty, William & Margery his wife, 502
Souche, *see* Zouche
Southam, John, alderman, 622, *615*
Southwark
  hospital of St. Thomas, master, Henry, 592
  priory of St. Mary Overey, prior (& convent), 582, 647
Sowyer, Richard le, 33
Spain (Ispania), Thomas de, 209
Spaldinge (Spaldyng), Joce de, & Joan his wife, 263, 288
Sparham, Peter de, 85
Spark
  Henry, 604

213

Index

Spark, *continued*
  William, 451
  William, armourer, & Maud his wife, 495
Speers (speres), screens for warding off air-draughts, 646; *see also* Entre-closewalls
Spelman (Speleman), Stephen, alderman, 661; sheriff, *645*
Spencer, Gilbert, 483
Sperling (Sperelyng)
  Edward son of Martin, 269
  Felicia, 269
  Maud daughter of Christine, 269
  Ralph, 269
Spersholte (Speresholte), William de, 234, 252; Alice his relict, 301
Spicer (Spycer)
  Richard, esquire, 649
  Simon le, lombard (*alias* Simon Lumbard, spicer), 520, 530; Emma his wife (relict), 530, 542
  Thomas, 574
  William le, skinner, 94
Spicer, *see* Trades
Sporon, Thomas, goldsmith, 333
Spot, William & Muriel his wife, 191
Sprot
  Adam, 511, 598
  John, 385
  John, chaplain, 415
  William, 297
Sprotburgh, Robert, rector of St. Margaret Fish Street Hill, 623
Spurrier, *see* Trades
Stable, Adam, alderman, 587, 591, 595, 597, 604, 618, *584–623*; mayor, *613*
Stables, *see* Buildings
Stacy
  Richard, 609–10
  William & Margery his wife, 483
Stafford, John, attorney, 648–50, 652
Stairs, *see* Buildings, steps
Stake, William atte, 335
Stakes, Alice atte, 60
Stalls, 219 & n, 396
Stamford, Andrew de, 147
Stanard, Stephen, 533
Standon (Staundone)
  Master Robert de, clerk, 34
  William, alderman, 631, *629–42*; mayor, 646, 660; sheriff, *633*
Stanes, William de, 317
Stanesfeld (Stansfeld), William de, parson of St. Stephen Walbrook, 370–1, 374
Stanford (Staneford, Staunford, *etc.*)
  Andrew de, 85, 101
  John de, pepperer, & Avice his daughter, 476
  Katherine relict of William de, 201, 282

Stephen de, 396
  William de, 280
Stanley, Adam de, abbot of Rewley, 570
Stansfeld, *see* Stanesfeld
Staples, *see* Buildings
Starre, John & Mary his wife, 91
Staundone, *see* Standon
Staunton, Alice relict of John de, kt., 511
Staynton, John de, 282–3
Stench, complaints of, xxv, 364, 485, 617, 644
Steps, *see* Buildings
Stertford (Sterteford), William de, 1, 3, 31
Steyndrop
  Agnes de, 503
  Gilbert de, sheriff, 429
Steynour, Christine relict of John, 652
Sthorn, Roger, 56
Stile, 606, 631
Stockfishmonger, *see* Trades
Stocks Market (les Stokkes), par., 289
Stodey(e)
  John (de), alderman, 432, 449, 476, 536, 587, 591, *434–605*; mayor, 492, 501–2, 528, 545, *492–502*
  William, vintner, 586
Stodle, William, rector of St. Benet Paul's Wharf, 533
Stoke, William (de), 511, 591; Margery his wife, 591
Stokes
  Henry de, 102
  Richard de, 525
  William, 526
Stokkes, les, *see* Stocks Market
Stokton, Roger, 642
Stomelhole, John, 660
Stone
  Gilbert atte, butcher, 555
  John, of London, hosteler, 654
Stone, use of, ix; *see also* Buildings, walls
Stonham, Richard & Margery his wife, 551
Storeys, *see* Buildings
Stortford (Storteford)
  John de, sheriff, 510
  Richard, 526
  Richard de, leatherseller, 591
  William de, sheriff, 510
Story, John, senior, 522
Stow, John, ix n
Strangers, visiting & staying, 521
Stratford
  John de, 97, 125; Belisant his wife, 97
  Robert de, def., 260; essoiner, 314; summoner, 447
  Roger de, rector of St. James Garlick-hithe, 443
Stratford Langthorne, Essex, abbot, 126, 393, 397
Stratton

Index

Nicholas, 660
William de, & Margaret his wife, 348
Straw, xi & n, 536
Streets, *see* Roads
Style, Richard, mason, 645–7, 661
Sudbery, Henry de, Alice his wife & Agnes his daughter, 327
Sudington, *see* Sodingtone
Suffolk, earl of, *see* Ufford, William de
Suffolk (Suthfolk)
   Elias de, 85; alderman, 233, 236, *225–32*
   Thomas de, 510
Summers, *see* Buildings, beams
Surgeon (Cirugien)
   Gilbert the, 115, 121; Felicia his wife, 115
   Master Peter le, 167
   see also Trades
Sutel
   Adam, 351
   Robert, 351
Suthfolk, *see* Suffolk
Sutton
   Henry de, & Isabel his wife, 334
   Henry de, guardian of the Friars Minor, 34
   Nicholas son of Alan de, *alias* Nicholas Ballard, 256
   Robert de, loriner, 355, 407
   Thomas de, dyer, 504
Suyte, Richard atte, 574
Swafham, Sampson de, 481
Swalclive (Swaleclive)
   John de, 429, 456
   Robert de, alderman [& recorder], *259, 280*
Swan
   Godfrey atte, 375
   Henry atte, 252
Swanlond
   Simon de, alderman, *313*; mayor, *307–10*
   Thomas, 619
Swift, John, tanner, 187
Swinfield, Richard, bishop of Hereford, 152
Syward
   John, alderman, 407, 416, *396*; sheriff, 385
   William, 231

Tables, 646
Taillour (Tailleur, Tayllour)
   Henry son of Philip le, 70
   John le, of Gracechurch, 203
   John son of Philip le, 11
   Richard le, & Margery his wife, 313
   Sabine relict of Philip le, 11, 70, 137
   William le, king's serjeant, 313
Tailor, *see* Trades

Tallow-chandler, *see* Trades
Talworthe (Taleworth), John de, 16, 193
Tanner, *see* Trades
Tannere, Brian, 522
Tanners' seld, 187
Tanrigge, William de, 222
Tapicer, *see* Trades
'Tappetrowe', *see* Trough
Tatersall, Robert, alderman, 653–4, *654*
Tatesfeld, Thomas de, essoiner, 4
Taunton, Gilbert de, 155, 158
Taverner, *see* Trades
Taverner, Peter le, *see* Herlyng
Tawyer, *see* Trades
Tayllehaste, Richard, 4
Tedenham, *see* Tudenham
Tedmar, John, 210
Tenements (named), *see* Barge, le; Bridge House; Cardinal's Hat; Converts, house of; Evesham Inn; Glean on the Hoop
Tenter-walls, *see* Tyghtyngwowes, le
Tenter-yard, 589
Tenting-frame, 643
Tenting-tun (thityngtunne), 277
Thame
   James de, 535; alderman, *514–22*; sheriff, *514*
   John de, 512
   Nicholas, 618
   Philip de, prior of St. John of Jerusalem, 436
   Robert de, 452, 476
   William de, 433
   William son of Robert de, & Juliana his wife, 571
Thames: xxiii, xxxii, 97, 292, 327, 352, 358, 392, 582, 645; roads (lanes) leading to, 85, 396, 401, 577; *see also* Wharves
Thames Street, 327, 392, 476, 577, 637
Thele, Henry de, & Maud his wife, 115
Tholosan, *see* Tullesan
Thomas, Roger son of, essoiner, 86
Thorneburgh, Thomas, recorder, *645*
Thorneye
   John, 575
   William de, xxxii, 324–6, 328; alderman, 376, *374–92*
Thornton, Thomas de, 525
Thorp
   Elias de, 169, 308
   John de, skinner, 363, 367
   Reginald de, 295
   Robert de, 446
   Master Walter de, canon of St. Paul's, 228
Thunderle(e)
   Adam de, 258
   John de, 258
   Reginald de, sheriff, 85, *87–102*

Index

Thurgod, Richard & Katherine his wife, 400
Thurkild, John, 618
Tiffeld
    John de, 385
    Thomas de, 416
Tiler, *see* Trades
Tiles, *see* Buildings
Timbermonger, *see* Trades
Tiryngton, John, 512
Toller, John, 631
Tonbridge, Kent, *see* Mustrel, Robert
Tondeby, Gilbert de, 117
Toppesfeld
    Stephen, 660
    William de, & Joan his wife, 145
Torches, wax, 544
Torgold, Walter, 641
Torkeseye, Robert de, barber, 223
Tornegold
    John, 396
    John de, alderman, 547, 613, *564–613*; fishmonger, 577; sheriff, 536
    see also Torgold
Torold
    Roger & Alice his wife, 507
    Roger son of Roger, 507
Totenham
    John de, carpenter, 304, 526–7
    John de, chandler, 407
    Lawrence de, 20
Totyng, John, 522
Tower of London, xxvii, xxix, 254
Trades & occupations, xxxi
    armourer (heumer), 344, 379, 400, 460, 495, 617, 623
    baker, 205, 257, 524, 561
    barber, 22, 124, 223
    brewer, 320, 424, 462, 466, 470–1, 498, 502, 505, 529, 576
    broderer, 502, 644
    butcher (bocher), 309, 546, 555, 569, 579, 584
    butler (botiller), 587
    capper, 594
    carpenter, 146, 346, 348, 482, 559, *see also* Viewers
    chandler, 407, 473, 568, 583, 592, 608, 614
    changer, 512
    cook, 583
    cooper, 622
    corder, 265
    cordwainer, 58, 199, 396, 532, 596
    cutler, 109
    draper, 233, 290, 292, 317, 429, 465, 472, 500, 527, 549, 564, 578, 584, 618, 647–8, 651
    dyer (dyghere), 351, 488, 504
    fellmonger, 465
    fishmonger (pessoner), 26, 78, 169, 331, 351–2, 357, 365, 372, 391, 419, 431, 475–6, 485, 513, 577, 580, 587, 629, 652
    furbisher (furbour), 234
    fuster (fuyster), 446
    girdler (zeinturer, gerdeler, *etc.*), 191, 293, 495, 581
    glazier, 656
    glover, 540
    goldbeater, 617
    goldsmith, 70, 85, 111, 151, 203, 219, 255, 305, 318, 333, 381, 430, 445–6, 460, 483–4, 501, 510, 515–16, 535, 602, 612, 617, 624–5, 657
    grocer, 551, 557, 617, 640, 648, 661
    haberdasher, 576, 581
    hanaper, 445, 483
    hosier, 317, 330
    hosteler, 596, 654
    ironmonger (ismongere), 545, 555, 592, 603
    joiner (ioignour), 228
    leatherseller, 591
    linendraper, 659
    lombard, 520, 542
    loriner, 246, 355, 407
    mason, 203, 323, 346, 621, *see also* Viewers
    mercer, 104, 236, 261, 318–19, 389, 405, 412, 435, 445, 494, 505, 511, 514, 516, 523–4, 602, 625, 631, 645–6
    merchant, 488, 645; Hanse, 444; Italian, 12
    nakerer, 309
    painter, 65, 68, 71
    paviour, xxx n, 249
    pepperer, 476
    pewterer (peutrer), 574, 617, 647
    pie-baker, 592, 627, 632
    potter, 28, 41, 81, 340–1, 418
    poulter, 400
    roper, 441
    saddler (seler), 110, 200, 355, 418
    shearman, 576
    skinner (peleter *etc.*), 94, 147, 173, 261, 362–3, 380, 400, 419–20, 442, 527, 573, 609, 617, 648, 651
    smith (ferrour, mareschall, *etc.*), 429, 519, 543, 610, 614, 617
    spicer, 405, 530, 554
    spurrier (sporier), 404, 406
    stockfishmonger, 350, 557
    surgeon, 185
    tailor, 12–13, 20, 86, 99, 144, 161, 169, 186, 190, 195, 203, 417, 496, 546, 559–60, 584, 599, 608, 617, 635, 639
    tallow-chandler, 651
    tanner, 187, 251, 359, 385
    tapicer, 647

Index

taverner, 139, 203, 234, 260
tawyer, 370, 499, 512, 524, 537, 566, 616
tiler, xx n
timbermonger, 524
vintner, 358, 414, 441, 488, 506, 509, 574, 586, 632, 642, 647
woodmonger, 244, 541
woolmonger, 548
Transoms, *see* Buildings, beams
Trappe, John, skinner, 362
Travers, Richard, 305
Traynel(l), Henry, 609–10, 616
Treasurer & Council, 174
Trees, 64, 279
Treier, *see* Treyere
Tremayn, John, recorder, *638*
Trent, William, 116; alderman, 154, *137–82*; def., 136, 179; pl., 159, 192
Trentemars, John, 89
Trethewe, John, 654
Treyere (Treier, Treyhere)
  Robert le, 289, 312
  Robert son of Robert le, 108, 151
Trig, William, 396
Triple, John (de), 169, 174
Trippelowe, John, essoiner, 355–6
Tristour, William, 655
Trough, with tap (tappetrowe), 583, 646
Tubs (tynes), 646
Tudenham (Tedenham), William (de), alderman, 476, 536, 545, 547, *424–547*; mercer, def., 523
Tulio, Master Arnold de, 146
Tullesan (Tholosan), Michael de, 30, 66
Tun (thityngtunne), 277
Turgis, Simon, 91
Turk
  Alexander, 599
  John, clerk, 599, 608
  Walter, alderman, 407, *384–96*; mayor, *419–24*
Turnham, Simon de, 396
Turret, *see* Buildings
Twyford
  Nicholas, alderman, 618, *609*; mayor, *635–7*; sheriff, 614, 616–17, 619, *615–18*
  William, 583
Twyn, Edmund, 659
Tyghtyngwowes, le (le Tythyngwowes, le Tytingwowes), plot of ground called, 298 & n, 488
Tylly, Christine, 266
'Tynes', *see* Tubs
Tyrp, John, essoiner, 559

Ufford, William de, earl of Suffolk, xxxi, 577, 620; Joan his wife, 577
Upton
  Ralph de, alderman, 333, *335–71*

Robert de, 85, 89–90; Margery his wife, 89–90
Stephen de, & Sybil his wife, 132
William de, draper, 317
Ussher
  Richard, tanner, 187
  Simon le, & Isabel his wife, 372
Utensils, leaden, 646
Uxbridge (Wexbregge, Woxebregg), Middx., *see* Waleys, Austin le

Vacant plot, unfenced, 394
Vagabonds, 250
Valence, Aymer de, earl of Pembroke, xxxi, 248–9
Vanner(e)
  Henry, alderman, 631, *631*
  Henry le, vintner, 358
  John le, 380
Vats, 646
Vault, *see* Buildings
Vauntage, William, girdler, 293
Vaux, John de, goldsmith, 305
Venour, William, alderman, *643*, *645*; mayor, *638*
Verneye, John le, 375
Vescy, widow of Geoffrey de, 176
Vessels: leaden, 583, 646; *see also* Aletuns; Barrels; Bin; Kimnels; Maltbin; Trough; Tubs; Tun; Vats
Victuals, 536, 613, 626, *see also* Ale; Fruit; Wheat; Wine
Viewers (masons & carpenters), xiv, xvii, xix–xx
Vigne, Maud atte, 417
Vilers, Francis de, kt., 183
Vines, 549
Vintner, *see* Trades
Vintry (Vinetria), John de (*alias* John le Coroner), alderman, *6–92*; clerk, pl., 18
Viroler, Roger le, 85
Vivien, Margaret relict of John, 270–1
Vyne
  John, alderman, 618, *616–19*
  John, mercer, 631

Wachyngton, Robert de, attorney, 531
Wade
  Adam, 130
  Alice, 214
  John, 659
  John, alderman, *641–2*; fishmonger, 629
Wakefeld
  Faukes de, tanner, 385
  John de, 607
Wakelee, John, alderman, *643*; vintner, 642
Walbrook (Walebroke, *etc.*), xxiii, xxviii, xxx, 15–16, 55, 109, 188, 198–200, 292,

Index

Walbrook, *continued*
   382–3, *198*; lane, 302; *see also* Marchal, John le
Walbrook ward, 510
Walcote, John, alderman, *637*; sheriff, 638
Walden, Essex, abbot & convent, 272
Walden (Waledene)
   John de, 142; another, 514
   Thomas de, 510
   Walter, spicer, 554
Waldern, William, mayor, 655, 659; sheriff, *643*
Waleworth, *see* Walworth
Waleys (Galeys)
   Austin le, & Maud his wife, 340–1
   Austin le, of Uxbridge, 349–51, 353–4
   Henry le, 500
   Henry le, mayor, 283, 312; def., 18; pl., 6–8
   Richard, attorney, 613
   Walter le, 318
   William, girdler, 581
Walisshman, Thomas, 381
Wall, City, *see* City Wall
Wall
   John atte, 477
   Walter atte, essoiner [? fictitious], 499
   William atte, 450
Wall-plates, Walls, *see* Buildings
Walpol, Adam, 381
Walrond, Master Philip, 24
Walsh (Walssh)
   Hugh le, 525
   John, goldsmith, 510
Walsyngham, Reginald de, & Mary his wife, 216
Walter, Robert son of, 107, 135
Waltham (Wautham)
   Hugh de, attorney, 312; assize adjourned by, xvi, 329; [common] clerk, 203, 234, 321; pl., 193, 203, 234, 273–5, 277–9, 307; Juliana his wife, 234, 273, 277, 307
   John de, 339, 375; attorney, 233
   Peter de, 270–1
   Roger de, 99
   Stephen de, & Joan his wife, 486, 506
Walton, Walter, (viewer), 656–8, *see also* Wylton, Walter
Walworth (Waleworth), William, alderman, 587, 595, 604, 613, *590–613*; mayor, *607*, *624*; pl., 597
Wangrave, *see* Wengrave
Wanlok, *see* Wenlok
War', John de, 597
Warburton, Robert, alderman, 631, *631*
Warde
   John, alderman, 574, 591, *589*; mayor, *606*, *608–11*; sheriff, *529–31*
   Stephen, carpenter, 620

William, draper, & Joan his wife, 648
Warden, William de, abbot of St. Mary Graces, 558
Wardmote: xi, xxvii, xxviii; held in a church, 454
Wardrobe, Giles of the, canon of St. Martin le Grand, 34
Ware
   Christine relict of Thomas de, stockfishmonger, 350, 354
   Henry de, 364
   John de, chandler, & Christine his wife, 568
   Lawrence de, *see* Bloseworth
   Peter de, 298
   Richard de, 456
   Thomas de, attorney, 360, 392–3, 395, 410, 412, 415; summoner, 361, 380
   Thomas de, skinner, 527
Warender, John, 448, 474; Alice his wife, 474
Warner, John, alderman, 660, *645*
Waryn, William, chandler, 614
Waryner, Thomas, 629
Wasshbourn, John de, 431
Wastel, William, 218
Watch-tower, *see* Buildings
Watercourse, 375, 625
Watere, William atte, butcher, 546
Waterford, xiin
Watergate, *see* East Watergate
Watford, John de, 186
Watling Street (Watlyngstrate), 617
Watlyngton, Robert (de), attorney, 519, 569–70, 572, 577, 605; def., 560; essoiner, 566, 614; summoner, 589, 605
Watton, *see* Wotton
Waudene, John de, 525
Wautham, *see* Waltham
Wax torches, 544
Wayte
   Ralph, 329
   Richard, 511
Wedon, William de, 329
Wegge, Thomas, 660
Welde, William (atte, de), alderman, 432, 449, 488, 501–2, 524–5, 545, 547, 574, *419–577*; sheriff, 439, 442
Welford (Weleford, Welleford, Wilford)
   Richard de, 451
   Richard de, sheriff, 174, *182–4*
   Robert de, 145
   Thomas, 607
   Thomas, alderman, 622, 631, *614–43*; sheriff, *641–2*
Welles (Wellis)
   John, alderman, 654, *653–4*
   Thomas de, 501
Wellesborn, Richard, coroner, 657

Index

Wells, xxiv, 219, 277, 307, 395, 534, 633
Wengrave (Wangrave), John de, alderman [& recorder], 85, 145, 149, 154, 206, *56–228*; arbitrator, 61; mayor, 233, 236, 240, *230–48*
Wenlok (Wanlok)
　Simon de, 395
　Walter de, 5, 46
Wentebrigg, John de, common serjeant, 536, 547; pl., 587, 607
Werlowe, Edmond, (viewer), 655
Westchep(e), *see* Cheapside
Westmelne, Robert de, broderer, 502
Westminster
　abbot & convent, 510
　chapel of St. Stephen, dean & chapter, 596; dean, *see* Sleford, William de
　hospital of St. James, 233
　king's council at, 629
　mayor & aldermen summoned to, xvi, 373, 629
Westmulne, Nicholas de, & Margaret his wife, 157
Weston
　Elias de, 618
　John, 659
　William, draper, 647
Westwode, W. de, essoiner, 189–90
Wetenhale, William, 630
Wetheresfeld
　Stephen de, essoiner, 1, 12
　William de, 351, 354
Wexbregge, *see* Uxbridge
Wharves & quays: xxxii, 97, 392, 453, 637, 645; for disposal of dung, & drawing water, 459; loading & unloading at, 327, 396; *see also* Byce, William
Wheat, 375
Whelpele, William, tawyer, 524
Whetele, William, tawyer, 537, 616–17
Whitcherch (Whytcherch), Thomas, tawyer, 537, 566
Whityngton, Richard, alderman, 659; mayor, 660
Whyte, Geoffrey, 483
Wichingham (Wichyngham, *etc.*), Geoffrey de, alderman, 407, *406*; mayor, *399–405*
Wickham (Wykham), ? Essex, rector, *see* Pikeman, John
Widden, Richard, cooper, 622
'Wikettes', *see* Buildings, windows
Wilehale (Wylehale, Wyrhale, *etc.*), Richard de, alderman, 154, *89–230*; pl., 40; Juliana his wife, 40
Wilemyn (Wylemyn), Master John, 184, 227
Wilford, *see* Welford
Willesdon, William, 606, 631
Willyngham, Robert, 615

Wiltshire, William, 639, 656–9
Windows, *see* Buildings
Wine, 617
Wintney (Wyntoneye), Hants., prioress, 269
Wircestre, *see* Worcester
Witham (Wytham)
　John de, canon of St. Martin le Grand, 34
　Richard de, mason, 53
Wockyngg, Geoffrey de, & Margery his wife, 432
Wode
　Henry atte, & Joan his wife, 418
　William atte, 518
Wodecok, John, mayor, 647
'Wodefyn', stack of wood, 524
Wodegate, William atte, essoiner [? fictitious], 481
Wodehous, William, alderman, *614–15*; sheriff, 607
Wolcherchehagh (Wollercherchehawe, *etc.*)
　Clarkin de, & Agnes his wife, 327
　William de, & Olive his wife, 510
Wolde, William atte, & Isabel his wife, 151
Wolfey (Wolphey), John, (viewer), 645–6, 647, 661
Wolleward (Woleward), Reginald, attorney, 27, 82, 276, 282; commonalty's attorney, 292, 299–300, 302; common serjeant, xxix
Wolmar, Richard, 312
Wood, stack of, 524; *see also* Firewood
Wood Street (Wodestrete), 71, 255, 454, 547–8, 612, 655; jury of the venue (named), 483; *see also* Palmer, Philip the
Woodmonger, *see* Trades
Woolmonger, *see* Trades
Worcester (Wircestre, Wyrcestre)
　Hugh de, 147
　William, serjeant of the Chamber, 614
　William de, 433, 436, 439
Worstede (Worthstede, Wurstede)
　Richard de, mercer, & Margaret his wife, 514
　Robert de, 85
　Simon, 631
　Simon (de), alderman (of Cripplegate ward), 449–50, 454, 474–6, 478, 483, 488, 501–2, *419–523*; (mercer), pl., 407, 411, 445, 516, 524; Alice his wife (relict), 445, 541, 552–3
Wotton (Watton)
　Nicholas, merchant, 645
　William, alderman, *637*
　William de, 597
Woxbregge, John, 658
Woxebregg, *see* Uxbridge

Index

Wrenge, Henry, 272
Wroth, John, alderman, 587, *536–611*; def., 399; mayor, 513, *511–13*; sheriff, 429; Juliana his wife, 399
Wrotham, Richard de, 501
Wurstede, *see* Worstede
Wyche, Thomas atte, 331
Wycoumbe, John de, 562
Wygth, Thomas de, taverner, 234
Wykham, *see* Wickham
Wylton, Walter, (viewer), 659, *see also* Walton, Walter
Wymbourne, Peter de, clerk, 151
Wymondham
  Adam (de), sheriff, 545, *546–7*
  John de, & Joan his wife, 275
Wynchecombe, Simon, alderman, 631, *626–7*; sheriff, 629, *629–31*
Wyndesore
  John de, 85; alderman, 145, 149, *124–85*
  John de, prior of Elsing Spital, 435
  Roger de, 266
Wyndon, Hamo de, & Joan his wife, 370

Wynton'
  Isabel relict of Eastmar de, 105–6
  John de, barber, 124
  Nicholas de, 351
  William de, 83
Wyntoneye, *see* Wintney
Wyrcestre, *see* Worcester
Wyrhale, *see* Wilehale
Wythome, William, 633

Yakesle, John de, 337
Yoman, William, smith, & Margery his wife, 610
Yonge
  Henry le, 403
  John le, 403
  Thomas & Alice his wife, 616–17
York, xiii
York, Robert de, 521
Yuele, Henry, 583

Zouche (Souche), William la, (kt.), (lord) of Harringworth, 539, 550

LONDON RECORD SOCIETY

The London Record Society was founded in December 1964 to publish transcripts, abstracts and lists of the primary sources for the history of London, and generally to stimulate interest in archives relating to London. Membership is open to any individual or institution; the annual subscription is £3·15, which entitles a member to receive one copy of each volume published during the year and to attend and vote at meetings of the Society. Prospective members should apply to the Hon. Secretary, Mr Brian Burch, c/o Leicester University Library, University Road, Leicester.

The following volumes have already been published:
1. *London possessory assizes: a calendar*, edited by Helena M. Chew (1965)
2. *London inhabitants within the Walls, 1695*, with an introduction by D. V. Glass (1966)
3. *London Consistory Court wills, 1492–1547*, edited by Ida Darlington (1967)
4. *Scriveners' Company Common Paper, 1357–1628, with a continuation to 1678*, edited by Francis W. Steer (1968)
5. *London Radicalism, 1830–1843: a selection from the papers of Francis Place*, edited by D. J. Rowe (1970)
6. *The London Eyre of 1244*, edited by Helena M. Chew and Martin Weinbaum (1970)
7. *The Cartulary of Holy Trinity Aldgate*, edited by Gerald A. J. Hodgett (1971)
8. *The Port and Trade of Early Elizabethan London: documents*, edited by Brian Dietz (1972)
9. *The Spanish Company*, by Pauline Croft (1973)

Price to members £3·15 each, and to non-members £4·50 each.

The following Occasional Publication is also available:
London and Middlesex Published Records, compiled by J. M. Sims (1970)
Price: free to members, and to non-members £1.

A leaflet describing some of the volumes in preparation may be obtained from the Hon. Secretary.